"This is a highly original book in a fi\
thinking and transformative approaches. Its originality lies in its sources, the nature of its case studies, its approach to analysing the problems of contemporary policing, and in its solution to the dangers we face. It is a bold manifesto for critical thinking and for radical change written by someone with both insider and outsider expertise."

Professor Tim Newburn, London School of Economics

"This is a highly original, thought provoking and challenging analysis of one of the major issues of our time. The legitimacy of the police as the agency charged with the state's domestic force is always a political balancing act. But in recent years it has been subject to increasing crises in the UK, US and elsewhere, culminating in calls not just for radical reform but for abolition. Rafe McGregor deploys a plethora of innovative conceptual and methodological tools to understand and tackle the problems besetting police and policing. These draw on philosophy, cultural and literary studies, and political economy to illuminate the requirements of good policing and how police leaders can restore these. This is essential reading for all students and practitioners of policing, and beyond that of our contemporary moral and political quagmire."

Emeritus Professor Robert Reiner, London School of Economics

"McGregor combines an innovative approach with a meticulously evidenced diagnosis of the transatlantic crisis of police legitimacy. However, this book doesn't stop at diagnosis and includes a radical yet practicable framework for change which skilfully addresses policing practices, institutions and their systemic context. This is a powerful manifesto for change."

Professor Sarah Charman, University of Portsmouth

"Drawing on policing scholarship and Rafe McGregor's own experience as a police officer, this book provides a sophisticated account of the factors that corrode the legitimacy of Anglo-American policing, offering an intelligent roadmap for the recovery of police legitimacy. Essential reading for legitimacy theorists."

Emeritus Professor Mike Hough, Birkbeck, University of London

"In his book, Recovering Police Legitimacy, Rafe McGregor tackles the most crucial issue facing police around the globe. Legitimacy is recognized as the foundation for effective policing and McGregor eloquently describes the "legitimacy" problem facing police in both the US and the UK. McGregor brings both academic and practitioner credentials to the task. He is the author 15 books and served as a police officer in Durban, South Africa and his tightly researched work deserves wide readership."

Captain Howard Rahtz, (RET.), Cincinnati Police Department

"Police legitimacy is essential in a healthy democracy. In this book, McGregor argues that police in the UK and the US are experiencing an unprecedented legitimacy crisis. To restore legitimacy, he recommends changes in policing as a practice, policing as an institution, and the systemic context of policing. His recommendations are thought-provoking and worthy of serious consideration."

Professor Ed Maguire, Arizona State University

RECOVERING POLICE LEGITIMACY

A Radical Framework

Rafe McGregor

LONDON AND NEW YORK

Designed cover image: Rafe McGregor
First published 2025
by Routledge
4 Park Square, Milton Park, Abingdon, Oxon OX14 4RN

and by Routledge
605 Third Avenue, New York, NY 10158

Routledge is an imprint of the Taylor & Francis Group, an informa business

© 2025 Rafe McGregor

The right of Rafe McGregor to be identified as author of this work has been asserted in accordance with sections 77 and 78 of the Copyright, Designs and Patents Act 1988.

All rights reserved. No part of this book may be reprinted or reproduced or utilised in any form or by any electronic, mechanical, or other means, now known or hereafter invented, including photocopying and recording, or in any information storage or retrieval system, without permission in writing from the publishers.

Trademark notice: Product or corporate names may be trademarks or registered trademarks, and are used only for identification and explanation without intent to infringe.

British Library Cataloguing in Publication Data
A catalogue record for this book is available from the British Library

Library of Congress Cataloging-in-Publication Data
Names: McGregor, Rafe, author.
Title: Recovering police legitimacy : a radical framework / Rafe McGregor.
Description: Abingdon, Oxon ; New York, NY : Routledge, 2024. | Includes bibliographical references and index.
Identifiers: LCCN 2024004417 (print) | LCCN 2024004418 (ebook) | ISBN 9781032546407 (hardback) | ISBN 9781032546414 (paperback) | ISBN 9781003425922 (ebook)
Subjects: LCSH: Police--United States--Public opinion. | Police--Great Britain--Public opinion. | Police training--United States. | Police training--Great Britain. | Police ethics--United States. | Police ethics--Great Britain. | Critical theory.
Classification: LCC HV8139 .M334 2024 (print) | LCC HV8139 (ebook) | DDC 363.2/0973--dc23/eng/20240229
LC record available at https://lccn.loc.gov/2024004417
LC ebook record available at https://lccn.loc.gov/2024004418

ISBN: 978-1-032-54640-7 (hbk)
ISBN: 978-1-032-54641-4 (pbk)
ISBN: 978-1-003-42592-2 (ebk)

DOI: 10.4324/9781003425922

Typeset in Sabon
by Taylor & Francis Books

CONTENTS

Acknowledgements ix

PART 1
The Problem 1

  1 The Crisis of Police Legitimacy 3

  2 Practice, Institution, and Context 34

PART 2
Methodology 59

  3 Autoethnography 61

  4 Critical Case Studies 86

PART 3
Case Studies 113

  5 Southern California, 2013–2014 115

6	West Yorkshire, 1980	151
7	Los Angeles, 1947–1958	191

PART 4
The Solution — 229

8	Public Protection and Police Legitimacy	231
9	Reviewing the Evidence	258
10	The Radical Framework	286

Index — *316*

ACKNOWLEDGEMENTS

I have been thinking, reading, and writing about this subject since 2016, when I published the first of four book reviews on police reform, driven by scepticism about the impact of the President's Task Force on 21st Century Policing in the US and the introduction of the Policing Education Qualifications Framework (PEQF) in the UK. My first 32 months of research were unpaid as I was a university teacher at my first institution and the project was not supported by my second. The remainder had institutional support, albeit without any relief from teaching or administration.

The reviews were published in the following journals:

1. McGregor, R. (2017). *To Protect and Serve: How to Fix America's Police* by Norm Stamper, *Policing: A Journal of Policy and Practice*, 11 (1), 118–119.
2. McGregor, R. (2017). *Race, Riots, and the Police* by Howard Rahtz, *Policing and Society: An International Journal of Research and Policy*, 27 (5), 580–582.
3. McGregor, R. (2018). *The War on Cops: How the New Attack on Law and Order Makes Everyone Less Safe* by Heather Mac Donald, *Journal of Applied Philosophy*, 35 (3), 634–636.

4. McGregor, R. (2020). *Evidence-Based Policing: Translating Research into Practice* by Cynthia Lum & Christopher S. Koper, *Police Practice and Research: An International Journal*, 21 (2), 204–205.

This book draws on two previously published articles, although they have both been subject to substantial revision:

5. McGregor, R. (2021). James Ellroy's Critical Criminology: Crimes of the Powerful in the *Underworld USA Trilogy*. *Critical Criminology: An International Journal*, 29 (2), 349–365.
6. McGregor, R. (2021). Four Characteristics of Policing as a Practice. *Policing: A Journal of Policy and Practice*, 15 (3), 1842–1853.

I was also provided with the opportunity to discuss autoethnography as a method in policing research in more detail than possible in this book, which was published as:

7. McGregor, R. (2023). Autoethnography: Analysing the World of Policing from Within. In: Fleming, J. & Charman, S. (eds). *Routledge International Handbook of Police Ethnography*. Abingdon: Routledge, 391–405.

There are several people I would like to thank, living and dead, many of whom are former or serving police officers or police staff. This book could not have been written without the assistance of: Thembinkosi Chiliza, Steven Cross, Shaun Hutt, Rensia Mathee, Sean Murray, Connie Oelofse, and Martin Wright. I am very grateful to: Iain Barr, Avi Brisman, David Churchill, Marianne Colbran, Karen Cummings, Ian Cummins, Gail Ennis, Scott Keay, Bill McClanahan, Keith McLachlan, Brian McNeill, Faheema Patel, Tom Sutton, Gali Perry, Owen West, and Tzachi Zamir. I would also like to thank: Matthew Bacon, Eleanor Carter, Sarah Charman, Jenny Fleming, Wally Insch, Serena Kennedy, Mandy Precious, Mario Slugan, Emily Spurrell, Jonathan Webber, and five anonymous referees (three from Routledge and two from the publisher that turned the proposal down). As usual, there are a handful of people (two in particular) who both helped and hindered the research, but I shall respect their privacy here. As always, I thank my wife, Linda, for her patience, forbearance, and resilience.

This book is a work of critical theory, defined by Bernard Harcourt in his monumental *Critique and Praxis: A Critical Philosophy of Illusions, Values, and Action* (published by Columbia University Press in 2020) as theory that aims to change rather than just interpret the world. The judgements I make are both approximate and temporary and I welcome revisions of my research that draw on and then discard it in working towards a more accurate understanding of what police legitimacy is and if and how it can be recovered in the US and the UK. My approximations are as accurate as I have been able to make them as of March 2024.

PART 1
The Problem

1
THE CRISIS OF POLICE LEGITIMACY

This book is about the crisis of police legitimacy in the US and the UK. More specifically, it is about how law enforcement agencies in the US and constabularies in the UK can recover at least some of the legitimacy that has been lost in the last decade. As such, it sets out a comprehensive framework for recovering police legitimacy, which is built from the bottom up, from the characteristics of policing as a practice to the political context within which the criminal justice system functions. The aim of this chapter is twofold: to diagnose the problem the book aims to solve and to review the existing solutions to that problem. The problem is the recent loss of public trust in the police as an institution whose purpose is to protect the public in both the US and the UK, a crisis of legitimacy. Police legitimacy is the public recognition of the right of law enforcement agencies and constabularies to exercise their legal powers, which is supervenient on trust and likely to be withdrawn in the event of either a reliance on coercion or a failure to protect the public. The Transatlantic crisis of legitimacy has been aggravated by the militarisation of the US police from the late 1980s and the politicisation of the UK police from the mid-1980s. The crisis was the subject of almost continuous media attention during the COVID-19 pandemic, during which two police officers – Derek Chauvin in the US and Wayne Couzens in the UK – were convicted of murder in high-profile cases. Broadly construed, there are three categories of solution. Reform aims to repair the institution of policing from within, making it more just and humane, usually by means of recruitment, training, discipline, and oversight. Three decades of substantial police reforms have, however, neither averted nor ameliorated the crisis. Defunding aims to redirect funding for the institution of policing to institutions that create sustainable safety for all, such as welfare, healthcare, and local government. The redirection is complicated by the fact that the increase in funding for other services must precede the decrease in police funding. Abolition aims to dismantle the institution of policing in its entirety, replacing law enforcement agencies and constabularies with community safety and conflict resolution in local, self-governing zones. Notwithstanding, the response to and investigation of violent crime would have to be by an institution that was trained and equipped in a very similar way to the police.

1.1 Legitimacy

'Police legitimacy' is a compound of two complex concepts, neither of which is easy to define. My concern with 'the police' as an institution and 'policing' as a practice is restricted to what Peter Manning (2010: 3) refers to as *Anglo-American Democratic Policing*: AADP nations are 'the bearers of the Peel legacy – the notion of a visible, reactive, bureaucratically organized means of state-based resolution of conflict with minimal force'.[1] He specifies these nations as the US, Canada, the UK, Australia, and New Zealand, all of which are English-speaking and all of which have a common law rather than civil law based criminal justice system (two features that distinguish them from most European nations). Policing in Anglo-American democracies is challenging in virtue of their combination of individual rights and collective diversity and Manning shares Robert Reiner's (2011, 2021) scepticism about the predication of democracy on inclusion and compliance rather than exclusion and conflict. My subject is US and UK policing exclusively, approached as two AADP nations in which the institution of policing is experiencing a crisis of legitimacy. The denotation of 'legitimacy' relevant to the police is conformity to a body of rules that are acknowledged as binding or conformity to a set of principles that are acknowledged as binding. Even this basic understanding recognises two distinct aspects of legitimacy, the legal (body of rules) and the moral (set of principles). The literature on the legitimacy of the police and the criminal justice system more broadly is dominated by procedural justice theory, which explores the relationships among the law, morality, and legitimacy in detail.

Tom Tyler (1990, 2011) introduced procedural justice theory by contending that laws are only effective if they induce voluntary compliance and that voluntary compliance is a product of the combination of morality and legitimacy. The former is an individual's view of right and wrong and the latter 'a quality possessed by an authority, a law, or an institution that leads others to feel obligated to obey its decisions and directives' (Tyler 2011: 34). In his study of chief officers' and senior leaders' justifications of police powers, Ian Shannon (2022: 43) provides a simpler but compatible definition of legitimacy as 'a right to exercise power'. David Beetham (1991) argues that there are three dimensions to legitimacy and that the exercise of power is only legitimate when it (1) conforms to rules based on (2) the shared beliefs of dominant and subordinate and (3) the consent of the latter to their subordination. The concept of consent is especially significant to policing. Shannon draws on Beetham to qualify legitimacy as a right to exercise power that is both based on rational rules and broadly accepted by those to whom the rules apply, which once again includes both the legal (rule-based) and moral (consensual) aspects of legitimacy. The idea of policing by consent is a fundamental part of what Manning refers to as the Peel legacy. Shannon notes that Peel's principles of policing, which are claimed to have been issued in the first General Instructions to the Metropolitan Police in 1829, are almost certainly the invention of historian Charles Reith in the middle of the 20th century. There are also a plurality of publics rather than a single, homogeneous public and each of these publics can either give or withhold consent. The probability that both the Peelian principles and policing by consent are legitimating myths does not, however, diminish their importance.

6 The Problem

Mike Hough (2021) summarises the relevance of procedural justice theory to police legitimacy as follows: procedural fairness rather than outcomes fairness produces trust, which in turn confers legitimacy. In other words, legitimacy is based on trust, which is a function of *how* the police do what they do, not *what* they actually do. Following Reiner, Hough recognises the significance of the police as symbolic of both the state and the law, in consequence of which police legitimacy is embedded in the broader contexts of judicial legitimacy and political legitimacy. Manning describes the crucial relationship between public trust and democratic governance, the necessity of public trust to the operation of the criminal justice system, and the importance of procedure to securing public trust in the police. Trust is not just crucial to democratic politics and bureaucracy, but inextricable from the notion of policing by consent. When trust is lost, consent is withdrawn. Shannon (2022: 137) quotes one of the (anonymous) deputy chief constables he interviewed, who explained consent in terms of trust alone: 'I think the trust is very hard won over lots of years and also rooted in tradition and it is very easily lost.' Former Cincinnati Police Department captain Howard Rahtz (2016: 53) reinforces this relationship by explaining trust in terms of a bank account: 'All police departments have a certain trust balance in their account. Actions by every officer – from those answering the phone to those responding to a call – will add to or subtract from this account.' According to Tyler (2004), this trust (or its absence) is in the motivation of the police, which I shall construe as public protection (more commonly 'public safety' in the US) and discuss in Chapter 2. One of the insights from procedural justice theory is that there is a reciprocal relationship among public trust, policing by consent, and police legitimacy.

Shannon found that chief officers justified their right to exercise power by means of a combination of the legitimating narratives of public protection, consensual policing, and policing that is both within the parameters set by law and accountable to the law. None of his interviewees claimed that any of these narratives was itself sufficient for legitimacy. Returning to my initial definition of the term, public protection and consensual policing are moral aspects of police legitimacy (set of principles) and operating within the bounds of the law the legal aspect of police legitimacy (body of rules).

Policing can be legal without being legitimate. One of the chief constables interviewed by Shannon (2022: 182) provided an example of the annual issuing of thousands of fixed penalty notices for cannabis possession: '"We were criminalising young people, perfectly within the law, simply to tick a box to satisfy HMIC [Her Majesty's Inspectorate of Constabulary] and the Home Office – that's not legitimate."' Manning (2010) makes a similar observation when he cites research on the Boston Gun Project (1996–1997). In spite of acknowledging the police as both competent and dependable, residents of high-crime areas did not recognise their legitimacy because of their tactics (failure to differentiate between the innocent and the guilty) and lack of respect (rudeness and dismissiveness). The response of the residents provides further evidence for Hough's claim that procedural fairness is more important than outcomes fairness with respect to police legitimacy. In the remainder of this book, I shall employ the following definition of *police legitimacy*: public recognition of the right of the institution of policing to exercise its legal powers. That recognition is supervenient on public trust in the police. It is likely to be withdrawn in the event of either a reliance on coercion or a failure to protect the public.

The importance of establishing and maintaining police legitimacy to the institution of policing, the criminal justice system, and democratic governance seems obvious, but has received relatively little attention in the US, where the crisis of legitimacy with which I am concerned is usually referred to as a 'crisis of confidence'. In his foreword to Hough's study of procedural justice in policing, Tyler (2021: ix) dates the US concern with 'popular legitimacy within policed communities' to 2004 and remarks on the belated acknowledgement of the importance of 'community trust in the police' by the President's Task Force on 21st Century Policing in 2015. An exception to the rule is Thomas Abt (2019), who draws on Beetham to delineate two categories of legitimacy: effectiveness and fairness. Effectiveness 'is judged by whether the primary purpose of the law – maintaining public safety and order – is achieved' (Abt 2019: 61). To achieve fairness, 'laws must also be enforced according to widely accepted values, including transparency, impartiality, proportionality, and equality, among others' (Abt 2019: 61). Taken together, these categories are consistent with my delineation of police legitimacy: lack of effectiveness corresponds to failure to protect the public and lack of fairness to a reliance on coercion. Abt maintains that loss of community confidence in the ability or will of the police to keep them safe results in a withdrawal of cooperation in which communities either protect themselves or rely on organised crime to maintain order. While there has been a dramatic overall decrease in violence in the US since 1994, it remains high in many communities of concentrated poverty, a large proportion of which are also communities of colour (a situation mirrored in the UK).[2] Abt (2019: 68) describes the legitimacy deficits in such communities as a catch-22: 'to improve safety, there must be trust, but to improve trust, there must be safety.' He argues that police legitimacy is essential to urban violence reduction and that the current crisis of legitimacy has – and continues to – cause loss of life.

1.2 Transatlantic Crisis

The 1990s saw a dramatic expansion of the crime control apparatus on both sides of the Atlantic, which David Garland (2001) attributes to the mass media response to rising crime in the UK from 1955 and in the US from 1960. The shift from a culture of welfarism to a culture of control was accelerated by the combination of neoliberal economic policies with conservative political policies. In the 1980s, Ronald Reagan and Margaret Thatcher inaugurated the reduction of social welfare and upper income taxation that set the US and the UK on trajectories to return to the peak income inequality of the early 20th century (Chancel et al. 2022). Thatcher treated striking miners as a threat to national security in 1984 and Reagan amplified the 'War on Drugs' in 1986. The expansion of crime control included the introduction of non-discretionary or zero-tolerance policing in the US (loosely underpinned by Broken Windows theory), the introduction of a more punitive youth justice system in the UK (following the Crime and Disorder Act 1998), and the rise of the prison populations of both countries to the extent that the US became the highest in the world in 2001 and the UK the highest in the European Union in 2002 (Walmsey 2002, 2003). One of the many problems with the expansion of policing is the extent to which the institution of policing is complicit in differential treatment, not only sustaining but aggravating socioeconomic disadvantage. This is especially pertinent to racism in the US and classism in the UK, but police in both countries have been accused of racism, classism, and sexism (Edwards 1989; Sherman, Schmidt & Rogan 1992; Wacquant 2004; Bowling, Reiner & Sheptycki 2019; Elliott-Cooper 2020; Vitale 2021). The aggravation of these and other inequalities is in direct contravention of what Manning (2010: xiii) regards as the linchpin of democratic policing, the *difference principle*: 'given the current range of inequalities in education, opportunity, income, and skills, any police practice, especially that shaped by policy, should not further increase extant inequalities.' The crisis of police legitimacy is a consequence of the violation of this principle, which has been facilitated by the processes of militarisation in the US and politicisation in the UK.[3]

1.2.1 Militarisation

Pete Kraska (1993, 2001) was one of the first academics to study the militarisation of the police in the US, documenting the impact of the War on Drugs on policing from the late 1980s and the blurring of the roles and responsibilities of the police and the military from the early 1990s. Militarisation undermines police legitimacy by relying on coercion rather than consensus to protect the public. Kraska's (2007: 505) research has focused on the proliferation and increased deployment of 'police paramilitary units' (PPU), more commonly known as Special Weapons and Tactics (SWAT) teams. This trend is a symptom of the militarist ideology created by the War on Drugs, which was exacerbated by the War on Terror in the new century. The results of this militarism were displayed in Ferguson in 2014, when mass and social media disseminated footage of armoured fighting vehicles supporting police officers in battle dress uniforms with military equipment alongside those armed and equipped for traditional public order policing. Radley Balko (2021) develops several of the themes pioneered by Kraska, including the concomitant proliferation of SWAT teams and no-knock warrants. The rationale for SWAT teams is the preference for the police rather than the military to deal with siege situations (such as the Texas Tower

Sniper in 1966) and hostage rescues (such as the Munich massacre in 1972), i.e. very-high-risk incidents that require specialist training and equipment for safe resolution. Notwithstanding, the first US SWAT team was formed by the City of Los Angeles Police Department (LAPD) in response to the Watts riots of 1965 and its first operation was a badly botched execution of arrest warrants on the Los Angeles chapter of the Black Panther Party in 1969 (Balko 2021). This initial link between militarisation and racism would persist and even increase as the decades progressed. By the 50th anniversary of the first SWAT raid, at least half of the US' approximately 18,000 law enforcement agencies had their own PPUs, a phenomenal figure when one considers that approximately 5,400 of those agencies have fewer than ten agents (Fleischer 2019; Reaves 2015).

One of several indicators of militarisation is the number of suspects killed by police. Notoriously, there is no official record of these killings in the US, with databases having been established by the abolitionist Campaign Zero (Mapping Police Violence, since 2013), the Fatal Encounters Dot Org charity (Fatal Encounters, since 2014), *The Washington Post* (Police Shootings Database, since 2015), and *The Guardian* (The Counted, since 2015). A qualitative rather than quantitative approach is, however, more revealing of the extent of the militarism. If one considers, for example, cases in which one or more police officers shot a Black man who was completely unarmed (without a firearm, replica, or other weapon) dead, then the following stand out: Jonathan Ferrell (2013, Charlotte, NC), Michael Brown (2014, Ferguson), Ezell Ford (2014, Los Angeles), Walter Scott (2015, North Charleston, SC), Samuel DuBose (2015, Cincinnati), Stephon Clark (2018, Sacramento), and Lindani Myeni (2021, Nuʻuanu, HI). In each of these incidents police officers responded to either flight, resistance, or assault with excessive rather than reasonable force. This reluctance to engage physically with suspects, using either defensive or offensive techniques for arrest, is part of the military mindset, which prioritises maximum force and has, in the US, been increasingly concerned with force protection ('officer safety') since the 1990s (Barry 2020; McChrystal 2013). There are two sets of evidence I cite for this claim, neither of which have received much attention: the number of rounds fired by police officers and the failure of police officers to administer first aid to suspects they have shot.

Each round fired by each officer should be independently justifiable. In cases where a suspect is wearing a ballistic vest or where it is unclear whether the round has hit the suspect, there may well be justification for a second round and possibly more. In cases where a police officer is under fire, the temptation to return fire with multiple – and poorly aimed – shots is completely understandable, albeit one that would ideally be resisted in urban areas. All of the above examples involve multiple shots being fired at unarmed suspects. An ABC News article provides some relevant statistics: the average number of shots fired by police officers in each of the City of New York Police Department's (NYPD) shooting incidents was five in 1995 and 3.2 in 2006 (Baram 2006).[4] There is no information on the circumstances of these shootings, but unless NYPD officers were attacked with lethal weapons on multiple occasions, even three rounds per officer per incident is high. Although every time a police officer fires a shot she must accept responsibility for an attempt to kill the suspect, the purpose of firing is to either protect life or facilitate arrest – not to kill. Killing is an unfortunate and foreseeable effect of police firearm use, but should never be the purpose of that use. In consequence, a police officer who has wounded a suspect (whether by shooting or another use of force) should administer first aid as soon as it is safe to do so. Typically, this would involve the officer approaching a suspect who has dropped to the ground, securing the suspect's weapon, holstering their own firearm, and then administering first aid. If the suspect continues to resist, this may not be possible, but the above examples involve officers either handcuffing a wounded suspect or standing guard while a wounded suspect bleeds to death. Institutional or legal action against officers who cause serious injury to a suspect and then fail to deliver first aid is extremely rare, even though it is a violation of the Eighth Amendment's prohibition of cruel and unusual punishment (Eldridge 2020; Williams 2020; US Department of Justice Civil Rights Division & US Attorney's Office District of Minnesota Civil Division 2023). In February 2022, former Minneapolis Police Department (MPD) Officers James Alexander Kueng and Thomas Lane were convicted for failure to render first aid to George Floyd and my hope is that the verdicts will set a national precedent for professional standards in police use of force.

1.2.2 Politicisation

There are two intersections of policing and politics that are related to but distinct from what I refer to as the politicisation of the police: governance and function. 'Governance' concerns the level at which police services and police chiefs are accountable to government officials where 'level' refers to local, regional, or national oversight. As an example, the majority of the US' thousands of law enforcement agencies are local, responsible to local or municipal authorities. In contrast, the majority of police personnel in the UK are employed in regional or metropolitan ('territorial') constabularies.[5] 'Function' refers to the distinction between high policing and low policing, described by Manning (2010: 46) as the difference between 'functions associated with national security' (for example, border control and counter terrorism) and the 'routine domestic functions' of policing (for example, emergency response and crime reduction). High policing is always carried out in the interests of the nation state, although national, regional, and local police services can all serve both a high and low function. My use of 'politicisation' refers to neither the level of governance nor the set of functions of AADP, but to the extent to which the institution is actually democratic, i.e. oriented to protecting the public rather than a particular interest group within that public. Ian Loader and Aogán Mulcahy (2003: 44) articulate this conception as protecting the general order, 'the preservation of basic standards of public tranquillity in which all social groups have a stake'. In the UK, politicisation has been associated with perceptions of the police as protecting the specific order of the incumbent political regime at the expense of the general order.[6] Politicisation undermines police legitimacy by failing to protect (all of) the public.

Ben Bowling, Robert Reiner, and James Sheptycki (2019) characterise the British police as undergoing a process of depoliticisation from 1856 to 1959, which was reversed from 1959 to 1992. Depoliticisation is based on two features: non-partisanship and accountability. Non-partisanship meant that the police as an institution was not subject to direct political control and that the various police authorities did not interfere in operational policing or in the policies underpinning operational policing. Regarding the second feature, Bowling, Reiner, and Sheptycki (2019: 80) describe how, by the middle of the 20th century, 'the police were purported to be accountable through an almost mystical process of identification with the British people, not the state'. Non-partisanship suffered in the 1970s, when both the Police Federation (the English and Welsh equivalent of a trade union) and Metropolitan Police Service (MPS) Commissioner Robert Mark (from 1972 to 1977) took active roles in political debate. Mark was openly critical of the Labour Party and resigned following a well-publicised dispute with the Home Secretary over the Police Act 1976. Identification with the police began to weaken in the 1960s, when they were seen as less representative of the public, a development that was intensified by race riots in London, Liverpool, Birmingham, Leeds, and Manchester in 1981.

The turning point in the politicisation of the police was their deployment in the interests of national security by the second Thatcher ministry during the Miners' Strike of 1984 to 1985 (McCabe & Wallington 1988; Milne 2004; Woodman 2018). Bowling, Reiner, and Sheptycki describe the last three decades of policing as being dominated by fiscal efficiency and 'value for money', but this is an extension of the politicisation begun by Thatcher, which was embraced by the four New Labour ministries from 1997 to 2010 and characterised by an increase in the control of the police by the Home Secretary and an increase in the targeting of anti-capitalist activists (Loader & Mulcahy 2003; Wilson & Walton 2019; Netpol 2020). The Police and Magistrates' Courts Act 1994 gave the Home Secretary the power to set national police objectives, which was exercised in a Home Office performance management regime based on the imposition of quantitative targets. The Police Act 1996 and the Police Act 2002 both yielded further control of operational policing to the Home Secretary. Public dissatisfaction with the policing of the 2009 G20 London summit protests and the reporting on the Spy Cops Scandal by *The Guardian* in 2010 was followed by the revelation that the police officer at the centre of the latter (Mark Kennedy) had also been present at the former, a high court ruling that police tactics at the protest were unlawful, and the launch of the ongoing Undercover Policing Inquiry (Wilson 2021). The police were also criticised for their use of force in response to the anti-fracking protests in England from 2016 to 2019 and for categorising Extinction Rebellion, a nonviolent environmental organisation, as politically extremist in 2020 (Gilmore et al. 2019; Wall 2021). Former Home Secretaries Priti Patel (from 2019 to 2022) and Suella Braverman (from 2022 to 2023) were the architects of the Police, Crime, Sentencing and Courts Act 2022 and the Public Order Act 2023, both of which limited the right to protest and increased the police's public order powers.

Patel was accused of attempting to control chief constables by amending the Policing Protocol, which was introduced with the Police Reform and Social Responsibility Act 2011 (Dodd 2022a). The act was a response to dual concerns about four decades of increasing government control and decreasing oversight by local police authorities. These authorities were replaced with Police and Crime Commissioners (PCCs, a category that includes Police, Fire and Crime Commissioners in some counties and the mayors of London, Manchester, and West Yorkshire), who are elected by the public every four years (Rogers 2017). PCCs were intended to reverse the totalising trend of centralisation and to provide a safeguard against chief constables who were not responsive to their publics. The new form of governance has succeeded in reducing the power of chief constables, who have lost the operational autonomy they held under police authorities (Shannon 2022).[7] The transfer of control advanced rather than reversed the totalising trend, however, as the elected officials divided along party lines. From 2012 to 2021, the proportion of independent PCCs decreased from 29% to zero and the Conservative Party majority increased from 39% to 77%, consolidating the Home Secretary's power (Hamilton 2021; Rix 2021; Casey et al. 2023).

1.2.3 COVID-19 Pandemic

The UK responded to the COVID-19 pandemic with three national 'lockdowns', the first of which began in March 2020 and the last of which ended in March 2021. All other restrictions, including those on socialising, were withdrawn in February 2022 (GOV.UK 2022).

The US responded at the state rather than federal level and although most of its 50 states were in lockdown by April 2020, the majority of lockdowns had been terminated by the end of the following month. By July 2022, all states had withdrawn almost all COVID-19-related restrictions (The New York Times 2022). The lockdowns presented at least a threefold challenge to the police. First, the police were required to deal with protests from libertarians, anti-vaccinationists, and conspiracy theorists, which began almost immediately in both the UK and US. There were violent protests in London in September 2020 and from March to August in 2021. Most of the protests in the US were peaceful, although many were attended by armed right-wing extremist groups (Ward 2020; Özdüzen, Bogdan & Ozgul 2021). Second, even when there was no organised resistance to lockdown, many people disobeyed the new laws, which the police were required to enforce. Third, there were concerns in the UK about how different constabularies were enforcing the new laws, with high numbers of fines issued by some and very few by others (Hough 2021). There was also concern about differential treatment due to the disproportionate fining of Black, Asian and Minority Ethnic (BAME) individuals, which was intensified in November 2021, when Prime Minister Boris Johnson, his Downing Street staff, and Conservative officials were accused of breaking the law on numerous occasions in the 'Partygate' scandal (BBC 2022; Slawson & Thomas 2022). A broad but accurate summary of the Transatlantic impact of the pandemic on policing is that it placed the police under greater public scrutiny at a time of heightened social tensions. In such circumstances, the actions of two police officers caused incalculable harm to police legitimacy in their respective countries.

On 25 May 2020 Officer Derek Chauvin and three of his colleagues in the MPD arrested George Floyd on suspicion of using a counterfeit bill. Chauvin, who is White, used excessive force against Floyd, who was Black, kneeling on his neck for 8 minutes and 46 seconds. The neck compression caused a fatal heart attack and Floyd's death was filmed by bystanders (The Washington Post 2020; The New York Times 2020). The video was shared on social media and attacks on police vehicles and stations began in Minneapolis the next day. By the end of May, there had been protests in 75 cities across 27 states, with 4,400 people arrested. By the end of June there had been protests in 2,000 cities across all 50 states, with up to 25 people killed, although the latter figure remains disputed (Taylor 2020; Burch et al. 2020). These protests spread to 60 countries worldwide, with at least four violent protests in London and Newcastle in the first two weeks of June. The difficulty of dealing with the protests was exacerbated by the presence of right-wing extremist counter-protesters in both countries. The number and size of the protests diminished as the year progressed, but they were reinvigorated in March 2021, when Chauvin's trial for murder started. Chauvin was found guilty on three charges, which included third-degree murder, on 20 April 2021 and sentenced to 22 and a half years in prison (Carter 2021).

On 9 March 2021 Constable Wayne Couzens, of the MPS' Parliamentary and Diplomatic Protection unit, was arrested on suspicion of kidnapping Sarah Everard, a 33-year-old marketing executive, the previous week. Couzens exploited COVID-19 legislation to detain Everard extrajudicially, after which he raped her, murdered her, and disposed of her corpse in a wood. Everard's remains were found the day after Couzens' arrest and she was identified by her dental records on 12 March (Morton 2021). An activist group called Reclaim These Streets organised a series of vigils to be held across the UK the following day. On the evening of 13 March, the MPS forcibly dispersed a group of several hundred people at a vigil on Clapham Common. Four mourners were arrested and video footage of police officers pushing and grappling with women was shared on social media (Dodd & Grierson 2021). The use of force was reasonable, proportionate, and supported by Her Majesty's Inspectorate of Constabulary and Fire & Rescue Services (HMICFRS, 2021), but the images of policemen from the same service as Couzens laying hands on women paying tribute to his victim did significant damage to the MPS' reputation. Couzens pleaded guilty to murder on 8 June and was sentenced to life imprisonment with a whole life order on 30 September (Alibhai 2021). On the same day, the Investigatory Powers Tribunal (IPT, 2021) handed down a judgement that the MPS had fundamentally breached the human rights of several women who were subjected to long-term surveillance in an undercover policing operation from 2003 to 2009 (by Kennedy and other police officers). Commissioner Cressida Dick resigned in February 2022 and the MPS was moved from routine to robust monitoring by HMICFRS in June 2022 (Dodd 2022b).

1.3 Reform, Defunding, and Abolition

The existence of a Transatlantic crisis in police legitimacy and its exacerbation by the circumstances of the COVID-19 pandemic are little disputed. The contribution of militarisation to the US crisis is similarly well known and while the significance of politicisation to the UK crisis has received much less academic attention, it is a recurring theme in the media. Broadly construed, three solutions have been proposed to date: reform, defunding, and abolition. Although many individual approaches to the crisis include aspects of all three, the categories remain useful because of their distinct goals. *Reform* aims to repair the institution of policing from within, making it more just and humane, usually by means of recruitment, training, discipline, and oversight. *Defunding* aims to redirect funding for the institution of policing to institutions that create sustainable safety for all, such as welfare, healthcare, and local government. *Abolition* aims to dismantle the institution of policing in its entirety, replacing police services with community safety and conflict resolution in local, self-governing zones. An exploration of the full extent, diversity, and merit of the versions of each of these solutions that have been proposed and published in the last 30 years is beyond the scope of my inquiry. I do not, however, wish to dismiss the solutions without recognising their value to my aim, which is to establish a comprehensive framework for the recovery of police legitimacy. My argument here is simply that regardless of the merits of individual solutions to the crisis of police legitimacy, each of the categories has at least one significant problem that must be overcome. In consequence of these problems my recommendation is to approach the crisis of police legitimacy from a completely different perspective, which I set out in Chapter 2.

1.3.1 Reform

Police reform aims to repair the institution of policing from within, making it more just and humane. This is usually achieved by means such as diversifying recruitment, improving initial and in-service training, streamlining service disciplinary procedures, and enhancing internal and external oversight, as in Ross Deuchar, Vaughn Crichlow, and Seth Fallik's (2021) recent study. While the literature on evidence-based policing (EBP) is not usually regarded as part of the reform agenda, it should not be ignored and Cynthia Lum and Christopher Koper (2017) provide an example of how the Evidence-Based Policing Matrix can increase police effectiveness and efficiency in the absence of changes usually associated with reform.[8] If Abt (2019) is correct in identifying effectiveness as a significant component of legitimacy, then EBP is a potential solution to the current crisis. More complex proposals for reform extend the repair required from police tactics to police strategy, as in Martin Innes and colleagues' (2020) study of the neighbourhood policing model. More complex still is the extension of the repair from the institution of policing to either the criminal justice system, such as in Michael Huemer's (2021) treatise on the US legal system, or, further still, to the political system, such as Bowling, Reiner, and Sheptycki's (2019) call for social democratic governance. What links all these approaches is that there are no substantial changes to the institutions or systems involved – policing, criminal justice, or political – they are all adjusted incrementally from within rather than reimagined or replaced. An obvious advantage of reform is that it is easier to implement than more fundamental changes. The problem with police reform is obvious: it does not – or, at least, *has not* – worked.

Two examples serve particularly well, the Christopher Commission on the LAPD and the Macpherson report on the MPS. The Christopher Commission (Independent Commission on the Los Angeles Police Department 1991) was established less than a month after the footage of LAPD officers using excessive force against Rodney King was released on 3 March 1991. Although it did not employ these terms, the Commission found the LAPD institutionally racist and over-militarised, the latter problem evinced by the widespread use of excessive force by officers and a departmental emphasis on crime control rather than crime prevention. The recommended reforms were delayed by rioting in April and May 1992, but pursued in earnest thereafter. These reforms did not, however, avert the Rampart scandal of 1997 to 1998, one of the largest and most notorious police corruption cases in the US, and the LAPD have been implicated in the current crisis with the killing of Ezell Ford in 2014 and Charley Leundeu Keunang in 2015 (Kirk & Boyer 2001). The Stephen Lawrence Inquiry (Macpherson et al. 1999) was launched in July 1997, four years after the murder of Black teenager Stephen Lawrence in a racially motived attack and following allegations that there had been major failings in the police investigation. The Macpherson report found that the MPS was institutionally racist and that there was a lack of confidence in the constabulary in BAME communities. In 2008, Assistant Commissioner Tarique Ghaffur, the highest-ranking BAME police officer in the UK, accused both the Commissioner, Ian Blair, and the MPS of racism, following which Blair was forced to resign by London Mayor Boris Johnson (Gray 2008). Three years later, inconsistencies in MPS reports of the fatal shooting of Mark Duggan, a Black man in possession of an illegal firearm, provided the catalyst for the 2011 England riots, a week of violent disorder in August (Lewis et al. 2011).

Returning to the US, the President's Task Force on 21st Century Policing (2015) was established in 2014, in response to the Ferguson protests, but the recommendations for the national implementation of community-oriented policing ('community policing' in the UK) prevented neither the murder of George Floyd nor the anger of the those who protested against it. The National Police Chiefs' Council and College of Policing's (2022) *Police Race Action Plan: Improving policing for Black people* aims to improve policing for Black communities in England and Wales and begins by admitting that anti-racist reform over the last quarter century has been neither substantial nor expeditious and that evidence of institutional racism remains. Tim Newburn (2022) criticises the Task Force in particular and the reform movement in general for being overly reliant on procedural justice as the solution to the crisis of police legitimacy. Regardless of whether this is an accurate assessment, no single set of reforms seem to have made a substantial difference in either the US or the UK. Neither procedural justice nor community-oriented policing averted or even ameliorated the crisis and there seems little point in continuing to pursue a solution with an apparently extensive history of failure.

1.3.2 Defunding

Police defunding aims to redirect funding for the institution of policing to other institutions. The idea is that other institutions, such as welfare, healthcare, and local government are both more effective at crime reduction than the police and capable of reducing crime without aggravating already existing inequalities. The largest and most vociferous defunding coalition is the Movement for Black Lives (M4BL, 2024), who articulate their demands in terms of divestment in local, state (regional), and federal (national) police and prisons and investment in local, state, and federal education, restorative justice, and employment, with the funding for the former being reallocated to the latter. Defunding can either be an end in itself or a means to the end of police abolition. Jennifer Cobbina (2019) is primarily concerned with the reduction of violence, specifically the reduction of police violence against minority communities, in consequence of which defunding is an end in itself. She argues that the most effective and efficient way to achieve this is to redistribute resources from criminal justice institutions to prevention and intervention programmes for at-risk young people. In contrast, Adam Elliott-Cooper (2020, 2021, 2023) regards the defunding of the criminal justice system as a means to the end of both police and prison abolition, citing statistics that are often lost in the comparison with the US: the English and Welsh prison population almost doubled from 1993 to 2016. The problem with police defunding is that the proposed redistribution of resources is not as straightforward as it seems.

Jennifer Fleetwood and John Lea (2022) are two of the few academics to have pointed out that 'defund the police' was official UK policy for at least five years and possibly nine, depending on the measurement employed. Conservative Prime Minister David Cameron responded to the Global Financial Crisis by decreasing public spending rather than increasing taxation and substantial budget cuts to the public sector were initiated with the Spending Review 2010. A decade of Conservative austerity politics followed, by the end of which the public sector was employing the smallest proportion of the country's workforce since 1945 (Toynbee & Walker 2020). The police experienced budget cuts along with the rest of the public sector and to take just one indicator of the extent of these cuts, the number of frontline police officers in England and Wales fell by 11% from 2010 to 2014 (National Debate Advisory Group 2015). The police budget reached a low in the 2015 to 2016 fiscal year and by the time Johnson announced his commitment to recruit more police officers in September 2019, numbers were 14% fewer than in 2009 (Home Office 2020). A decrease of between 11% and 14% may not sound like very much, but the problem was – and still is – a dramatic increase in workload and calls for service after the decrease in the provision of health, education, and social services.

Andrew Millie and Karen Bullock (2012: 17) describe this situation as 'the "policification" of social policy'. Referring to similar austerity politics in the US, Alex Vitale (2022) states: 'It[']s about defunding communities and using police to paper over the problems that result.' Chief constables in the UK are faced with a situation where they have to do more with less and are simply unable to meet public expectations of police services (Boulton et al. 2017; Lumsden & Black 2018; Dodd 2022c; Casey et al. 2023). Clearly, none of this is what is intended by defunding as a response to the crisis of police legitimacy. The defunding of the police must be matched with an increase in funding to the types of services mentioned above, not a corresponding decrease, which will inevitably lead to an expansion of the police function. Crucially, the increase in funding to the other services must *precede* police defunding in order to avoid replicating the UK's austerity experiment, which – paradoxically – makes defunding an expensive solution to the crisis. Kraska (2021) suggests the term 'de-policing' instead, which he uses to refer to the reduction of the police function, specifically retraction from schools, traffic, mental health, and drug abuse. I shall refer to solutions to the crisis of police legitimacy that involve the reduction of the police function as *depolicing*, which is a more accurate description of what is supposed to happen (and which may or may not be accompanied by defunding).[9] Depolicing is also used to describe a reduction in proactive police practice and while there is evidence that this actually increases effectiveness there are concerns that the withdrawal of police patrols from neighbourhoods could lead to the problem with abolition I discuss below (Deuchar, Crichlow & Fallik 2021; Abt 2019).[10]

1.3.3 Abolition

Police abolition aims to dismantle the institution of policing in its entirety. The police abolition movement emerged from the prison abolition movement, which was initiated in the US in the 1970s with the work of Thomas Mathiesen (1974) and Faye Honey Knopp (1976) and popularised with subsequent work by Angela Davis (2003) and Ruth Wilson Gilmore (2007), among others. Prison abolitionists promote either mass decarceration or the complete elimination of the prison system. Police abolitionists identify AADP as either an adaptation or development of colonial policing, which was initially performed by the military and included militias in the British Caribbean and slave patrols in the Southern states of the US (Siegel 2018; Balko 2021; Cunneen 2023). Colonial policing was both militarised and politicised and abolitionists promote the replacement of police services with community safety and conflict resolution, often in local, self-governing zones. Vitale (2021: 28) is probably the best-known contemporary abolitionist, a position he justifies with clarity and conviction: 'American police function, despite whatever good intentions they have, as a tool for managing deeply entrenched inequalities in a way that systematically produces injustices for the poor, socially marginal, and nonwhite.'[11] He provides specific examples of the violation of Manning's difference principle in the policing of homelessness, sex work, drugs, and gangs. Derecka Purnell's (2021) approach is somewhat broader, regarding the police as part of a prison-industrial complex that should be eliminated and basing her abolition on a shocking research finding: only 4% of calls for police service are about violent crime. She makes the persuasive claim that the widespread dissemination of these and related statistics would cause a large proportion of the population to reconsider their views on the need for the police.

Like police reform, the problem with police abolition is obvious: if not the police, then whom – or what? Unlike reform, abolition has not been implemented in the US or the UK so there is no conclusive evidence either way. While I am in favour of mass – or, at the very least, substantial – decarceration, I am not a prison abolitionist, unlike many of my colleagues in criminology. When asked why not, I respond with the question: what would you do with Wayne Couzens? The public needs to be protected from Couzens and the only way to do that appears to be incapacitation by means of a custodial sentence. While prison is far from ideal, it is more morally acceptable than alternative historical solutions such as execution and exile. Both Vitale and Purnell's research provide evidence for the possibility of a dramatic reduction in the size and the functions of the institution of policing, but not for the elimination of the entire institution. It seems uncontroversial to state that the police are the appropriate institution to respond to violent crime – if not the police, it would have to be a similar institution that is trained and equipped to respond to violence with reasonable force. While such calls for service may only be a tiny percentage of uniformed police work, those incidents must be investigated – and, again, if not by police detectives, then by whom?

There is also another concern, about what happens when police withdraw from a community completely. An example of this can be seen in the Capitol Hill Occupied Protest (CHOP), an autonomous zone that existed in Seattle for three weeks of June 2020. Following a week of violent clashes with residents protesting Floyd's murder, the Seattle Police Department abandoned its East Precinct in Capitol Hill in an attempt to de-escalate the situation. Six city blocks around the precinct were declared a 'no-cop zone' on 8 June and described as resembling a street fair and a commune by observers (Garcia 2020). There were no elected leaders in the zone, with most decisions made by groups of community members, although mayoral candidate Nikkita Oliver and hip hop artist Raz Simone received considerable media coverage. The impromptu 23-day experiment in police abolition created a situation that seemed to achieve the conviviality at which most late modern cities aim during the day, but was reported as being unsafe at night (Burns 2020). On 20 June, two men were shot in two separate incidents, one of whom died. Two more men were shot in two further incidents over the next two days. On 29 June, one teenager was shot dead and another wounded and on 1 July the police returned in force, dismantling barricades and arresting protesters who refused to disperse (Abrams 2020). Though the circumstances of the establishment of CHOP very likely contributed to the problem, the persistence of gun violence in a self-declared, self-governing, and self-policing community is indicative of the challenges facing police abolition.

Several points emerge from my very brief summary of existent solutions to the crisis of police legitimacy. First, the wide variation in even the tiny sample I have selected. These range from minor changes to police tactics to eliminating the entire institution of policing. Second, all of the approaches in my sample have both merits and flaws. None of the reforms that have been implemented have survived the litmus test of the pandemic and none of the approaches that have not been implemented are without genuine legal or moral difficulties. Third, all three categories of solution recognise that the institution of policing is part of the criminal justice system. This suggests that the crisis of police legitimacy may not reflect public perceptions of the police in isolation and that there are at least two levels at which police legitimacy may be undermined. My thesis is that there are three levels at which police legitimacy is undermined: the practice of policing, the institution of policing, and the systemic context of policing. As such, any comprehensive framework for recovering police legitimacy must respond to the sets of problems at each of these levels. In the next chapter, which concludes Part 1 of the book, I describe these levels in detail. I set out my methodology in Part 2, beginning with an autoethnography that identifies four characteristics of the practice of policing. These characteristics provide a lens for the analysis of the relationships among policing as a situated practice, public protection, and police legitimacy, which are explored using an epistemology of narrative fiction. Part 3 presents the three critical case studies: Southern California, 2013–2014; West Yorkshire, 1980; and Los Angeles, 1947–1959. I summarise and review the evidence from the case studies in Part 4, concluding with an elaboration of my framework for recovering police legitimacy that includes recommendations for both the US and the UK.

Notes

1 Robert Peel was Home Secretary of the United Kingdom of Great Britain and Ireland from 1822 to 1830 (with a temporary resignation in 1827), took over as Prime Minister when Charles Grey resigned in 1834, and served a full term as Prime Minister from 1841 to 1846. His title was Sir Robert Peel, 2nd Baronet.
2 For details of the decrease in violent crime in the US and the UK from the early 1990s to the mid-2010s, see: Garland (2001); Sharkey (2018); Miles and Buehler (2022).
3 There are arguments of varying degrees of strength for the militarisation and politicisation of the police in both countries, for example: Lea and Young 1993; Wacquant 2004; Neocleous 2014, 2021; Gordon 2022. I shall restrict my focus to militarisation in the US and politicisation in the UK on the basis of the excess of evidence available.
4 The article is about the phenomenon of 'contagious shooting', which is a specific instance of the wider process with which I am concerned. It nonetheless provides several more examples of multiple rounds being fired unnecessarily by police officers.
5 I discuss the institution of policing and the police establishment in the US and UK in Chapter 2.
6 For an early discussion of the relevance of the distinction between the general and specific orders, see: Marenin (1982).
7 The chief officers interviewed by Shannon (2022) were particularly perturbed by the PCCs' authority to both appoint and dismiss chief constables.
8 The UK equivalent of the EBP Matrix is the Crime Reduction Toolkit (What Works Centre for Crime Reduction 2024).
9 For an early argument for depolicing, see: Black (1980).
10 A similar concern about the reduction of proactive policing has been called the 'Ferguson effect', but this is a deliberate conflation of several phenomena for political purposes – as Abt (2019) makes very clear.
11 Notwithstanding his reputation as an abolitionist, Vitale (2021) provides equal support for depolicing in *The End of Policing*.

References

Abrams, R. (2020). Police Clear Seattle's Protest 'Autonomous Zone'. 23 July. *The New York Times*. Available at: www.nytimes.com/2020/07/01/us/seattle-protest-zone-CHOP-CHAZ-unrest.html.

Abt, T. (2019). *Bleeding Out: The Devastating Consequences of Urban Violence – and a Bold New Plan for Peace in the Streets*. New York: Basic Books.

Alibhai, Z. (2021). Wayne Couzens: Judge's sentencing remarks in full. 30 September. *The Independent*. Available at: www.independent.co.uk/news/uk/crime/wayne-couzens-judge-sentencing-remarks-b1929914.html.

Balko, R. (2021). *Rise of the Warrior Cop: The Militarization of America's Police Forces.* 2nd ed. New York: Public Affairs.

Baram, M. (2006). How Common is Contagious Shooting? 29 November. ABC News. Available at: https://abcnews.go.com/US/LegalCenter/story?id=2681947&page=1.

Barry, B. (2020). *Blood, Metal and Dust: How Victory Turned into Defeat in Afghanistan and Iraq.* Oxford: Osprey Publishing.

BBC (2022). Partygate: A timeline of the lockdown gatherings. 19 April. *BBC News.* Available at: www.bbc.co.uk/news/uk-politics-59952395.

Beetham, D. (1991). *The Legitimation of Power.* London: Palgrave Macmillan.

Black, D. (1980). *The Manners and Customs of the Police.* New York: Academic Press.

Boulton, L., McManus, M., Metcalfe, L., Brian, D. & Dawson, I. (2017). Calls for police service: Understanding the demand profile and the UK police response. *The Police Journal: Theory, Practice and Principles,* 90 (1), 70–85.

Bowling, B., Reiner, R., Sheptycki, J. (2019). *The Politics of the Police.* 5th ed. Oxford: Oxford University Press.

Burch, A.D.S., Cai, W., Gianordoli, G., McCarthy, M. & Patel, J.K. (2020). How Black Lives Matter Reached Every Corner of America. 13 June. *The New York Times.* Available at: https://acleddata.com/special-projects/us-crisis-monitor.

Burns, K. (2020). The violent end of the Capitol Hill Organized Protest, explained. 2 July. *Vox.* Available at: www.vox.com/policy-and-politics/2020/7/2/21310109/chop-chaz-cleared-violence-explained.

Carter, M. (2021). George Floyd and the Global Fight for Black Lives. *African American Intellectual History Society.* 26 May. Available at: www.aaihs.org/george-floyd-and-the-global-fight-for-black-lives.

Casey, L., Caddie, D., Callan, S., Fisher, I., Gilbert, C., Hilton, L., Kincaid, S., Lumley, J., Mohan, N., O'Connor, N., Rahman, N. & Williams, S. (2023). *Baroness Casey Review: Final Report: An independent review into the standards of behaviour and internal culture of the Metropolitan Police Service.* March. Metropolitan Police. Available at: www.met.police.uk/SysSiteAssets/media/downloads/met/about-us/baroness-casey-review/update-march-2023/baroness-casey-review-march-2023a.pdf.

Chancel, L., Piketty, T., Saez, E., Zucman, G., Bajard, F., Burq, F., Moshrif, R., Neef, T. & Robilliard, A. (2022). *World Inequality Report 2022.* Cambridge, MA: Belknap Press.

Cobbina, J.E. (2019). *Hands Up, Don't Shoot: Why the Protests in Ferguson and Baltimore Matter, and How They Changed America.* New York: New York University Press.

Cunneen, C. (2023). *Defund the Police: An International Insurrection.* Bristol: Policy Press.

Davis, A.Y. (2003). *Are Prisons Obsolete?* New York: Seven Stories Press.

Deuchar, R., Crichlow, V.J. & Fallik, S.W. (2021). *Police-Community Relations in Times of Crisis.* Bristol: Bristol University Press.

Dodd, V. (2022a). Priti Patel accused of 'power grab' over new policing proposals. 16 May. *The Guardian.* Available at: https://amp.theguardian.com/uk-news/2022/may/15/priti-patel-accused-of-power-grab-over-new-policing-proposals.

Dodd, V. (2022b). Met police placed in special measures due to litany of new 'systemic' failings. 28 June.*The Guardian.* Available at: www.theguardian.com/uk news/2022/jun/28/met-police-placed-special-measures-series-scandals?CMP=Share_iOSApp_Other.

Dodd, V. (2022c). Child in mental health crisis lived at police station for two days, chief reveals. 27 November. *The Guardian.* Available at: www.theguardian.com/uk-news/2022/nov/27/child-in-mental-health-crisis-lived-at-police-station-for-two-days-chief-reveals.

Dodd, V. & Grierson, J. (2021). Priti Patel wanted police to stop people gathering at Sarah Everard vigil. 19 March. *The Guardian.* Available at: www.theguardian.com/uk-news/2021/mar/19/priti-patel-wanted-police-stop-people-gathering-sarah-everard-vigil.

Edwards, S.S.M. (1989). *Policing 'Domestic' Violence: Women, the Law and the State.* London: Sage Publications.

Eldridge, T.E. (2020). Cops Could Use First Aid to Save Lives. Many Never Try. 15 December. *The Marshall Project.* Available at: www.themarshallproject.org/2020/12/15/cops-could-use-first-aid-to-save-lives-many-never-try.

Elliott-Cooper, A. (2020). 'Defund the police' is not nonsense. Here's what it really means. 2 July. *The Guardian.* Available at: www.theguardian.com/commentisfree/2020/jul/02/britain-defund-the-police-black-lives-matter.

Elliott-Cooper, A. (2021). *Black Resistance to British Policing.* Manchester: Manchester University Press.

Elliott-Cooper, A. (2023). Abolishing institutional racism. *Race & Class*, 65 (1), 100–118.

Fleetwood, J. & Lea, J. (2022). Defunding the police in the UK: Critical questions and practical suggestions. *The Howard Journal of Crime and Justice.* Available at doi:10.1111/hojo.12468.

Fleischer. M. (2019). Opinion: 50 years ago, LAPD raided the Black Panthers. SWAT teams have been targeting Black communities ever since. 8 December. *Los Angeles Times.* Available at: www.latimes.com/opinion/story/2019-12-08/50-years-swat-black-panthers-militarized-policinglos-angeles.

Garcia, A. (2020). Seattle's protest is the latest in a long history of experimental living. 16 June. *The Washington Post.* Available at: www.wa

shingtonpost.com/outlook/2020/06/16/seattles-protest-is-latest-long-history-experimental-living.

Garland, D. (2001). *The Culture of Control: Crime and Social Order in Contemporary Society*. Oxford: Oxford University Press.

Gilmore, J., Jackson, W., Monk, H. & Short, D. (2019). *Protesters' experiences of policing at anti-fracking protests in England, 2016–2019: a national study*. Centre for the Study of Crime, Criminalisation and Social Exclusion. Available at: https://researchonline.ljmu.ac.uk/id/eprint/11633/1/Gilmore%20Jackson%20Monk%20and%20Short%202019%20National%20Report%20small%207.pdf.

Gilmore, R.W. (2007). *Golden Gulag: Prisons, Surplus, Crisis, and Opposition in Globalizing California*. Oakland, CA: University of California Press.

Gordon, D. (2022). *Policing the Racial Divide: Urban Growth Politics and the Remaking of Segregation*. New York: New York University Press.

GOV.UK (2022). UK Summary. *Coronavirus (COVID-19) in the UK*. Available at: https://coronavirus.data.gov.uk.

Gray, S. (2008). Tarique Ghaffur settles out of court with Met. 25 November. *The Guardian*. Available at: www.theguardian.com/uk/2008/nov/25/ian-blair-tarique-ghaffur-police.

Hamilton, F. (2021). Priti Patel faces little resistance as Tories sweep police elections. 12 May. *The Times*. Available at: www.thetimes.co.uk/article/tory-sweep-in-police-elections-boosts-priti-patels-reform-plans-8t7x520sg.

Her Majesty's Inspectorate of Constabulary and Fire & Rescue Services (HMICFRS) (2021). The Sarah Everard vigil: An inspection of the Metropolitan Police Service's policing of a vigil held in commemoration of Sarah Everard on Clapham Common on Saturday 13 March 2021. Available at: www.justiceinspectorates.gov.uk/hmicfrs/wp-content/uploads/inspection-of-mps-policing-vigil-commemoration-sarah-everard-clapham-common.pdf.

Home Office (2020). Police workforce, England and Wales, as at 30 September 2019. Available at: https://assets.publishing.service.gov.uk/government/uploads/system/uploads/attachment_data/file/861800/police-workforce-sep19-hosb0220.pdf.

Hough, M. (2021). *Good Policing: Trust, Legitimacy and Authority*. Bristol: Policy Press.

Huemer, M. (2021). *Justice before the Law*. London: Palgrave Macmillan.

Independent Commission on the Los Angeles Police Department (1991). Report of the Independent Commission on the Los Angeles Police Department. July. Los Angeles: Weingart Foundation. Available at: https://archive.org/details/ChristopherCommissionLAPD.

Innes, M., Roberts, C., Lowe, T. & Innes, H. (2020). *Neighbourhood Policing: The Rise and Fall of a Policing Model*. Oxford: Oxford University Press.

Investigatory Powers Tribunal (2021). Wilson v (1) Commissioner of Police of The Metropolis (2) National Police Chiefs' Council. 30 September. Available at: www.ipt-uk.com/judgments.asp?id=61.

Kirk, M. & Boyer, P.J. (2001). L.A.P.D. Blues: The story of Los Angeles' gangsta cops & the corruption scandal that has shaken the once great L.A.P.D. 15 May.PBS. Available at: www.pbs.org/wgbh/pages/frontline/shows/lapd/bare.html.

Knopp, F.H. (1976). *Instead of Prisons: A Handbook for Abolitionists*. Syracuse, NY: Prison Research Education Action Project.

Kraska, P.B. (ed.) (1993). *Altered States of Mind: Critical Observations of the Drug War*. New York: Garland Publishing.

Kraska, P.B. (ed.) (2001). *Militarizing the American Criminal Justice System: The Changing Roles of the Armed Forces and the Police*. Boston, MA: Northeastern University Press.

Kraska, P.B. (ed.) (2007). Militarization and Policing – Its Relevance to 21st Century Police. *Policing: A Journal of Policy and Practice*, 1 (4), 501–513.

Kraska, P.B. (ed.) (2021). I prefer de-policing as opposed to defund. 28 February. Twitter. Available at: https://twitter.com/Peterkraska/status/1366080463798996996. Accessed 3 March 2024.

Lea, J. & Young, J. (1993). *What Is To Be Done About Law and Order? Crisis in the Nineties*. London: Pluto Press.

Lewis, P., Newburn, T., Taylor, M., McGillivray, C., Greenhill, A., Frayman, H. & Proctor, R. (2011). *Reading the Riots: Investigating England's summer of disorder*. London: The London School of Economics and Political Science and The Guardian. Available at: https://eprints.lse.ac.uk/46297/1/Reading%20the%20riots(published).pdf.

Loader, I. & Mulcahy, A. (2003). *Policing and the Condition of England: Memory, Politics, and Culture*. Oxford: Oxford University Press.

Lum, C. & Koper, C.S. (2017). *Evidence-Based Policing: Translating Research into Practice*. Oxford: Oxford University Press.

Lumsden, K. & Black, A. (2018). Austerity Policing, Emotional Labour and the Boundaries of Police Work: An Ethnography of a Police Force Control Room in England. *The British Journal of Criminology: An International Review of Crime and Society*, 58 (3), 606–623.

McCabe, S. & Wallington, P. (1988). *The Police, Public Order, and Civil Liberties: Legacies of the Miners' Strike*. Abingdon: Routledge.

McChrystal, S. (2013). *My Share of the Task: A Memoir*. New York: Penguin Group.

Macpherson, W., Cook, T., Sentamu, J. & Stone, R. (1999). *The Stephen Lawrence Inquiry*. February. London: GOV.UK. Available at: https://assets.publishing.service.gov.uk/government/uploads/system/uploads/attachment_data/file/277111/4262.pdf.

Manning, P.K. (2010/2016). *Democratic Policing in a Changing World*. New York: Routledge.

Marenin, O. (1982). Parking tickets and class repression: The concept of policing in critical theories of criminal justice. *Contemporary Crises*, 6 (3), 241–266.

Mathiesen, T. (1974). *The Politics of Abolition*. London: Martin Robertson & Company.

Miles, C. & Buehler, E. (2022). The homicide drop in England and Wales 2004–2014. *Criminology & Criminal Justice*, 22 (1), 3–23.

Millie, A. & Bullock, K. (2012). Re-imagining policing post-austerity. *British Academy Review*, 19 (January), 16–18.

Milne, S. (2004). *The Enemy Within: The Secret War Against the Miners*. 2nd ed. London: Verso Books.

Morton, S (2021). Sarah Everard: How Wayne Couzens planned her murder. 30 September. *BBC News*. Available at: www.bbc.co.uk/news/uk-58746108.

Movement for Black Lives (M4BL) (2024). 2020 Policy Platform. Available at: https://m4bl.org/policy-platforms.

National Debate Advisory Group (2015). Reshaping policing for the public. June. Criminal Justice Inspectorates. Available at: www.justiceinspectorates.gov.uk/hmicfrs/wp-content/uploads/reshaping-policing-for-the-public.pdf.

National Police Chiefs' Council & College of Policing (2022). Police Race Action Plan: Improving policing for Black people. 24 May.College of Policing. Available at: www.college.police.uk/print/pdf/node/3145.

Neocleous, M. (2014). *War Power, Police Power*. Edinburgh: Edinburgh University Press.

Neocleous, M. (2021). Kettle Logic. *Critical Criminology: An International Journal*, 29 (2), 183–197.

Netpol (2020). Police to finally stop calling us Domestic Extremists. 1 September.The Network for Police Monitoring. Available at: https://netpol.org/2020/09/01/police-to-finally-stop-calling-us-domestic-extremists.

Newburn, T. (2022). The inevitable fallibility of policing. *Policing and Society: An International Journal of Research and Policy*, 32 (3), 434–450.

Özdüzen, Ö., Bogdan, I. & Ozgul, B. (2021). Freedom or self-interest? Motivations, ideology and visual symbols uniting anti-lockdown protesters in the UK. *Political Studies Association Blog*. 14 September. Available at: www.psa.ac.uk/psa/news/freedom-or-self-interest-motivations-ideology-and-visual-symbols-uniting-anti-lockdown.

President's Task Force on 21st Century Policing (2015). *Final Report of the President's Task Force on 21st Century Policing*. Washington, DC: Office of Community Oriented Policing Services.

Purnell, D. (2021). *Becoming Abolitionists: Police, Protests, and the Pursuit of Freedom*. London: Verso Books.

Rahtz, H. (2016). *Race, Riots, and the Police*. Boulder, CO: Lynne Rienner Publishers.

Reaves, B.A. (2015). Local Police Departments, 2013: Personnel, Policies, and Practices. Bureau of Justice Statistics. Available at: https://bjs.ojp.gov/content/pub/pdf/lpd13ppp.pdf.

Reiner, R. (2011/2016). *Policing, Popular Culture and Political Economy: Towards a Social Democratic Criminology*. Farnham: Ashgate Publishing.

Reiner, R. (2021). *Social Democratic Criminology*. Abingdon: Routledge.

Rix, B. (2021). PCC Elections 2021: Results and analysis. 11 May. *Policing Insight*. Available at: https://policinginsight.com/features/analysis/pcc-elections-2021-results-and-analysis.

Rogers, C. (2017). *Plural Policing: Theory and practice*. Bristol: Policy Press.

Shannon, I. (2022). *Chief Police Officers' Stories of Legitimacy: Power, Protection, Consent and Control*. Cham, Switzerland: Palgrave Macmillan.

Sharkey, P. (2018). *Uneasy Peace: The Great Crime Decline, the Renewal of City Life, and the Next War on Violence*. New York: W.W. Norton & Company.

Sherman, L.W., Schmidt, J.D. & Rogan, D.P. (1992). *Policing Domestic Violence: Experiments and Dilemmas*. New York: Free Press.

Siegel, M. (2018). *Violence Work: State Power and the Limits of Police*. Durham, NC: Duke University Press.

Slawson, N. & Thomas, T. (2022). Met police did not initially investigate No 10 parties because nobody admitted taking part, legal paper shows – as it happened. 11 February. *The Guardian*. Available at: www.theguardian.com/politics/live/2022/feb/11/cressida-dick-resigns-sadiq-khan-boris-johnson-uk-politics-live.

Taylor, D.B. (2020). George Floyd Protests: A Timeline. *The New York Times*. 10 July. Available at: www.nytimes.com/article/george-floyd-protests-timeline.html.

The New York Times (2020). District Court State of Minnesota Transcript. 15 June. Available at: https://int.nyt.com/data/documenthelper/7070-exhibit-final07072020/4b81216735f2203a08cb/optimized/full.pdf.

The New York Times (2022). Coronavirus in the U.S.: Latest Map and Case Count. *The Coronavirus Pandemic*. Available at: www.nytimes.com/interactive/2021/us/covid-cases.html.

The Washington Post (2020). The death of George Floyd: What video shows about his final minutes. 30 May. *YouTube*. Available at: www.youtube.com/watch?v=FMGUAHBFmjk.

Toynbee, P. & Walker, D. (2020). The lost decade: the hidden story of how austerity broke Britain. 3 March. *The Guardian*. Available at: www.theguardian.com/society/2020/mar/03/lost-decade-hidden-story-how-austerity-broke-britain.

Tyler, T. (1990). *Why People Obey the Law*. New Haven, CT: Yale University Press.

Tyler, T. (2004). Enhancing Police Legitimacy. *The Annals of the American Academy of Political and Social Science*, 593, 84–99.

Tyler, T. (2011). *Why People Cooperate: The Role of Social Motivations*. Princeton, NJ: Princeton University Press.

Tyler, T. (2021). Foreword. In: Hough, M. *Good Policing: Trust, Legitimacy and Authority*. Bristol: Policy Press, vii–xii.

US Department of Justice Civil Rights Division & US Attorney's Office District of Minnesota Civil Division (DOJ & USAO) (2023). Investigation of the City of Minneapolis and the Minneapolis Police Department. 16 June.US Department of Justice. Available at: www.justice.gov/d9/2023-06/minneapolis_findings_report.pdf.

Vitale, A. (2021). *The End of Policing*. 2nd ed. London: Verso Books.

Vitale, A. (2022). This is what liberal austerity politics looks like. 10 February. Twitter. Available at: https://twitter.com/avitale/status/1491840768813805568. Accessed 3 March 2024.

Wacquant, L. (2004/2009). *Punishing the Poor: The Neoliberal Government of Social Insecurity*. Trans. anonymous. Durham, NC: Duke University Press.

Wall, T. (2021). Wrong to label Extinction Rebellion as extremists, says Home Office adviser. 21 August. *The Guardian*. Available at: www.theguardian.com/environment/2021/aug/21/wrong-to-label-extinction-rebellion-as-extremists-says-home-office-adviser.

Walmsey, R. (2002). World Prison Population List. 3rd ed. *Findings*, 166. Available at: https://static.prisonpolicy.org/scans/rds/r166.pdf.

Walmsey, R. (2003). World Prison Population List. 4th ed. *Findings*, 188. Available at: https://static.prisonpolicy.org/scans/rds/r188.pdf.

Ward, A. (2020). Anti-lockdown protests aren't just an American thing. They're a global phenomenon. 20 May. *Vox*. Available at: www.vox.com/2020/5/20/21263919/anti-lockdown-protests-coronavirus-germany-brazil-uk-chile.

What Works Centre for Crime Reduction (2024). Crime reduction toolkit. College of Policing. Available at: www.college.police.uk/research/crime-reduction-toolkit.

Wilson, K. (2021). Kate Wilson: after spy cops case the Met is beyond redemption. 30 September. *The Guardian*. Available at: https://amp.theguardian.com/uk-news/2021/sep/30/kate-wilson-after-spy-cops-case-the-met-is-beyond-redemption.

Wilson, T. & Walton, R. (2019). Extremism Rebellion: A review of ideology and tactics. Policy Exchange. Available at: https://policyexchange.org.uk/wp-content/uploads/2019/07/Extremism-Rebellion.pdf.

Williams, K. (2020). Why Police Have a Legal Duty to Provide Medical Aid to People They Shoot. *Ohio State Journal of Criminal Law*, 18 (1), 391–407.

Woodman, C. (2018). Spycops in context: A brief history of political policing in Britain. December. Centre for Crime and Justice Studies. Available at: www.crimeandjustice.org.uk/sites/crimeandjustice.org.uk/files/Spycops%20in%20context%20%E2%80%93%20a%20brief%20history%20of%20political%20policing%20in%20Britain_0.pdf.

2
PRACTICE, INSTITUTION, AND CONTEXT

My approach to the problem of the crisis of police legitimacy begins with the identification of three different levels at which police legitimacy is undermined: the practice of policing, the institution of policing, and the systemic context of policing. My starting point is Alasdair MacIntyre's (2007) philosophical, sociological, and political critique of modernity, to which the distinction between practices and institutions is crucial. Practices are complex, coherent, and cooperative human activities that realise a set of excellences in pursuit of a particular aim. The practice of Anglo-American Democratic Policing (AADP) has an almost unlimited range of functions in contemporary society, but its aim can nonetheless be summarised as public protection or public safety. Institutions are structures of power and status that sustain practices by acquiring and distributing money and material resources. The institutions of policing in the US and the UK are radically different, with the former comprising approximately 18,000 law enforcement agencies, two-thirds of which operate at the local or municipal level, and the latter comprising 69 constabularies, two-thirds of which operate at the regional or metropolitan level. Significantly, the aim of the institution of policing is not to protect the public but to sustain the practice of policing. My approach extends MacIntyre's distinction

DOI: 10.4324/9781003425922-3

between practices and institutions to the systemic context within which institutions and practices are situated. The systemic context of policing includes both the criminal justice system and the political system within which justice is administered. The criminal justice system is comprised of three institutions – policing, judicial (courts), and penal (prisons and probation) – but there are 51 separate legal systems in the US and three in the UK. Both countries are liberal rather than social democracies, in consequence of which there are high levels of inequality, which exacerbate existing problems with police legitimacy. The value of this three-tiered approach to the crisis of police legitimacy is in drawing attention to the significance of all of the levels, which has been overlooked in most of the literature to date. A framework for recovering police legitimacy must include all of the levels and identify the different ways in which legitimacy is undermined at each.

2.1 MacIntyre's Social Theory

MacIntyre's (2007) *After Virtue: A Study in Moral Theory* is a comprehensive philosophical, sociological, and political critique of modernity, which was initially published in 1981 and reissued with supplementary material in 1984 and 2007. MacIntyre begins by identifying the turn of the 19th century as a period of social fragmentation in Europe, the cause of which was a twofold shift of emphasis in philosophy and politics, from ethics to morality in the former and from the state to the individual in the latter. The philosophical difference is between ethics as a concern with social values and the good life and morality as a set of rules based on either the intention of the agent, the act itself, or the consequences of the act.[1] The political difference is between the role of the state as either promoting a particular conception of the good life or facilitating the coexistence of individual conceptions of the good life. The moral emphasis on the individual and her motivations and actions and the liberal democratic prioritisation of individual freedom over collective responsibility combined to create a society in which morality was little more than one personal preference among many and in which there was no longer any conception of the common good (beyond the coexistence of individual pursuits of the good life). MacIntyre

(2007: 1) describes this situation as an unrecognised 'catastrophe' and argues for a neo-Aristotelian approach to the good life based on the pursuit of human excellence, the narrative structure of human being, and the significance of socially embodied living traditions.

The first living tradition discussed by MacIntyre is the heroic society, which was pan-European in the pre-Socratic and pre-Christian eras. Courage was the most important excellence of character in the heroic society because it was essential to sustaining a community. Human beings are aware of their mortality and a vital component of courage is the struggle made in the face of the failure represented by death. MacIntyre (2007: 126–127) draws two lessons from the heroic society for contemporary ethics: that 'all morality is always to some degree tied to the socially local and particular' and 'that there is no way to possess the virtues [excellences] except as part of a tradition in which we inherit them and our understanding of them'. Moving on to the living tradition of the Golden Age of Athens, MacIntyre points out that there is no distinction between the good person and the good citizen, in consequence of which the concept of excellence is necessarily rather than contingently political. The excellences are qualities of character and qualities of the intellect that facilitate the achievement of *eudaimonia* (the good life) and although each individual exercises the excellences to a greater or lesser extent, the political character of these excellences means that they can only be realised as part of a community (the specific community being the city-state of Athens).[2] MacIntyre explores Aristotle's four central (or cardinal) excellences – *andreia* (courage), *sōphrosunē* (self-restraint), *dikaiosunē* (integrity), and *phronēsis* (judgement) – noting first that judgement belongs to a distinct category (as an excellence of the intellect rather than an excellence of character) and then that the four are inextricably integrated such that any ethical evaluation of a person must regard the excellences as a single complex whole.

MacIntyre's (2007: 148) discussion of the relationship between the good life and the excellences is where he introduces 'good' as a concept and he employs it to differentiate between two goals after an exploration of the living tradition of medieval Christianity. Human activity can be directed towards either external goods or internal goods. External goods are resources that are limited such that when they are acquired by one individual or group they are denied to another. To adapt one of MacIntyre's two examples, if I were to purchase J.M.W. Turner's painting *Snow Storm* (1842) and display it in my home, then I would be denying the public the access they currently enjoy courtesy of the Tate Britain gallery. Internal goods are resources that are not limited in this way, in consequence of which their acquisition benefits the community beyond the successful individual or group (MacIntyre 2007: 191): 'So when Turner transformed the seascape in painting or W.G. Grace advanced the art of batting in cricket in a quite new way their achievement enriched the whole relevant community.' Turner's achievement benefitted society as a whole rather than art lovers at the expense of those who are indifferent to art, but my purchase of his painting benefits me at the expense of art lovers. The distinction between external goods and internal goods is crucial to the most significant element of MacIntyre's social theory for my study, which is the distinction between institutions and practices.

MacIntyre makes two caveats before he defines practices. The first is that the exercise of the excellences is not exclusive to practices. The second is that he is creating a new denotation of *practice*. This denotation is defined in terms of internal goods (MacIntyre 2007: 187–188):

> By a 'practice' I am going to mean any coherent and complex form of socially established cooperative human activity through which goods internal to that form of activity are realized in the course of trying to achieve those standards of excellence which are appropriate to, and partially definitive of, that form of activity, with the result that human powers to achieve excellence, and human conceptions of the ends and good involved, are systematically extended. Tic-tac-toe is not an example of a practice in this sense, nor is throwing a football with skill; but the game of football is, and so is chess. Bricklaying is not a practice; architecture is. Planting turnips is not a practice; farming is. So are the enquiries of physics, chemistry and biology, and so is the work of the historian, and so are painting and music. In the ancient and medieval worlds the creation and

sustaining of human communities – of households, cities, nations – is generally taken to be a practice in the sense in which I have defined it. Thus the range of practices is wide: arts, sciences, games, politics in the Aristotelian sense, the making and sustaining of family life, all fall under the concept.[3]

Extending MacIntyre's examples, making an arrest is not a practice, but policing is. Practices are constituted by a specific set of excellences and a specific set of technical skills the combination of which is required to achieve the internal goods towards which the practice is directed. The excellences and technical skills can only be achieved by subordinating oneself to other practitioners, recognising one's own inadequacies, and taking self-endangering risks. There is no other way to achieve the internal goods because attempts to, for example, cheat at chess make the practice nothing more than a means to the end of acquiring status, money, and whatever other external goods grandmasters enjoy. Although practices can flourish in societies with different values, they cannot flourish in societies where the foundational values of cooperation, self-awareness, risk-taking, and fairness are not respected.

MacIntyre (2007: 194) contrasts practices with *institutions*, which are defined in terms of external goods:

> Practices must not be confused with institutions. Chess, physics, and medicine are practices; chess clubs, laboratories, universities and hospitals are institutions. Institutions are characteristically and necessarily concerned with what I have called external goods. They are involved in acquiring money and other material goods; they are structured in terms of power and status, and they distribute money, power and status as rewards. Nor could they do otherwise if they are to sustain not only themselves, but also the practices of which they are the bearers. For no practices can survive for any length of time unsustained by institutions. Indeed so intimate is the relationship of practices to institutions – and consequently of the goods external to the goods internal to the practices in question – that institutions and practices characteristically form a single causal order in which

the ideals and the creativity of the practice are always vulnerable to the acquisitiveness of the institution, in which the cooperative care for common goods of the practice is always vulnerable to the competitiveness of the institution.

The relationship between institutions and practices is that the former characteristically and necessarily sustain the latter. Crucially, the purpose of an institution is distinct from the purpose of the practice it sustains; the purpose of hospitals is not to restore or preserve health, but to sustain the practice of medicine, whose purpose is to restore or preserve health (which is, of course, an internal good), by sustaining itself. In consequence, institutions share a common purpose – sustaining practices by self-sustenance – with one another rather than with the practices they sustain. In contrast, each practice has a purpose that is distinct from both the institution that sustains it and from other practices. Whatever the purpose of the practice of policing, the purpose of the institution of policing is to sustain the practice of policing by sustaining itself. Returning to the excellences, MacIntyre notes that while they are essential to the achievement of the internal goods at which practices are directed, they may frustrate the acquisition of external goods, which suggests that successful practice is distinct from institutional success and that being, for example, a good doctor not only fails to guarantee promotion, progression, and other types of institutional recognition, but may hinder them.

The narrative character, narrative form, or narrative structure of human life is an essential component of MacIntyre's critique as it provides the link among excellences, practices, and the living traditions within which practices and institutions exist. The key feature of the narrative concept of selfhood for MacIntyre (2007: 215) is that it is teleological:

> We live out our lives, both individually and in our relationships with each other, in the light of certain conceptions of a possible shared future, a future in which certain possibilities beckon us forward and others repel us, some seem already foreclosed and others perhaps inevitable.

To work towards this shared future is to undertake a self-selected and self-conscious quest. MacIntyre (2007: 219) deploys narrative understanding to argue that the good life is 'the life spent in seeking for the good life for man [*sic*]'. Narrative identity links the excellences to the good life and one's own good life to the good lives of others. One's own narrative is only discrete to the extent that it cannot be directly experienced by others because one's life story is characteristically and necessarily embedded in the social relations that constitute the community with which one identifies. When one follows the modern imperative to narrate one's identity in isolation from others, one cuts oneself off from not only one's present but also one's past, undermining the whole process of identity creation. The liberal democratic ideal of the state as facilitating the coexistence of individual conceptions of the good life is thus counterproductive in precluding the conditions conducive to wellbeing and flourishing. MacIntyre (2007: 222) refers to the social relations within which narrative identity is embedded as a living tradition:

> A living tradition then is an historically extended, socially embodied argument, and an argument precisely in part about the goods which constitute that tradition. Within a tradition the pursuit of goods extends through generations, some through many generations. Hence the individual's search for his or her good is generally and characteristically conducted within a context defined by those traditions of which the individual's life is a part, and this is true both of those goods which are internal to practices and of the goods of a single life.

My concern is with policing as a practice and policing as an institution as the terms are defined by MacIntyre. I have nonetheless presented an overview of his entire theory in order to provide a more comprehensive account of practices and institutions and because of the relationship between practices and the excellences, to which I return in Chapter 3.

2.2 Policing as a Practice and Institution

2.2.1 Practice

'Policing' is clearly *a coherent and complex form of socially established cooperative human activity through which goods internal to that form of activity are realised in the course of trying to achieve those standards of excellence which are appropriate to, and partially definitive of, that form of activity*, i.e. a practice as defined by MacIntyre. This practice is sustained by 'the police', which is *involved in acquiring money and other material goods; structured in terms of power and status, and distributes money, power, and status as rewards*, i.e. an institution as defined by MacIntyre. In Chapter 1, I identified my subject as the practice and institution of what Peter Manning (2010) refers to as AADP: *the bearers of the Peel legacy – the notion of a visible, reactive, bureaucratically organised means of state-based resolution of conflict with minimal force*. The practice of AADP occurs across the US, Canada, the UK, Australia, and New Zealand, which are distinguished from other democratic nations by being English-speaking and having a common law rather than civil law-based criminal justice system. I then restricted my interest to the practice of AADP in the US and the UK. The Peel legacy is derived from the Peel model, conceived in 1829 and described by Manning (2010: 47) as 'the epitome of democratic policing – focused on deterrence and prevention, reactive and responsive to public concerns, works, uniformed, visible, and order maintaining at best'. This model can be understood in terms of three features: authority, paradigm, and function.

AADP is public policing rather than private policing, the *state-based resolution of conflict* rather than conflict resolution by private individuals or by private or third sector organisations. Law enforcement agents and constables are empowered by the government (at various levels, which I discuss below), which distinguishes them from private security guards and private investigators, whose powers are standardly no more than those of any citizen (Kakalik & Wildhorn 1977; Johnston 1992; Button 2019). Public policing is both *focused on deterrence and prevention* and *reactive and responsive to public concerns*, i.e. composed of two paradigms, proactive and reactive, which are distinguished by the determination of the definition of order. In proactive policing, which originated with uniformed night patrol in the early 19th century, order is defined by the police, who decide whether or not to intervene. In reactive policing, which originated with plainclothes daytime detection, order is defined by the public, who decide whether or not to call the police to intervene (Elmsley 1983; Waddington 1993; Maguire 2000; Churchill 2017). Finally, public policing is proactive and reactive with respect to two distinct functions, high policing and low policing. Recall from Chapter 1 that high policing is the set of functions concerned with national security, such as border control and counter terrorism and low policing the set of routine domestic functions, such as emergency response and crime reduction (Brodeur 2010; Manning 2010; Bowling & Sheptycki 2012).These two sets of functions draw attention to the question of the purpose of the practice of AADP: if policing is a practice in MacIntyre's sense then it must realise internal goods, i.e. be aimed at achieving a specific purpose that benefits a community, population, or nation.

Ben Bowling, Robert Reiner, and James Sheptycki (2019: 66) present three distinct accounts of the origins of AADP in their history of policing in the UK: the orthodox thesis, the revisionist antithesis, and their preferred synthesis, which they refer to as 'neo-Reithian'.[4] In other words, the Peel model was either a response to the increased fear of crime that accompanied industrialisation and urbanisation, a strategy for advancing the interests of the socioeconomic elite, or motivated by a combination of consensus-seeking and political conflict. Depending on which account one prefers, the function of the proactive paradigm of policing could be regarded as either crime prevention, social control, or keeping the peace. Similarly, the function of the reactive paradigm of policing could be regarded as either detecting crime, crime control, or enforcing the law. Referring to the pioneering work of Egon Bittner (1970, 1990), Bowling, Reiner, and Sheptycki complicate the question by drawing attention to the almost unlimited range of services the police provide. Bittner's (1970) own answer is that the core function of the practice of policing is the legitimate use of responsive force. This may well distinguish the practice of AADP from other practices, but it also misrepresents that practice, in which the actual use of force is the exception rather than the norm, and fails to reflect the variety highlighted by Bowling, Reiner, and Sheptycki (Muir 1977; Manning 1997; Pearson & Rowe 2020).

A meaningful identification of the internal good towards which the practice of AADP is aimed must be concise enough to avoid listing a set of services and imprecise enough to avoid the imposition of a preconceived idea onto the practice. I shall take the internal good towards which the practice of policing is aimed to be 'public protection', used as a synonym for 'public safety', which is more common in the US (Bittner 1970, 1990; Goldstein 1977; Skolnick 1999; Bowling, Reiner & Sheptycki 2019). Having established the internal good at which the practice of AADP is aimed, no finer description of the practice can be found than that of Manning (2010: 200, emphasis in original) himself, which I take pleasure in citing in full:[5]

> Policing is an art. Policing has an emotional effect, as do police officers. Policing is an aesthetic form. That is, it produces a response in audiences and in those who police, that is, it is sentimental and emotional in consequence. As an *aesthetic object* and a creator of aesthetic objects, criminals, and the other diverse objects of policing's attention, policing has a place in a larger political economy of emotions and energies that stimulate, simulate, animate, and consummate power relationships in a society. It is dramatic. Much of what policing does and produces is drama or the appearance of order and compliance with abstract, distant, unknown laws, regulations, and rules. The masterful turn of modern policing is [to] connect law, abstract morality and propriety and convince the public that they are one, and that the police alone can respond to these complex matters of morality and justice. In a more general sense, it has long been the concern of theorists of mass society to point out that politics and aesthetics become fused in some fashion when direct material and class interests are blurred or misplaced. The spectacle of policing, what the media present, and the imagery that frames police actions replace the reality of its mundane actions. The politics of policing is rooted in a simple drama of good and evil reproduced daily on television. Policing reflects

what a society expects of itself. It reflects on the taken-for-granted form of interpersonal conflicts and how they should be resolved. It is a reflexive operation, but it is not only reflexive; it is also cybernetic in the sense that it is a closed system of evaluation that keys off itself to differentiate internally.

2.2.2 Institution

In explaining policing as a practice, I noted that it was sustained by the institution of policing. As an institution in MacIntyre's terms, the police acquire money and other material goods, are structured in terms of power and status, and distribute money, power, and status as rewards: law enforcement agencies and constabularies are funded by government bodies, structured in terms of rank and grade, and reward their membership by means of promotion and progression. Crucially, and this is one of the reasons MacIntyre's account of practices and institutions is so insightful, the purpose of the institution of policing is not identical with the purpose of the practice of policing. Where the purpose of the practice of policing is public protection, the purpose of the institution of policing is to sustain the practice of policing and it achieves this purpose by sustaining itself. This distinction creates an immediate tension – or, at least, potential for tension – because there is no reason to expect complete compatibility between the goals of public protection and institutional self-sustenance. In fact, given the foundational distinction between internal and external goods, it seems likely that conflicts will emerge and examples of those conflicts are explored in Parts 3 and 4 of this book. Manning (2010: 206; emphasis in original) does not use MacIntyre's distinction, but describes policing as '*a situated practice*', which he contrasts with institutional or organisational processes and politics. I shall employ this term to describe the relationship between policing as a practice on the one hand and the combination of institution and systemic context in which the practice is located on the other hand. Manning is clear that the processes and politics of the institution do not fully determine the sense making and interpersonal tactics of the practice. He (Manning 2010: 206) maintains that institutional rhetoric and practical sense making are only 'loosely coupled' and that attempts to represent the relationship between the two as being closer are deliberately misleading, aimed at maintaining police legitimacy.

The institution of policing can refer to both particular institutions (for example, the City of New York Police Department, City of Los Angeles Police Department, Metropolitan Police Service, or Greater Manchester Police) or to a geographical collective of law enforcement agencies and constabularies (for example, US law enforcement, US federal law enforcement, the UK police, or the English and Welsh police). The practice of policing is the practice of public rather than private policing and, as such, the institution of policing is funded by government bodies (which are themselves institutions). Government can be at one of four different levels: international or global, national or federal, regional or metropolitan, and local or municipal. Although there is a sense in which both AADP and my concern with AADP in the US and UK are international, none of the institutions in which I am interested are funded or governed by international institutions (like, for example, the United Nations or the North Atlantic Treaty Organisation).[6] This leaves three levels at which the institutions of policing operate and there are national or federal, regional or metropolitan, and local or municipal law enforcement agencies and constabularies in both the US and the UK.

Across the federal, state (regional), county (regional or local), and municipal levels, the US has approximately 18,000 different law enforcement agencies (Banks et al. 2016; Rushin 2017; Li, Calderón & Eads 2022). These agencies employ a total of approximately 780,000 full-time law enforcement agents. Approximately 66% of these agencies are local police departments, employing approximately 61% of the agents. In contrast, federal agencies account for only 0.5% of law enforcement agencies in the US, employing 17% of the nation's agents (Brooks 2022a, 2022b; Goodison 2022). Perhaps the most interesting statistic about the institution of policing in the US is that 46% of local departments – and thus 30% of law enforcement agencies – employ less than ten agents. When one considers that 24-hour-coverage usually requires at least three shifts or watches and that a quarter to a third of officers are likely to be unavailable for patrol or investigation in consequence of annual leave, sick leave, training, or administrative duties at any one time, this is a remarkable figure.[7] Across the national, regional, and local levels, the UK has 69 constabularies, employing a total of approximately 186,000 full-time equivalent police officers (National Audit Office 2013, 2020; Her Majesty's Inspectorate of Constabulary 2015; Button & Wakefield 2018; Brown 2021; Allen & Mansfield 2022; Downer 2022). Approximately 65% of these constabularies are 'territorial' (regional) and they employ approximately 88% of the nation's police officers. The are seven national police services (which includes three 'special police forces') and 17 'miscellaneous' constabularies, which are local to ports, cathedrals, parks, and an airport and employ less than 500 police officers in total.[8]

While the practice of policing is common to both the US and the UK, the institution of policing in each national could not be more different. The first point to consider is the different populations of each country. Over the last few decades, the UK's population has remained approximately 20% of the US's population, in spite of net growth in both countries, a statistic confirmed by the most recent census in each: the US population was approximately 331 million in 2020 and the UK population approximately 67 million in 2021 (United States Census Bureau 2021; Office for National Statistics 2022). In consequence, one might expect to find five times (actually 4.9) the number of law enforcement agents in the US compared to police officers in the UK, but the ratio is closer to four to one (actually 4.2). This is a sizeable difference in terms of numbers of officers, but may not be particularly significant in consequence of geographical differences between the countries and the different criteria and methods for measuring law enforcement agency and constabulary strength. The conspicuous – and apparently more significant – difference is the way in which the practice of these law enforcement agents and police officers is sustained by the respective institutions. The US has approximately 18,000 law enforcement agencies and the UK 69 constabularies. Allowing for the 4.2:1 ratio the magnitude of the distinction can be understood in the following terms:

(1) If the US institution of policing was organised along UK lines, the 780,000 law enforcement agents would be employed by 290 law enforcement agencies, not 18,000.

(2) If the UK institution of policing was organised along US lines, the 186,000 police officers would be employed in 4,286 constabularies, not 69.

Within the context of the vast difference in the number of law enforcement agencies and constabularies that constitute the institution of policing in each nation, 61% of law enforcement agents in the US are employed by law enforcement agencies responsible to local or municipal authorities whereas 88% of police officers in the UK are employed by constabularies responsible to regional or metropolitan authorities. If one includes the 54% of Sheriffs' Offices with less than 24 deputies as policing at the local rather than regional level, then 63% of US law enforcement agents are responsible to local or municipal authorities (Brooks 2022b; Goodison 2022). The fact that the US has 261 times the number of law enforcement agencies as the UK has constabularies is a reflection of the difference between the local structure of the former and regional structure of the latter.

2.3 The Systemic Context of Policing

For MacIntyre (2007), the context of institutions and the practices they sustain is the living tradition, which provides individuals with their identity and unites them in a socially embodied and historically extended collective. The relationship among living traditions, institutions, and practices is that living traditions determine the goods that are worth pursuing, those goods are pursued by means of practices, and practices are sustained by institutions. MacIntyre presents relatively little detail about living traditions when compared to practices and institutions and the concept is closely tied to his notion of narrative identity, which is controversial.[9] As such, the living tradition is useful in drawing attention to the fact that practices and institutions exist in a context rather than sketching the character of that context. Manning's (2010) situated practice, which I introduced in the previous section, is more promising. He contrasts the practice of policing with institutional and organisational processes and politics, which explicitly establishes a distinction between practices and institutions while implicitly pointing to the context within which they both exist, the political economy mentioned in his extended description of the practice. The institution of policing is one of three institutions constituting a particular country's criminal justice system, alongside the judicial institution (the courts) and the penal or correctional institution (prisons and probation). All three of these institutions are regulated by a combination of parliamentary legislation and government policy (Joyce 2017; Davis 2019; Pakes 2019). I shall refer to the criminal justice system as the *juridical context* of the practice and institution of policing. Politics in both the US and UK, at all levels of government, has become increasingly concerned with fear of crime, law and order, and crime and its control in the last three decades and people standing for office exploit these concerns to secure election votes, very often advocating a 'tough on crime' punitive agenda (Garland 2001; Reiner 2007; Stuntz 2011). I shall refer to liberal democratic governance as the *political context* of the practice and institution of policing.

2.3.1 Juridical Context

The criminal justice system combines a set of government institutions with a set of legal ideals for the purpose of resolving conflict by identifying those who are deserving of punishment (Hillyard et al. 2004; Stuntz 2011; Faulkner & Burnett 2012). David Faulker and Ross Burnett (2012) describe the guiding principles of the institutions as integrity, transparency, and mutual trust within the system and humanity, dignity, and reciprocal respect in the system's relations with the public. William Stuntz (2011) describes the legal ideals as the avoidance of discrimination, the protection of the portion of the public that is most vulnerable, and balancing the twin goals of crime control and reasonable punishment. I have to some extent pre-empted an introduction to the criminal justice systems in the US and UK by introducing one of its constitutive institutions, policing, in the previous section so the first of the two main differences between the criminal justice systems – their structure – will come as no surprise. The diversity of the institution of policing in the US is partly a reflection of the diversity of the juridical context within which it is situated. The US has 51 separate legal systems, one at the federal level and 50 at the state level. Over 95% of criminal cases are tried at the state rather than the federal level and the US criminal justice system is thus primarily regional rather than national. A well-known but nonetheless striking feature of the US criminal justice system is that 97% of the criminal cases brought before both state and federal courts do not result in a trial in consequence of guilty pleas (Stuntz 2011; Davis 2019; Huemer 2021).

In the UK, there are three separate legal systems, one for England and Wales, one for Scotland, and one for Northern Ireland. The three serve populations of vastly different sizes: 60 million in England and Wales, 5 million in Scotland, and 2 million in Northern Ireland (Faulkner & Burnett 2012; Joyce 2017; Office for National Statistics 2022). This explains why both Scotland and Northern Ireland have a single constabulary and their respective criminal justice systems can be regarded as regional while the English and Welsh criminal justice system is more accurately described as national. In England and Wales, pre-trial guilty pleas account for approximately 91% of criminal cases, with a similar proportion in Scotland, but significantly less in Northern Ireland (Criminal Justice Inspection Northern Ireland 2013; Nobles & Schiff 2020; Gormley 2022). The second difference between the criminal justice systems of the US and the UK is procedural. Most chief prosecutors, judges, police chiefs, and sheriffs in the US are either elected or appointed by elected politicians whereas prosecutors, judges, and chief constables in the UK are career civil servants (Pakes 2019; Tonry 2020; Shannon 2022). There is disagreement as to whether the election of prosecutors, judges, and police chiefs makes them more accountable to the public they serve or undermines the fundamental democratic separation of legislative, executive, and judiciary power. The fact that there is no widely accepted answer to the question raised by this important procedural difference is indicative of a significant feature shared by both criminal justice systems, that they are extremely complex.

Jake Monaghan (2023: 30) defines complex systems as 'highly coupled systems with many parts'. Coupled systems are systems constituted by numerous distinct but interacting parts such that failure in one of the parts can cause failure in another and the more coupling in a system, the more opportunities there are for failure.

The criminal justice system is a complex system constituted by the institution of policing, the judicial institution, and the penal institution, all of which are coupled with the legal system, which is coupled with the political system, which is influenced by the institution of the media, which has become exponentially diverse with the rise of social media as a counterpart to mass media. Coupling makes the consequences of changes to one part of the system very difficult to predict and raises the risk of catastrophic failure. Monaghan uses the example of well-motivated legal and procedural reforms to the policing of domestic abuse in Washington, DC. In order to solve the twin problems of victims being reluctant to press charges and the police not taking domestic abuse seriously enough, police officer discretion as to how to deal with the perpetrator has been replaced with a policy of mandatory arrest.[10] A predictable result of the reform is that arrests for domestic abuse have increased; an unpredictable – or at least less obvious – result is that some victims of domestic abuse are now less likely to report it to the police, which may result in an increase in intimate partner homicides. If mandatory arrest did cause an increase in homicide (the existing evidence is mixed), then this would be a catastrophic failure of the criminal justice system. Monaghan (2023: 32) also observes that 'the policy appears to deter calling for service for some subset of the population, so the failure of the policy may disproportionately burden some groups.' This is true of so many aspects of policing, the courts, prisons and probation, and the criminal justice system in its entirety, where there is differential treatment of both perpetrators and victims in spite of the equality that respect for individual rights is intended to guarantee.

2.3.2 Political Context

Democracy is famously characterised by the French motto 'Liberté, Egalité, Fraternité' and freedom, equality, and cosmopolitanism are secured by free elections, the rule of law, and the protection of minority rights in both liberal and social democracies (Derrida 2003; Pemberton 2015; Raymen 2022). Reiner (2021) provides a pithy description of the difference in terms of two distinct conceptions of justice: the liberal sense of facilitating that meritorious individuals receive what they have earned against the social sense of facilitating that all individuals receive the necessities required for a worthwhile life. Reiner's terminology for the social democratic prioritisation of collective responsibility over individual freedom is the primacy of the ethical and he regards the ethical as inseparable from the economic because poverty, inequality, and unemployment cause crime by weakening social bonds and by encouraging competition over cooperation. As such, social democracy is also materialist rather than idealist, i.e. focused on the conditions in which people actually live rather than their entitlement to rights they may never be able to exercise (Marx 1845; Beauvoir 1963; Davies 2015). Consequent to their focus on individual freedom and individual rights, liberal democratic countries are characterised by high levels of inequality. In a comparative study of the differences in income between the wealthiest 20% and poorest 20% of the populations of the world's 50 richest nations, Richard Wilkinson and Kate Pickett (2009) identified the four biggest gaps as: Singapore, the US, Portugal, and the UK. These gaps were exacerbated by the impact of the Global Financial Crisis, including the austerity policies of the Conservative governments in the UK, which began in 2010 and have yet to be reversed (Cooper & Whyte 2017). In a subsequent comparative study of health and social problems, Wilkinson and Pickett (2018) identified the three rich nations with the worst conditions as: the US, Portugal, and the UK. These conditions were, once again, exacerbated by the COVID-19 pandemic. Writing of the differential impact of the pandemic in the US, Adam Tooze (2021: 29) notes that people in low-income areas were already twice as likely to die of influenza as those in high-income areas before the outbreak of COVID-19: 'It would be too much to say that these probabilities enjoy general acceptance. They are, on their face, a scandal. They give the lie to any idea that our collective priority is keeping people alive [...].' One might well wonder what inequality has to do with policing in general and with police legitimacy in particular.

The first point is the causal relation between inequality and health and social problems. Almost all of the conditions Wilkinson and Pickett (2009, 2018) studied are likely to have a direct or indirect impact on policing: trust, mental illness, life expectancy, infant mortality, obesity, educational performance, teenage births, homicide rates, imprisonment rates, and social mobility.[11] Second, inequality reinforces Monaghan's (2023: 45) crucial point that just policing is undermined by the complex juridical and political systems within which it is required to function: 'Policing institutions are coupled with key social arrangements basically everywhere, such that pathologies in other social arrangements can affect the justice of police practices and vice versa.' In spite of the ideals espoused by defenders of liberal democracy, who extend well beyond the Republican Party in the US and the Conservative Party in the UK, the political systems in both countries have produced societies that are unequivocally unequal and arguably unjust – and that is before any interaction with the police. Manning (2010: xii, emphasis in original) very astutely picks up on this point by delineating the police as *an agency for the redistribution of life chances in a population* and then defining good policing in terms of his difference principle, which I cited in Chapter 1 and is an application of John Rawls' (1999) distributive justice principle of the same name. Manning refers to his application as a framework for the consequences of police actions and although he does not use Monaghan's terms, it is a heuristic for keeping policing just in an unjust system: *given the current range of inequalities in education, opportunity, income, and skills, any police practice, especially that driven and shaped by policy, should not further increase extant inequalities.*

The purpose of identifying the systemic context of policing is not to absolve police officers or police chiefs from their roles in and responsibility for creating the Transatlantic crisis of police legitimacy, but to demonstrate the complexity of the juridical and political systems of which both the institution and practice are a part and to make two preliminary observations.[12] First, even the brief description I have provided in this chapter suggests that the practice, institution, and systemic context of policing can all come into conflict with one another and thus exist in tension with one another. The recognition of both the three levels themselves and the tensions among them has not received sufficient attention to date and Tim Newburn (2022: 441) is exceptional in having published on its impact, which he describes as the 'inevitable fallibility of policing'. The levels identified by Newburn are the interactional, organisational, and politico-economic – a near perfect match for those I derived from MacIntyre.[13] My second observation is that, tensions aside, it seems highly likely that police legitimacy can be undermined at all three of these levels and, indeed, Newburn's concern with fallibility is precisely a concern with legitimacy. If police legitimacy can be undermined at all three of the levels of practice, institution, and systemic context, then what I require is an analytic tool that is valid across all three, which is the subject of the next chapter.

Notes

1 The *locus classicus* of this distinction is Georg Wilhelm Friedrich Hegel's critique of Immanuel Kant's *Moralität* (morality) in terms of *Sittlichkeit* (ethical life) in first the *Phenomenology of Spirit* (1807) and then the *Elements of Philosophy of Right* (1820).
2 There is no direct English translation of '*eudaimonia*'. MacIntyre (2007: 148) mentions 'blessedness, happiness, prosperity', but 'wellbeing' or 'flourishing' are more illuminating for contemporary readers. *Aretē* can be translated as either 'virtue' or 'excellence' and I shall use the latter in order to avoid the Christian connotations of the former. For the same reason, I prefer 'self-restraint' to 'temperance' for *sōphrosunē* and 'judgement' to 'prudence' for *phronēsis*. *Phronēsis* is also translated as 'practical wisdom' and *dikaiosunē* as 'justice', but both of these denotations are redundant in the context of the practice of policing. I discuss the excellences in Chapter 3.
3 *Politics in the Aristotelian sense* is a reference to the political character of the excellences and the identity of good personhood with good citizenship mentioned above.
4 The term is derived from Charles Reith, a now forgotten police historian from Scotland who published several important works from 1938 to 1956 and is believed to have invented the Peelian principles of policing, as noted in Chapter 1.
5 In the remainder of this book, I shall use 'the practice of policing' as an abbreviation of 'the practice of AADP' and 'the institution of policing' as an abbreviation of 'the institution of AADP' unless otherwise specified.
6 International or global policing in the sense in which I am using it here is distinct from transnational policing, which involves cooperation of the police in different countries for the purpose of preventing, reducing, or controlling criminal activity that crosses international borders. Following globalisation at the end of the 20th century, transnational policing is

an increasingly important feature of public protection (see: Bowling & Sheptycki 2012; McDaniel, Stonard & Cox 2020).
7 This figure decreased by 2% from 2013 to 2020, a point to which I return in Chapter 10 (Reaves 2015; Goodison 2022).
8 This figure was reached by augmenting Mark Button and Alison Wakefield's (2018) research with a series of internet searches conducted in March 2022. As the websites used were not all completely reliable, I have not cited them and the figure should be regarded as an estimate only. The important point is that even if it is not entirely accurate, a minute proportion of the UK's police officers are employed by local constabularies.
9 MacIntyre regards the construction of a narrative identity as beneficial to both the individual and the society in which she lives, of similar value to an internal good, but it is far from obvious that narrative identity is always – or even largely – beneficial to either (see: Presser 2008; Goldie 2011; Lamarque 2014).
10 Although there is no mandatory arrest policy in the UK, the College of Policing's Authorised Professional Practice on Domestic Violence requires police officers to take 'positive action' when attending domestic abuse incidents and Geoff Pearson and Mike Rowe (2020: 142) note that this has been interpreted as mandatory arrest by many officers.
11 See also: College of Policing (2020).
12 I return to the question of absolving police officers and police chiefs from responsibility in Chapter 9, where I address it as a potential objection to my framework for recovering police legitimacy.
13 Daanika Gordon (2022: 1) deploys a similar tripartite analysis of policing in her study of the pseudonymous 'River City Police Department' in the US – micro, meso, and macro – although she is not explicitly concerned with police legitimacy.

References

Allen, G. & Mansfield, Z. (2022). Police Service Strength. December. House of Commons Library. Available at: https://researchbriefings.files.parliament.uk/documents/SN00634/SN00634.pdf.

Banks, D., Hendrix, J., Hickman, M. & Kyckelhahn, T. (2016). National Sources of Law Enforcement Employment Data. October. US Department of Justice. Available at: https://bjs.ojp.gov/content/pub/pdf/nsleed.pdf.

Beauvoir, S. de (1963/1965). *Force of Circumstance*. Trans. R. Howard. London: André Deutsch and Weidenfeld & Nicolson.

Bittner, E. (1970). The Functions of the Police in Modern Society. US Department of Justice: Office of Justice Programs. Available at: www.ojp.gov/pdffiles1/Digitization/147822NCJRS.pdf.

Bittner, E. (1990). *Aspects of Police Work*. Boston, MA: Northeastern University Press.

Bowling, B., Reiner, R., & Sheptycki, J. (2019). *The Politics of the Police*. 5th ed. Oxford: Oxford University Press.

Bowling, B. & Sheptycki, J. (2012). *Global Policing*. London: Sage Publications.

Brodeur, J.P. (2010). *The Policing Web*. New York: Oxford University Press.

Brooks, C. (2022a). Federal Law Enforcement Officers, 2020 – Statistical Tables. September. US Department of Justice. Available at: https://bjs.ojp.gov/sites/g/files/xyckuh236/files/media/document/fleo20st.pdf.

Brooks, C. (2022b). Sheriffs' Offices Personnel, 2020. November. US Department of Justice. Available at: https://bjs.ojp.gov/sites/g/files/xyckuh236/files/media/document/sop20.pdf.

Brown, J. (2021). *Policing in the UK*. September. House of Commons Library. Available at: https://researchbriefings.files.parliament.uk/documents/CBP-8582/CBP-8582.pdf.

Button, M. (2019). *Private Policing*. 2nd ed. Abingdon: Routledge.

Button, M. & Wakefield, A. (2018). 'The Real Private Police': Franchising Constables and the Emergence of Employer Supported Policing. In: Hucklesby, A. & Lister, S. (eds), *The Private Sector and Criminal Justice*. London: Palgrave Macmillan, 135–159.

Churchill, D. (2017). *Crime Control and Everyday Life in the Victorian City: The Police and the Public*. Oxford: Oxford University Press.

College of Policing (2020). Policing in England and Wales: Future Operating Environment 2040. 11 August. Available at: https://assets.college.police.uk/s3fs-public/2020-08/future-operating-environment-2040.pdf.

Criminal Justice Inspection Northern Ireland (2013). The Use of Early Guilty Pleas in the Criminal Justice System in Northern Ireland. February. Available at: www.cjini.org/getattachment/6bf65923-3cab-4dee-a2a3-717cee809e80/report.aspx.

Cooper, V. & Whyte, D. (eds) (2017). *The Violence of Austerity*. London: Pluto Press.

Davies, W. (2015). *The Happiness Industry: How the Government and Big Business Sold Us Well-Being*. London: Verso Books.

Davis, F.T. (2019). *American Criminal Justice: An Introduction*. Cambridge: Cambridge University Press.

Derrida, J. (2003/2005). *Rogues: Two Essays on Reason*. Trans. P.A. Brault & M. Naas. Stanford, CA: Stanford University Press.

Downer, A. (2022). *Independent Review of Border Force*. July. Home Office. Available at: www.gov.uk/government/publications/independent-review-of-border-force/an-independent-review-of-border-force-accessible-version.

Elmsley, C. (1983). *Policing and its Context 1750–1870*. London: The Macmillan Press Ltd.

Faulkner, D. & Burnett, R. (2012). *Where Next for Criminal Justice?* Bristol: The Policy Press.

Garland, D. (2001). *The Culture of Control: Crime and Social Order in Contemporary Society*. Oxford: Oxford University Press.

Goldie, P. (2011). Life, Fiction, and Narrative. In: Carroll, N. & Gibson, J. (eds), *Narrative, Emotion, and Insight*. University Park, PA: The Pennsylvania State University Press, 8–22.

Goldstein, H. (1977). *Policing a Free Society*. Cambridge, MA: Ballinger Publishing Company.

Goodison, S.E. (2022). Local Police Departments Personnel, 2020. November. US Department of Justice. Available at: https://bjs.ojp.gov/sites/g/files/xyckuh236/files/media/document/lpdp20.pdf.

Gordon, D. (2022). *Policing the Racial Divide: Urban Growth Politics and the Remaking of Segregation*. New York: New York University Press.

Gormley, J. (2022). The Inefficiency of Plea Bargaining. *Journal of Law and Society*, 49 (2), 277–293.

Her Majesty's Inspectorate of Constabulary (2015). An inspection of the National Crime Agency. July. Criminal Justice Inspectorates. Available at: www.justiceinspectorates.gov.uk///hmicfrs/wp-content/uploads/inspection-of-the-national-crime-agency-terms-of-reference-2015.pdf.

Hillyard, P., Pantazis, C., Tombs, S. & Gordon, D. (eds) (2004). *Beyond Criminology: Taking Harm Seriously*. London: Pluto Press.

Huemer, M. (2021). *Justice before the Law*. London: Palgrave Macmillan.

Johnston, L. (1992). *The Rebirth of Private Policing*. Abingdon: Routledge.

Joyce, P. (2017). *Criminal Justice: An Introduction*. 3rd ed. Abingdon: Routledge.

Kakalik, J.S. & Wildhorn, S. (1977). *The Private Police: Security and Danger*. New York: Crane, Russak & Company.

Lamarque, P. (2014). *The Opacity of Narrative*. London: Rowman & Littlefield International.

Li, W., Calderón, A.R. & Eads, D. (2022). See If Police in Your State Reported Crime Data to the FBI. 15 October.The Marshall Project. Available at: www.themarshallproject.org/2022/08/15/see-if-police-in-your-state-reported-crime-data-to-the-fbi.

McDaniel, J.L.M., Stonard, K.E. & Cox, D.J. (eds). (2020). *The Development of Transnational Policing: Past, Present and Future*. Abingdon: Routledge.

Maguire, M. (2000). Policing by risks and targets: Some dimensions and implications of intelligence-led crime control. *Policing and Society: An International Journal*, 9 (4), 315–336.

MacIntyre, A. (2007). *After Virtue: A Study in Moral Theory*. 3rd ed. London: Duckworth Books.

Manning, P.K. (1997). *Police Work: The Social Organization of Policing*. 2nd ed. Prospect Heights, IL: Waveland Press, Inc.

Manning, P.K. (2010/2016). *Democratic Policing in a Changing World*. Abingdon: Routledge.

Marx, K. (1845/2000). The Holy Family. Trans. R. Dixon. In: Marx, K., *Karl Marx: Selected Writings*. Oxford: Oxford University Press, 145–170.

Monaghan, J. (2023). *Just Policing*. New York: Oxford University Press.

Muir, W.K. (1977/1979). *Police: Streetcorner Politicians*. Chicago: University of Chicago Press.

National Audit Office (2013). The Border Force: securing the border. September. Home Office. Available at: www.nao.org.uk/wp-content/uploads/2013/09/The-Border-force-securing-the-border.pdf.

National Audit Office (2020). Immigration Enforcement. June. Home Office. Available at: www.nao.org.uk/wp-content/uploads/2020/06/Immigration-enforcement.pdf.

Newburn, T. (2022). The Inevitable Fallibility of Policing. *Policing and Society: An International Journal of Research and Policy*, 32 (3), 434–450.

Nobles, R. & Schiff, D. (2020). The Supervision of Guilty Pleas by the Court of Appeal of England and Wales – Workable Relationships and Tragic Choices. *Criminal Law Forum*, 31 (4), 512–552.

Office for National Statistics (ONS) (2022). Population estimates for the UK, England, Wales, Scotland and Northern Ireland: mid-2021. December. Available at: www.ons.gov.uk/peoplepopulationandcommunity/populationandmigration/populationestimates/bulletins/annualmidyearpopulationestimates/mid2021.

Pakes, F. (2019). *Comparative Criminal Justice*. 4th ed. Abingdon: Routledge.

Pearson, G. & Rowe, M. (2020/2022). *Police Street Powers and Criminal Justice: Regulation and Discretion in a Time of Change*. Oxford: Hart Publishing.

Pemberton, S. (2015). *Harmful Societies: Understanding Social Harm*. Bristol: Policy Press.

Presser, L. (2008). *Been a Heavy Life: Stories of Violent Men*. Champaign, IL: University of Illinois Press.

Rawls, J. (1999). *A Theory of Justice*. Revised ed. Cambridge, MA: Harvard University Press.

Raymen, T. (2022). *The Enigma of Social Harm: The Problem of Liberalism*. Abingdon: Routledge.

Reaves, B.A. (2015). Local Police Departments, 2013: Personnel, Policies, and Practices. May. US Department of Justice. Available at: https://bjs.ojp.gov/content/pub/pdf/lpd13ppp.pdf.

Reiner, R. (2007). *Law and Order: An Honest Citizen's Guide to Crime and Control*. Cambridge: Polity Press.

Reiner, R. (2021). *Social Democratic Criminology*. Abingdon: Routledge.

Rushin, S. (2017). *Federal Intervention in American Police Departments*. Cambridge: Cambridge University Press.

Shannon, I. (2022). *Chief Police Officers' Stories of Legitimacy: Power, Protection, Consent and Control*. Cham, Switzerland: Palgrave Macmillan.

Skolnick, J.H. (1999). On Democratic Policing. *Ideas in American Policing*. August. Washington, DC: Police Foundation. Available at: www.policinginstitute.org/wp-content/uploads/2015/06/Skolnick-1999-On-Democratic-Policing.pdf.

Skolnick, J.H. & Fyfe, J.J. (1993). *Above the Law: Why Police Use Excessive Force and What to Do About It*. New York: The Free Press.

Stuntz, W.J. (2011). *The Collapse of American Criminal Justice*. Cambridge, MA: The Belknap Press.

Tonry, M. (2020). *Doing Justice, Preventing Crime*. New York: Oxford University Press.

Tooze, A. (2021). *Shutdown: How Covid Shook the World's Economy*. London: Penguin Books.

United States Census Bureau (2021). 2020 Census Apportionment Results. April. Available at: www.census.gov/data/tables/2020/dec/2020-apportionment-data.html.

Waddington, P.A.J. (1993). *Calling the Police: The Interpretation of, and Response to, Calls for Assistance from the Public*. Aldershot: Avebury Publishing.

Wilkinson, R. & Pickett, K. (2009). *The Spirit Level: Why Greater Equality Makes Societies Stronger*. New York:Bloomsbury Press.

Wilkinson, R. & Pickett, K. (2018). *The Inner Level: How More Equal Societies Reduce Stress, Restore Sanity and Improve Everyone's Well-being*. London:Allen Lane.

PART 2
Methodology

3
AUTOETHNOGRAPHY

This study employs a methodology that combines autoethnography, which is the subject of this chapter, and case studies, which are discussed in Chapter 4. Autoethnography is deployed to outline the characteristics of policing as a practice, which provide an analytic tool for determining the different ways in which police legitimacy is undermined. An autoethnography, which can be either evocative or analytic, is a study of an observer's own culture from within that culture. Evocative autoethnography is a method of self-investigation and analytic autoethnography a method of social investigation through the self. For a variety of operational, legal, and ethical reasons, only three monograph-length police autoethnographies are currently available in English, all within the analytic paradigm. My analytic autoethnography was published as a journal article and is based on my service in the Durban City Police (DCP) in South Africa from 1992 to 1998. Although South Africa is not an Anglo-American Democratic Policing (AADP) nation, the similarities between my service and contemporary US policing are substantial, including: a common language and system of government, shared legal roots in English common law, commensurate urban population densities, and equivalent levels of gun crime. The findings of my autoethnography,

DOI: 10.4324/9781003425922-5

expanded here and extrapolated from the US to the US and the UK, are that the practice of policing not only requires mastery of a set of excellences and a set of skills, as suggested by Alasdair MacIntyre (2007), but has four distinguishing characteristics. The practice is a heroic struggle because its purpose, public protection, can never be achieved in full. The practice is edgework because it involves a high risk of injury, which can be reduced by competence in a specific skill set and is accompanied by a specific sensation and set of emotions. The practice is an absolute sacrifice because public protection requires continuous self-sacrifice, which is accompanied by an accumulated weight of responsibility. The practice is worldmaking because public protection requires the re-creation of social reality. The characteristics of the practice can either contribute to or detract from public protection. As the characteristics are emergent from the tensions among the practice of policing, the institution of policing, and the systemic context of policing, they constitute an analytic tool that can determine the different ways in which public protection is undermined at all three levels.

3.1 Autoethnography

Karl Heider (1975: 3) coined 'auto-ethnography' to describe an ethnographic study in which he asked members of the Grand Valley Dani in Indonesia to give accounts of their own culture. 'Auto-ethnography' in this sense is distinct from both 'ethnography' and the contemporary use of 'autoethnography': instead of researching another culture by embedded participant observation (ethnography) or employing someone who was part of that culture to conduct research (autoethnography), Heider used his embedded participant observation to record his subjects' descriptions of their own culture (auto-ethnography). Another early use of the term is by David Hayano (1979: 99), who defined auto-ethnographies as a new development in which 'anthropologists conduct and write ethnographies of their "own people"'. He (Hayano 1979: 103 fn.2) distinguishes between auto-ethnographic research and 'self-ethnographic' research, in which the researcher analyses her own life by means of the ethnographic method. 'Autoethnography' as it has been used since the publication of Arthur Bochner and Carolyn Ellis' (2001) landmark edited collection, *Ethnographically Speaking: Autoethnography, Literature, and Aesthetics*, combines both Hayano's 'auto-ethnography' and 'self-ethnography'. In the new century, the emphasis switched to the latter, to what Bochner and Ellis refer to as 'evocative autoethnography'. *Evocative autoethnography* combines 'the systematic, "scientific" methodologies of ethnography with the evocative, creative, and artistic elements and forms of storytelling' (Bochner & Ellis 2016: 67). 'Evocative' is closely associated with 'emotive' and evocative autoethnography involves the production of a vivid and resonant impression of the social scientist's reality in order to communicate what it is like to have a particular experience or a particular set of experiences to others.

If Hayano's 'self-ethnography' evolved into 'evocative autoethnography', then his 'auto-ethnography' evolved into 'analytic autoethnography'. Leon Anderson (2006a: 374) acknowledges the value of evocative autoethnography as the dominant paradigm of autoethnographic research in the 21st century, but proposes an alternative, which he defines in terms of five key features. First, the analytic autoethnographer is a 'complete member researcher' (CMR), a researcher who is a fully-fledged participant of the group being observed (Anderson 2006a: 378). The CMR is thus an integral participant who (also) records fieldnotes rather than an embedded participant observer. Second, analytic autoethnographers employ 'analytic reflexivity', framing their accounts with personal reflection and recognising the impact of the process of representation on their personal identity (Anderson 2006a: 378). Analytic reflexivity is also characteristic of ethnographic research, but has the potential for a much deeper and richer reciprocity in autoethnographic research because of the researcher's status as a CMR. Third, 'the researcher is a highly visible social actor within the written text' (Anderson 2006a: 384). The CMR includes her own experiences and emotions in her research although, significantly, they are not the focus of the autoethnography. Fourth, analytic autoethnography involves 'dialogue with informants beyond the self' (Anderson 2006a: 378). Finally, and most importantly, analytic autoethnography is characterised by its 'commitment to the analytic agenda' (Anderson 2006a: 386).

Autoethnography employs inductive logic, using the data collected from the specific sample to draw conclusions about the broader population to which the sample belongs in the manner of conventional social science. Analytic autoethnographies are thus essentially about others, about the experiences of the population under study rather than the experiences of the CMR as an individual within that population. Stephen Wakeman (2014: 708), who recognises the significance of artistic modes of representation and the expression of emotion, captures the priority of this outward focus when he states that *analytic autoethnography* 'is not so much a method of self-investigation, but a technique of *social* investigation conducted *through* the self'.

Anderson's (2006b) respect for the work of evocative ethnographers is not reciprocated and he notes that they are united in their opposition to his realist epistemology and symbolic interactionist assumptions. The basis of the rejection of analytic autoethnography by evocative autoethnographers is Anderson's extrapolation from the empirical to the theoretical, i.e. his reliance on induction. While both paradigms are committed to internal validity, it is only analytic autoethnography that makes a commitment to external validity. This commitment does not, however, require a commitment to positivism, understood as an approach to social science that assumes the social world is an external reality, that social facts have a truth value, and that researchers can gain access to the reality to discover the truth values. Instead, analytic autoethnography requires a commitment to realism, understood as an approach to social science that assumes the social world is an external reality and that social facts have a truth value, but that researchers can only ever gain partial access to the reality (Perri 6 & Bellamy 2011). Within this approach, traditional and innovative methods of social science research advance knowledge by producing increasingly accurate approximations of reality without aspiring to achieve complete correspondence with reality. As a realist, I do not share the evocative autoethnographic reservations about analytic autoethnographic assumptions. I am also more sceptical of the value of evocative autoethnography to social science than Anderson. My concern is that in the absence of the analytic agenda, autoethnography is essentially about the self, another genre of life writing alongside autobiography. As a method of self-investigation, the scope for social investigation seems much more limited than a method that employs the self as a conduit for social investigation.

For a variety of ethical, legal, and operational reasons, very few police autoethnographies have been published to date. Autoethnography raises the same ethical issues as all research involving human participants and autoethnographers typically follow ethical imperatives to avoid harm, deception, and invasion of privacy. In police autoethnography, there are also legal consequences that may prevent the author from publishing all the relevant information, at least some of which may incriminate the author or others in legal or procedural breaches that could be investigated retrospectively. In addition, there are operational considerations, such as the protection of the identities of witnesses and informants. There is a further complication in that a study of the police by a serving police officer is not necessarily an autoethnography, evocative or analytic. For example, Journalist Valentin Gendrot (2020) joined the *Police nationale* for two years to research *Flic: Un journaliste a infiltré la police*, a book on police culture in France that includes elements of both autoethnography and autobiography, but is a work of investigative journalism.[1] Nor are Simon Holdaway's (1983) *Inside the British Police: A Force at Work* and Malcolm Young's (1991) *An Inside Job: Policing and Police Culture in Britain* autoethnographies. Holdaway and Young were police scholars who conducted covert insider research and published their results as monographs. In both cases, the studies are correctly classified as covert ethnographies, a research method that contravenes the ethical principle of informed consent, rather than autoethnographies. At the time of writing, there are only three monograph-length police autoethnographies available in English: Peter Moskos' (2008) *Cop in the Hood: My Year Policing Baltimore's Eastern District*, Jonathan Wender's (2008) *Policing and the Poetics of Everyday Life*, and Tom Tooth's (2019) as-yet-unpublished PhD thesis, *Becoming Special: Occupational socialisation in volunteer police officers*.

Moskos' (2008) original intention was to undertake an ethnographic study of the Baltimore Police Department, but he was persuaded to join as an officer and served in that role for two years. While *Cop in the*

Hood provides a great deal of insight into what it is like to be a police officer in Baltimore, it is primarily concerned with drug prohibition and the need to change policies at the municipal and national levels. Wender (2008) published a retrospective study of policing based on his 15 years of service in the Mountlake Terrace Police Department in the Pacific Northwest. He uses phenomenological aesthetics to sketch a programme of police reform that takes everyday encounters between the police and the public as its starting point. Tooth (2019: 4) conducted an autoethnography of his recruitment, training, and first 14 months of deployment as a special constable (a part-time, fully sworn role) in the pseudonymous 'Westshire Constabulary'. His study is aimed at illuminating the complex relationship between the Special Constabulary and police culture. All three are analytic autoethnographies, Tooth's explicitly so and Moskos' and Wender's implicitly. They are distinguished from evocative autoethnographies not just by their style of writing or intended audience, but by taking others as their respective subjects. Each author uses his experience to illuminate the lives of others and uses inductive logic to reach conclusions that extend beyond the individual and his peers to the practice of policing in the US (Moskos and Wender) and to the Special Constabulary in the UK (Tooth).

To return to Wakeman's description of analytic autoethnography, the technique involves *social investigation through the self*. The criterion for social rather than self-investigation is Anderson's (2006a: 387) delineation of 'analytic social science' in terms of extrapolating from the empirical to the theoretical, i.e. an aspiration to external validity. Social investigation through the self is sufficient to distinguish analytic autoethnography from evocative autoethnography, but not from journalism such as Gendrot's or police autobiographies such as Thomas Jackson's (2017) *Policing Ferguson, Policing America: What Really Happened – And What the Country Can Learn From It* and Rosa Brooks' (2021) *Tangled Up in Blue: Policing the American City*. Gendrot, Jackson, and Brooks' works all extrapolate from the specific sample (the author's experience) to the broader population to which the sample belongs (policing in France and the US respectively). What distinguishes Moskos, Wender, and Tooth's studies from those of Gendrot, Jackson, and Brooks is that the former: (1) investigate the social through the self by (2) deploying a theoretical framework and (3) providing corroborating evidence for their claims. These three conditions are jointly sufficient to distinguish analytic autoethnography from evocative autoethnography as well as from journalistic and autobiographical nonfiction. They are also the conditions I aimed to meet in my own analytic autoethnography, 'Four Characteristics of Policing as a Practice' (McGregor 2021), which was published in *Policing: A Journal of Policy and Practice* in June 2021 and which provides the foundation on which I build in this book.

When I joined the DCP in 1992 I was well aware that I was living through a watershed in South African history and my service did indeed extend from the dismantling of apartheid (1989 to 1994) to the first democratic elections in South Africa (April 1994) and Nelson Mandela's presidency (1994 to 1999). In consequence, I started taking fieldnotes in the form of a series of scrapbooks that were filled with cuttings from in-service magazines and local, regional, and national newspapers; with pasted pages from training manuals, memoranda, Standing Orders, and municipal regulations; and with personal documents and photographs. In March 1995, a Town & Regional Planning student from Technikon Natal conducted an ethnographic study of the Public Transport Unit for his dissertation on the post-apartheid minibus industry, producing a 60-minute documentary film that included an interview with one of my two police mentors, Police Constable Siza Menye.[2] In September of the following year my other mentor, Senior Constable Chris Cray, and I participated in a ceremonial parade and I was given a VHS tape of both the documentary film and the parade. By the time I left the police in 1998 my fieldnotes consisted of two videotapes, six 192-page A4 notebooks, and one 96-page A3 sketchbook. My initial inclination was to use my fieldnotes to write a crime novel and I began researching a police procedural in 2002, commissioning a company called Rhino Research to provide me with newspaper and journal articles on policing in Durban during apartheid two years later. That novel was never written, but the research inaugurated the archive I would curate over the next 17 years as a supplement to my fieldnotes.

At the end of 2007, I spent two weeks with Chris in Auckland. He had moved there in 2006 and I made notes of approximately 12 hours of conversations we had about his service before and after mine (he joined the DCP in 1987 and left in 2006), the years of our joint service, and our partnership together in the Dog Section (from October 1995 to November 1996). In 2014, I was contacted by Carl Mitchell, a close friend of Chris who had also moved to Auckland. Carl had been one of my two role models in the police and wanted help creating a history of his service (1988 to 2010).[3] My contribution was co-authoring a detailed diary of the period from March 1995 to January 1998. In the summer of 2019, I spent a long weekend with Chris in York, during which I made notes on three hours of conversation about the similarities and differences between his service in the DCP and his service in the New Zealand Police (which he had joined in 2008). It was after Chris' visit that I began my autoethnographic research. By that time my archive included the commissioned material; five rare books on policing in South Africa; three hard-to-find magazine articles on dog units in Durban; five clips of news footage from Durban in the 1990s; 15 hours of interviews with Chris, and the co-authored diary with Carl. My only reservation was the 21-year hiatus between my service and my study. I was, however, confident that the combination of fieldnotes, archive, and memory provided me with a firm empirical basis for my autoethnography and the editor and referees of *Policing* concurred. Although there are obvious disadvantages to conducting autoethnographic research after one's service, there is an advantage in that the temporal distance provides a perspective on the people, places, and events which is likely to be lacking if they are still part of one's everyday experience (Emerson, Fretz & Shaw 2011; Dillard 2008). David Peace (2010), whose *Red Riding Quartet* is the basis of my West Yorkshire, 1980 case study (Chapter 6), makes a similar observation about temporal and spatial distance in writing fiction and his four novels were all written and published while he was living in Tokyo.

3.2 Durban City Police

The DCP is South Africa's oldest police service, though it has been known by three different names: Durban Borough Police

(1854 to 1936), Durban City Police (1936 to 2000), and Durban Metropolitan Police Service (2000 to present). Policing in South Africa was reorganised in 1912, with two national police forces – the South African Police (SAP) and the South African Mounted Riflemen (SAMR) – and two local police forces (in Durban and Pietermaritzburg). The national forces were typical of colonial police forces in having both policing and military functions, with the SAMR a 'regular military force' that would fight in wartime and police the Black population in peacetime (King & Portman 2000: 12). By 1936 the SAP had taken over the SAMR and Pietermaritzburg police, but the Durban council was successful in resisting pressure to incorporate the local force into a single, national, organisation (Jewell 1989). The SAP nonetheless became the main police force in Durban (constituting about 90% of the city's police officers) and the lead agency responsible for crime prevention, relegating the newly christened DCP to the lead agency for traffic control and by-law enforcement. In 1993, the Durban City Council recognised crime prevention as the primary function of the DCP, a decision that may have been an attempt to take advantage of speculation that the African National Congress government-in-waiting would disband the SAP in consequence of its role in enforcing apartheid. The SAP was in fact reorganised by the new government as the South African Police Service (SAPS) in 1995 and remains the lead agency for crime prevention. Unlike the SAP, the DCP was modelled on the Metropolitan Police Service rather than colonial police forces, never used military ranks, and was never paramilitary in orientation (Rauch, Shaw & Louw 2001). As a local force responsible for policing the only South African city where the majority of the White population was English- rather than Afrikaans-speaking, the DCP had a very limited role in the maintenance of apartheid. The force was deployed on internal security duties on a single occasion during the National Party's rule, being jointly responsible with the SAP for suppressing the violent protest against the creation of a Tricameral Parliament in the city centre in 1985. There were no deaths in the DCP sector and the Truth and Reconciliation Commission's (1998) regional report does not mention the force at all.

I arrived at DCP headquarters in Old Fort Place on the evening of Monday 14 September 1992, aged 19, to begin my induction as an auxiliary constable (a part-time, fully sworn role). There were three other recruits in the class and I remember doing my best to conceal my nerves from a soft-spoken but nonetheless intimidating training sergeant. I had wanted to join the DCP as a police constable (fully sworn and full-time), but there were no vacancies and I had to wait until June 1993, when – along with one of my classmates – I joined the force a second time. I was promoted to senior constable in June 1997, by which time I had qualified as a dog handler. I returned to headquarters to terminate my final tour of duty shortly after midday on Friday 30 January 1998, a few days before my 25th birthday, mildly disappointed that I had not been able to interest either the force field unit or the local detective branch in raiding the mid-sized 'chop-shop' (premises where stolen motor vehicles were processed before being sold) my partner and I had discovered that morning. My service actually finished the next day, but I had been removed from the weekend rota (because I wasn't working the Sunday) and the control room sergeant allowed me to sign on and off duty from home. My five years of service can be summarised as follows: one year of basic and specialist training; one year of general uniform patrol (divided between foot and van patrol); one year in the Public Transport Unit (a plainclothes community liaison role); and two years in the Dog Section (divided equally between being a driver and a handler). A year is a long time to spend in training, but that includes been trained as both an auxiliary constable and police constable (the latter period prolonged in consequence of local politics and operational requirements) and specialist training as a police pursuit driver and patrol dog handler.

The DCP expanded steadily during my service. By the time I left, there were over 500 police officers, including auxiliary constables. The force did not recruit women as police officers until 1993 and the proportion of women police officers had reached about 5% by 1998. The ethnic mix of the force reflected the ethnic mix of the municipal patrol area, roughly one third Black, White, and South Asian (known as 'Indian' under apartheid).[4] Most of the 15 senior officers (Inspector, Chief Inspector, Deputy Chief Constable, and Chief

Constable) were White, however, including all four of the chief officers (two of whom were born in the UK and a third in the Republic of Ireland). The force consisted of three divisions: general uniform patrol, specialist operations, and support services. Specialist operations and support services were based at headquarters and general uniform patrol distributed among headquarters (central), Chatsworth (south), and Phoenix (north). There was no criminal investigation department and all police detectives in South Africa were in the SAPS, as the lead agency for crime prevention. There were four shifts, which included either a 30- or 60-minute break: early (0600–1430), day (0900–1800), late (1400–2230), and night (2200–0630). Constables and sergeants worked a 48-hour week, which was only four more than the norm in South Africa, but they were on duty for 12 days and off for two, i.e. off duty every second weekend. The 12-day duty stretches consisted of two shifts, one lasting five days and the other seven; for example, a day shift from Monday to Friday, followed by an early shift from Saturday to the next Friday. DCP pay was better than SAPS pay, but poor by international standards. My final salary (two points below the maximum for a constable) was 59% of the starting salary of an English police constable (excluding London) in real terms. Paid overtime was almost always available and occasionally compulsory. My most common overtime shift was 0600–1800 as I didn't find it much more onerous than a day shift. My longest tour of duty lasted 32 hours, beginning at 0600 on New Year's Eve in 1997 and concluding at 1430 the next day.

Durban was then and is still the third largest city in South Africa, behind Johannesburg and Cape Town. Although the municipality was considerably smaller, the DCP responded to calls for service from the metropolitan area, which had a population of three million. Gun ownership (legal and illegal) was common and gun crime high. There were nearly 2,000 murders in 1997, a murder rate of about 67 per 100,000. Combining several sources which are themselves approximates, this puts Durban well above the currently most dangerous city in the UK (London, 2), on a par with the currently most dangerous city in the US (St Louis, 65), below Johannesburg and Cape Town at the time (both in the 70s), and well below the currently most dangerous city in the world (Colima, 184, in Mexico) (Special Task Force South Africa 1999; Suneson & Comen 2020; Fieldstadt 2022; Forbes Staff 2023; Allen & Mansfield 2023). I do not recall how many police officers were shot in Durban during my service because only the small proportion that died received any significant media coverage. I do recall that the highest number of police officers killed in South Africa in a single year was 371 (in 1995 or 1996, I am not sure which), a substantial proportion of which were killed off duty. The likelihood of being killed on duty in Durban was less than in rural areas, although police officers incurred a higher-than-average risk of injury or death in motor vehicle collisions. These risks were accepted as part of the job and stress was not sanctioned as a reason for sick leave until the final year of my service. I do not know what the official statistics were, but there was a high rate of suicide among police officers in both the DCP and SAPS (six whom I knew personally, four men and two women). As a rough guide, my experience of policing was for the most part similar to that of Moskos (2008), with one major exception: the illegal drug trade in Durban in the 1990s was not lucrative. In consequence, organised crime was focused on the minibus taxi industry (Durban was plagued by 'Taxi Wars' from 1995 to 1997), armed robberies (of business premises, banks, and cash-in-transit), and motor vehicle theft (almost all of which was of motor cars). There were no regional police units exclusively dedicated to organised crime, but many of the related investigations were conducted by the senior criminal investigation branch, Murder and Robbery, which consisted of about 50 detectives.

The DCP was and is one of the institutions of policing in South Africa. As such, its purpose is not to protect the public, but (as explained in Chapter 2) to sustain the practice of policing in a particular place (Durban) at a particular time (1854 to the present). The purpose of the practice of policing into which I was inducted in 1992 was (as also explained in Chapter 2) the internal good of public protection. To be a 'good cop' was to be good at protecting the public and being good at protecting the public required mastery of the excellences of the practice and mastery of a specific set of skills, as suggested by MacIntyre (2007). The specific set of skills required for public protection – competence in physical confrontations, delivering first aid, driving in adverse conditions, and with several types of firearm – were the subject of training modules and in-service assessments.[5] The excellences of the practice of policing were, in contrast, assimilated while 'on the road' (doing police work). At no time during either my year of basic and specialist training or my two years of being mentored by first Siza and then Chris were the excellences explained, discussed, or even mentioned by name. Excellences were, instead, identified indirectly, by their absence, using an informal vocabulary. As such, they are a product of informal occupational norms, summarised by Holdaway (1983: 134) as the social construction of policing by the lower ranks, 'which means not that it is concocted out of thin air but that the various legal and policy instruments available to the staff are modified as the rules in the book are translated into rules in use o[n] the ground'.[6] Cops who lacked the excellence of physical courage were labelled as 'scared', which did not mean feeling fear – most of us were scared some of the time – but failing to overcome fear. Courage, physical courage especially but also moral courage, was the most valued of all the excellences of the practice and once a reputation for being scared was acquired it was almost impossible to elude. The absence of the excellence of self-restraint was called 'getting involved' and there were several officers with reputations for escalating confrontations unnecessarily. Cops who were untrustworthy were known as 'thrillers', a lack of the excellence of integrity that comprised a combination of exaggeration and apathy. Thrillers were typically lazy, 'only here for the 27th' (the monthly payday), and would try to conceal their neglect of duty by embellishment, falsification, or both. The absence of the excellence of judgement was referred to as being 'stupid', regardless of the individual's education or intellectual ability. Typically, stupid cops were those who were unable to balance the at times conflicting demands of proactive and reactive policing within their practice.

In addition to these four excellences, there were three other features of the practice of policing that were recognised and accepted without ever being the subject of discussion. Perhaps the most important was the understanding that being a good cop required a combination of skill, excellence, and luck. My 13-month partnership with Chris is an instructive example: though our level of commitment remained consistent, we were afflicted with bad luck for the first six months (to the extent that our colleagues spoke of 'the curse of Cray') and gifted with good luck for the rest (during which Chris was lauded as 'one-shot Cray' for his self-restraint). If one was not dogged by misfortune, then there were two ways to fail to be a good cop, through choice or weakness. Those who chose not to aspire to the excellences of the practice had usually joined the police for either the opportunity to exercise power or for job security. Those who aspired to the excellences of the practice but failed to achieve them were well-intentioned, but lacking in one or more of courage, self-restraint, integrity, or judgement.[7] This type of failure need not be permanent. Joseph Wambaugh (1971) provides a gripping account of excellences being achieved relatively late in careers in his novel *The New Centurions*, which is based on his own service as a police officer. Finally, being a good cop was accompanied by pleasure in dedication to duty, by reciprocal respect for other good cops, and by genuine friendship. Cops who were lacking in the excellences were not respected by their colleagues and seemed to derive little satisfaction from their practice of policing.

3.3 The Four Characteristics

My (McGregor 2021) published analytic autoethnography presented three findings. First, that analytic autoethnography is a valuable method for social scientists to deploy in policing research. Second, that there is a significant distinction between policing as a practice and policing as an institution, on which I have elaborated considerably in my discussion of policing as a situated practice in Chapter 2. The third and most important finding of my study is that the practice of policing not only requires mastery of the excellences of the practice and a specific set of skills, but is distinguished from other practices by a specific set of characteristics. My experience of the practice of policing is that it had four characteristics, which I shall explain by means of the following concepts: heroic struggle, edgework, absolute sacrifice, and worldmaking. Excellences are, as discussed in the previous section, the personal qualities required to perform the practice and they are excellences rather than deficiencies because their object, public protection, is an internal good that is valued in and by society (MacIntyre 2007). As constitutive of the practice, they are essential to it. Characteristics as I conceive of them here are features of the practice of AADP that arise from its situation in both an institution and a systemic context.[8] As such, they are features of the contingent relations among the practice and the institution and context within which it is situated. In Orson Welles' *Touch of Evil* (1958: 57:04–57:07), protagonist Mike Vargas (played by Charlton Heston) sums up the tension between the pursuit of public protection and the situation of that pursuit nicely: 'A policeman's job is only easy in a police state.' Given my concern with police legitimacy, it is worth noting that the original title of the film (and of the novel from which it was adapted) was *Badge of Evil*.

3.3.1 Heroic Struggle

'Heroic' has several related meanings, one of which refers to the pre-Socratic and pre-Christian society that preceded the classical age in Western Europe, which I discussed in Chapter 2. The definitive feature of this society is acknowledgement that all human endeavour ends in failure rather than success (MacIntyre 2007). The individual understands that whatever she does, she will fail to achieve all of her goals, even if for no other reason than that death will cut them short. AADP is a *heroic struggle* in the same sense because the aim of that practice, protecting the public, can never be achieved in full. Peter Manning (2010: 202) describes this characteristic when he states: 'Police actions only reduce what might be worse; they cannot alter the causal factors – class, age, education, family, and school effects – that lie outside officers' control.' If public protection involves the prevention of some harm and the reduction of other harm, then both the proactive and reactive paradigms of policing are implicated in the inevitable failure of the practice. In proactive policing, the officer who intervenes cannot predict precisely what the consequences of her intervention will be in terms of net harm, especially when one considers the aftereffects of that intervention. In reactive policing, the harm has already been inflicted and public protection has already failed so the best the officer can hope for is to reduce the consequences of that harm. Police officers strive to prevent and reduce as much harm as possible, but understand that their impact is always limited. Lois Presser (2008) draws attention to both the extent to which epic struggles are celebrated in Western culture and the extent to which heroism is the dominant model of masculinity in that culture. She argues that heroism is criminogenic when the struggle against impossible odds is conflated with another meaning of heroism, being acclaimed or admired for greatness. Toxic masculinity frames the difficulty of the struggle as the moral justification of the struggle, i.e. the hero is acclaimed or admired solely for embarking on an impossible endeavour without considering whether that endeavour is in fact worthwhile. The moral mismatch can be made by both agents of the criminal justice system and those who believe they are victimised by it.

The most important prosecution in which Chris and I were involved was the premeditated murder of a middle-aged woman by a group of six youths. The crime scene was a freeway after midnight and we found the victim dead, but all suspects in attendance. As soon as they saw me, they fled into the thick bush on either side of the road and Chris used his patrol dog to track and apprehend one of them. Within 24 hours the local detectives arrested the leader, but he would not give up any accomplices. In the first few seconds of my arrival, I was in a position to apprehend all six and could have done so had I not been concerned about using deadly force unnecessarily. Whenever I think about the incident, it is always about the four suspects that escaped, not the two that went to trial, in spite of my retrospective confidence in making the right choice in the circumstances.

3.3.2 Edgework

Edgework is the term Stephen Lyng (1990) uses to describe the phenomenon of voluntary risk taking in contemporary society, which includes sports such as skydiving and motor racing and occupations such as a policing and combat roles in the military. Edgework has two key features: (1) it involves a high risk of injury or death; and (2) this risk can be reduced by the edgeworker achieving competence in a certain skill set. Policing is clearly edgework. William Ker Muir (1977: 263) cites Jerome Skolnick (1966) on the dangers of police work and describes patrolling as 'lonely, dangerous, and preoccupied with human suffering'. Police officers in the most peaceful countries in the world or on the most uneventful beats can be confronted with life-or-death situations in which they are required to intervene at any time during any shift and such intervention is often at great personal risk. This risk can be minimised by means that are both within and without the practice of policing. The former category includes mastery of the specific skill set I mentioned in the previous section, which includes maintenance of an above average level of fitness, with a focus on at least one of strength, speed, or endurance. The latter category, which is by far the safer, includes tactics such as failing to respond to certain calls for service, employing excessive force, and treating every member of the public as a potential assailant. Lyng notes that edgework is accompanied by a euphoric sensation and a specific set of emotions. The sensation is of self-actualisation or self-determination and the emotional sequence proceeds from fear to exhilaration. The goal of edgework is to subject oneself to a dangerous experience and to survive that experience. Skolnick's (1966) theory of working personality depicts a similar situation, in which police officers experience both intimidation and enjoyment in the face of danger.[9] The euphoria and exhilaration of survival can, I suggest, become addictive, particularly when the work itself is demanding in terms of time, commitment, and lifestyle. If 'the idea of self-actualization serves to designate the essential condition of the edgework experience' as Lyng (1990: 878) claims, then it becomes all too easy to crave this sensation.

My colleagues and I worked a 48-hour week, which was not in itself particularly arduous, but the 96-hour fortnight was spread across 12 days, with every second weekend off duty. Even in the absence of planned overtime and with only eight-hour shifts, the two-week stretch was often tiring in consequence of either the unpredictability of the edgework (unplanned overtime), the swap between shifts, or both. Police officers without family responsibilities tended to spend their days off in one of two ways, either exhausted collapse or extravagant recreation, and I indulged in both. Collapse involved sleeping for as much of the weekend as I could manage, staying in bed for ten to 16 hours at a time. Recreation consisted of afternoons, evenings, and nights of socialising, almost always accompanied by heavy alcohol consumption. What I remember most clearly, however, is those weekends off as *waiting* – just killing time until the next pair of shifts started.

3.3.3 Absolute Sacrifice

Jacques Derrida (1992) uses the biblical narrative of the sacrifice of Isaac to articulate a conception of self-sacrifice. Self-sacrifice in his terms is both authentic and absolute. *Authentic sacrifice* involves a recognition of the ethical bond among all human beings and a willingness to act on this bond by sacrificing one's own interests for that of another. Muir (1977: 178) acknowledges this bond in the 'tragic perspective', the appreciation of human suffering, one of his two criteria for the professional police officer (the other is moral calm, the appreciation of the relationship between coercion and justice). Becoming a police officer is essentially a sacrifice of one's own interests to those of the public good and the practice of policing requires that police officers sacrifice their interests on a continuous rather than occasional basis. While the ultimate sacrifice, of one's own life in exchange for another's, is rare in most countries, police officers necessarily exchange their safety for those of others while on and off duty and often sacrifice their mental health (Henry 2004). *Absolute sacrifice* involves the recognition that one can never achieve authentic sacrifice because of the extent of the demands made by the ethical bond. We can only help so many people in the course of our lives and that number is always exponentially smaller than the number of people who would have benefitted from our help. When we recognise this, we move beyond the concern with the sacrifice of our own interests to a concern with why we make some sacrifices but not others. In Derrida's (1992: 71) terms, absolute sacrifice is not about the self, but about the others we sacrifice: 'I can respond to the one (or to the One), that is to say to the other, only by sacrificing to that one the other.' In other words, once we accept the demand for continuous self-sacrifice, we are no longer sacrificing our own interests for the interests of others, but sacrificing the interests of some others (those whom we choose not to help) for the interests of other others (those whom we choose to help). Muir (1977: 218) refers to the second-guessing produced by this recognition as the acquisition of 'moral baggage', which suggests the deteriorative effects of long-term participation in such activity.

I mentioned the frequency of police suicides in the previous section and the causes were no doubt both diverse and complex, comprising the combination of a wide variety of life and work pressures. The death that stands out for me is that of Police Constable Themba Radebe, who shot himself a few months before the freeway murder I described. He and I were of a similar age, had joined the Dog Section together, and approached our police practice with the same seriousness and enthusiasm. Themba was liked by his colleagues, respected by senior officers, and had an enviable career trajectory ahead of him. His funeral was very well attended and his suicide blamed on a broken engagement, albeit with little conviction. Whatever else may have contributed, I think that absolute sacrifice and its accompanying degree of responsibility – the accumulated weight of the moral baggage of police work – simply wore him down.

3.3.4 Worldmaking

Amia Srinivasan (2019: 145) defines *worldmaking* as 'the transformation of the world through a transformation of representational practices'. Representational practices are important because the way in which the social world is represented determines our experience of that world as well as our understanding of our own selfhood. Representations are created by individuals and institutions and often employed to create a representational order whose purpose is to oppress a particular group of people. Worldmaking is a transformation that consists of two stages, diagnosis and redescription. The first involves perceiving that the social world is not a consequence of randomness, but of a created representational order, and perceiving our own role in relation to that order. The second involves realising that we can exercise our agency to create our own representations individually or collectively and, in so doing, remake the social world. Srinivasan advocates collective feminine worldmaking over individualistic masculine worldmaking, but it is the latter rather than the former that characterises policing. The police officer has a peculiar relation to power. AADP is almost entirely reliant on discretion and this alone provides the individual police officer with substantial power over the public, including the power of life and death in rare circumstances. Egon Bittner (1970: 39) describes the police as 'nothing else than a mechanism for the distribution of situationally justified force in society' and certain situations may justify deadly force. As noted in Chapter 2, Manning (2010) goes even further, stating that the police *operate as an agency for the redistribution of life chances in a population.* Individual police officers remake the social worlds of the people with whom they interact and police officers collectively remake the social world of the public they are sworn to protect. In contrast, the police officer in an AADP nation is an insignificant part of the criminal justice system as a whole, often as powerless as members of the protected public. The contrast between powerlessness and power reaches its apotheosis in uniformed patrol, which is where most officers begin their practice. Police officers worldmake when they decide whether or not to employ their discretion and there is a strong temptation to worldmake beyond the bounds of one's authority, which may be motivated by either self-interest or self-sacrifice.

My most blatant exceeding of authority was also one of my best exercises of judgement. While working in the Public Transport Unit, I responded to a report of a peaceful protest by about a dozen minibus taxi drivers near the docks. I had just dropped Siza off at the magistrates' court when we were called on the radio, which meant that I was both on my own and less than two minutes away. I arrived, in plainclothes and an unmarked car, before the protest had gathered momentum and managed to persuade the drivers to remove their vehicles from the traffic lanes. The blockade was still being dismantled when the local SAP station commander, a major, appeared, also on his own, and ordered me to arrest the ringleader. I made a show of looking for the man (who was standing on the pavement next to his parked minibus), reported that he had already left, and said that I had no way of ascertaining his identity. The major was convinced by my performance and I emerged from the incident neither charged with insubordination nor praised for de-escalation.

What is striking about these characteristics of the practice of policing is that they can either contribute to or detract from the internal good of public protection. Police officers who appreciate the practice as a heroic struggle may well be more realistic in their goals and consequently more effective in actually achieving them. On the other hand, that same appreciation could lead to either cynicism or a blunting of moral emotion. Similarly, appreciation of the absolute sacrifice the practice demands could prepare officers for the weight of the responsibility they will have to bear or produce indifference or despair.[10] The balance between power and powerlessness that must be negotiated by police officers could – again – produce a worldmaker who is well-acquainted with her role within the justice system or one who strives to impose her own brand of justice outside that system. Understanding the practice of policing as edgework prepares officers for the dangers they will face, but the addictive quality of those dangers can encourage officers to take unnecessary or illegal risks. Heroic struggle, edgework, absolute sacrifice, and worldmaking are thus not only emergent from the tension between the practice and its situation in an institution and a systemic context, but features that are neither intrinsically helpful nor intrinsically harmful with respect to the aim of that practice, public protection. In consequence of their origin in the tension between practice and situation, the four characteristics can be employed as an analytic tool for determining the different ways in which police legitimacy is undermined at all three levels: policing as a practice, policing as an institution, and the systemic context of policing. In Part 3, which begins with Chapter 5, I explore the characteristics of the practice in detail, considering their implications for public protection at each of the levels.

Notes

1 For a similar albeit not identical example from the UK, see: Lloyd-Rose (2023).
2 I have changed the names of all six of the former colleagues whom I mention in this book.
3 My other role model was Detective Inspector Carl Devlin, who was only a year older than me and killed on duty in January 2004.
4 Under apartheid all babies had their 'race' recorded on their birth certificates in one of the following four categories: 'White', 'Coloured'

(mixed race), 'Indian' (South Asian), or 'Black'. Durban and the DCP had a very small mixed-race population during my service (under 10%).

5 A notable absence from this abbreviated skill set is effective verbal communication, which is essential to police practice but was acquired by means of informal occupational norms in the DCP. A more accurate summary of the contemporary skill set required for public protection in both the US and the UK is: effective communication, physical prowess, technical proficiency, and first aid.

6 These informal occupational norms are often referred to as 'cop culture', which I define as *a patterned set of understandings that shapes beliefs, attitudes, and behaviours that are either emergent, enduring, or extinguished over time and in to which successive generations of police officers are socialised* in Chapter 9. I am sceptical of the explanatory power of cop culture as it has been represented in most of the literature to date, in consequence of which my preference is to retain 'informal occupational norms' to describe the means by which the excellences of the practice of policing are acquired.

7 I do not wish to suggest that my own practice of policing was not lacking in one or more of the excellences described – on the contrary, I was probably lacking in all of them at one time or another.

8 My preliminary findings included two claims that subsequent research revealed as oversimplifications. First, I identified the characteristics of the practice as emergent from the tension between the practice of policing and the institution of policing rather than the tensions among the practice, institution, and systemic context of policing. Second, I identified the population of the autoethnography as US city policing rather than UK policing (in virtue of the legal and social similarities between the US and South Africa) and UK policing (in virtue of the DCP being modelled on the MPS) (McGregor 2021; see also: McGregor 2023).

9 I return to Skolnick's (1966) theory in my discussion of cop culture in Chapter 9.

10 The blunting of moral emotion and indifference and despair as responses to suffering are all explored in the literature on police 'compassion fatigue'; see: Andersen and Papazoglou (2015); Papazoglou et al. (2020); Russo et al. (2020).

References

Allen, G. & Mansfield, Z. (2023). Homicide Statistics. 11 July. House of Commons Library. Available at: https://researchbriefings.files.parliament.uk/documents/CBP-8224/CBP-8224.pdf.

Andersen, J. P. & Papazoglou, K. (2015). Compassion fatigue and compassion satisfaction among police officers: An understudied topic. *International Journal of Emergency Mental Health and Human Resilience*, 17 (3), 661–663.

Anderson, L. (2006a). Analytic Autoethnography. *Journal of Contemporary Ethnography*, 35 (4), 373–395.
Anderson, L. (2006b). On Apples, Oranges, and Autopsies: A Response to Commentators. *Journal of Contemporary Ethnography*, 35 (4), 450–465.
Bittner, E. (1970). The Functions of the Police in Modern Society: A Review of Background Factors, Current Practices, and Possible Role Models. *Crime & Delinquency Issues*. November. Chevy Chase, MD: National Institute of Mental Health. Available at: www.ncjrs.gov/pdffiles1/Digitization/147822NCJRS.pdf.
Bochner, A.P. & Ellis, C. (eds) (2001). *Ethnographically Speaking: Autoethnography, Literature, and Aesthetics*. Lanham, MD: AltaMira Press.
Bochner, A.P. & Ellis, C. (eds) (2016). *Evocative Autoethnography: Writing Lives and Telling Stories*. New York: Routledge.
Brooks, R. (2021). *Tangled Up in Blue: Policing the American City*. New York: Penguin.
Derrida, J. (1992/2008). The Gift of Death. In: Derrida, J. *The Gift of Death (Second Edition) and Literature in Secret*. Trans. D. Wills. Chicago: University of Chicago Press, 1–116.
Dillard, C.B. (2008). Whole Sense of Self, a Whole Sense of the World: The Blessings of Spirituality in Qualitative Research and Teaching. *International Review of Qualitative Research*, 1 (1), 81–101.
Emerson, R.M., Fretz, R.I. & Shaw, L.L. (2011). *Writing Ethnographic Fieldnotes*. 2nd ed. Chicago: University of Chicago Press.
Fieldstadt, E. (2022). Murder Map: Deadliest U.S. Cities. 23 February. *CBS News*. Available at: www.cbsnews.com/pictures/murder-map-deadliest-u-s-cities.
Forbes Staff (2023). Colima es la ciudad más violenta del mundo: informe. 20 February, *Forbes México*. Available at: www.forbes.com.mx/colima-es-la-ciudad-mas-violenta-del-mundo-informe.
Gendrot, V. (2020). *Flic: Un journaliste a infiltré la police*. Paris: Éditions Goutte D'Or.
Hayano, D. (1979). Auto-Ethnography: Paradigms, Prospects, and Problems. *Human Organization*, 38 (1), 99–104.
Heider, K.G. (1975). What Do People Do? Dani Auto-Ethnography. *Journal of Anthropological Research*, 31 (1), 3–17.
Henry, V.E. (2004). *Death Work: Police, Trauma, and the Psychology of Survival*. New York: Oxford University Press.
Holdaway, S. (1983). *Inside the British Police: A Force at Work*. Oxford: Blackwell.
Jackson, T. (2017). *Policing Ferguson, Policing America: What Really Happened – And What the Country Can Learn From It*. New York: Skyhorse Publishing.

Jewell, J. (1989). *A History of the Durban City Police*. Durban, South Africa: Rotary Club of Durban Musgrave.

King. T. & Portman, A. (2000). *Gallantry Awards of the South African Police 1913–1994: Including a Complete Roll of Honour*. Germiston, South Africa: Rhino Research.

Lloyd-Rose, M. (2023). *Into the Night: A Year with the Police*. London: Picador Books.

Lyng, S. (1990). Edgework: A Social Psychological Analysis of Voluntary Risk Taking. *American Journal of Sociology*, 95 (4), 851–886.

McGregor, R. (2021). Four Characteristics of Policing as a Practice. *Policing: A Journal of Policy and Practice*, 15 (3), 1842–1853.

McGregor, R. (2023). Autoethnography: Analysing the World of Policing from Within. In: Fleming, J. & Charman, S. (eds), *Routledge International Handbook of Police Ethnography*. Abingdon: Routledge, 391–405.

MacIntyre, A. (2007). *After Virtue: A Study in Moral Theory*. 3rd ed. London: Duckworth Books.

Manning, P.K. (2010). *Democratic Policing in a Changing World*. Abingdon: Routledge.

Moskos, P. (2008). *Cop in the Hood: My Year Policing Baltimore's Eastern District*. New Jersey: Princeton University Press.

Muir, W.K. (1977/1979). *Police: Streetcorner Politicians*. Chicago: University of Chicago Press.

Papazoglou, K., Marans, S, Keesee, T. & Chopko, B. (2020). Police Compassion Fatigue. *FBI Law Enforcement Bulletin*. 9 April. Available at: https://leb.fbi.gov/articles/featured-articles/police-compassion-fatigue.

Peace, D. (2010). Audible Interview. In: Peace, D., *Nineteen Seventy Four*. 29 June. Available at: www.audible.co.uk/pd/Nineteen-Seventy-Four-Audiobook/B004FT6SIK.

Perri 6 & Bellamy, C. (2011). *Principles of Methodology: Research Design in Social Science*. London: Sage Publications.

Presser, L. (2008). *Been a Heavy Life: Stories of Violent Men*. Champaign, IL: University of Illinois Press.

Rauch, J., Shaw, M. & Louw, A. (2001). *Monograph 67: Municipal Policing in South Africa. Development and Challenges*. Institute for Security Studies. 1 November. Available at: https://issafrica.s3.amazonaws.com/site/uploads/Mono67.pdf.

Russo, C., Aukhojee, P., McQuerrey Tuttle, B., Johnson, O., Davies, M., Chopko, B.A., & Papazoglou, K. (2020). Compassion Fatigue & Burnout. In: Papazoglou, K. & Blumberg, D.M. (eds). *Power: Police Officer Wellness, Ethics, and Resilience*. London: Academic Press, 97–115.

Skolnick, J.H. (1966). *Justice Without Trial: Law Enforcement in Democratic Society*. New York: Wiley.

Special Task Force South Africa (1999). *Episode* 1. Date of original release unknown. Available at: www.youtube.com/watch?v=rUlk7XGqFCM&t=748s. Accessed 3 March 2024.

Srinivasan, A. (2019). Genealogy, Epistemology and Worldmaking. *Proceedings of the Aristotelian Society*, CXIX (2), 127–156.

Suneson, G. & Comen, E. (2020). The Most Dangerous Cities in the World. *24/7WallSt*. 9 July. Available at: https://247wallst.com/special-report/2020/07/09/the-most-dangerous-cities-in-the-world-3/6/.

Tooth, T.R. (2019). *Becoming Special: Occupational socialisation in volunteer police officers*. PhD thesis. University of Bristol. Available at: https://research-information.bris.ac.uk/ws/portalfiles/portal/215127572/Becoming_Special_definitive_edit_TT.pdf.

Touch of Evil (1958). Directed by Orson Welles. US: Universal-International.

Truth and Reconciliation Commission of South Africa (1998). *Truth and Reconciliation Commission of South Africa Report: Volume Three (Natal and KwaZulu)*. Department of Justice and Constitutional Development. Available at: www.justice.gov.za/trc/report/finalreport/Volume%203.pdf.

Wakeman, S. (2014). Fieldwork, Biography and Emotion: Doing Criminological Autoethnography. *The British Journal of Criminology: An International Review of Crime and Society*, 54 (5), 705–721.

Wambaugh, J. (1971). *The New Centurions*. New York: Little, Brown, and Company.

Wender, J.M. (2008). *Policing and the Poetics of Everyday Life*. Champaign, IL: University of Illinois Press.

Young, M. (1991). *An Inside Job: Policing and Police Culture in Britain*. Oxford: Clarendon Press.

4
CRITICAL CASE STUDIES

My methodology consists of two core elements: autoethnography, which was discussed in Chapter 3, and case studies, which are the subject of this chapter. I begin with Bent Flyvbjerg's (2001) delineation of phronetic social science in terms of nine features that prioritise the analysis of value-laden praxis over the proof of predictive theory in the investigation of social reality. Case studies are the primary method of phronetic social science and a critical case study is defined as having strategic significance with respect to the problem under scrutiny, being narrative in form, and including thick descriptions that reveal the full extent of social complexity. Within the phronetic approach to social science, I follow what Ashely Rubin (2021) describes as the fieldwork model of research for case selection and data sampling. In order to determine my criteria for case selection, I combine Derek Matravers' (2014) research on thickness in representation with Gregory Currie's (2010) research on narrativity in representation to demonstrate first that the epistemic distinction between nonfiction and fiction is widely misunderstood and then that fiction has a greater potential for providing phenomenological knowledge than nonfiction. As such, I regard nonfiction and fiction as complementary epistemic endeavours in a similar manner to that in which Flyvbjerg regards the social sciences and natural sciences as complementary. In consequence of the centrality of the lived experience of policing to my study of the crisis of police legitimacy, the cases I select are all fictional explorations of the four characteristics of policing and of policing as a situated practice. My initial selection is: James Ellroy's (1987, 1988, 1990, 1992, 1995, 2001, 2009, 2014, 2019) unfinished hendecad, nine novels about police and political corruption in the US from 1941 to 1972; David Peace's (1999, 2000, 2001, 2002) *Red Riding Quartet*, four novels about the murders of 19 women and girls in the UK from 1969 to 1983; and HBO's *True Detective* (2014–2019), a television series about three sets of murder investigations in the US from 1980 to 2015. They are so replete with data, however, that it is necessary to distinguish the case from the context within each series by means of further selection and sampling. My final selection, in the order in which they will be presented, is: Southern California, 2013–2014 (*True Detective 2*); West Yorkshire, 1980 (Peace 2001); and Los Angeles, 1947–1958 (Ellroy 1987, 1988, 1990).

4.1 Phronetic Social Science

This book is a study of the Transatlantic crisis of police legitimacy that aims to set out a comprehensive framework for the recovery of legitimacy in both countries. As such, it is an investigation into social rather than natural reality and although I am suspicious of attempts to create an impermeable division between the two, I am clearly conducting a social scientific rather than a natural scientific inquiry (Derrida 1967a, 1967b, 1967c; Bhaskar 1975, 1987, 1989). Bent Flyvbjerg (2001) describes the social and natural sciences as complementary endeavours in which the weaknesses of each are compensated by the strengths of the other. Where the natural sciences excel at providing predictive theories, the social sciences provide reflexive analyses of values, interests, and power. Recall from my discussion of Alasdair MacIntyre's (2007) social theory in Chapter 2 that *phronēsis* (judgement or practical wisdom) is distinct from Aristotle's other central virtues in being an excellence of the intellect rather than an excellence of character. Flyvbjerg (2001) draws on Aristotle's exploration of the intellectual excellences to identify three distinct types of knowledge: *episteme* (scientific causal knowledge), *techne* (technical know-how), and *phronesis* (value-laden praxis). He (Flyvbjerg 2001: 57, emphasis in original) identifies *episteme* as the goal of natural science and *phronesis* as the goal of social science, describing the latter as follows:

> *Phronesis* thus concerns the analysis of values – 'things that are good or bad for man [*sic*]' – as a point of departure for action. *Phronesis* is that intellectual activity most relevant to praxis. It focuses on what is variable, on that which cannot be encapsulated by universal rules, on specific cases. *Phronesis* requires an interaction between the general and the concrete; it requires consideration, judgment, and choice. More than anything else, *phronesis* requires *experience*. [1]

If phronesis is the goal of social science, then the practice of social science should embrace value-laden praxis rather than strive for scientific causal knowledge that it will never achieve in full. Noting, as I did in Chapter 2, that there is no direct English translation of *phronesis*, Flyvbjerg refers to his preferred approach as *phronetic social science*.

Phronetic social science is distinguished from natural science and from much social science as it is currently practised by its point of departure, methodology, and purpose. Phronetic social science begins with the following four questions (Flyvbjerg 2001: 145):

(1) Where are we going [...]?
(2) Who gains, and who loses, by which mechanism of power?
(3) Is it desirable?
(4) What should be done?

These questions are answered using a methodology with nine features. The first, which is explicit in the definition of *phronesis* as a type of knowledge, is that phronetic social science focuses on values (rather than, again, striving for a value-neutrality it will never achieve). The second feature is explicit in the second of the four questions: power is placed at the centre of reflexive analysis. Third, phronetic social science aims for relevance to social reality by avoiding *so what?* research, i.e. research whose results will make no difference to society. Fourth, the approach shares the phenomenological concern with minutiae, even when specific details seem trivial, because of the crucial connection between value-laden praxis and lived experience. Fifth, the approach takes activity and practice as its subject rather than language and discourse, notwithstanding the linguistic construction of social reality. Sixth, the primary method of phronetic social science is the case study (to which I return below) and researchers recognise the significance of the relation between (each) case and (its) context. Flyvbjerg makes explicit reference to MacIntyre (2007) for the seventh feature, which is that phronetic social science simultaneously prioritises the questions *why?* and *how?* and maintains this dual priority by deploying narrative analysis and prioritising narratology over both epistemology and ontology. Eighth, phronetic social science avoids focusing on one side of the agency-structure dichotomy at the expense of the other by focusing on the relation between the two and treating them as aspects of a complex whole. Finally, phronetic social scientific research involves dialogue with a polyphony of voices in order to reach an objectivity characterised by variation in perspectives and interpretations rather than by assumed or actual disinterest on the part of the researcher. Having established these methodological guidelines, Flyvbjerg (2001: 167) identifies the purpose of phronetic social science as 'to contribute to society's practical rationality in elucidating where we are, where we want to go, and what is desirable according to diverse sets of values and interests'. My investigation of the crisis of police legitimacy adopts the phronetic approach and this book is a work of phronetic social science.[2]

Flyvbjerg's sixth methodological guideline for phronetic social science is that it is best served by the case study, i.e. the primary method for the investigation of social reality should be the case study. Rubin (2021) similarly argues that all qualitative research methods follow the fieldwork model of research. Within this model, she draws attention to the overlap and imprecision of the use of two pairs of key terms: case/site and selection/sampling. Where a *case* 'can refer to a population, event, state/province/country, organization, some phenomenon common in a particular period, or court case', a *site* 'usually refers to a specific location' (Rubin 2021: 86). As the inclusion of the latter in the definition of the former suggests, the difference is not significant to Rubin, but she notes that the convention is to distinguish sites and cases on the basis of the former being visited and the latter studied remotely. A sample is simply the researcher's immediate source of data, regardless of how it is acquired or accessed. Sampling occurs at two levels: at the level of the case, which is usually called *selection*, and at the level of immediate data collection, which is usually called *sampling*. As with the (lack of) difference between cases and sites, selection and sampling are essentially the same process and Rubin refers to both as sampling. Although I agree with Rubin's reductive approach, I shall retain the conventional distinctions between case and site and case selection and data sampling for the sake of clarity. Rubin (2021: 91 & 92) claims that the most vociferous criticism of the fieldwork model of research is directed at sampling:

(1) Generalisability (case selection): 'Is your sample going to be representative of some larger population that we care about?'
(2) Selection bias (data sampling): 'Are you systematically (and perhaps unknowingly) overrepresenting pieces of data that have an atypical representation of or relationship with the thing you care about?'

She maintains that both these concerns are overemphasised and that critics of the fieldwork model of research place pressure on individual qualitative studies that they would not place on individual quantitative studies. All research, whether quantitative or qualitative in method or natural or social in subject, is conducted in the context of other research and of science as a practice and an institution (to use MacIntyre's terminology). As such, each study should be evaluated in terms of its contribution to the practice of science rather than its self-sufficiency, a point to which I return in the next section. Rubin's (2021: 93) rejoinder is pithy, albeit perhaps a little too dismissive: 'The goal of any individual study is not to solve the world's mysteries, but to get us one step closer to that goal.'

Flyvbjerg (2001) confronts the same problem from a different perspective, expanding the challenges to the case study to include all three of theory, reliability, and validity and providing a more robust response, which requires two sets of distinctions. The first is between random case selection and information-oriented case selection. The purpose of random case selection, which involves either random or stratified data sampling, is to avoid systematic bias and the generalisability of randomly selected cases is determined by the size of the sample. The purpose of information-oriented selection is to maximise the utility of the information acquired from a minimal sample and the basis for selection is the expectation of informational content. There are four types of cases that can be selected – extreme, maximally variant, paradigmatic, and critical – and each has a different function. Extreme cases acquire information about unusual examples and are used to convey findings in a memorable manner. Maximally variant cases acquire information about the relationship between circumstances and outcomes and are used for comparison. Paradigmatic cases acquire information about general characteristics of practices and cultures and are used to create metaphors for disciplines. Finally, 'a critical case can be defined as having strategic importance in relation to the general problem' and is used to make a particular type of logical deduction (Flyvbjerg 2001: 78). Flyvbjerg acknowledges that there are no universal methodological principles for identifying critical cases and that their selection requires relevant researcher experience. A rule of thumb for the selection of cases with strategic significance is seeking those that are either likely to clearly confirm or irrefutably falsify hypotheses. Strategic selection underpins the formulation of the following type of logical deduction (Flyvbjerg 2001: 78):

> a generalization of the sort 'if it is valid for this case, it is valid for all (or many) cases.' In its negative form, the generalization would be 'if it is not valid for this case, then it is not valid for any (or only a few) cases.'

Flyvbjerg emphasises extreme, paradigmatic, and critical cases, which are not mutually exclusive categories, and my study employs *critical cases*.

Flyvbjerg's taxonomy of case studies enables his refutation of the challenges to the method, which are also the most significant challenges to phronetic social science as an approach. Broadly construed, Rubin's (2021) concerns about generalisability and selection bias are equivalent to Flyvbjerg's (2001: 77, 86 & 84, emphases in originals) concerns about theory and validity and he responds to scepticism about the theory, reliability, and validity of case studies as follows:

(1) One can often generalize on the basis of a single case, and the case study may be central to scientific development via generalization as supplement or alternative to other methods. But formal generalization is overvalued as a source of scientific development, whereas 'the power of the good example' is underestimated.
(2) It is correct that summarizing case studies is often difficult, especially as concerns process. It is less correct as regards outcomes. The problems in summarizing case studies, however, are due more often to the properties of the reality studied than to the case study as a research method. Often it is not desirable to summarize and generalize case studies. Good studies should be read in their entirety.
(3) The case study contains no greater bias toward verification of the researcher's preconceived notions than other methods of inquiry. On the contrary, experience indicates that the case study contains a greater bias towards falsification of preconceived notions than toward verification.

Although it is not part of his argument for the value of case studies, Flyvbjerg remarks on their centrality to Karl Marx, Charles Darwin, and Sigmund Freud, which I take to be indicative of the value of the method both within and without phronetic social science given the incalculable influence of each of their oeuvres. Flyvbjerg concludes his discussion of the power of example by reiterating the need for systematic exemplar production, which requires, in turn, a substantial amount of thorough case studies.

4.2 Narrative Fiction

4.2.1 Complex Narratives

In the previous section, I framed Flyvbjerg's (2001) response to concerns about the irreducibility of case studies as a challenge to the reliability of the method. He begins his discussion of irreducibility with the close relation between case studies and narrative representation. Flyvbjerg (2001: 84) argues that this feature is a strength rather than a weakness: 'To the researcher practicing *phronesis* [...] a particularly "thick" and hard-to-summarize narrative is not necessarily a problem. Rather, it may be a sign that the study has uncovered a particularly rich problematic.' As such, it is curious that criminology has been so reluctant to embrace narrative as a tool for understanding, explaining, and reducing crime and harm. The initial criminological interest in narrative representation was developed in the Department of Sociology at the University of Chicago, where Clifford Shaw (1930) published *The Jack-Roller: A Delinquent Boy's Own Story*. In his introduction to the 1966 edition, Howard Becker laments that Shaw's method, the life history, never became one of the discipline's standard research tools. He accounts for this failure in terms of the growing professionalisation of the discipline, one of the consequences of which was (and remains) an increasing requirement for the self-sufficiency of studies. This recalls Rubin's (2021) response to criticism of the fieldwork model of research, cited in the previous section, and Becker's (1966: xvii) commentary is worth revisiting:

> It has led people to ignore the other functions of research and, particularly, to ignore the contribution made by one study to an overall research enterprise, even when the study, considered in isolation, produced no definitive results of its own.

Whether Becker's explanation is correct or not, only a handful of criminological studies deploying narrative methods were conducted in the remainder of the 20th century. At the beginning of the new century, Shadd Maruna (2001) published *Making Good: How Ex-*

Convicts Reform and Rebuild Their Lives, a study of the life narratives of offenders that is a direct descendant of Shaw's seminal work. Narrative criminology as a framework within the discipline was inaugurated with Lois Presser's (2008) *Been a Heavy Life: Stories of Violent Men* and followed relatively quickly by Sveinung Sandberg and Willy Pedersen's (2009) *Street Capital: Black Cannabis Dealers in a White Welfare State*, Presser's (2013) *Why We Harm*, Jennifer Fleetwood's (2014) *Drug Mules: Women in the International Cocaine Trade*, Thomas Ugelvik's (2014) *Power and Resistance in Prison: Doing Time, Doing Freedom*, and Presser's (2018) *Inside Story: How Narratives Drive Mass Harm*.

Presser (2013: 29; 2018: 2) defines the narrative criminological framework as one 'where the main explanatory variable is one's story' and as 'the study of the relationship between narratives and harmful actions and patterns'. As the lineage from Shaw to Maruna to Presser suggests, narrative criminologists typically focus on the life stories of offenders and typically regard the narratives communicated as constitutive rather than representational, i.e. as shaping lived experience rather than providing evidence of events or of the way in which events are experienced. Presser and her colleagues thus avoid the need to distinguish between nonfiction and fiction, but the life stories of offenders would be categorised as the former. The reluctance of criminology to embrace narrative as a tool for understanding is one of the reasons the discipline has resisted engaging with fiction. To date, the overwhelming majority of published studies have treated fiction as a source of information about the society in which it is produced and consumed rather than as a source of information about the content that it represents.[3] Another reason for this resistance to fiction is belief in an exact and impermeable distinction between fiction and nonfiction that is not shared by disciplines such as cultural studies, literary studies, film studies, and philosophy. To take a representative example of each: Stuart Hall (1973) argues that documentaries and dramas are both subject to the fallible processes of encoding and decoding; Michael Riffaterre (1990) examines a variety of senses of 'truth' in his critique of the established relation between referentiality and realism in linguistic representation; Roger Odin (2000) maintains that fictional films are distinguished from documentaries by differences in the way in which audiences interact with each mode of cinema; and Matravers (2014) regards the distinction between thick narratives and thin narratives as more fundamental than the distinction between fictional narratives and nonfictional narratives.

Matravers (2014: 47) sets out his position as follows:

> My view, in short, is that representations can be put to different uses: to teach, to persuade and to entertain being three of them. Representations also come in two varieties, thin and thick; or, rather, representations exist along a continuum from the very thin to the very thick. The traditional distinction, between representations that are fiction and representations that are nonfiction, is entirely unhelpful.

Matravers' use of 'thick' and 'thin' is best-known to social scientists from the work of anthropologist Clifford Geertz (1973: 312), who introduced 'thick description' to ethnographic practice. Geertz's source was the philosopher Gilbert Ryle (1968), who distinguished between two different descriptions of an identical action. Ryle's example, which Geertz discusses in detail, is two boys who each contract the eyelids of their right eyes, one of whom is twitching and the other of whom is winking. Ryle claims that unlike the twitcher, the winker does two things: contracts his eyelid *and* winks. The *contraction of the eyelid* is a thin description of the action and *wink* (and the other possibilities) a thick description of the action. Geertz (1973: 312) maintained that thick descriptions produced the 'stratified hierarchy of meaningful structures' at which ethnographic inquiry aims. Matravers argues that reading Leo Tolstoy's *War and Peace* (1869, a historical novel) and reading Faber de Faur's *With Napoleon in Russia* (1831–1843, an illustrated memoir) are thick experiences. What is important about the novel and the memoir is that they are both *thick representations* – i.e. vivid, rich, and gripping – not that the former is a fictional representation and the latter a nonfictional representation. In *Narrative Justice* (McGregor 2018), I combined Matravers' insights on the thin/thick continuum with Currie's (2010) insights on the minimal/exemplary continuum of narrative representation to argue for the epistemic value of complex narratives, regardless of whether they are fictional or nonfictional.

Like thickness, narrativity is a gradational property of representation that exists in a continuum from basic narratives to non-basic narratives to complex narratives to very complex narratives. A *basic narrative* is the product of an agent that represents one or more agents and two or more events which are connected. In other words, narratives are – like all representations – created by human beings rather than found in nature and the minimal criteria for a narrative are a single character who takes part in two events that are connected in some way. 'I typed this sentence and took a sip of coffee' is thus a basic narrative. There is one character (me) who performed two actions (typing and sipping) that are connected (by the second immediately following the first). These kinds of narrative have typically been of little interest to critics or philosophers, although Presser (2018) has drawn attention to the significance of basic narratives following their proliferation on social media in the second decade of the 21st century. My concern is with complex narratives and a *complex narrative* is the product of an agent that is high in narrativity in virtue of representing one or more agents and two or more events which are causally connected, thematically unified, and conclude. The crucial difference between complex and basic narratives is the thematic unity and closure of the former. A causal connection requires events earlier in the sequence to either cause or contribute to events later in the sequence, but the connection is so strong in complex narratives that it contributes to their thematic unity, which is a common thread on which the representation focuses. Complex narratives also conclude rather than terminate, providing readers or audiences with a tangible and meaningful sense of an ending. The combination of causal connectivity, thematic unity, and closure produces a representation that is essentially perspectival, i.e. presents people, places, and events from a particular point of view. The perspective that constitutes a complex narrative produces a framework, which Currie (2010: 86) defines as 'a preferred set of cognitive, evaluative, and emotional responses to the story'. In this way, the creators of narratives invite those who experience them to adopt certain emotional responses and evaluative attitudes to the characters, actions, and settings represented, which is precisely the thick experience with which Matravers is concerned. Complex narratives can be verbal or visual (or some combination of the two, like De Faur's memoir) and fictional or nonfictional (or some combination of the two, as is often claimed of Tolstoy's novel).

4.2.2 Phenomenological Knowledge

One of my key interests in *Narrative Justice* was the way in which complex narratives provide *phenomenological knowledge*, which I (McGregor 2018: 75) defined as 'the realisation of what a particular lived experience is like'. I contended that complex narratives provide phenomenological knowledge by means of their frameworks and regardless of whether they are fictional, nonfictional, or somewhere in-between.[4] The controversial part of my claim is that the phenomenological knowledge in complex narrative fictions, such as *War and Peace*, is knowledge of actual lived experience rather than the fictional lived experience of a character invented by an author, such as Pierre Bezukhov. The idea that there is a correspondence between representation and reality in nonfiction that is absent in fiction is the standard way of distinguishing the two types of representation. The relationship between correspondence and nonfiction is usually conceptualised in one of three ways. On the first and most naïve, nonfictional representations are characteristically true and fictional representations characteristically false. The approach runs into immediate problems due to 'false' being a pejorative term, denoting either accidental error or deliberate deception (Lamarque & Olsen 1994). To accuse Tolstoy of being in error in *War and Peace* because he tells a story about Bezukhov, a person that did not actually exist, is to misunderstand the production and consumption of fiction. The representation of Bezukhov could not be in error because there is no particular person with which it could or should correspond and it is not deceptive because both Tolstoy and his readers were and remain aware of its fictionality. A second way of approaching the distinction is to focus on the relationship between the representation and the readers or audiences that experience the representation. In this account, nonfictional representations invite audiences to believe their content and fictional representations invite audiences to make-believe or imagine their content (Matravers 2014). The distinction is applied as follows: where De Faur invites his readers to believe that he and his comrades fought the Russians at Smolensk, Valutino, and Borodino, Tolstoy invites his readers to imagine that Bezukhov was a wealthy Russian aristocrat. This is precisely where Matravers deploys his thin/thick continuum, arguing that all thick narratives (whether fictional or nonfictional) produce a thick experience that activates the imagination.

The third approach distinguishes nonfiction and fiction by means of their content, which is (or was) existent in nonfiction and is invented in fiction (Attridge 2015). The distinction is insufficiently robust because there is an important sense in which the content of *War and Peace* is existent and the content of *With Napoleon in Russia* invented. Fictional representations are always *about* something of relevance to human beings and the relation between fictional people, places, and events and the world can be understood in terms of reference to universals (McGregor 2016). The notion is from Aristotle's famous observation on the superiority of poetry over history: history refers to what has happened (particulars) and poetry to the kinds of thing that can happen (universals). For example, although *War and Peace* does not represent the search for meaning of an actual Russian aristocrat (particular), Bezhukov's attempts to make his life meaningful by first joining the Freemasons and then planning the assassination of Napoleon is true to life, lifelike, or realistic in virtue of representing the actions that someone with his background and personality (universal) would be likely to take in similar circumstances. The phenomenological knowledge is thus knowledge of the actual lived experience of *people like Bezukhov* rather than the fictional lived experience of Bezukhov himself. The blurring of the boundary between existence and invention is also evident in the opposite direction, between invention and nonfiction. Complex narratives represent reality in an opaque rather than transparent manner in consequence of the selectivity essential to narrative representation. Narratives standardly ignore, omit, or condense those parts of the sequence of events that lack relevance to the plot, unity, or coherence of the representation. Once again, this notion extends back to Aristotle, who praises Homer for his unity of plot in the *Odyssey*, where the sequence of events takes place over a decade (McGregor 2016). De Faur does not just represent the sequence of events in which he was involved in *With Napoleon in Russia*, but transforms them into a complex narrative by means of emplotment, selecting the most significant in order to create a narrative framework and thus to at least some extent fictionalising the reality.

My conclusion in *Narrative Justice* was that with respect to the epistemic value of complex narratives – specifically, the extent to which they provide phenomenological knowledge – their complexity takes priority over their fictionality. Where Matravers argues that all thick narratives activate the imagination (regardless of whether they are fictional or nonfictional), my argument is that all complex narratives provide phenomenological knowledge (regardless of whether they are fictional or nonfictional). My argument was restricted to phenomenological knowledge – *knowing what* (something is like) – as distinct from two other types of knowledge, which are identified by Dorothy Walsh (1969: 96, emphasis in original) as '*knowing that* (such and such is so) and [...] knowing in the sense of *knowing how* (to perform some act)'.[5] The complexity of narratives takes priority over their fictionality in knowledge-what, but not in knowledge-that or knowledge-how. Notwithstanding, the distinction is not as clear cut for either knowledge-that or knowledge-how. The status of *War and Peace* as a fiction does not prevent Tolstoy from representing how to comport oneself in a duel in 19th-century Russia any more than the status of *With Napoleon in Russia* as nonfiction prevents De Faur from accidentally or deliberately misrepresenting details of the retreat from Moscow. There is, of course, an expectation of a closer correspondence between representation and reality in nonfiction and a greater tolerance for inventiveness, imaginativeness, and fabrication in fiction, which makes nonfiction a much more reliable source of knowledge-that and knowledge-how. On the other hand, the freedom accorded to the creators of fiction facilitates a capacity for realising what particular lived experiences are like that is difficult (but not impossible) to replicate in nonfiction.

This may seem implausible, but consider whether any historical or contemporary documentary can match the second scene of Steven

Spielberg's *Saving Private Ryan* (1998) for providing knowledge of what it was like to be on Omaha Beach on D-Day. If you were lucky enough to watch it on the big screen, with surround sound and without any spoilers, like I was, then you have a vivid, rich, and gripping idea of how unlucky the 2nd Ranger Battalion was on 6 June 1944 (see: McGregor 2012). Neither Robert Capa's famous photographs nor John Ford's film footage of the actual event convey the desperate, visceral, and harrowing nature of the amphibious assault to the same extent as Spielberg's carefully crafted cinematic experience. My position is that nonfiction and fiction are complementary epistemic endeavours, like Flyvbjerg (2001) on the natural and social sciences, where the weaknesses of each are compensated by the strengths of the other. Nonfiction excels at providing knowledge-that and knowledge-how and fiction excels at providing knowledge-what. The conclusion I have reached about the relationship between complex narratives (whether nonfictional or fictional) and phenomenological knowledge may be too counterintuitive for some readers to accept so I offer an alternative that might be more appealing. One can differentiate between two types of truth: accuracy and authenticity. A complex narrative is accurate when the people, places, and events it represents correspond with reality. A complex narrative is authentic when the people, places, and events it represents cohere with lived experience. On this account, nonfictions are accurate or inaccurate and fictions authentic or inauthentic – though both nonfiction and fiction have the potential for accuracy and authenticity, in the same way that both nonfiction and fiction can provide knowledge-that, knowledge-how, and knowledge-what.

4.3 Selection and Sampling

4.3.1 Selection

My study of the crisis of police legitimacy is an investigation of social reality and, as such, best approached as phronetic social science, i.e. as an analysis of praxis rather than causation. The primary method of phronetic social science is the case study, which has the capacity for thickness and narrativity. My system of methods begins with a previously published analytic autoethnography (McGregor 2021c) that provides a foundation for further analysis, in consequence of which my investigation of social reality is bottom up, based on the lived experience of police practice. In the previous section I argued that nonfiction and fiction are complementary epistemic endeavours, the former excelling at providing knowledge-that and knowledge-how and the latter excelling at providing knowledge-what. The combination of this theory with my focus on lived experience meant that I was more likely to find the knowledge-what I was seeking in a complex fictional narrative than in a complex nonfictional narrative and fictionality became my first criterion for the selection of case studies. I decided that critical case studies were the most suitable for my investigation because they would enable me to make the generalisation *if it is valid for this case, then it is valid for many cases*. I established the following three criteria to ensure that the selected cases had strategic significance to the problem: cases that would (a) clearly confirm my hypothesis; (b) explore the four characteristics of policing as a practice; and (c) explore policing as a situated practice, including both the institution and systemic context of policing. In order to provide a more rigorous justification for the extrapolation from the specific sample to the wider population, I was determined to use multiple probes to search for answers, i.e. triangulate my results (Rubin 2021). If I selected three critical case studies, then at least one should be from the US and at least one from the UK. I now had a set of criteria for case selection:

(1) three complex narrative fictions
(2) each of which is a critical case study of the four characteristics of the practice of policing and of policing as a situated practice
(3) at least one of which is from the US and at least one of which is from the UK.

My interest in crime fiction, crime drama, and crime film has extended across six decades, from well before I joined the police to the present day. My first encounter with the genre was my parents reading the Sherlock Holmes short stories to me, followed by my own efforts with

The Hardy Boys (1979–1985) easy readers (which may now be classified differently). We did not own a television until after I started school so my first encounter with the genre on screen, ABC's *Chopper One* (1974), came later, followed closely by what I think was Philip D'Antoni's *The Seven-Ups* (1973). I started writing crime fiction of my own just over two decades ago, published two novels (one in 2009 and one in 2017) and a collection of short stories (in 2017), and reviewed crime fiction semi-professionally from 2006 to 2021. It is thus no exaggeration to state that I have read, watched, and more recently listened to literally thousands of short stories, novellas, novels, graphic novels, feature films, and television series about police officers, police and private detectives, criminals, and spies. These thousands of complex narrative fictions constitute the subset of the population of all the crime fiction, drama, and film ever published and released from which my sample for this study was drawn. Matching this expertise with my criteria for case selection, I thought it highly unlikely that any single work – a novel, film, or television season – would contain sufficient detail on both the four characteristics of the practice of policing and policing as a situated practice so I narrowed my search to series and franchises.

I have been thinking, reading, and writing about police legitimacy since 2017, when I published the first of four book reviews on police reform (in *Policing: A Journal of Policy and Practice*), driven by scepticism about the impact of the President's Task Force on 21st Century Policing in the US and the introduction of the Policing Education Qualifications Framework in the UK. After completing *Narrative Justice* (McGregor 2018), I started considering whether complex narrative fictions might be a source of data and published 'James Ellroy's Critical Criminology: Crimes of the Powerful in the *Underworld USA Trilogy*' (McGregor 2021b), which was about the ways in which complex fictions could actually be works of criminology, in 2019. Meanwhile, my work on police legitimacy changed direction as I began the autoethnographic research for what would later be published as 'Four Characteristics of Policing as a Practice' (McGregor 2021c). At this point I thought I was working on two different projects, an autoethnographic study of police practice and a narrative study of crime fiction as criminology. It was only after the publication of 'Four Characteristics of Policing as a Practice' in 2021 that I began to see the two articles as part of the same project, though I had yet to flesh out the methodology I would use. I also realised that I had already found my first critical case study – not Ellroy's (1995, 2001, 2009) *Underworld USA Trilogy*, but the wider history of police and political corruption of which it is a part (discussed below). This left two more to select, one or both of which should be set in the UK, and I composed a shortlist for re-reading and re-watching while keeping abreast of new publications and releases. It would be tedious and pointless to list all of the novels, films, and television series I considered, but the following six, which were shortlisted but not selected, are indicative: the five police procedurals Joseph Wambaugh published from 1975 to 1985; Derek Raymond's *Factory* novels (1984–1993); Bill James' *Harpur and Iles* novellas (1985–2019); ABC's *High Incident* (1996–1997); HBO's *The Wire* (2002–2008); and BBC One's *Happy Valley* (2014–2016).[6]

My first critical case study is, as already mentioned, Ellroy's history of police and political corruption, which is planned as a hendecad that will consist of two quartets and a trilogy. He (Ellroy 2019: 585) has published nine of the novels to date and the three series 'span thirty-one years and will stand as one novelistic history'. The hendecad has not been published in chronological order. The *Second L.A. Quartet* (Ellroy 2014, 2019) begins with *Perfidia* (Ellroy 2014), which opens the day before the attack on Pearl Harbor in 1941, continues with *This Storm* (Ellroy 2019), which concludes in 1942, and has yet to be completed. The *L.A. Quartet* begins with *The Black Dahlia* (Ellroy 1987) in 1943, continues with *The Big Nowhere* (Ellroy 1988) and *L.A. Confidential* (Ellroy 1990), and concludes with *White Jazz* (Ellroy 1992) in 1958. The *Underworld U.S.A. Trilogy* begins with *American Tabloid* (Ellroy 1995) in 1958, continues with *The Cold Six Thousand* (Ellroy 2001), and concludes with *Blood's a Rover* (Ellroy 2009) in 1972, a little over a week after the death of J. Edgar Hoover. Ellroy's (1995: 5, emphasis in original) explicit intention with the *Trilogy*, which applies to the hendecad as a whole, is '*to demythologise an era*', focusing on the local in the *L.A. Quartet* (Los Angeles), the national and international in the *Trilogy* (the US, Cuba, and South Vietnam), and the glocal in the *Second Quartet* (as Los Angeles goes to war). My only concern about the hendecad as a critical case study was that the publication of the next novel in the *Second L.A. Quartet* might alter the history of police and political corruption as represented in the first nine and thus invalidate some of the data. Reflecting on this possibility, I decided that the history established by and in the nine published novels was unlikely to be altered in any significant way by the remaining two. Ellroy launched a new series in 2021 with *Widespread Panic*, which continued in 2023 with *The Enchanters*, so it is not clear if he intends to follow through with his commitment to completing the hendecad.

My second critical case study is David Peace's *Red Riding Quartet*, which consists of four novels about the murders of six girls and 13 women in West Yorkshire from 1969 to 1983: *Nineteen Seventy-Four* (Peace 1999), *Nineteen Seventy-Seven* (Peace 2000), *Nineteen Eighty* (Peace 2001), and *Nineteen Eighty-Three* (Peace 2002). The two sets of crimes are linked by the formation of a cabal composed of seven corrupt police officers, a construction magnate affiliated with organised crime, and a famous architect in 1972. My third critical case study is HBO's *True Detective* (2014–2019), a television series consisting of three seasons of eight episodes of between 54 and 87 minutes, released in 2014, 2015, and 2019. The series is about three sets of police and private investigations from 1980 to 2015: a murder in Vermilion Parish, Louisiana (*True Detective 1*); a murder on the Pacific Coast Highway (*True Detective 2*); and the disappearance of two children in West Finger, Arkansas (*True Detective 3*). *True Detective* is an anthology series, meaning that each season features different detectives investigating a different case, but the three are united by the creative vision of screenwriter and novelist Nic Pizzolatto, who was permitted an extraordinary amount of creative control over the series (Cohen 2015; Monagle 2018). Shortly after I completed my case selection, rumours of a fourth season began circulating and *True Detective: Night Country* was released in January 2024. As Pizzolatto has publicly distanced himself from the project, which is the creation of Issa López, I did not include it as part of the critical case study (Hadadi 2024).

4.3.2 Sampling

Although I selected cases rather than sites, I employed Rubin's (2021) fieldwork model of research and was determined to follow all three of its principles in my sampling: (1) reflexivity (self-reflection on my data collection); (2) fieldnotes (making detailed notes as I read or watched each case); and triangulation.[7] My initial reflection on the three critical studies was that there was far too much data in each to analyse in a single chapter of a research monograph, even in a disproportionately long chapter. Taken together, the nine published novels of Ellroy's hendecad are approximately one and a half million words in length and although Peace's quartet is considerably shorter, it is still approximately half a million words long. *True Detective* combines the verbal with the visual in its mode of representation and the series running time of approximately 24 hours provides an equivalent excess of data. The main problem is not the respective word counts or running time, but the apparently unfathomable complexity of each set of narratives. Indeed, each case is so replete with thick description and phenomenological detail that one is highly unlikely to collect all of the relevant data on a first – or even second or third – reading or viewing. I did not keep a record of how many times I read or watched each novel or season in each series, but it was a minimum of three for each, at least one of which involved extensive notetaking. I decided to follow Flyvbjerg (2001) by distinguishing the case from its context in each of the studies. The case would be the source of information for data on policing as a practice and on policing as a situated practice and the context would supplement the data on policing as a situated practice. I now had to select my case within each of the contexts and this proved surprisingly easy.

Ellroy's hendecad consists of three separate series so I decided that the case would be one of the series. I discounted the *Second L.A. Quartet* in virtue of it remaining unfinished, which left the first *L.A. Quartet* and the *Underworld U.S.A. Trilogy*. Where the *Trilogy* is focused on the politics of the 1960s, the *Quartet* is focused on policing in Los Angeles in the 1940s and 1950s and was the obvious choice. Each novel in the *Quartet* takes a single police investigation as its primary subject: the Black Dahlia murder (1947) in *The Black Dahlia*, the Wolverine Prowler murders (1949–1950) in *The Big Nowhere*, the Nite Owl massacre (1953) in *L.A. Confidential*, and the Kafesjian burglary (1958) in *White Jazz*. *The Black Dahlia* and *White Jazz* are narrated in the first person by a single protagonist and *The Big Nowhere* and *L.A. Confidential* are narrated in the third person with three protagonists each. While the first three novels each have at least one character who aspires to excellence in his police practice (the protagonists are all men), the protagonist and narrator of the fourth does not. David Klein is a detective lieutenant in the City of Los Angeles Police Department, qualified attorney, and decorated war hero. He has been a police officer for 20 years, but has been in the employ of organised crime for half of that, most recently as a contract killer. As such, Klein is not participating in the practice of policing as defined and developed in Chapters 2 and 3 and *White Jazz* is not as relevant to my study of the characteristics of that practice as the first three novels. In consequence, I selected *The Black Dahlia*, *The Big Nowhere*, and *L.A. Confidential* as my case and included *White Jazz* as part of the context of the case, along with the *Underworld U.S.A. Trilogy* and the two novels of the *Second L.A. Quartet*. Like the *L.A. Quartet*, the *Red Riding Quartet* includes two novels with a single protagonist and two novels with multiple protagonists. *Nineteen Seventy-Four* is narrated by a journalist and *Nineteen Eighty* by a police detective. The police detective is involved in two simultaneous investigations – the Yorkshire Ripper inquiry and a police anti-corruption inquiry – so *Nineteen Eighty* was another obvious choice. The other three novels provide the context for this case. The decision was more difficult when it came to *True Detective*. Each season has multiple protagonists: two police officers in *True Detective 1*, three police officers and a career criminal in *True Detective 2*, and two police officers and an author (who is married to one of the officers) in *True Detective 3*. *True Detective 2* seemed the most likely to be useful in representing the police practice of three rather than two officers and when I realised that it was also the most complex of the three investigations, I chose it as the case and the other two seasons as the context.

At the end of this procedure, I was left with the following three critical case studies:

(1) Los Angeles, 1947–1958: *The Black Dahlia* (Ellroy 1987), *The Big Nowhere* (Ellroy 1988), and *L.A. Confidential* (Ellroy 1990);
(2) West Yorkshire, 1980: *Nineteen Eighty* (Peace 2001); and
(3) Southern California, 2013–2014: *True Detective 2* (2015).

As the Los Angeles case study is the most complex of the three, I decided to present them in reverse chronological order, which has the advantage of beginning with a case and context in which the circumstances are very similar to contemporary policing and then moving backwards across eight decades to a world that is less familiar (albeit strikingly similar in many ways). Once selected, I realised that the three cases have a further advantage I had not previously considered: each involves a blend of fact and fiction. Most conspicuously, *Nineteen Eighty* is a fictionalised account of the murders of 13 women by Peter Sutcliffe, known as the Yorkshire Ripper, from 1975 to 1980, and *The Black Dahlia* a fictionalised account of the murder of Elizabeth Short, which was never solved, in 1947. Ellroy's hendecad is populated with a mix of historical and fictional characters (the *Trilogy* in particular) and Peace's (2006) publisher, Faber and Faber, settled out of court after they were sued for libel in consequence of their publication of his sixth novel, *The Damned Utd* (Dart 2010). Peace (2000: 50, emphasis in original) even has a fictionalised version of criminologist Leon Radzinowicz (who founded the Institute of Criminology at the University of Cambridge in 1959), called '*Raazinowicz*', in *Nineteen Seventy-Seven*. Vinci, the setting of *True Detective 2*, is based on Vernon, a tiny city on the southern edge of downtown Los Angeles that was embroiled in a series of corruption scandals from 2009 to 2012 (Becerra & Vives 2015). Given my positions on the priority of complexity over fictionality and nonfiction and fiction as complementary epistemic endeavours, I do not require such explicit anchors to reality as a rationale. I offer them here, however, for the same reason I offered the pairing of accuracy and authenticity at the end of the previous section, for readers who cleave to the naïve distinction between nonfiction as reality and fiction as fantasy. Having established my system of methods, set of principles, and theory of research in this part of the book, I proceed to the next, which begins with the first of the three critical case studies.

Notes

1 Flyvbjerg also emphasises the epistemic significance of experience in his most recent monograph; see: Flyvbjerg and Gardner (2023).

2 The book is also a work of critical theory, as explained in the acknowledgements. See: Harcourt (2020).
3 The few exceptions prove the rule; see: Ruggiero (2003, 2020); Frauley (2010); Cavender and Jurik (2012); Brisman and South (2014); and my own work (McGregor 2018, 2021a, 2021d, 2023; Grčki & McGregor 2024).
4 For a simplified version of this argument, see: McGregor (2021a), Chapter 4.
5 Walsh's taxonomy of knowledge is distinct from Flyvbjerg's (2001), which was set out in the previous section, but they are at the very least compatible. Consider, for example, the extent to which knowledge-that, knowledge-how, and knowledge-what are equivalent to scientific causal knowledge, technical know-how, and value-laden praxis respectively.
6 The third and final season of *Happy Valley* was released in February 2023, after I made my selection.
7 There is a strong sense in which I had already used all three of these principles to guide my case selection, which provides evidence for Rubin's scepticism about the extent to which selection and sampling are discrete activities.

References

Attridge, D. (2015). *The Work of Literature*. Oxford: Oxford University Press.

Becerra, H. & Vives, R. (2015). 'True Detective' setting based on California city with a corrupt past. 19 June. *Los Angeles Times*. Available at: www.latimes.com/local/california/la-me-vernon-true-detective-20150619-story.html.

Becker, H.S. (1966). Introduction. In: Shaw, C.R. *The Jack-Roller: A Delinquent Boy's Own Story*. Chicago: University of Chicago Press, v–xviii.

Bhaskar, R. (1975). *A Realist Theory of Science*. London: Verso Books.

Bhaskar, R. (1987). *Scientific Realism and Human Emancipation*. London: Verso Books.

Bhaskar, R. (1989). *Reclaiming Reality: A Critical Introduction to Contemporary Philosophy*. London: Verso Books.

Brisman, A. & South, N. (2014). *Green Cultural Criminology*. Abingdon: Routledge.

Cavender, J. & Jurik, N.C. (2012). *Justice Provocateur: Jane Tennison and Policing in Prime Suspect*. Champaign, IL: Illinois University Press.

Cohen, R. (2015). Can Nic Pizzolatto, True Detective's Uncompromising Auteur, Do It All Again? 11 June. *Vanity Fair*. Available at: www.vanityfair.com/hollywood/2015/06/nic-pizzolatto-true-detective-season-2-better-than-season-1.

Currie, G. (2010). *Narratives & Narrators: A Philosophy of Stories*. Oxford: Oxford University Press.

Dart, T. (2010). John Giles sets record straight on Brian Clough and Leeds. 12 November. *The Times*. Available at: www.thetimes.co.uk/article/john-giles-sets-record-straight-on-brian-clough-and-leeds-w9g59qnwd22.
Derrida, J. (1967a/1978). *Writing and Difference*. Trans. A. Bass. London: Routledge.
Derrida, J.(1967b/2011). *Voice and Phenomenon: Introduction to the Problem of the Sign in Husserl's Phenomenology*. Trans. L. Lawlor. Evanston, IL: Northwestern University Press.
Derrida, J. (1967c/1976). *Of Grammatology*. Trans. G.C. Spivak. Baltimore, MD: Johns Hopkins University Press.
Ellroy, J. (1987/1988). *The Black Dahlia*. London: Mysterious Press.
Ellroy, J. (1988). *The Big Nowhere*. New York: The Mysterious Press.
Ellroy, J. (1990). *L.A. Confidential*. New York: The Mysterious Press.
Ellroy, J. (1992). *White Jazz*. New York: Alfred A. Knopf.
Ellroy, J. (1995). *American Tabloid*. London: Arrow Books.
Ellroy, J. (2001/2010). *The Cold Six Thousand*. London: Windmill Books.
Ellroy, J. (2009/2010). *Blood's a Rover*. London: Windmill Books.
Ellroy, J. (2014). *Perfidia*. London: William Heinemann Ltd.
Ellroy, J. (2019). *This Storm*. London: William Heinemann Ltd.
Fleetwood, J. (2014). *Drug Mules: Women in the International Cocaine Trade*. Basingstoke: Palgrave Macmillan.
Flyvbjerg, B. (2001). *Making Social Science Matter: Why Social Inquiry Fails and How It Can Succeed Again*. Cambridge: Cambridge University Press.
Flyvbjerg, B. & Gardner, D. (2023). *How Big Things Get Done: The Surprising Factors Behind Every Successful Project, from Home Renovations to Space Exploration*. New York: Random House.
Frauley, J. (2010). *Criminology, Deviance, and the Silver Screen: The Fictional Reality and the Criminological Imagination*. New York: Palgrave Macmillan.
Geertz, C. (1973). *The Interpretation of Cultures*. New York: Basic Books.
Grčki, D. & McGregor, R. (2024). *An Epistemology of Criminological Cinema*. Abingdon: Routledge.
Hadadi, R. (2024). Issa López Responds to Nic Pizzolatto Criticism of *True Detective: Night Country*. 31 January. *Vulture*. Available at: www.vulture.com/2024/01/true-detective-night-country-nic-pizzolatto-issa-lopez.html.
Hall, S. (1973/2019). Encoding and Decoding in the Television Discourse. In: Hall, S. *Essential Essays: Volume* 1. Durham, NC: Duke University Press, 257–276.
Harcourt, B.E. (2020). *Critique and Praxis: A Critical Philosophy of Illusions, Values, and Action*. New York: Columbia University.
Lamarque, P. & Olsen, S.H. (1994). *Truth, Fiction, and Literature: A Philosophical Perspective*. Oxford: Clarendon.

MacIntyre, A. (2007). *After Virtue: A Study in Moral Theory*. 3rd ed. London: Duckworth Books.

McGregor, R. (2012). The Problem of Cinematic Imagination. *Contemporary Aesthetics*, 10, article 13. Available at: https://digitalcommons.risd.edu/liberalarts_contempaesthetics/vol10/iss1/13.

McGregor, R. (2016). *The Value of Literature*. London: Rowman & Littlefield International.

McGregor, R. (2018). *Narrative Justice*. London: Rowman & Littlefield International.

McGregor, R. (2021a). *A Criminology of Narrative Fiction*. Bristol: Bristol University Press.

McGregor, R. (2021b). James Ellroy's Critical Criminology: Crimes of the Powerful in the Underworld USA Trilogy. *Critical Criminology: An International Journal*, 29 (2), 349–365.

McGregor, R. (2021c). Four Characteristics of Policing as a Practice. *Policing: A Journal of Policy and Practice*, 15 (3), 1842–1853.

McGregor, R. (2021d). *Critical Criminology and Literary Criticism*. Bristol: Bristol University Press.

McGregor, R. (2023). *Literary Theory and Criminology*. Abingdon: Routledge.

Maruna, S. (2001). *Making Good: How Ex-Convicts Reform and Build Their Lives*. Washington, DC: American Psychological Association.

Matravers, D. (2014). *Fiction and Narrative*. Oxford: Oxford University Press.

Monagle, M. (2018). 'True Detective' and the Unadaptable Nic Pizzolatto. 3 April. *Film School Rejects*. Available at: https://filmschoolrejects.com/the-unadaptable-nic-pizzolatto.

Odin, R. (2000). *De la fiction*. Louvain-la-neuve: De Boeck Supérieur.

Peace, D. (1999/2009). *Nineteen Seventy-Four*. London: Quercus Books.

Peace, D. (2000/2009). *Nineteen Seventy-Seven*. London: Quercus Books.

Peace, D. (2001/2009). *Nineteen Eighty*. London: Quercus Books.

Peace, D. (2002/2009). *Nineteen Eighty-Three*. London: Quercus Books.

Peace, D. (2006). *The Damned Utd*. London: Faber & Faber.

Presser, L. (2008). *Been a Heavy Life: Stories of Violent Men*. Champaign, IL: University of Illinois Press.

Presser, L. (2013). *Why We Harm*. New Brunswick, NJ: Rutgers University Press.

Presser, L. (2018). *Inside Story: How Narratives Drive Mass Harm*. Oakland, CA: University of California Press.

Riffaterre, M. (1990). *Fictional Truth*. Baltimore, MA: The Johns Hopkins University Press.

Rubin, A.T. (2021). *Rocking Qualitative Social Science: An Irreverent Guide to Rigorous Research*. Stanford, CA: Stanford University Press.

Ruggiero, V. (2003). *Crime in Literature: Sociology of Deviance and Fiction.* London: Verso Books.

Ruggiero, V. (2020). *Visions of Political Violence.* Abingdon: Routledge.

Ryle, G. (1968). The Thinking of Thoughts: What is "Le Penseur" Doing? In: Ryle, G., *Volume II: Collected Essays 1929–1969.* London: Hutchinson & Co. Ltd., 480–496.

Sandberg, S. & Pedersen, W. (2009). *Street Capital: Black Cannabis Dealers in a White Welfare State.* Bristol: Policy Press.

Saving Private Ryan (1998). Directed by Steven Spielberg. US: DreamWorks Pictures.

Shaw, C.R. (1930/1966). *The Jack-Roller: A Delinquent Boy's Own Story.* Chicago: University of Chicago Press.

True Detective (2014–2019). Originally released 12 January. US: HBO.

True Detective(season 1) (2014). Originally released 12 January.US: HBO.

True Detective(season 2) (2015). Originally released 21 June.US: HBO.

True Detective(season 3) (2019). Originally released 13 January.US: HBO.

Ugelvik, T. (2014). *Power and Resistance in Prison: Doing Time, Doing Freedom.* Basingstoke: Palgrave Macmillan.

Walsh, D. (1969). *Literature and Knowledge.* Middletown, CT: Wesleyan University Press.

PART 3
Case Studies

5

SOUTHERN CALIFORNIA, 2013–2014

This chapter presents the first critical case study of the characteristics of policing as a practice and of policing as a situated practice. The case takes place in Southern California from October 2013 to January 2014 and is about the murder of a man on the Pacific Coast Highway. The context of the case is two sets of police and private investigations from 1980 to 2015, a murder in Vermilion Parish, Louisiana and the disappearance of two children in West Finger, Arkansas. The critical case study comprises two diachronic investigations conducted by three police officers. Both investigations are initiated by the California Department of Justice (CA DOJ). The first is a special detail to solve the murder of Benjamin Caspere, City Manager of Vinci. The second, which begins two months after the conclusion of the first, is a confidential special investigation to reopen the Caspere case. The three police officers involved are: Detective Sergeant Antigone Bezzerides of the Ventura County Sheriff's Office (VCSO), Detective Raymond Velcoro of the Vinci Police Department (VPD), and Officer Paul Woodrugh of the California Highway Patrol (CHP). Both investigations are complete failures and the second concludes with Woodrugh's murder and Bezzerides and Velcoro forced to flee the country for their safety. The focus on Bezzerides, Velcoro, and Woodrugh demonstrates the

DOI: 10.4324/9781003425922-8

significance of heroic struggle, edgework, absolute sacrifice, and worldmaking to police practice and provides insight into the different ways in which each can both contribute to and detract from public protection. An exploration of the tensions from which the four characteristics of the practice of policing are emergent in the case and its context provides insight into the ways in which the institution of policing and the systemic context of policing can detract from public protection. Taken together, the three sets of police and private investigations draw attention to the impact of competition between different law enforcement agencies, competition between different institutions within the criminal justice system, and the relative impunity of powerful individuals or groups.

5.1 Case Summary

5.1.1 Special Detail

When Caspere's mutilated corpse is found in a rest stop on the Ventura Pacific Coast Highway, the Attorney General (AG) of California, Richard Geldof, and his deputy, Katherine Davis, establish a special detail to solve the murder. Their motive is to use the detail to conduct a covert investigation of the VPD and Vinci mayor's office and Woodrugh, the CHP officer who discovered the body, is recruited as a state attorney's investigator for the purpose of gathering evidence for a grand jury on municipal corruption. The detail is led by Bezzerides, who was the senior VCSO detective on call. She is told to recruit Velcoro, who was investigating Caspere's disappearance for the VPD, as a state witness for the grand jury. In the presence of the Mayor of Vinci, Austin Chessani, Velcoro is ordered by Chief William Holloway and Lieutenant Kevin Burris to protect the interests of the city at all costs, over and above detecting the murderer. The fourth member of the detail is Detective Teague Dixon of the VPD, who has been an accomplice of Holloway and Burris since they were all in the City of Los Angeles Police Department (LAPD) together. Dixon is assigned to the detail as a safeguard, to conceal any incriminating evidence that Velcoro misses. Velcoro is an associate of Frank Semyon, an organised crime group

(OCG) executive, who tells him that Caspere was involved in illegal transactions pertaining to the purchase of land in a lucrative rail corridor and directs him to a house Caspere owned in West Hollywood, which is where he was murdered. Bezzerides and Velcoro learn that Caspere made extensive use of sex workers, at the house and at elite sex parties, and that he was last seen alive at one of the latter with a sex worker named Tasha. Bezzerides and Woodrugh open Caspere's safe deposit box and find documents incriminating him in illegal activity related to the planned California Central Rail Corridor, a $68 billion investment, and four distinctive blue diamonds. Velcoro employs traffic cameras to track the car that drove Caspere from West Hollywood to the Pacific Coast Highway via a long and circuitous route. The car was stolen from a film set and is found by Bezzerides and Velcoro when they interview a transport worker from the production company.

Meanwhile, Woodrugh and Dixon discover a watch and a set of blue diamond cufflinks that were stolen from Caspere's house in a pawnshop. The woman who sold them is identified as Irina Rufo and the fingerprints of Ledo Amarillo, a repeat offender with a history of violence, are also found on the watch. Dixon suggests that Amarillo was selling Irina's sexual services to Caspere, realised how wealthy he was, and tortured him to death for his money and valuables. He claims to have located Amarillo, who is living in a rented warehouse with his cousin, by means of a confidential informant. There is no tactical unit available, but Bezzerides does not want to risk losing him so she plans a raid involving the special detail, two other VPD detectives, and four uniformed VPD officers. As Bezzerides and her squad approach the warehouse, they are ambushed by four heavily armed suspects. The extended firefight that follows – in which all of the suspects, at least two of the police officers (including Dixon), and several innocent bystanders are killed – is filmed by a news crew and becomes known as the Vinci Massacre. Geldof terminates the special detail on the grounds that Amarillo was guilty of Caspere's murder, clears all the officers involved in the massacre of any misconduct, and closes the case. Bezzerides is returned to uniform and assigned to work in the VCSO evidence locker after being charged with sexual misconduct. Velcoro resigns from the VPD and goes to work for Semyon as one of his collectors. Woodrugh receives a commendation for his bravery and is promoted to detective, working in CHP Insurance Fraud.

5.1.2 Confidential Special Investigation

Bezzerides receives photographs of the elite sex parties and Caspere's diamonds from a missing sex worker named Vera Machiado and learns that the diamonds have been stolen from evidence control. Velcoro suspects some kind of collusion because he does not believe that Amarillo killed Caspere and discovers that Tony Chessani (the mayor's son) and Irving Pitlor (Caspere's psychiatrist) are involved in the sex trade. Two months after the Vinci Massacre, Davis recruits Bezzerides, Velcoro, and Woodrugh for a confidential special investigation. The investigation is ostensibly intended to locate Rufo, who remains missing, but actually intended to solve Caspere's murder and uncover evidence of collusion among the VPD, mayor's office, and Geldof, who is now running for Governor of California. Velcoro subjects Pitlor to an extrajudicial interrogation and he confesses conspiring with Tony and Caspere to host the elite sex parties, procuring sex workers through human trafficking, and increasing their value with cosmetic surgery. The parties are where the land deals have been made – by Tony and Caspere, various OCG executives, and Jacob McCandless, who is president of the Catalyst Group, the consortium that will manage the rail corridor. The parties also provide material for the blackmail of corrupt politicians and business executives should it be needed. Bezzerides and Woodrugh are looking for Machiado in Guerneville when they find a crime scene where a woman (later revealed to be Tasha) has been tortured and murdered (for trying to blackmail Caspere). Woodrugh discovers that $2.5 million worth of blue diamonds were stolen from Sable Fine Jewellers in a murder and robbery during the 1992 Los Angeles riots. The married couple who owned the shop, the Ostermans, were shot dead, and their two young children, Leonard and Laura, placed in foster care.

Bezzerides decides to infiltrate the next sex party, which is being held in Monterey, undercover, by posing as a sex worker. The guests include Geldof, Holloway, and an OCG executive named Osip Agranov. Velcoro and Woodrugh observe Agranov sign a deal with McCandless and

Woodrugh enters the premises to retrieve the documents. Bezzerides recognises Machiado, who is semi-conscious, decides to escape with her, and kills a security guard who tries to stop her. The detectives flee the scene, taking Machiado to a motel for safety. Bezzerides is officially on leave from the VCSO and becomes a person of interest in the security guard's death. Woodrugh returns to work and learns that Holloway, Burris, Dixon, and Caspere (in a civilian role) all worked at the same LAPD station in 1992. Velcoro meets Davis to provide her with a progress report, but finds her corpse instead. Woodrugh is killed by Burris and Velcoro framed for both Wooodrugh and Davis' murders. Bezzerides works out that Burris and Dixon killed the Ostermans and that Burris, Holloway, and Caspere used the money from the sale of the diamonds to buy their positions in Vinci. She recognises a sex worker in one of the photographs taken by Tasha, Velcoro identifies her as Caspere's secretary, and they suspect she is Laura Osterman. Velcoro remembers one of the photographers on the film set bearing a resemblance to Laura and speculates that he is her brother, Leonard. Bezzerides suggests the children killed Caspere to avenge their parents' murder. Bezzerides and Velcoro find Laura in Leonard's house and she confirms their suspicions. Leonard is meeting Holloway at the train station, where he plans to kill him. While Velcoro goes to intercept Leonard, Bezzerides puts Laura on a bus and tells her to leave Los Angeles and never come back. Velcoro fails to stop Leonard, a shootout ensues in which both Holloway and Leonard are killed, and Velcoro and Bezzerides flee for the second time. Velcoro maintains that they have no option other than leaving the country and does one last job for Semyon to raise the money. When Bezzerides attempts to continue the investigation, she learns that both Austin Chessani and Pitlor have allegedly committed suicide and that Tony has disappeared. Convinced she has no other option, Bezzerides agrees to leave for Venezuela, but Velcoro is killed by Burris before he can join her.

5.1.3 Bezzerides, Velcoro, and Woodrugh

The critical case study focuses on the practices of the three police officers recruited to both the special detail and the confidential special investigation: Bezzerides, Velcoro, and Woodrugh. Bezzerides, who abbreviates her given name to 'Ani', is in her mid-30s and divorced. She lives on her own and has only two close relationships – with her sister, Athena, and her Major Crimes Bureau partner, Elvis Ilinca – both of which are strained in consequence of her emotional reticence. She is a dedicated, conscientious, and shrewd detective and a capable commander. Bezzerides was brought up in a New Age commune in Guerneville and her father, Elliot, became one of the movement's leaders. He currently runs the Panticapaeum Institute, a spiritual retreat on the Ventura County coast. When she was a young child, Bezzerides was abducted by one of the men who visited the commune and taken to a remote cave for four days. She was drugged and cannot remember what happened there, although it seems unlikely that she was physically or sexually abused. Bezzerides blames Elliot for her mother's suicide, which happened when she was 12, and for her sister's drug addiction, which has been funded with sex work. She is plagued with guilt because she left home with her abductor voluntarily and because she believes she has failed to protect Athena from harm. Bezzerides is short, slim, and athletic, maintaining her fitness with martial arts and surfing. She has both physical and moral courage and is resilient, determined, and tenacious. Bezzerides has had casual relationships with several male colleagues and when she ends her affair with one of them because he wants more commitment, he reports her to VCSO Internal Affairs for initiating a sexual relationship with a junior officer. Bezzerides drinks heavily on occasion and smokes cigarettes and electronic cigarettes, but is not addicted to either alcohol or tobacco. She is, however, addicted to gambling and while she has accrued some debt, it is insufficient to interfere with her practice of policing.

Velcoro is in his early 40s and has an 11-year-old son named Chad with Gena, his ex-wife. He lives on his own and his only personal relationships are with his son and his father, Eddie, a retired LAPD sergeant. Velcoro was a deputy in the County of Los Angeles Sheriff's Department for eight years, during which time Gena was raped, and Chad's paternity is uncertain. He agreed to work for Semyon's OCG in exchange for information about the rapist and murdered the man once he discovered his identity (without realising that both he and Semyon had been misinformed). Velcoro has never recovered from perpetrating this crime and the combination of his guilt and his increasing involvement with Semyon changed his personality and destroyed his marriage. After Gena divorced him, he transferred to the VPD as a detective because the better pay and more regular hours made it easier to maintain his relationship with Chad. Gena is attempting to have his visitation rights restricted due to his emotional instability, poor self-control, and substance abuse. When Velcoro refuses to cooperate, she applies for sole custody and tells him that she will have Chad's paternity tested if he contests her claim. Velcoro's lack of self-control is matched by a profound self-awareness and recognition that he ruined both his personal and professional lives when he committed murder. He is also aware that his career could implode at any moment and has applied for a private investigator's licence. Velcoro employs daily combinations of alcohol, hard and soft drugs, and tobacco to cope with the rigours of his police practice, illegal activity for Semyon, and personal problems. He is nonetheless able to abstain for periods of varying lengths and has not yet lost his physical capability, skill with firearms, or cardiovascular endurance.

Woodrugh is in his early 30s and has a girlfriend named Emily. His mother, Cynthia, did not know his father and he was neglected to the point of abuse as a child. Woodrugh nonetheless supports Cynthia, who lives in a trailer park and draws disability benefit for carpal tunnel syndrome, financially. He has been an officer in the CHP for three years and is assigned to motorcycle patrol, which he enjoys, riding his own motorcycle off duty. Prior to joining the police, he worked for a private military company named Black Mountain, following service in the US Armed Forces. Woodrugh has extensive combat experience from operations in the Middle East and has maintained his military skill set, including a very high level of physical fitness. Although he does not identify as gay, he is androphilic and struggles to maintain a physical relationship with Emily in consequence of his lack of sexual attraction to women. While Woodrugh and his friend, Miguel, were cut off from their Black Mountain unit they had a sexual relationship of which Woodrugh is deeply ashamed. He deals with his repressed homosexuality and his guilt at withholding emotional intimacy from Emily by throwing himself into his police practice. When work fails to provide sufficient distraction, he drinks alcohol and smokes tobacco heavily, although his only addiction is to the exhilaration of combat, which he secretly misses. Woodrugh is devastated when he is suspended from the CHP after being falsely implicated in war crimes committed by Black Mountain and falsely accused of abusing his authority to coerce an actress into having sex with him. He is contemplating committing suicide on his motorcycle when he finds Caspere's corpse on the Pacific Coast Highway and eagerly accepts Davis' offer to join the special detail. The police practice of Woodrugh, Velcoro, and Bezzerides provides insight into the different ways in which heroic struggle, edgework, absolute sacrifice, and worldmaking contribute to and detract from public protection.

5.2 Characteristics of the Practice

5.2.1 Heroic Struggle

The practice of policing is a heroic struggle because its purpose, public protection, can never be achieved in full. This limitation is underpinned by the unpredictability of the consequences of proactive policing and the inability of reactive policing to reduce anything more than the consequences of harm that has already been inflicted. No such nuance is required to understand the heroic struggle in the Caspere murder investigation, which consists of three stages, each of which is less likely to succeed than the previous one and each of which is more dangerous for the detectives involved. The whole critical case study is, in fact, a series of increasingly heroic struggles in the classical sense in that only Bezzerides survives, albeit at great professional and personal cost. The first stage is the initial investigation conducted by the special detail. In spite of the clandestine goals set for all four of the detectives by their superiors, Bezzerides, Velcoro, and Woodrugh make quick progress on the murder, learning about Caspere's frequent use of sex workers, identifying the crime scene and the car used to transport his corpse, and discovering that he visited various sites in the rail corridor where farmland had been contaminated by mines. As soon as they uncover evidence linking the murder to the land purchases, however, Dixon sabotages the investigation, setting up Amarillo as the prime suspect. Dixon is himself set up by Holloway and Burris, leading to the Vinci Massacre, after which Geldof colludes with Austin Chessani to terminate the investigation.

The second stage commences when Davis recruits Bezzerides, Velcoro, and Woodrugh to her confidential special investigation. The confidential special investigation is considerably more difficult than the special detail because Davis intends to achieve more with less. The aim of the investigation is twofold: to solve Caspere's murder and to uncover evidence of corruption at the municipal and state levels. In order to maintain operational security, Davis keeps her team of investigators as small as possible. When she is murdered, the chances of bringing the case to court decrease exponentially: the team is now completely reliant on Woodrugh's official status and the framing of Velcoro by Burris means that both he and Bezzerides are suspects in murder investigations. Woodrugh's murder brings the confidential special investigation to an end. The third stage commences when Bezzerides and Velcoro, who have become lovers, decide to continue to seek evidence of corruption in spite of the murders of Davis and Woodrugh. This private investigation is considerably more difficult than the confidential special investigation because it intends to achieve the same aim with even fewer resources. Velcoro, who has less faith in the criminal justice system than Bezzerides, recommends they make contingency plans after Davis' murder (*True Detective 2*, episode 7: 46:27–46:32): 'We need an exit strategy ... get out of the country. There's no way they'll let us go to trial.' Bezzerides and Velcoro only commit to escaping after Leonard's death and even then Bezzerides attempts to take statements from Tony Chessani, Betty Chessani (Tony's sister), and Pitlor. Velcoro suggests that once they are safe in Venezuela, they can send the information they have to Dan Hauser, a staff writer at the *Los Angeles Times* who is investigating corruption in Vinci. Velcoro is killed by Burris, but Bezzerides meets Hauser in Venezuela a year later. Although she tells him the details of the case and gives him all the files and photographs she has, she refuses to come back to the US to testify in order to protect the son she has had with Velcoro.

A less dramatic, but more specific example of the limitations of public protection is Bezzerides' relationship with Vera Machiado. Prior to the formation of the special detail, Bezzerides and Ilinca deliver a foreclosure notice to a woman named Danielle Delvayo. Delvayo tells them that she has been trying to get hold of Machiado, her 24-year-old younger sister, for a month. Machiado's phone was disconnected and she left her rented apartment without a forwarding address. Delvayo reported the disappearance to the City of Ventura Police Department, but never heard back from them. Machiado's most recent employment was as a cleaner at the Panticapaeum Institute, which piques Bezzerides' interest as it is run by her father. Bezzerides and Ilinca interview two of the cleaners at the institute, who tell them that Machiado handed her notice in two months ago for a better job, on the 'club circuit' in the Bay Area (*True Detective* 2, episode 1: 31:25–31:26). While Bezzerides is assigned to the special detail, Ilinca interviews Machiado's roommate, who had received a phone call from her from an address in Guerneville shortly after she gave notice at the Panticapaeum Institute. In the period after the Vinci Massacre and before the confidential special investigation, Delvayo contacts Bezzerides, expressing her disappointment at not hearing back from her. Delvayo has received a package that Machiado left in a post office box, containing photographs of a party, photographs of blue diamonds, and an admission ticket for a party. Bezzerides identifies Caspere and a state senator in the photographs and discovers that Caspere's diamonds are missing from the evidence locker. Once the confidential special investigation has begun, Bezzerides and Woodrugh go to the address in Guerneville and find the crime scene where Tasha was tortured and murdered.

Bezzerides then makes use of her sister's contacts in the sex trade to take her place at the next elite sex party for the purpose of conducting an undercover investigation. She is forced to take 3,4-Methylenedioxymethamphetamine (MDMA) at the party and goes to the bathroom to vomit. Bezzerides finds Machiado in a semiconscious state, under the influence of MDMA and champagne, tells her that she is a friend of her sister, and escapes from the party with her after killing a security guard. Bezzerides, Velcoro, and Woodrugh take Machiado to their motel and Bezzerides interviews her once she is fully recovered. Machiado explains that the package was probably sent to her by Tasha, who was taking covert photographs of the parties in order to blackmail Caspere, Tony Chessani, and Pitlor. She tells Bezzerides that Chessani and his men found a camera on Tasha when she was in Guerneville and took her to the cabin in the woods. Bezzerides asks Machiado if she will testify in court and she says no, retracting her verbal statement. She adds that she was never missing, had no intention of leaving the party circuit, and was angry with Tasha for trying to involve her in her scheme. When Delvayo arrives at the motel and Bezzerides tells Machiado to stay with her until the case is solved, Machiado blames both of them for putting her in danger in the first place. Concerned that Machiado may go straight to Chessani, Bezzerides threatens to let him know that she has talked to the police if she does not comply. As such, Bezzerides is caught between Delvayo, who wants her sister back, and Machiado, who wants to continue her employment as a sex worker. Bezzerides also killed a man who tried to prevent her removing someone from a premises she did not want to leave, which has placed her in an ambiguous legal position. In spite of not only good intentions on Bezzerides' part, but also astute, committed, and dangerous police work, all three of her, Machiado, and Delvayo are worse off than if Bezzerides had done nothing, like the Ventura police.

5.2.2 Edgework

The practice of policing is edgework because it involves a high risk of injury, which can be reduced by competence in a specific skill set and is accompanied by a specific sensation and set of emotions. These emotions can become addictive, especially when the work is demanding in terms of time, commitment, and lifestyle. The most obvious example of edgework in the Caspere murder investigation is the Vinci Massacre. Amarillo becomes the prime suspect when his fingerprints are found on the jewellery pawned by Rufo and the special detail is augmented with four other detectives and four uniformed officers from the VPD for the purpose of finding him. The next morning, Dixon reports that one of his confidential informants has found Amarillo, who is with his cousin in a rented room above a warehouse and has just returned home. Unbeknownst to Bezzerides, Velcoro, and Woodrugh, Dixon has framed Amarillo. Unbeknownst to all of the special detail, Dixon is being set up to be murdered by Burris because he is blackmailing Burris and Holloway over the Osterman murder and robbery. Bezzerides assembles her squad to execute the arrest warrant, stating that the CHP tactical unit would take too long to arrive. Burris, who wants the special detail as defenceless as possible, asks her if she requires the full complement of police officers (ten) and Bezzerides replies (*True Detective* 2, episode 4: 45:04–45:05): 'Better safe than something else.' Bezzerides completes her briefing at the scene. The building has three floors and Amarillo's cousin rents the top two, above a business premises. None of the police officers are aware that there is a methamphetamine hydrochloride (crystal meth) laboratory on the second floor. The squad approaches the front of the warehouse on foot and Bezzerides orders the officers to their places.

While the squad is deploying, a suspect leans out of a first-floor window and opens fire with an assault rifle, hitting two uniformed officers with the first burst. The rest take cover behind parked cars and although Bezzerides, Velcoro, and Woodrugh are all obviously afraid, they remain calm and return fire as precisely as possible, taking care to minimise the risk to the public. Woodrugh is particularly impressive, negotiating the entire firefight with dispassionate competence and assisting and organising his colleagues in the initial response to the ambush and the subsequent pursuit of the suspects. The crystal meth laboratory ignites and explodes while the officers are still pinned down behind the cars. Woodrugh leads the police advance and Dixon, who has been too scared to return fire, is shot dead as soon as he breaks cover. Woodrugh shoots the suspect in the window (the only one they have seen thus far) and while he and Velcoro advance to the front door, Bezzerides very shrewdly and courageously runs through the warehouse on her own, to the rear of the premises, where the officers were unable to deploy before the ambush. When she reaches the rear, she sees a sports utility vehicle (SUV) with tinted windows pulling away and a suspect leans out with an assault rifle and fires at her, beginning the second stage of the firefight. Bezzerides informs the rest of the squad by radio, returns fire, and pursues the SUV on foot, able to keep it in sight as the driver is required to avoid obstacles in a relatively narrow alleyway. Woodrugh and Velcoro run to her assistance. As soon as the SUV leaves the alleyway it crashes into a bus, which draws a crowd of bystanders. Three suspects emerge from the SUV, firing assault rifles and sidearms at Woodrugh, Velcoro, Bezzerides, the other police officers, and the crowd. A close-quarter battle ensues, during which Woodrugh, Velcoro, and Bezzerides continue to remain calm. Velcoro wounds the driver, who panics and runs towards Bezzerides and another detective. The detective shoots a bystander by mistake and Bezzerides shoots the driver, incapacitating him. The detective is then shot dead by a second suspect and Bezzerides realises she has run out of ammunition. She prepares to attack the suspect with a knife, but Woodrugh shoots him. Amarillo, the only suspect still at large, takes a bus passenger hostage. Neither Velcoro nor Woodrugh are able to take a safe shot at Amarillo, who shoots the hostage in the head. While his revolver is still in his hand, the detectives open fire, killing him. Of the police squad, only Bezzerides, Velcoro, and Woodrugh are alive and unwounded. Bezzerides and Velcoro are shaken by the experience, while Woodrugh's composure returns almost as soon as he holsters his sidearm.

Bezzerides is acutely aware of her vulnerability as not only a woman, but a short, slim woman, in the face of the physical challenges posed by the practice of policing. She understands that being a short, slim woman increases both her risk of being assaulted and the injuries she is likely to sustain in the event of an assault. Velcoro observes that she carries two concealed knives in addition to her sidearm and asks her about them when they are getting to know one another at the start of the special detail (*True Detective 2*, episode 2: 39:42–40:08):

VELCORO: Then what's with all the knives?
BEZZERIDES: Could you do this job if everyone you encountered could physically overpower you? I mean, forget police work, no man could walk around like that without going nuts.
VELCORO: So they're equalisers. Makes sense.
BEZZERIDES: No, I'd still wear 'em, even if I wasn't on the job. Fundamental difference between the sexes is that one of them can kill the other with their bare hands. A man of any size lays hands on me, he's going to bleed out in under a minute.

The brief conversation is interesting for at least two reasons. First, it reveals Bezzerides' recognition of the significance of edgework to policing and of its enhanced challenge for women police officers in consequence of the combination of sex differences, gender stereotypes, and toxic masculinity. Although individual females are stronger, faster, or fitter (or, indeed, all three) than individual males, males are, on average, stronger, faster, and fitter than females, sex differences that underpin the segregation of most competitive sport. Gender is mostly, albeit not always, supervenient on sex and gender stereotypes represent women as physically and mentally weaker than men. What this means is that regardless of the reality of individual variation, toxically masculine men perceive women as easier to overpower and intimidate. Second, notwithstanding Bezzerides' dismissal of Velcoro's claim, the rest of her response reveals both that the knives are equalisers and that the equalisation is necessary because of the link between the violence directed at police officers and the violence directed at women. As a woman, Bezzerides runs the risk of being a victim of misogynistic violence, whose likelihood is increased by the fact that she is perceived as being easy to overpower. This hazard is exacerbated for woman police officers because of the disproportionately high number of men that commit crime. The point Bezzerides is making is that all women need equalisers in order to defend themselves from men and that women police officers just need them more than other women. As such, Bezzerides' practice of martial arts is not merely for the sake of maintaining her fitness, but part of the skill required to minimise the risk of injury while performing her duties as a police officer.

5.2.3 Absolute Sacrifice

The practice of policing is an absolute sacrifice because public protection requires continuous self-sacrifice and the sacrifice of the interests of some others to other others, both of which are accompanied by an accumulated weight of responsibility. The most conspicuous example of absolute sacrifice takes place in the third stage of the Caspere murder investigation, when Davis and Woodrugh have been killed and Bezzerides and Velcoro are fugitives from the criminal justice system. Having concluded that Caspere was killed to avenge the murder of the Ostermans by Burris and Dixon in 1992, Bezzerides and Velcoro locate Lauren Osterman in her brother's house. Her brother has handcuffed her to the fireplace in order to prevent her from interfering with his plan to murder Holloway. Leonard Osterman does not know who killed his parents, only that Caspere and Holloway were both involved. When Velcoro learns that the murder is imminent, he tells Bezzerides to keep Laura safe and goes to the train station, where Leonard is waiting for Holloway. Bezzerides is having second thoughts about using Laura as a witness, but Velcoro leaves before they can discuss the issue. Bezzerides follows Velcoro to the transport hub, taking Laura to the bus station and buying her a ticket to Seattle. She tells Laura to leave forever, forget about Caspere and her brother, and take the opportunity to avoid any further involvement with the case. When Laura asks why Bezzerides is letting her go, she replies that she does not deserve to be punished for what she has done. Although Laura did not kill anyone herself, she assisted her brother in the planning and commission of Caspere's murder and withheld evidence when she was first questioned by Velcoro and Dixon (who were investigating his disappearance). Bezzerides feels that she has suffered enough, from witnessing her parents' murder to being separated from her brother, to leaving her foster parents for the sex trade at 16. She does not want Laura to have to endure the consequences of entanglement in the criminal justice system, which will definitely involve giving evidence in court, probably involve being exposed by the media, and possibly involve threats to her life. In making this decision, Bezzerides is knowingly placing all her and Velcoro's hopes of solving the case on Leonard and on Velcoro's ability to apprehend him before he can kill Holloway.

Velcoro finds Leonard waiting for Holloway and convinces him to help secure evidence of Holloway's guilt rather than kill him. Leonard covertly records a conversation between Holloway and Velcoro in which Holloway implicates himself, Tony Chessani, and Geldof in corruption and murder. When Holloway reveals that Caspere was Laura's father, Leonard is overcome with rage and attacks him with a knife, initiating a shootout in which Burris tries to kill Velcoro,

Bezzerides wounds Burris, and Leonard and Holloway are shot dead by uniformed police officers. Velcoro and Bezzerides escape, but the recording of the conversation is destroyed. Without either Laura or Leonard Osterman available as witnesses, there is no way to bring the case to trial. In deciding to let Laura go, Bezzerides sacrificed her own interests to hers, an authentic sacrifice that recognises the ethical bond among all human beings. That same decision is also an absolute sacrifice because Bezzerides understands that she has not only sacrificed her and Velcoro's interests to those of Laura, but Leonard's interests to Laura. While Velcoro's consent to sacrifice his interests might be assumed, given that he is a state investigator, Leonard is as much a victim of Burris and Dixon as Laura, perhaps even more so as he was sent to a group rather than private home as a child. Bezzerides' sacrifice of Leonard to Laura is short-lived as he is killed in the train station, in consequence of which her decision is ultimately responsible for the need for her and Velcoro to leave the country. Velcoro does not blame her for their misfortune, suggesting his tacit consent, although she has already revealed that she feels guilt for the harm he has suffered (after he is framed for Davis' murder).

The weight of the accumulated responsibility that accompanies absolute sacrifice is revealed during the confidential special investigation, when Woodrugh interviews Deiffenbach, the retired LAPD detective who investigated the double murder and diamond robbery at Sable Fine Jewellers in 1992. Deiffenbach is in his mid-50s, has not aged well, and appears to be an alcoholic and a heavy smoker. In spite of the two decades that have passed, the case is etched in his memory and he can recall specific details with ease, including Margaret Osterman's first name and the fact that she was pregnant (with Caspere's second child). Deiffenbach tells Woodrugh the shop was looted immediately after the robbery (of $2.5 million worth of blue diamonds), which was committed by professionals, who executed the Ostermans and removed the security tape, destroying all the evidence that could incriminate them. Woodrugh hands him a picture of the Osterman children to assist his memory, but it is not necessary (*True Detective 2*, episode 6: 16:48–18:23):

DEIFFENBACH: *Christ...* you had to show me this? They were hiding; one of the display cabinets; had to stay like that for a long time. Hiding with their parents lying there like... I had quadruple my normal caseload. Riots overwhelmed the system – something, didn't close fast... moved on.

WOODRUGH: Kids couldn't offer up anything?

DEIFFENBACH: They could barely talk. The girl was maybe four; the boy a little older. Men wore masks. That's about it. Ended up in the foster system. Got kids?

WOODRUGH: One on the way.

DEIFFENBACH: Oh, God. Those kids fucked me up. Coming from where they did going into the system. All that and the city burning to the fucking ground.

Deiffenbach is visibly upset by his absolute sacrifice, the sacrifice of those cases that wouldn't close quickly to those that would. The sense of responsibility he expresses in *those kids fucked me up* is, however, more than just failing Leonard and Laura for not solving their parents' murder. Deiffenbach also feels responsible for what happened to them afterwards, knowing what the foster system would be like for children who had grown up in an apparently loving and stable home. This is, of course, irrational because the intersection of his life with theirs only began after the murder. The children would have been placed in foster care regardless of whether he solved the case or not and it seems highly unlikely that they would have taken any solace in the conviction of Burris and Dixon when one considers their ages and the traumatic nature of the change they experienced. Deiffenbach's exaggerated sense of guilt is another feature of absolute responsibility, a vicious circle of second-guessing and moral baggage. Had he realised the real reason for Woodrugh's investigation – that Leonard and Laura are suffering further harm as they enact their revenge – there is no doubt that he would have felt significantly more guilt because his failure to solve the 1992 case is a direct cause of this harm (if he had solved the case, Leonard would not have needed to torture Caspere to find out who killed his parents). Deiffenbach and Woodrugh are separated by at least two decades in age, but are broadly similar in appearance –

White men with blond hair and the same face and body shapes – and it takes very little stretch of the imagination to see the former as a future incarnation of the latter, after 20 years of absolute sacrifice have taken their mental and physical toll.

5.2.4 Worldmaking

The practice of policing is worldmaking because its goal, public protection, requires the re-creation of social reality. This re-creation is achieved by negotiating the relationship between power and powerlessness by means of the exercise of authority and the employment of discretion. The formation of the confidential investigation is an act of worldmaking by Davis, aimed at protecting the public from corrupt municipal and state officials by re-creating the social reality created by Geldof, the Chessanis, and Holloway. The most striking example of worldmaking within the confidential special investigation is Bezzerides' decision to infiltrate one of the elite sex parties hosted by Tony Chessani and Pitlor undercover, as a sex worker. She is briefed in full by her sister, who explains that Bezzerides will be searched for defensive, communication, or surveillance devices before she is allowed to enter the party and will then be expected to have sex with any guest who propositions her. In consequence of Davis' prioritisation of operational security over investigative effectiveness, Bezzerides will only be supported by Velcoro and Woodrugh. Bezzerides was first recruited as an undercover officer by Davis during the special detail, when she was instructed to enlist Velcoro as a state witness, but disobeyed the order with the support of her VCSO supervisor. The circumstances in the confidential special investigation are, however, entirely different. Following the discovery of the crime scene in Guerneville (Tasha's torture and murder), it appears as if the sex parties are the key to both of the confidential special investigation's aims, solving Caspere's murder and finding evidence of systemic corruption. Bezzerides worldmakes when she decides to achieve these aims (as well as increase her chances of finding Machiado) by going undercover in spite of the very high risk.

All Bezzerides is able to conceal on her person is a transponder, whose primary purpose is to facilitate Velcoro and Woodrugh being able to follow her to the correct address, a heavily guarded mansion in Monterey. Velcoro and Woodrugh arrive at the premises shortly after Bezzerides, infiltrate the grounds, and incapacitate one of the guards. As they search for a place to establish an observation post, Woodrugh sees Agranov closing a deal with McCandless. Woodrugh and Velcoro worldmake when they decide to break into the room and retrieve the documents, aware that while they may assist the detectives in solving the case, they will be inadmissible in court. Inside the mansion, Bezzerides is forced to take MDMA and then paraded in front of the most important guests with the other sex workers. She recognises Geldof and Holloway, although she is disorientated by the effects of the drug. Bezzerides is propositioned by a guest and removes a knife from a buffet, concealing it in her dress as he escorts her to the first floor. She begins hallucinating and tells the guest that she needs to go to the bathroom. Bezzerides forces herself to vomit in an attempt to detoxify and recognises a semi-conscious Machiado. Machiado objects when she is pulled to her feet, but the objection appears to be in response to being disturbed rather than being rescued.

As they are leaving, Bezzerides is accosted by the guest who propositioned her. She throws him to the floor and stamps on his groin. This draws the attention of a security guard, who grabs Bezzerides by the throat. She draws her knife and slashes him several times across the torso before he disarms her, lifts her off her feet, and pins her against a wall. Bezzerides is defenceless and struggling to breathe when the guard drops her, making one last attempt to grab her before collapsing in a pool of his own blood. She drags Machiado to the ground floor and exits the premises to find Woodrugh waiting. Bezzerides, Machiado, and Woodrugh reach Velcoro's car under fire and all four of them escape unscathed. Notwithstanding the legality of the undercover operation, the worldmaking of all three detectives has placed them in a precarious position. Though the security guard was significantly bigger and stronger than Bezzerides, she stabbed him multiple times while he was still dragging her away from Machiado and it is not completely clear that her life was in danger (albeit highly probable). Similarly, she cannot claim that she was defending Machiado as it is later revealed that Machiado did not actually want to leave the party. With respect to the evidence the detectives have acquired, Bezzerides' consumption of MDMA makes her an unreliable witness and the documents retrieved by Woodrugh were seized illegally. The only evidence likely to withstand cross-examination is Woodrugh's witnessing of the transaction between Agranov and McCandless. While the undercover operation improves the detectives' grasp of the corruption linked to the California Central Rail Corridor, it does not provide any clues to the solution to Caspere's murder. The operation also fails to achieve the purpose of the practice of policing by the taking of a life in circumstances that were avoidable.

Velcoro has never recovered from murdering the man he was led to believe raped his wife, which was an extrajudicial act of worldmaking. He resigns from the VPD after the Vinci Massacre, accepting that he is no longer able to meet the demands of the practice of policing and understanding that his failure to meet these demands is damaging his mental health beyond repair. When Davis summons Velcoro, Bezzerides, and Woodrugh to the scene of the Vinci Massacre and explains her plan for a confidential special investigation, Velcoro is antagonistic. He asks Davis if she is trying to secure evidence to blackmail Geldof, then asks her if she has been persuaded by Bezzerides' desire to find Machiado (neither of which he believes), and finally asks Woodrugh if he is simply craving excitement (which is at least partly true). When Velcoro turns Davis down, she offers to assist him with his custody battle for Chad and he accepts without hesitation. Before Bezzerides and Woodrugh take their leave, Bezzerides says (*True Detective 2*, episode 5: 39:46–39:51), 'Think it over, Velcoro. Never too late to start all over again.' This is exactly what he does, personally and professionally, reaching an out of court settlement with Gena, redefining the parameters of his relationship with Semyon, and rededicating himself to public protection. Velcoro's return to the practice of policing reinvigorates his tendency to worldmake both within and without the bounds of the law and his first act as a state investigator is trespass and battery. He waits until Pitlor is alone in his clinic after hours and commences a brutal and systematic extrajudicial interrogation. Velcoro begins with the threat of violence and proceeds to punching him when he refuses to answer questions about his participation in the sex trade. Pitlor claims that he is only involved in the cosmetic surgery and Velcoro escalates his violence, using a sap. Pitlor confesses that the elite sex parties are run by him, Caspere, and Tony Chessani and being used to make the rail corridor deals because of their potential for blackmail. Velcoro ends the interrogation with a punishment beating after Pitlor discloses his complicity in Austin Chessani's long-term physical and psychological abuse of his wife. None of the evidence is admissible, but Velcoro's worldmaking provides the first breakthrough in the case, revealing the links between the purchase of cheap farmland ruined by mining run-off and the elite sex party circuit. The recognition of the core role of the sex parties leads, in turn, to the solution of the investigation into the corruption at municipal and state levels.

5.3 Situated Practice

5.3.1 Institution

Heroic struggle, edgework, absolute sacrifice, and worldmaking are characteristics of the practice of policing, the purpose of which is public protection. That practice is a situated practice, situated in both an institution and a systemic context. As the characteristics are emergent from the tensions among practice, institution, and systemic context, the Caspere murder provides insight into the complexity of the relations among the characteristics of the practice of policing, policing as a situated practice, and public protection. An exploration of the tensions in the investigations of the Caspere murder, the murder in Vermilion Parish, and the disappearances in West Finger provides insight into the ways in which the institution of policing and the systemic context of policing can detract from public protection. The tensions among the practice of policing, the institution of policing, and the systemic context of policing are exacerbated by conflicts of interests among different institutions of policing or among policing and juridical institutions, as the Caspere murder investigation makes clear. After Caspere is absent from work for two days and fails to attend an important meeting about the rail corridor, Holloway opens a missing person case. Velcoro is placed in charge of the investigation and told to work with Dixon. He is unenthusiastic about both the case (suspecting deep-seated corruption) and Dixon's abilities as a detective. When he expresses his reservations about the latter, he is told the partnership is not optional. Dixon has been selected because of his involvement in the Osterman murder and robbery, in consequence of which Holloway and Burris believe – erroneously, it turns out – that he is loyal to them. Velcoro and Dixon arrive at Caspere's house to find it ransacked and his desktop computer stolen. Velcoro thinks the evidence points to kidnapping, concludes that Holloway and Burris are already aware of the crime, and remains reluctant to investigate. Late that night Caspere's corpse is found by Woodrugh, who is off duty and suspended pending investigation of the allegations made by the actress. The rest stop on the Pacific Coast Highway is in the jurisdiction of the VCSO and Bezzerides and Ilinca are the detectives on call. Velcoro is notified because the missing person case has already been opened by the VPD. In virtue of the location of the crime scene and her seniority to Ilinca, Bezzerides takes charge of the investigation initially, but the following morning there is a meeting of VCSO, VPD, and CA DOJ officials.

Assistant Sheriff James O'Neal claims the case is straightforwardly the VCSO's as the corpse was found in their jurisdiction. Burris states that the VPD have already opened a missing persons case, found Caspere's house burgled, and will continue to investigate that crime on their own if necessary. Geldof reveals the CA DOJ's investigation into the allegations of corruption made by Hauser in the *Los Angeles Times* and Davis argues that it was a state law enforcement agent who discovered the corpse. As a compromise, a special detail comprising officers from all three agencies is formed. At first, this cooperation appears to be in the interests of public protection as the investigation seems likely to cross jurisdictional boundaries. Davis places Bezzerides in command of the special detail, tells her that Velcoro will be her deputy, and issues the following instruction (*True Detective 2*, episode 2: 08:37–08:46): 'Vinci detective with you – word is, he's bent. Work him, leverage something to turn him. We'll have a full state probe up inside a week. Caspere's death is a window, into everything.' In other words, Davis is prioritising the investigation into corruption over the detection of Caspere's murderer and Bezzerides is expected to follow suit by focusing on recruiting Velcoro as a witness against the VPD rather than on solving the case. Bezzerides presents her first report to O'Neal after opening Caspere's safe deposit box, during which Davis asks what progress she has made with Velcoro. Bezzerides evades the question by calling him a 'burnout' (*True Detective 2*, episode 3: 22:42). Davis is not satisfied, however, and tells Bezzerides to seduce Velcoro. O'Neal intervenes, saying that Bezzerides is in Major Crimes, not in Internal Affairs or working as an undercover officer. What is noteworthy is that O'Neal is not objecting to seduction being used as an intelligence-gathering tactic by police officers, but to Bezzerides being told to use it when her primary role is that of a homicide detective (Marx 1988; Joh 2009; Nathan 2022). Davis then offers Bezzerides a promotion if she is able to recruit Velcoro in addition to solving the case. Bezzerides has no interest in recruiting Velcoro for the probe and maintains exclusive focus on solving the murder. The distinction between Bezzerides' reluctance to seduce Velcoro and her commitment to the practice of policing is indicative of a conflict between undercover policing as a type of policing and policing as a practice. Bezzerides does not consider seduction to be a requirement of that practice and there is ample evidence of the tension between the practice of policing and undercover policing during the confidential special investigation.

Velcoro receives his orders from Burris in the presence of Holloway and Austin Chessani (*True Detective 2*, episode 2: 09:51–09:59): 'State's gonna use the homicide to dig into whatever they can, Ray. Wherever the Caspere case goes, we need you running point. Control the sprawl, control the flow of information.' After being briefed, Velcoro asks whether he is supposed to solve the murder or not and is told to prioritise municipal interests. Much like the CA DOJ, the VPD has no interest in detecting the murderer, only in protecting the reputation of the institution and in concealing the corruption of individual officers. Velcoro is unaware of the full extent of the corruption in the VPD and mayor's office and does not realise that Holloway and Burris are keeping Dixon on the special detail as a safeguard, i.e. in case Velcoro either fails to follow his orders or is unsuccessful in restricting the CA DOJ's intelligence-gathering. Like Bezzerides, Velcoro ignores his orders and pursues the investigation to the best of his ability. Dixon also ignores his orders and threatens to expose the corruption of Caspere, Holloway, and Burris unless he is financially compensated. Burris decides that it is safer to have Dixon killed and the ensuing Vinci Massacre has the unintended but welcome consequence of ending the homicide investigation. When Woodrugh is recruited as a state investigator, Geldof tells him that although Caspere's murder is the public investigation, his confidential mandate is to investigate the VPD and gather intelligence for a grand jury. He leaves no doubt as to which of the two is the priority (*True Detective 2*, episode 2: 07:47–07:49): 'This probe is very important to the Governor's Office.' Geldof not only draws attention to the greater authority of the state when compared to the city, but refers directly to the head of government at the superior level. Like Bezzerides, Woodrugh has little interest in the CA DOJ's probe and focuses exclusively on solving the homicide, learning the skills of detection from his more experienced colleagues. Municipal corruption, particularly of the scale on which it takes place in Vinci, may well be more significant to public protection than a murder investigation, but the CA DOJ's prioritisation of the former over the latter nonetheless undermines the ability of the VCSO to solve the murder. Similarly, while the VPD's priority is – courtesy of its venal chief – the concealment of corruption, this concealment is part of the broader motive of the protection of the reputation of public institutions, particularly police institutions, which is an important part of the means by which those institutions and the practices they support are sustained (Mawby 2002; Lee & McGovern 2014; Colbran 2022).

In November 1980, Arkansas State Police (ASP) Major Crimes Division detectives Wayne Hays and Roland West are called to West Finger, Washington County, to investigate the disappearance of two children. Will, who is 12, and his sister Julie, who is ten, have been reported missing by their father, Tom Purcell. The following day Hays discovers Will's corpse in a cave, prompting county prosecutor Gerald Kindt to establish a joint ASP-Federal Bureau of Investigation (FBI) task force in which the detectives will lead the homicide investigation and the special agents the search for Julie. Will's corpse was found in the vicinity of two straw dolls and Hays and West learn that Julie received a similar doll on Halloween. Hays wants to put the entire town under surveillance for three days, during which every householder will be asked for permission to search their premises. Kindt vetoes the plan because he does not want to anger his constituents close to re-election. Where Hays is primarily motivated by Julie's safety, Kindt's motivation as a prosecutor is to secure a conviction for Will's murder (Davis 2019; Pakes 2019; Huemer 2021). He ignores Hays' plea to protect Julie and holds a televised interview that reveals details of the police investigation and creates a panic in West Finger. Many residents (most of whom are White) turn their attention to Brett Woodard, a mentally ill Native American Vietnam veteran, and the investigation comes to a violent and untimely end when nine vigilantes attack Woodard. Woodard has booby-trapped his property with explosives, in consequence of which a three-way firefight among him, the vigilantes, and the police leaves 12 people dead, including Woodard himself. When Will's backpack and the remains of Julie's shirt are recovered from the crime scene, Kindt closes the investigation and announces his intention to try Woodard for the murder of both children *in absentia*. Hays is certain that Woodard is not guilty, but is dismissed from the criminal investigation division (CID) and demoted after leaking information to the press.

In March 1990, Julie's fingerprints are found at a burglary in Sallisaw, Oklahoma, and Woodard's children petition to have his conviction overturned. Two months later, the Purcell case is reopened with West, who has been promoted to detective lieutenant in Major Crimes, leading the investigation. West's commander, Major Blevins, gives him his orders in the presence of Kindt, who is now Arkansas AG (*True Detective 3*, Episode 3: 23:30–23:36): 'The mandate of this unit is to vindicate the original conviction for Will Purcell's murder.' Neither the AG nor the ASP have anything to gain by uncovering the truth, but West and Hays prioritise the search for Julie. In a repeat of the initial investigation, Hays' concerns about operational security are overridden by Kindt, who holds another televised interview. Hays works out that Will's backpack was planted at the Woodard crime scene and missed because both the police and prosecutor were satisfied with the early resolution. The police hotline receives a call from Julie, who asks her father to leave her alone and implies that he killed Will. Kindt's main interest remains the protection of his personal reputation and he suggests that Purcell colluded with Woodard. Blevins is more open to an admission of error, but nonetheless wants a quick resolution and suggests that Purcell planted the evidence. West and Hays suspect the real culprit was an ASP officer named Harris James, who has been working as head of security for the wealthy Hoyt family since 1981. Purcell takes the law into his own hands at this point, discovering that his late wife sold Julie to Isabel Hoyt as a replacement for her dead daughter. When he breaks into the Hoyt mansion to exact revenge, he is murdered by James and his death arranged to look like a suicide. Kindt holds another press conference stating that Purcell is guilty of Will's murder and that Woodard's conviction is going to be overturned. The combination of Kindt's political ambition and two senior police officers' desire to protect the reputation of the ASP brings the case to a premature and erroneous conclusion on two separate occasions.

In January 1995, Louisiana State Police (LSP) homicide detectives Martin Hart and Rustin Cohle are called to a crime scene outside Erath, in Vermilion Parish, by Sheriff Tate. They open an investigation into the murder of Dora Lange, a sex worker whose naked corpse has been found in a sugar cane field, posed post-mortem, adorned with deer antlers, and painted with a crooked spiral. The evidence indicates an occult connection and the case attracts immediate media attention. When Hart briefs his squad their commanding officer, Detective Major Ken Quesada, is clear about the pressure placed on them by the media, which has in turn aroused the interest of their chief officers and local church groups. Hart and Cohle begin interviewing Erath residents to look for potential witnesses and discover that a ten-year-old girl, Marie Fontenot, went missing five years ago. They suspect the two cases are related. Tate tells them that Ted Childress was sheriff at the time and that the missing person report was filed as being made in error because Fontenot had gone to live with her father. Shortly after the first press briefing, the Reverend Billy Lee Tuttle visits CID to inform Hart and Cohle that his cousin – Edwin Tuttle, the Governor of Louisiana – is following their progress closely. Captain Speece, the Vermilion troop commander, adds that he is considering setting up an Anti-Christian Crimes Task Force to take over the case. Several weeks later, Hart and Cohle meet the task force, three LSP detectives detailed to investigate a spate of animal mutilations and cemetery defilements. Quesada wants Hart to share the case file with them despite the apparent absence of any link to the murder.

When Hart and Cohle are reluctant, Quesada calls them into his office (*True Detective 1*, episode 2: 50:05–50:48):

QUESADA: We work under command, right? And our betters want a public, high profile show of response. Shit, I got a state senator, he's trying to label Satanic graffiti as a hate crime.
HART: That has nothing to do with our DB [dead body] and that's... the fact of it.
QUESADA: OK, OK, fine, let's say that's true, alright? Let's say that you guys get the case all to yourselves. You ever solve a murder been in the red more than a week? You ever clear one when two rounds of questions didn't hand you the fucking answer?
HART: No, come on –
QUESADA: No, you got leads, you got a timeline – you know what I got? I got a whodunnit where my two detectives are stalling... and I got a brand new task force wants to take it off our hands.

Quesada recommends that Hart hand the case over given the pressure from the governor, the media, and Speece. When Hart asks to keep it, Quesada sets a deadline of two weeks. The only lead Hart and Cohle have on a suspect is a tall man with burn scars with whom Lange went to church. Cohle remains convinced that the murder and the disappearance are linked and wants to search for more unsolved murders in the period between the two. Hart tells him they have to pursue the lead they have on the suspect, however slim, because if they begin again the case will definitely be handed over to the task force. Cohle investigates on his own and finds another victim, Rianne Olivier, who was believed to be drowned in a flood. At the same time, Quesada tells Hart their remaining time has been cut to two days, which precludes further inquiry into the possibility of a linked series of murders. Hart and Cohle find two suspects, but mishandle the arrest, resulting in the death of both men and the closure of the case. Like the West Finger case, the closure is premature and erroneous. The irony is that closure motivated by the protection of institutional reputations becomes completely counterproductive if institutional failure is subsequently exposed (Batts, deLone & Stephens 2014; Davis & Leo 2017; Norris & Mullinix 2020).

5.3.2 Systemic Context

I have already described the way in which the situation of the practice of policing in a systemic context can undermine public protection in my discussion of institutions above, specifically the way in which the competing interests of the institutions of the VCSO, VPD, and CA DOJ undermine the detection of Caspere's murder. The special detail is formed precisely because the AG wants to use the murder as a means to the end of his investigation into municipal corruption, with little concern as to whether the murder is solved. As I noted in that discussion, the investigation into municipal corruption may well be more significant to public protection than the investigation of a single murder, but the former should not be at the expense of the latter. The VPD is only invited to join the special detail so that Bezzerides can recruit Velcoro as a state witness and Geldof is aware that Velcoro has been ordered to sabotage the investigation. The fact that Geldof is able to pervert the course of an investigation into the most serious and highest profile crime handled by the police to suit his own ends is indicative of the disproportionate power wielded by prosecutors in the US. Compared to other Anglo-American Democratic Policing (AADP) countries, local, regional, and federal prosecutors in the US have a greater involvement in and influence on police investigations (Davis 2019; Pakes 2019). They also have absolute powers of discretion over which cases will be taken to trial and are very rarely investigated for misconduct and even more rarely punished for it, even when that misconduct constitutes blatant corruption (Stuntz 2011; Huemer 2021). The combination of failure to separate police and juridical institutions with the power differential between detectives and prosecutors reduces the ability of the two sets of institutions to serve as checks and balances for one another, which is fundamental to the administration of criminal justice in a democracy. The problem is exacerbated by another feature of the US criminal justice system that distinguishes it from other AADP countries: most chief prosecutors, judges, sheriffs, and police chiefs are elected or appointed by elected politicians rather than being career civil servants (Stuntz 2011; Tonry 2020). While making these officials directly responsible to their electorates (or to officials who are directly responsible to their electorates) appears to promote justice, it also increases the likelihood of corruption by aggravating an already present vulnerability to the influence of the wealthy, who are able to fund the political campaigns of juridical officials.

Geldof's probe into Vinci's corruption seems to be motivated by either a genuine concern for public protection or the desire to enhance his personal reputation in preparation for the next election (the two are not, of course, mutually exclusive). As a city police chief, Holloway reports directly to the mayor, Austin Chessani, a chain of command intended to provide a safeguard against the abuse of police power. Chessani is elected by Vinci's public (or, more accurately, a proportion of that public) and it is therefore in his interests to use his oversight of the police to ensure that the VPD follows its function, which is to sustain both itself and the practice of policing, whose function is the protection of (all of) Vinci's public. The problem is that all three of the chief, mayor, and city manager are corrupt, colluding with one another for mutual benefit. In situations such as this, where the municipal authorities cease to work in the interests of the public, the existence of an institution at a distinct level of political authority – the CA DOJ, a state department – promotes justice by providing a second safeguard, built in to the criminal justice system (albeit limited by the close collaboration between prosecutors and detectives noted above). When Davis recruits Bezzerides, Velcoro, and Woodrugh to the confidential special investigation she divulges that Geldof announced his intention to run for Governor of California shortly after closing the Caspere case and that his campaign is extremely well-funded. Her position is unequivocal (*True Detective* 2, episode 5: 37:37–37:43): 'Geldof's actions are the clearest indication of collusion between the ... Vinci power structure and the larger state institutions.' The evidence suggests Geldof either closed the case in order to curry favour with the mayor or threatened to continue the investigation if the mayor did not fund his campaign for governor. Velcoro, who has little confidence in the criminal justice system, suspected the latter as soon as the special detail was formed, warning Bezzerides that 'the state investigation's a shakedown' and speculating that Geldof wanted part of the land development profit (*True Detective* 2, episode 4: 7:37–7:39). He also warned her about the influence and endurance of the Chessanis, who have been the most powerful family in this part of California for a century.

Davis intends to solve Caspere's murder and acquire evidence of collusion among the VPD, mayor's office, AG, and any other state institutions involved, but the fatal flaw in the confidential special investigation is manifest on its formation: the need to prioritise operational security over investigative effectiveness. Given the ambition and scope of the investigation, the team of four is woefully inadequate. Their effectiveness is further diminished by Davis and Woodrugh having to investigate Caspere's murder while meeting their existing responsibilities in the CA DOJ and CHP respectively. Even worse, Bezzerides and Velcoro have no institutional support beyond that provided by Davis and Woodrugh because Bezzerides is recruited as a confidential investigator (while she is on leave from the VCSO) and Velcoro is a private investigator (following his resignation from the VPD). Davis is only able to initiate and direct the confidential special investigation in consequence of the lack of oversight she enjoys as a prosecutor. Her judgement in prioritising security over effectiveness is sound because the extension of corruption from the municipal level (the mayor's office and VPD) to the state level (the AG) removes the second built-in safeguard and substantially increases the power of those involved. The secrecy that protects the investigation also places it at risk, however, as revealed when the detectives conduct an undercover operation without adequate levels of surveillance or support. Davis' operational security facilitates the detection of the murderer, but not the acquisition of the evidence she is seeking and is ultimately self-defeating. When Bezzerides breaks her cover at the sex party, the corrupt officials realise Davis is leading a confidential special investigation. The level of confidentiality she has maintained means that the entire investigation can be terminated by removing her. In a repeat of his decision to have Dixon killed, Burris decides that killing Davis is the safest option and frames Velcoro for the murder. Without Davis, there is no confidential special investigation and the three detectives lose their official status. As neither Velcoro nor Bezzerides have institutional support, Woodrugh becomes the sole hope for a judicial resolution of the case. After the success of Davis' murder, Burris murders Woodrugh, once again framing Velcoro. Where the special detail shows the need for the diffusion of institutional power among different levels of criminal justice administration, the confidential special investigation shows that corruption across these levels is exponentially more difficult to detect and prosecute. Bezzerides has more faith in the criminal justice system than Velcoro and intends to take the case to the FBI. With the corruption having spread from the municipal to the state level, the federal level is the best option available, but she is unable to secure sufficient evidence.

Hart and Cohle only solve the Lange case in 2012, 17 years after her murder, by which time they have both left the police. Cohle has long suspected the existence of a state-wide conspiracy of paedophiles who prey on girls under the guise of a homicidal cult. He and Hart identify Errol Childress as the high priest of the cult and caretaker of the holy site where the girls are raped and murdered. The cult has remained undetected for so long because of the extent to which the Tuttle family (and its Childress offshoot) is embedded in different levels of the political and criminal justice systems. The problem is exacerbated by the progression of individuals through those systems by means of nepotism, cronyism, and other forms of patronage. Patronage establishes strong and stable networks of influence that are either implicitly or explicitly corrupt and whose power is exerted across both space and time (Bellow 2003; Tolchin & Tolchin 2011; Harcourt 2020). The impact of patronage in the political and criminal justice systems is evident in the changing circumstances of the Lange murder investigation from 1990 to 2012. Edwin Tuttle, cousin to Billy

Lee, is initially the Governor of Louisiana and then one of the state's senators. Errol Childress is related to both Ted Childress, who was Sheriff of Vermilion Parish in 1990, and a deputy detailed to Vermilion Parish Jail in 2002. Steve Geraci, who is not part of the conspiracy but facilitates its continued existence by following orders without question, began his career in the Vermilion Parish Sheriff's Office, was promoted to the rank of detective in the LSP in the early 1990s, and was subsequently appointed Sheriff of Iberia Parish.

The integration of the conspiracy into different levels of governance and law enforcement not only makes it more difficult to detect, but easier to protect. Before Cohle and Hart set out to interview Childress in 2012, Cohle prepares ten packages and asks an associate to post them if he does not hear from him in 24 hours. Each package contains copies of a videotape of Fontenot's murder, the case files, and Cohle and Hart's depositions. They are addressed to: the FBI New Orleans, LSP CID, Louisiana State AG, US Attorney Western District of Louisiana, two national newspapers, two local newspapers, and two national news channels. Cohle feels that this is necessary to ensure the case is investigated if he and Hart are killed. Although they survive their confrontation with Childress, they are both wounded and the packages posted. Two weeks later media reports describe Childress as a serial killer who has murdered dozens of people. Strictly speaking, they are correct in that Childress' actions fit the FBI's definition of serial murder, but the connotation is that he was a lone predator, working in isolation, which is clearly false (Behavioral Analysis Unit 2008). The AG and FBI deny that he is related to Edwin Tuttle, which is an outright lie as they are both relatives of Sam Tuttle, Billy Lee's father. While Cohle and Hart are still in hospital, they reflect on the limited nature of their success, in spite of apprehending Childress and releasing information about the conspiracy to the press (*True Detective 1*, episode 8: 44:46–44:58):

COHLE: Tuttles, the men in the video... we didn't get 'em all.
HART: Yeah and we ain't gonna get 'em all, that ain't what kind of world it is, but we got ours.

Hart recognises the relationship between the power exerted by individuals and the standard of evidence required to bring them to trial and his prediction is confirmed in 2015 when it is revealed that 'the case never went wider' (*True Detective 3*, episode 7: 22:20–22:22).

AG Kindt closes the Purcell case in 1990 on the grounds that Purcell killed Will and that Julie is an adult whose privacy should be respected. Working on his own, Hays finds evidence implicating James in planting the evidence in 1980, killing Julie's mother in 1988, and possibly killing Purcell. Hays knows that the only way to acquire evidence on which Blevins and Kindt will act is to secure a confession, which can only be achieved by extrajudicial means. Hays and West abduct James, take him to a black site, and kill him after bungling his interrogation. They decide to cover up their crime and bury his body. Early the next morning Hays receives a phone call from Edward Hoyt, the family patriarch, who is parked outside his house with four security guards. Hoyt takes Hays to a remote rural location and demands to know where James is, disclosing his possession of closed-circuit television footage of Hays and West following James and the existence of a Global Positing System chip in James' pager. Despite the threat to himself and his family, Hays remains motivated by Julie's safety and replies by asking Hoyt what he knows about her. Hoyt not only has personal information about Hays, but classified information about the investigation and proposes a truce in which Hays ceases his search for Julie and he ceases his search for James. Hays refuses and only agrees to drop the case when Hoyt first guarantees Julie's safety and then states that if Hays does not drop it, Julie will be killed precisely because he is looking for her. In a final display of the power differential between them Hoyt terminates the interview by leaving Hays in the woods, miles from home. Hays resigns from the police to protect his family and the investigation is dormant for 25 years.

In 2015, a television broadcaster interviews Hays, who is now 70. She is working on a story about large-scale paedophile rings, including the case investigated by Hart and Cohle, and suspects that Julie's disappearance is part of a wider conspiracy because of the straw dolls – which may, like the crooked spiral, be a symbol used by such groups – and the disproportionate number of deaths associated with the investigation. With Hoyt having died of natural causes, Hays and West (who has also retired) make a final attempt to locate Julie. They find Junius Watts, Isabel's accomplice, who tells them Will was accidentally killed by Isabel during Julie's abduction. When Watts learned that Isabel was drugging Julie with lithium, he helped her escape. Julie failed to rendezvous with him, however, and after more than a decade of looking for her, he discovered she had died at a convent in Fort Smith in 1995. Hays and West visit Julie's grave, where Hays recognises the convent landscaper, who was a childhood friend of hers. He realises that the nuns faked Julie's death for her own safety, drives to her address for confirmation, and then forgets why he is there due to his progressive memory loss. The case is thus finally solved 35 years after it began, but was only ever likely to be solved after Hoyt's death. Although Hoyt is not part of any conspiracy, the influence he is able to exert in virtue of his wealth extends beyond Hays and his family to different levels of the criminal justice system, an influence that is aggravated by the personal ambition of various people at different levels and in different institutions within that system. The delayed resolution of the case suggests the relevance of the level of inequality in a society to the differential treatment of suspects within that society's criminal justice system. As with the Vermilion Parish case, the systemic context of the West Finger case demonstrates the close relationship between the criminal justice and political systems. In liberal democracies with high levels of wealth inequality, there is likely to be a commensurate inequality in the treatment of suspects (Wacquant 2004; Neocleous 2021; Reiner 2021). The three sets of police and private investigations thus draw attention to the different ways in which competition between different law enforcement agencies, competition between different institutions within the criminal justice system, and the relative impunity of powerful individuals or groups detracts from public protection.

References

Batts, A.W., deLone, M. & Stephens, D.W. (2014). Policing and Wrongful Convictions. *New Perspectives in Policing*, August, 1–31. Available at: www.ojp.gov/pdffiles1/nij/246328.pdf.

Behavioral Analysis Unit (2008). Serial Murder: Multi-Disciplinary Perspectives for Investigators. Federal Bureau of Investigation. www.fbi.gov/stats-services/publications/serial-murder/serial-murder-july-2008-pdf.

Bellow. A. (2003). *In Praise of Nepotism: A Natural History*. New York: Bantam Books.

Colbran, M. (2022). *Crime and Investigative Reporting in the UK*. Bristol: Policy Press.

Davis, D. & Leo, R.A. (2017). A Damning Cascade of Investigative Errors: Flaws in Homicide Investigation in the USA. In: Brookman, F., Maguire, E.R. & Maguire, M. (eds), *The Handbook of Homicide*. Malden, MA: Wiley-Blackwell, 578–598.

Davis, F.T. (2019). *American Criminal Justice: An Introduction*. Cambridge: Cambridge University Press.

Harcourt, B.E. (2020). *Critique and Praxis: A Critical Philosophy of Illusions, Values, and Action*. New York: Columbia University.

Huemer, M. (2021). *Justice Before the Law*. London: Palgrave Macmillan.

Joh, E.E. (2009). Breaking the Law to Enforce It: Undercover Police Participation in Crime. *Stanford Law Review*, 62 (1), 155–199.

Lee, M. & McGovern, A. (2014). *Policing and Media: Public Relations, Simulations and Communications*. Abingdon: Routledge.

Marx, G.T. (1988). *Undercover: Police Surveillance in America*. Oakland, CA: University of California Press.

Mawby, R.C. (2002). *Policing Images: Policing, Communication and Legitimacy*. Cullompton: Willan Publishing.

Neocleous, M. (2021). *A Critical Theory of Police Power: The Fabrication of Social Order*. 2nd ed. London: Verso Books.

Nathan, C. (2022). *The Ethics of Undercover Policing*. Abingdon: Routledge.

Norris, R.J. & Mullinix, K.J. (2020). Framing innocence: an experimental test of the effects of wrongful convictions on public opinion. *Journal of Experimental Criminology*, 16 (2), 311–334.

Pakes, F. (2019). *Comparative Criminal Justice*. 4th ed. Abingdon: Routledge.

Reiner, R. (2021). *Social Democratic Criminology*. Abingdon: Routledge.

Stuntz, W.J. (2011/2013). *The Collapse of American Criminal Justice*. Cambridge, MA: Belknap Press.

Tolchin, M. & Tolchin, S.J. (2011/2016). *Pinstripe Patronage: Political Favoritism from the Clubhouse to the White House and Beyond*. Abingdon: Routledge.

Tonry, M. (2020). *Doing Justice, Preventing Crime*. New York: Oxford University Press.

True Detective (2014–2019). Originally released 12 January. US: HBO.

True Detective (season 1) (2014). Originally released 12 January. US: HBO.

True Detective (season 2) (2015). Originally released 21 June. US: HBO.

True Detective (season 3) (2019). Originally released 13 January.US: HBO.
Wacquant, L. (2004/2009). *Punishing the Poor: The Neoliberal Government of Social Insecurity*. Trans. anonymous. Durham, NC: Duke University Press.

6

WEST YORKSHIRE, 1980

This chapter presents the second critical case study of the characteristics of policing as a practice and of policing as a situated practice. The case takes place in West Yorkshire during the last three weeks of 1980 and is about the murder of 13 women in the North of England from 1975 to 1980. The context of the case is the murder of six girls in the North of England from 1969 to 1983 and case and context are linked by the formation of a cabal composed of seven corrupt police officers, a construction magnate affiliated with organised crime, and a famous architect in 1972. The critical case study comprises two synchronic investigations conducted by two police officers: Assistant Chief Constable (ACC) Peter Hunter and Detective Sergeant (DS) Helen Marshall, both of Greater Manchester Police (GMP). Following the murder of the 13th victim of the Yorkshire Ripper, Hunter is recruited to lead a covert Home Office investigation of the West Yorkshire Metropolitan Police (WYMP) under the guise of being part of a brains trust attached to the Ripper Squad. The Ripper inquiry is brought to a successful conclusion by a patrol officer rather than a squad detective and the covert inquiry is thwarted by the combination of the independent efforts of the cabal and the chief constables of the WYMP and GMP. The focus on

Hunter and Marshall demonstrates the significance of heroic struggle, edgework, absolute sacrifice, and worldmaking to police practice and provides insight into the different ways in which each can both contribute to and detract from public protection. An exploration of the tensions from which the four characteristics of the practice of policing are emergent in the case and its context provides insight into the ways in which the institution of policing and the systemic context of policing can detract from public protection. Taken together, the two sets of crimes draw attention to the prioritisation of reputation risk management by the institution of policing, the vulnerability of the institution of policing to organised corruption, the impact of competition between government institutions, and the extent to which the criminal justice system is unfit for purpose.

6.1 Case Summary

6.1.1 Ripper Inquiry

On Wednesday 10 December 1980 the serial murderer known as the Yorkshire Ripper kills his 13th victim, a student nurse named Laureen Bell, in Leeds. The following day, the Home Office and Her Majesty's Inspectorate of Constabulary (HMIC) create 'a *brains trust*, a *Super Squad*' to assist the WYMP's Ripper Squad (Peace 2001: 14, emphasis in original). The Super Squad consists of Deputy Chief Constable Leonard Curtis of Thames Valley Police; William Meyers, National Coordinator of the Regional Crime Squads; Commander Donald Lincoln, the Deputy Chief Inspector of Constabulary; Dr Stephen Tippet of the Forensic Science Service; and ACC Hunter of GMP. Their mandate is to provide the WYMP with short-term advice until either the Christmas break or the end of the year and Hunter is given responsibility for reviewing the Ripper inquiry. In order to achieve this colossal task, he is offered a choice of up to seven detectives, but prioritises operational security and selects four: Detective Chief Superintendent (DCSI) John Murphy, Detective Chief Inspector (DCI) Alec McDonald, Detective Inspector (DI) Mike Hillman, and Marshall. Hunter's team arrive in Leeds late on Friday to an inhospitable reception as neither Chief Constable

(CC) Ronald Angus nor Temporary ACC Peter Noble, who has just taken over the Ripper inquiry from ACC George Oldman, want their assistance. Hunter insists on beginning his review the next day and Noble insists on the appointment of a liaison to his team, ostensibly to guide them through the huge archive of evidence but actually to monitor and control the information they receive. Hunter is not happy about Noble's choice, Detective Superintendent (DSI) Robert Craven, who was suspected of misconduct during a multiple murder at the Strafford Arms public house in Wakefield in December 1974.

The Ripper's first victim was murdered in June 1975, but the 'Prostitute Murder Squad' was only established after the fourth, in May 1977, because of the similarities with the first and third murders (Peace 2001: 113). Most of the murders were of sex workers in the West Yorkshire Built-Up Area (Leeds, Bradford, Huddersfield, and Wakefield), but four were further afield (two in Manchester and two in Preston) and the three most recent victims were, respectively, two university students and a bank clerk. On Monday 15 December, Hunter provides Noble with a profile: the Ripper is local, married, drives for a living, has never been in prison, and has already been interviewed by the police – all of which will turn out to be accurate. Hunter's recommendation that the WYMP revisit every statement where a suspect was given an alibi by his wife is ignored. The second and sixth victims – Clare Strachan, murdered in Preston in November 1975, and Janice Ryan, murdered in Bradford in June 1977 – were only connected to the Ripper after a series of communications by him to the press in 1977. There is doubt as to whether Strachan and Ryan were Ripper victims and speculation that, if not, they were murdered by the same person. By the beginning of his second week on the Super Squad, Hunter suspects the Ripper inquiry has been complicated by either misconduct or corruption. On Sunday 21 December, he interviews two long-term Ripper Squad detectives, DSI Richard Alderman and DSI James Prentice, who inadvertently reveal that DS Robert Fraser, who committed suicide in 1977, was suspected of murdering Ryan.

That same day, the Manchester *Daily Mirror* receives a telephone call from a man claiming to be the Ripper and threatening to kill again on Tuesday. There is no murder and Hunter's team leave for a four-day break on Wednesday evening. On Friday 26 December, Hunter is removed from the Super Squad following vague and false accusations of corruption. Two days later, the Ripper – Peter David Williams of Heaton, Bradford – is arrested in Hillsborough, Sheffield, for using false number plates. He is taken to his local police station, Dewsbury, on Monday and DS Mike Ellis contacts the Ripper Room. Following the results of a blood test and the recovery of weapons at the scene of the arrest, Williams is interviewed by Alderman, Prentice, and Ellis on Tuesday 30 December. Hunter arrives in time for the second interview, by Alderman and Prentice, during which Williams admits to being the Ripper. In the third interview, Noble, Alderman, and Prentice work through a long list of the names of women who were murdered or assaulted in the North of England and Williams admits to 13 murders, but not the same 13 identified by the Ripper Squad: he denies killing Strachan and Ryan and includes two previously unrecognised victims, his ninth in Bradford in November 1978 and his 12th in Harrogate in August 1980. Hunter notices that Craven is the only senior detective missing from the station and finds him in the Strafford Arms, where he has committed suicide.

6.1.2 Covert Inquiry

When Hunter is summoned to the home of Philip Evans, the Regional Inspector of Constabulary for Yorkshire and the North East, early on Thursday 11 December, he is introduced to Sir John Reed, the Chief Inspector of Constabulary, and Michael Warren, who is 'from the Home Office' (Peace 2001: 11). Hunter is asked to lead a covert Home Office inquiry into the WYMP's handling of the Ripper inquiry under the guise of the Super Squad, reporting directly and exclusively to Evans. He asks why the review is covert and is told that neither the public nor the WYMP will accept two synchronous investigations into the Ripper murders and that public revelations of misconduct or incompetence would exacerbate existing problems with police morale. Hunter arrives in Leeds on Friday to find that Angus not only knows about the covert inquiry, but has outlined its terms of reference so that Hunter reports to him rather than Evans.

Hunter phones Evans for clarification the next morning and receives a supportive but evasive reply. When he phones Evans back to protest about Craven being assigned to his team, he is told he is unavailable. On Monday 15 December, Hunter is contacted by Elizabeth Hall, the widow of DI Eric Hall, who was the head of Bradford Vice and the target of a planned anti-corruption investigation when he was murdered in June 1977. Hall tells Hunter that her husband knew Ryan and was convinced she had been killed by Fraser, a Ripper Squad detective with whom she was having an affair. Eric kept a personal archive of notes and tapes that Elizabeth gave to the detectives investigating his murder, but she never heard back from them and wants Hunter to reopen the case using her duplicate of the archive.

Hunter works through Hall's collection and finds a recording in which he tells an unidentified man that he is being blackmailed over a pornographic magazine called *Spunk*. Issue 13 of the magazine (March 1976), which features a photoshoot of Ryan, is included in the archive. As *Spunk* is out of print, Hunter visits the publisher and distributor, MGM Ltd, in Manchester on Saturday 20 December. Although the company has moved, he discovers that the building is owned by Richard Dawson, a friend of his who has just been arrested for financial fraud, raising the possibility that *Spunk* links the Ripper inquiry to the recent murder of Dawson's security consultant, Robert Douglas, an ex-WYMP police officer who was partnered with Craven. Hunter reports this information to his CC, Clement Smith, who responds by asking him if he wants to continue with the covert inquiry. The next day, Hunter locates MGM's new premises, in Batley. He confides in Marshall about the significance of *Spunk*, breaks into the building, and retrieves a collection of ten magazines, which means he is missing only issues 3 and 9. Marshall agrees to help Hunter keep the premises under 24-hour surveillance and he returns to Leeds on Monday, to a reprimand from Angus for not sharing the *Spunk* discovery with Noble. At midnight, three explosions ignite a fire that destroys MGM. A corpse is discovered in the debris and subsequently identified as Dawson.

Hunter's house is burned down on Christmas Day, he is relieved of command of the covert inquiry on Boxing Day, and he meets an anonymous informant in Preston on Sunday 27 December. While waiting for the informant – Barry James Anderson, a witness to the Strafford Arms shootings – Hunter opens his mail and finds photographs of him and Marshall walking her dog, evidence of the affair they were having earlier in the year. Anderson hands Hunter a photocopied page from *Spunk* issue 3 (January 1975), featuring Strachan, and tells him that she and her sister (who worked at the Strafford Arms) were killed by a cabal of corrupt WYMP officers (who are also pursuing Anderson). Anderson claims the cabal is taking direct action against Hunter, pointing out the extent to which his removal from Leeds and the Ripper inquiry has been overdetermined. Hunter is interviewed by Angus on Monday, when he succeeds in dismissing several of the accusations against him. Having heard the Ripper's confession the following day, Hunter decides to return home on Wednesday 31 December. While he is packing up, Marshall arrives and tells him that Craven is blackmailing both of them. Convinced that Craven killed Strachan and Ryan, Hunter finds him in the Strafford Arms, where he has committed suicide. Hunter has, however, been followed by Murphy and Alderman and when he realises that Murphy is part of the cabal, he does not defend himself against them. After murdering Hunter, Murphy and Alderman tamper with the crime scene so that the evidence implicates Craven, preserving the cabal from detection for a further three years.

6.1.3 Hunter and Marshall

The critical case study focuses on the practices of the two police officers involved in both the review of the Ripper inquiry and the *Spunk* magazine investigation: Hunter and Marshall. Hunter is 40 years old and has been married to Joan, who is 38, for 15 years. They have a large property in Alderley Edge, an affluent village on the outskirts of Manchester. They both want children, but Joan had several miscarriages from 1972 to 1977, after which they decided to stop trying. She wants to adopt a Vietnamese child instead and Hunter is enthusiastic about the idea. While he loves his wife, he is also in love with Marshall, with whom he had an affair that he recently ended out of respect for both women. Hunter was brought up as a Catholic, but became sceptical of organised religion and renounced religious practice. He has no living family, maintains a good relationship with Joan's family, and has the social circle one would expect of a chief officer in a metropolitan constabulary. Hunter has had a remarkably successful career, a DS by 25 and the ACC for crime by 40, and is on a trajectory to lead his own constabulary. Although he worked on the Moors murders case in 1965, Hunter's reputation has been made with A10, the UK police's first anti-corruption unit, working on the Flying Squad and Dirty Squad cases in London and the Strafford Arms shooting in West Yorkshire from 1972 to 1977 (Root 2019). His commitment to and expertise in anti-corruption investigations has earned him the contempt of many junior and senior colleagues, who refer to him as 'Saint Cunt' (Peace 2001: 123). Hunter is physically capable, does not smoke, and drinks alcohol in moderation. He suffers from chronic back pain that is getting progressively worse and from chronic insomnia. He is also guilt-ridden, plagued with remorse for his personal and professional failings.

Marshall is in her early 30s and single. She lives in Fallowfield, a suburb south of downtown Manchester with a high proportion of university student residents. She has no close family, no friends outside of work, and keeps a dog as a pet. In the last two years she has had two intimate relationships with senior officers, one with Hunter for six to nine months and the other with Craven for a year or more. Although Marshall has not told Hunter, she is three months pregnant with his child when he recruits her to the covert inquiry. During the first week of the inquiry, she meets the Reverend Martin Laws, a psychopathic Anglican priest who thrives on human suffering, and confides in him. Laws encourages Marshall to terminate the pregnancy in secret and she is absent without leave for a day making the necessary arrangements. She has the abortion three days after Christmas. Marshall has also had a remarkably successful career, but it has been severely handicapped by institutional sexism. When GMP was created in 1974, women police officers were segregated from men in the Uniformed Women's Branch, had their ranks prefixed with 'Policewoman', and constituted only 5% of the constabulary (Richards 1975: 29).[1] Although women were fully integrated into the service following the Sex Discrimination Act 1975, restrictions of various types remained until the mid-1990s

(GMP Museum & Archives 2024). Marshall was recruited to the Vice Squad in 1970 and became one of the first women in Manchester and Salford Police (MSP) to specialise when she worked as an undercover officer. She subsequently transferred to the Drug Squad and is currently a DS in the Serious Crime Squad. Marshall is physically fit and has no addictions. The police practice of Marshall and Hunter provides insight into the different ways in which heroic struggle, edgework, absolute sacrifice, and worldmaking contribute to and detract from public protection.

6.2 Characteristics of the Practice

6.2.1 Heroic Struggle

The practice of policing is a heroic struggle because its purpose, public protection, can never be achieved in full. This limitation is underpinned by the unpredictability of the consequences of proactive policing and the inability of reactive policing to reduce anything more than the consequences of harm that has already been inflicted. Anti-corruption, internal affairs, or professional standards investigations are a crucial component of public protection because they protect the public from predatory, brutal, and dishonest police officers. Heroism is criminogenic when there is a mismatch between the difficulty and the morality of the struggle. The former replaces the latter as justification and individuals are acclaimed or admired exclusively for their struggle regardless of whether it is worthwhile. Anti-corruption work presents a related mismatch, in which police officers are condemned or despised exclusively for the morality of the struggle regardless of its difficulty. If anti-corruption investigations succeed, detectives damage the reputation of the institution by drawing attention to its corruption and are condemned by colleagues for their disloyalty. If anti-corruption investigations fail, detectives are despised by colleagues for both disloyalty and ineffectiveness and must, in addition, reconcile their practice of policing with its corrupt institutional situation. Hunter joined A10 because of his commitment to public protection rather than for career advancement, but has been rewarded with rapid – and much-deserved – promotion to

ACC. He is well aware of the cost of this commitment, the extent to which he is reviled and feared by junior colleagues and isolated from his fellow chief officers, and fully prepared for the lack of cooperation, sustained incivility, and open hostility he receives from the WYMP. Notwithstanding, Hunter underestimates Smith's antipathy to the covert inquiry. The selection of Hunter and his team from GMP implies at least tacit approval on Smith's part, which makes him vulnerable to the contempt of his colleagues. Smith is rude to Hunter when he reports to him on Friday 12 December and closes their meeting by expressing his lack of enthusiasm for GMP's involvement (Peace 2001: 25):

> Clement Smith nods and goes back to the work on his desk.
> I walk to the door.
> 'Peter,' he says.
> I turn around.
> 'You made up your mind pretty quickly?'
> 'Not something I felt I could refuse.'
> 'You could have,' he says. 'I would have.'
> 'I think it's an honour, sir. An honour for the Manchester force.'
> He goes back to the work on his desk again.
> I open the door.
> 'Peter,' he says again.
> I turn around.
> 'Let's hope so,' he says. 'Let's hope so.'

Smith's antipathy is problematic for Hunter because it contributes to the overdetermination of his removal from Leeds and the Ripper inquiry. All three of the cabal, the WYMP, and GMP want Hunter off the case and take independent steps to achieve their shared goal. The cabal, whose existence is unknown to Angus and Smith, is able to manipulate senior officers from both constabularies in order distract and discredit Hunter. This manipulation is particularly successful in destroying Hunter's reputation for integrity, creating a paradigm of heroic struggle in which the closer he comes to detecting organised corruption in the WYMP, the more his professional and public status deteriorates. On Monday 22 December, Hunter is set up for a fake press interview by two men using false identities who push him to reveal confidential information about Eric Hall and Ryan and to comment on alleged rumours that he is being removed from the Super Squad because of his relationship with Dawson. On Friday, the Clerk to the Greater Manchester Police Authority informs Hunter that Angus will be investigating allegations made against him. Hunter phones Smith to ask for details and Smith directs him to Angus. Smith's refusal is appropriate in the circumstances, but his failure to protest the appointment of Angus – whose constabulary is the subject of an ongoing investigation by Hunter – as investigating chief officer is, at best, highly unethical. Angus immediately dismisses Hunter from the covert inquiry and when Hunter asks him for details of his accuser (to which disciplinary regulations entitle him) at their second meeting, on Saturday 27 December, he stalls. That evening, Hunter's suspension is the *Manchester Evening News* headline, even though he has not actually been suspended (because of the lack of incriminating evidence). Hunter is not intimated by threats to either his reputation or his safety, but his official dismissal from the covert inquiry and public shaming by the press greatly reduces his effectiveness in detecting organised corruption, which suits all three of the cabal, the WYMP, and GMP. While Smith does not actively participate in the destruction of Hunter's reputation and career, he facilitates it by failing to provide him with institutional support. Smith's inaction is motivated by his distaste for anti-corruption investigations and his desire to distance both himself and GMP from the stigma they attach.

Marshall's heroic struggle is made more difficult by the interpersonal and institutional sexism she faces in GMP, which handicaps her capacity for public protection.[2] Five years after the criminalisation of gender discrimination in the workplace in 1975, the proportion of women police officers in England and Wales increased to 9%, but a mere 2% of police sergeants were women and GMP did not appoint a woman chief officer until 2007 (Jones 1986; GMP Museum & Archives 2024). As such, Marshall is required to overcome the challenges of sexism in addition to and as part of the challenge posed by heroic struggle. The former include being perceived as an inferior police officer by most of her colleagues, sexual harassment from those colleagues, and institutional gender discrimination. These challenges are almost continuous for Marshall and Hunter is one of the few colleagues to take her seriously as a police officer and treat her as an equal. Murphy is more typical, patronising and disparaging when Marshall responds to Hunter's concerns about witness discrepancies in the Ripper inquiry (Peace 2001: 246, emphasis in original):

> 'If this wasn't Joanne [Thornton] and the Ripper, then this couple have yet to come forward. If it was Ripper and victim, then the description is at odds with previous ones.'
> 'Unless there were two of them,' whispers Marshall.
> 'That's what I said,' winks Murphy.
> 'No, not two separate Rippers. Two of them together – doing the killings together.'
> 'What? A bloody tag-team.'
> 'Yes,' she says. 'A bloody tag-team.'
> No-one speaks, eyes moving from her to me and back again until –
> Until there's a knock on the door and a uniform says: 'Mr Hunter, Detectives Prentice and Alderman are here.'

Murphy simply assumes that Marshall is repeating the already-established likelihood that Strachan and Ryan were murdered by a second man. When he realises that Marshall is providing a new explanation – that there are two men hunting women together – his response is scornful. Murphy's scepticism is pure sexism, the product of the idea's source (Marshall, an inferior detective in virtue of being a woman) rather than its plausibility (which is supported by available evidence). Significantly, neither McDonald nor Hillman make a contribution and all three men look to Hunter for guidance on whether to include the explanation as a possibility.

6.2.2 Edgework

The practice of policing is edgework because it involves a high risk of injury, which can be reduced by competence in a specific skill set and is accompanied by a specific sensation and set of emotions. These emotions can become addictive, especially when the work is demanding in terms of time, commitment, and lifestyle. Hunter's risk of injury is heightened by the cabal, who deploy a complex and escalating series of countermeasures against him. The cabal opens its strategy by initiating the investigation into Dawson's financial irregularities, carefully calculating the cost of his peripheral affiliation with them against the benefit of his friendship with Hunter. They then orchestrate a series of encounters designed to distract and intimidate Hunter, which begin on Saturday 13 December when one of their associates, Peter McCardell, tries to cast doubt on Marshall's loyalty. On Sunday, Hunter is placed under intermittent but overt surveillance by two men with access to GMP headquarters. When Douglas and his daughter are murdered on Tuesday, Douglas' corpse is posed with an audio cassette recording in which Hunter is mentioned by name, providing both Evans and Smith with an opportunity to remove Hunter from the covert inquiry. Smith makes the offer to Hunter, but he refuses. From Tuesday 23 December, the cabal targets Hunter's safety as well as his reputation, sending him a letter purporting to be from the Ripper and threatening to kill his wife and (non-existent) children. They make one last attempt to avoid direct action by sending him photographic evidence of his affair with Marshall, but – unbeknownst to them – he does not receive it until Sunday 28 December (in consequence of working between two offices). On Christmas Day, Hunter's house is burned down while he and Joan are out. The cabal's initial manoeuvre bears fruit the following day when Hunter is dismissed from the covert inquiry, though he remains undeterred and meets Anderson on Sunday.

Hunter seals his own fate on Monday 29 December by telling Murphy about his progress with Anderson (Peace 2001: 398):

> 'What you going to do?' says Murphy.
> 'What do you mean?'
> 'You going to tell anyone?'
> 'Like who?'
> 'Alderman? Smith?'
> 'Why? What will they do?'
> He shakes his head: 'What will you do?'
> 'You wait and see.'
> 'What?'

'Wait and see, John.'
'You're going to rip this thing open, aren't you? The whole fucking place?'
'Wait and see,' I smile. 'Wait and see.'
'Fuck, Pete.'
I nod.
'Fuck, fuck, fuck.'

As their previous efforts at distraction and intimidation have all failed, the cabal's sole remaining option is to kill Hunter. The risk of detection accompanying the murder of an ACC is mitigated by the fact that Hunter has not yet revealed details of his investigation to anyone. Murphy has taken over as the cabal's main enforcer and understands that the task will fall to him. Whatever he has planned for Hunter is delayed by the Ripper interviews on Tuesday, but the cabal has a stroke of luck when Hunter unwittingly sets himself up on Wednesday. After learning that Craven is blackmailing both him and Marshall, he decides to confront him at the Strafford Arms. Craven has already committed suicide, leaving evidence that suggests he misdirected the Ripper inquiry by means of letters and tapes to the press and police. Hunter is reflecting on the implications of his discovery, sitting on a table with Craven's shotgun across his knees, when he hears a car pull up and footsteps crossing the car park (Peace 2001: 471–472, emphasis in original):

> They step inside –
> A rotting, eaten mattress against a window –
> They walk down the passage to the front –
> To the bar –
> They pull open another door –
> The door to the bar –
> The last door –
> Two figures in the doorway –
> Two shotguns –
> Two figures and two shotguns:
> Alderman and Murphy –
> Richard Alderman and John Murphy –

> The shotgun across my knees –
> The silent sixes, the shadows –
> Wings, huge and rotting things –
> Big black raven things that –
> That weigh me down, heavy and burnt
> That stop me standing –
> That stop me –
> Stop me –
> – *a shot*.

The last minute of Hunter's life is an intersection of all four characteristics of the practice of policing: the re-creation of social reality to reveal the links between the Ripper inquiry and the Strafford Arms shooting; the failure of the anti-corruption investigation courtesy of Murphy's betrayal; the black wings of Hunter's guilt for his professional and personal shortcomings; and the realisation of the risk of death.

Marshall is also the target of countermeasures by the cabal and one of the mysteries of the critical case study is whether her risk of injury is increased by her participation in the covert inquiry. Marshall is physically and morally courageous, refuses to be intimidated by men whether they are suspects or colleagues, and retains her composure under pressure. She was recruited to the MSP's Vice Squad very early in her career and worked as an undercover officer. In 1974 she was involved in an undercover operation against McCardell and his organised crime group (OCG) that resulted in his conviction for publishing pornography and procuring sex workers. Marshall infiltrated the OCG by masquerading as a pornographic model named '*Helen Mills*' for an extended period with limited support (Peace 2000: 300, emphasis in original). As is often the case in undercover operations, however, she was unable to maintain her cover for long enough to acquire the necessary evidence without undertaking the activities demanded by the role. In consequence, she posed for *Spunk* magazine and appeared in its third issue, which was published in January 1975 and included a photoshoot of Strachan. Notwithstanding the success of the operation in securing the conviction of McCardell and closing down *Spunk*, it did not penetrate to the magazine's financing by the cabal. It is not clear how the cabal became aware that Helen Mills was Helen Marshall, but it seems likely that either Murphy or Craven recognised her from the magazine.

Once the identification was made, Craven decided to pursue a sexual relationship with Marshall, following the example of his former partner Douglas, who married 17-year-old *Spunk* model Sharon Pearson in 1973. Marshall's relationship with Craven was longer than her relationship with Hunter and although there may have been an overlap between the two, it probably finished late in 1979 and started some time in 1978. Despite being an experienced and astute detective, Marshall grew close to Craven, deceived by his superficial charm and pathological lying. She ended the relationship after recognising his misogyny and psychopathy, but retained his habit of abbreviating 'don't mention it' to 'mention it' in conversation. She uses the phrase twice in quick succession while she and Hunter are watching MJM on Monday 22 December and he almost makes the connection between her and Craven in a brief exchange with Craven a few hours later (Peace 2001: 267):

> I'm the first out the door, heading back next door, when there's an arm on mine –
> Bob Craven: 'The Chief Constable asked me to have you meet him in Assistant Chief Constable Noble's office after the briefing.'
> 'Thank you very much, Inspector,' I say.
> 'Don't mention it,' he mutters, walking off.
> 'What?' I say –
> He turns: 'Pardon?'
> 'I said what did you say?'
> 'Don't mention it,' he smiles –
> 'Don't mention it?'
> 'Yes,' he says, walking away. 'Don't mention it.'

Hunter is preoccupied – and perhaps startled by Craven's proximity – addressing him by the wrong rank (he is a superintendent). Craven appears to be aware of Marshall's adoption of the phrase 'mention it' and of Hunter's suspicions, taunting him by repeating

166 Case Studies

'don't mention it' a second time. Though Craven's blackmail of Marshall includes a death threat (the photocopy of her *Spunk* shoot has a line drawn through her eyes), she refuses to be intimidated and warns Hunter about him.

6.2.3 Absolute Sacrifice

The practice of policing is an absolute sacrifice because public protection requires continuous self-sacrifice and the sacrifice of the interests of some others to other others, both of which are accompanied by an accumulated weight of responsibility. Marshall's sacrifice is not only absolute, but tragic, as she has forfeited her private life to a profession that does not value her because of her gender. She has no close family, no close friends outside of work, and does not even have anyone who can look after her dog when she is recruited to the covert inquiry. Marshall is almost completely isolated: from society in virtue of being a police officer and from the majority of her colleagues in virtue of being a woman. As a heterosexual woman working antisocial hours in an overwhelmingly masculine occupation, it is unsurprising that her intimate relationships have been with colleagues and she has recently made two poor choices. In addition to being five ranks her senior, Hunter is the chief officer commanding her division, creating a conflict of interest that could damage both of their careers. While he is in love with Marshall, cares for her deeply, and treats her with respect, he has no intention of leaving his wife, with whom he is also in love. They kept their relationship secret and a clandestine affair with one of her chief officers cannot have been very emotionally satisfying for Marshall. Her relationship with Craven is a danger to her physical and mental health, albeit less likely to harm her professionally (he is three ranks her senior in a different constabulary). Craven is a violent psychopath and vicious misogynist who has murdered or conspired to murder several people on behalf of the cabal, including at least two women, Strachan and Ryan. Instead of dispatching Strachan quickly, Craven violated her with his teeth and a milk bottle, raped her multiple times (one of which was post-mortem), and then kicked her to death. He was able to restrain himself with Ryan, but nonetheless chose the same slow means, kicking her to death. Whatever comfort and support Marshall received from him must have been extremely limited and entirely false, exacerbated by the relationship being conducted at a distance and kept private. Although Marshall ended the relationship once she recognised Craven's misogyny and psychopathy, she still experiences acute emotional discomfort in his presence.

Marshall's work on both the Ripper and covert inquiries involves further self-sacrifice in that she is required to pore over the details of the misogynistic violence suffered by the victims and interview Elizabeth Hall, who was subjected to an almost unimaginable ordeal by the gangsters who murdered her husband. She is also required to share a cramped office with Craven, which does not stop her from working her usual long hours. It is through Elizabeth Hall that Marshall meets Laws, a paedophile and sadist who has honed his abilities to perceive pain and manipulate people in pain to harm themselves or their loved ones. Laws discerns Marshall's vulnerability instantly, promptly establishes a rapport with her, and persuades her to confide in him. Misled by his apparent concern for her wellbeing and social status as a priest, she discloses details of her relationship with Hunter and his relationship with Joan. After Hunter ended their relationship, Marshall discovered that she was pregnant with his child and decided not to tell him. Her decision was based on her conviction that he would not leave his wife and her desire to protect him from personal and professional complications. Once the covert inquiry is underway, she has further reason to avoid sharing the news, not wanting to distract him from an investigation whose success is crucial to the protection of women in the North of England. Laws encourages Marshall to keep the pregnancy secret and have an abortion. This may well be what she wants, given her commitment to her career and her selfless love for Hunter, but Laws wants to consolidate their own relationship and make her more vulnerable to his manipulation in the future. Marshall terminates the pregnancy on 28 December and returns to work on 31 December, as soon as she hears about the Ripper's arrest, in spite of not being due back from annual leave until 5 January. The first thing she does is find Hunter, warning him about the blackmail and

Craven. He demands to know Craven's whereabouts and leaves before she can offer to accompany him.

Although Hunter has also sacrificed much of his personal life to his profession, working long hours, taking work home with him, and working away from home for months at a time, he has been able to maintain a for the most part happy marriage and a social circle beyond the police. Aside from Joan and Marshall, however, his relationships are not close, in consequence of which he has no idea that Dawson is involved with an OCG or that Murphy is part of the cabal. Two decades of police practice have taken a mental and physical toll on Hunter, who has chronic insomnia and chronic back pain. Notwithstanding his conspicuous courage, he suffers from anxiety, with recurring nightmares about work and nuclear war (Peace 2001: 9):

A shot –
I'm awake, sweating and afraid.
Downstairs the telephone is ringing, before the dawn, before the alarm.
The LED display says 5:00, my head still full of murder and lies, nuclear war:
The North after the bomb, machines the only survivors.
I get out of bed and go downstairs and take the call.

Hunter's mental health has also been affected by the quantity and quality of violence (murder) and corruption (lies) to which he has been exposed. On his first return home from Leeds, he tries and fails to have sex with Joan, but then has an erotic dream in which he is one of the participants in Elizabeth Hall's abuse and torture. Later that week, he has a similar dream in which Marshall is the victim.

While Hunter is not a practising Catholic, Catholicism continues to exert a powerful influence on his thoughts and emotions. He rehearses silent prayers in times of stress, appeals for God's assistance in creating order from chaos, and has an imagination saturated with Christian imagery (including demonic wings and the number 666). Hunter's dedication to public protection is accompanied by an accumulated weight of responsibility that is exacerbated by the significance of guilt to the Catholic Church (Tangney & Dearing 2002). He feels responsible for every anti-corruption and other case he failed to solve as well as cases to which he was never assigned, such as the Ripper inquiry. He is also aware of the extent to which his investigations cause rather than reduce harm, sacrificing the feelings and interests of some victims and witnesses to those of other victims and witnesses in the pursuit of sufficient evidence to secure a conviction. Hunter has a particularly intense pang of conscience while travelling between the interview of two vulnerable witnesses (Peace 2001: 298–299, emphasis in original):

> And then somewhere over the Moors again, I remember it's almost Christmas and I hate myself afresh, wondering what the fuck I thought I was doing, what the fuck I thought I was going to do, the bad dreams not leaving, just staying bad, like the headaches and the backache, the murder and the lies, the cries and the whispers, the screams of the wires and the signals, like the voices and the numbers:
> 666.

6.2.4 Worldmaking

The practice of policing is worldmaking because its goal, public protection, requires the re-creation of social reality. This re-creation is achieved by negotiating the relationship between power and powerlessness by means of the exercise of authority and the employment of discretion. Hunter has internalised the collective failure of the institution of policing to protect the public from the Ripper, which is not unique to him, as Reed points out (Peace 2001: 14, emphasis in original):

> 'I think like most senior detectives in this country, I think you feel West Yorkshire have lost the plot, that the *Ripper Tape* is bollocks, that he's laughing at us, the British police, and that you'd like nothing more than to have a crack.'

In addition to this collective failure, both of Hunter's anti-corruption investigations of the WYMP failed. The Strafford Arms shooting inquiry was closed in 1975 after two months without progress. A10 received an anonymous tip-off about Bradford Vice at the beginning of June 1977, but the inquiry was closed two weeks later, before it had even started, when Hall was murdered. Hunter's desire to revisit these inquiries is intensified by the personal losses that accompanied both professional failures. Joan miscarried in February 1975 and the Strafford Arms shooting inquiry was taken over by DCI Mark Clark, Hunter's friend, who had a heart attack from which he never recovered. Joan miscarried for the last time in June 1977, while Hunter was in the preliminary stages of the Bradford Vice corruption inquiry. He only grasps the degree to which the professional and personal have coalesced when he arrives in Leeds on Friday 12 December (Peace 2001: 38, emphasis in original):

> And sitting here, staring into the black marks, the dog hairs, I realize how long I've been waiting –
> Waiting for it all to stop:
> *Five years –*
> *Five years to come back and right the wrongs, to make it right, make it all worthwhile –*
> *The five years of marriage and miscarriage, of wet pillows and bloody sheets, of doctors and priests, of the drugs and the tests, the broken promises and plates –*
> *Five years of –*
> 'Manchester? You can go up.'

Hunter hopes that the resolution of his professional failures will make his personal failures meaningful and his recruitment by Reed, Evans, and Warren provides him with the opportunity to resolve the three failures for which he feels most guilty: the Ripper murders, the Strafford Arms shooting, and the Bradford Vice corruption. Hunter has a brief conversation with Joan after receiving Evans' summons (Peace 2001: 9, emphasis in original):

> After a few minutes I say: 'I've got to go to Whitby.'
> 'It was him then?' she asks, face still away.
> 'Yes,' I say, thinking –
> *Everyone gets everything they want.*

As such, the critical case study is a sustained evaluation of Hunter's worldmaking in terms of its public, professional, and personal benefits, costs, and consequences.

Hunter began his worldmaking on both the Ripper and covert inquiries prior to his recruitment by Reed, Evans, and Warren. He has been investigating the Ripper inquiry from a home office he built in his garden and calls 'The War Room' (Peace 2001: 21). When he was placed on compassionate leave after Joan's final miscarriage in 1977, he staked out Eric Hall's funeral and discovered that most of the attendees were from the Leeds division of the WYMP rather than the Bradford division. Once he has official sanction, Hunter conducts both inquiries to the highest legal and ethical standards until the start of the *Spunk* investigation on 20 December. He gains access to the Asquith and Dawson company records using questionable means and then removes the file on MJM illegally, motivated by the combination of the connection to Dawson and the significance of *Spunk* to the organised corruption. The following night, he breaks into the new premises in Batley and removes one of each available issue of the magazine (Peace 2001: 259–260, emphasis in original):

> I close the cupboard door and gather the magazines –
> I turn off the light with my elbow and walk back down the hall –
> I kick open the door and close it with my back –
> It won't lock and they'll know I've been –
> But that's OK:
> I WANT THEM TO KNOW I'VE BEEN HERE.

By this stage of the inquiry, Hunter suspects that countermeasures have been deployed against him. Even though the evidence he has retrieved will not be admissible in court, it seems likely to help him uncover the organised corruption. When Hunter is permanently removed from both inquiries on 26 December, Angus invites him to take extra leave for a month, but he continues the covert inquiry on his own and joins his colleagues in Dewsbury as soon as he learns of the Ripper's arrest. On arrival at the Strafford Arms in search of Craven, Hunter removes a hammer and a can of petrol from his car boot. While the hammer is a reasonable precaution given that he is unarmed, the petrol can suggests his intention is to kill rather than arrest Craven and thus commit murder himself. Hunter never has to make the choice, however, as Craven has already committed suicide.

Marshall's capacity for re-creating reality is much more limited than Hunter's, but her worldmaking just as interesting, if not more so. The difference in their respective capacities is a function of Marshall's gender, the creation of a representational order in which her contribution to public protection is marginalised and minimised, rather than their difference in rank. Although Hunter is a chief officer, Marshall is a DS in the constabulary's most senior investigative unit, a hard-earned and prestigious position that would be accompanied by preference and privilege were she a man. In spite of her mastery of the excellences and skills of the practice of policing and her commendable character, Marshall is not taken seriously by most of her colleagues and has been denied the prospects available to Hunter by her institution. This lack of professional and institutional support restricts her re-creation of reality, but there is also a sense in which her worldmaking is qualitatively distinct from Hunter's, an instantiation of collective feminine worldmaking rather than individualistic masculine worldmaking. Marshall dedicates her police practice to the success of Hunter's re-creation of reality rather than her own, supporting him immediately and wholeheartedly. She does not hesitate when Hunter asks to her to join the covert inquiry, notwithstanding the demanding nature of the workload and the risk that an anti-corruption investigation might aggravate both her marginalisation and alienation. When he asks for her assistance in pursuing *Spunk* as a lead, she agrees again, albeit with less enthusiasm (Peace 2001: 260–261):

> 'We're going to have to watch this place twenty-four hours.'
> 'What about the others?'
> I shake my head: 'Maybe later, but for now I want it to be just you and me.'
> 'Me, you mean.'
> 'If you don't want to do it, just say.'
> 'No, it's fine,' she says, like it's not.
> 'Thank you,' I say –
> 'Mention it,' she says.

Marshall's reluctance is because she anticipates the need to return to Manchester to arrange her pregnancy termination and because of the conflict of interest created by her desire to keep her identity as a pornographic model hidden from Hunter. Withholding this information from Hunter extends her support of his worldmaking from the professional to the personal by reducing the likelihood that his residual feelings for her will interfere with his progress on either of the two inquiries. In contrast to individualistic worldmaking, collective worldmaking requires the forfeiture of one's own re-creation of reality for a co-created representational order, which suggests a more robust link with sacrifice. Marshall's worldmaking is thus a product of power (her active support of Hunter's re-creation of reality) and powerlessness (the limitation of her re-creation of reality by sexism) and consequently more complex than Hunter's.

6.3 Situated Practice

6.3.1 Institution

Heroic struggle, edgework, absolute sacrifice, and worldmaking are characteristics of the practice of policing, the purpose of which is public protection. That practice is a situated practice, situated in both an institution and a systemic context. As the characteristics are emergent from the tensions among practice, institution, and systemic context, the Ripper and covert inquiries provide insight into the complexity of the relations among the characteristics of the practice of policing, policing as a situated practice, and public protection. An exploration of the tensions in the investigations of the murders of 13 women from 1975 to 1980 and the murders of six girls from 1969 to 1983 provides insight into the ways in which the institution of policing and the systemic context of policing can detract from public protection. As an institution, the WYMP has little to gain from the assistance of either the Super Squad or the covert inquiry. Public pressure to solve the murders of women in Leeds increased in May 1977, once they were identified as a linked series. The coining of the sobriquet '*Yorkshire Ripper*' by *Yorkshire Post* reporter Jack Whitehead elevated interest in the crimes from the local to the national by comparing the perpetrator to the most infamous criminal in British history, Jack the Ripper (Peace 2000: 87, emphasis in original). The sobriquet also raised the possibility of WYMP failure as the original Ripper murders were never solved (Sugden 1994). The murder of Rachel Johnson in Leeds in June 1977 (believed to be the Ripper's fifth victim, but actually his fourth) had a much more significant impact on public interest than Whitehead's comparison.

The first four murder victims were described by ACC Oldman as '*prostitutes or women of loose moral character*', but Johnson was a 16-year-old shop assistant (Peace 2001: 273, emphasis in original). Public pressure to solve the case increased again with the murder of Joanne Thornton in Morley in May 1979 (believed to be the 11th victim, but actually the tenth) and continued to mount with the following two victims: Dawn Williams, murdered in Bradford in September 1979, and Laureen Bell, murdered in Leeds in December 1980. Thornton, Williams, and Bell were, respectively, a bank clerk, a university student, and a student nurse. Oldman went as far as to describe the murder of Thornton as '*a terrible mistake*' and the Ripper as '*attacking innocents*' (Peace 2001: 244, emphasis in originals). The obvious implication is that the other victims were not innocent and thus in some way complicit in their own murders, which make his comments a clear case of victim-blaming (Ryan 1971). The relationship among police officers, victims of crime, and public opinion is, however, complicated by DCSI Maurice Jobson, who investigated the first two murders, in a conversation with Hunter (Peace 2001: 137–138):

'But Theresa and Joan, they were slags Pete. Whores, as they say over here. And no-one mourns a whore, except her kids, her husband, her mates, and bloody coppers that have to look at her dead fucking body in the snow. So no-one was right bothered, except me and my lads […].'

The rationale for both the Super Squad and the covert inquiry is the increased public pressure consequent on the murder of three women whose *moral character* is unquestionable and the apparent deterioration of Oldman's mental health after leading the investigation for three and a half years. When interviewed by the *Yorkshire Post* the week before Bell's murder, Oldman stated (Peace 2001: 13, emphasis in original): '*To me, he's like a bad angel on a mistaken journey and, while I could never condone his methods, I can sympathize with his feelings.*' The *Post* put ethical considerations above financial gain and contacted the Home Office instead of going to press. It is not apparent whether the Super Squad is actually intended to contribute to the Ripper inquiry or if it is simply a cover for the covert inquiry: Reed's comments to Hunter suggest the former, but the failure of one of its five members to attend its inauguration and the failure of the other three to liaise with Hunter suggest the latter. Either way, the creation of the Super Squad draws attention to the fact that the WYMP took two years to recognise the murders as a linked series and has made no progress after 13 murders in five and a half years. If the Super Squad is intended to assist the WYMP, then neither a negative nor a positive result benefits the institution's reputation. If the Super Squad fails to provide the Ripper Squad with any new leads, the stigma of its creation and the increased media attention to the WYMP's failure to protect the public remain. If the Super Squad's assistance results in the immediate or short-term detection of the Ripper, then they will receive the credit for solving the case. The Ripper Squad has been working without success since May 1977 so any progress that follows the Super Squad's intervention is likely to be attributed to the Super Squad.

The covert inquiry is even more of a threat to the WYMP than the Super Squad. Hunter's mandate is to review the whole inquiry and, once again, neither a negative nor a positive result will benefit the institution's reputation. If Hunter fails to provide the Ripper Squad with any new leads and fails to uncover any incompetence or corruption, then the stigma of the covert inquiry remains for those privy to its existence – which seems to be an increasingly large circle of senior police officers and senior civil servants. If Hunter's review results in the immediate or short-term detection of the Ripper, but fails to uncover any incompetence or corruption, then the WYMP retain the stigma of the covert inquiry without any credit for solving the case. If Hunter's review uncovers incompetence or corruption, then the reputation of the WYMP will suffer substantially given the media coverage of and public interest in the case. While the WYMP will gain in the sense of being provided with the opportunity to correct errors and eradicate corruption, CC Angus believes that any benefit to the institution's effectiveness and efficiency is outweighed by the cost to the institution's reputation. He is consequently uncooperative at the institutional level and antagonistic at the systemic level. At the institutional level, Angus and Noble deploy several tactics to undermine both of Hunter's investigations, beginning before his arrival in Leeds on Friday 12 December. Hunter and his team are provided with unsuitable accommodation and have no office in which to start their work on Saturday. An office is procured after Hunter complains, though there is a delay and he is not given keys for the filing cabinets. Noble exploits the question of access to the Ripper inquiry files to create further delays and to appoint Craven as Hunter's liaison officer. The appointment is for the practical purpose of keeping both investigations under surveillance, in addition to which Craven has symbolic significance because of his involvement in the Strafford Arms shooting. Noble has selected Craven precisely because Hunter does not trust him and his attachment to Hunter's team is an affront that is simultaneously subtle and public. Hunter and his team are eventually able to begin their review at 1700 on Sunday. When Hunter arrives at the office on Monday morning, he finds that someone has unlocked it overnight. After Hunter and Murphy interview Prentice and Alderman the following Sunday, Noble accuses Hunter of misconduct and reports him to Angus, who reports him to Evans, all of which cause further delay and discouragement. In essence, Angus and Noble do everything they can to hinder the progress and minimise the impact of Hunter's investigations short of failing to comply with Evans' orders.

The most significant influence on the investigations of the murders of 13 women from 1975 to 1980 and the investigations of the murders of six girls from 1969 to 1983 is neither CC Angus as an individual nor the wider institutional protection of the WYMP's reputation, but the existence of organised corruption within the WYMP. The core component of the organised corruption is a cabal consisting of seven police officers, an architect, and a builder. The cabal has its origins in a meeting between the two most senior officers and the architect and builder in July 1969, during the investigation of the disappearance of Jeanette Garland from Castleford. DSI William Molloy and DI Jobson meet John Dawson, Richard's brother and the '*Prince of Architecture*', and Donald Foster, '*Yorkshire's Construction King*', at the site of Dawson's future home (Peace 2002: 196, emphasis in originals). Although Molloy and Foster are already acquainted, the formation of the cabal gets off to a poor start when Jobson suspects both Dawson and Foster of providing George Marsh, one of Foster's foremen, with a false alibi.[3] Jobson remains ambivalent and retains some professional integrity until the cabal is threatened with exposure by journalist Edward Dunford in December 1974, after which he commits in full, murdering the Strafford Arms shooting witnesses with Molloy.

The cabal is formed *in camera* at the wedding reception of Sergeant Fraser and Louise Molloy (William's daughter) at the Marmaville Club in Mirfield (a small town between Dewsbury and Huddersfield) on 25 March 1972. Its purpose is to generate income by setting up an OCG run by police officers (Peace 2002: 324):

'Controlled vice,' says Bill [Molloy], quietly. 'Off the streets and out the shop windows, under our wing and in our pocket.'
Smiles.
'The whole of the North of England, from Liverpool to Hull, Nottingham up to Newcastle – it's ours for the taking: the girls, the shops, the mags – the whole bloody lot.'

A proportion of the profits from the controlled vice will be invested in The Swan Centre, which will be the biggest shopping centre in Europe and provide the cabal with a potentially inexhaustible source of legitimate income. Molloy is retiring to run the cabal full-time and Jobson will be promoted to DCSI and take over as head of Leeds City Police's Criminal Investigation Department (CID; Jobson is later head of the WYMP's CID).[4] The other police officers involved are DIs (later DSIs) Prentice and Alderman; Sergeant (later DI) John Rudkin and Constable (later DSI) Craven, two 'hard m[e]n just out of uniform'; and DI (later DCSI) John Murphy, of MSP (later GMP) (Peace 2002: 259). The cabal is inaugurated with a toast

(Peace 2002: 326): 'Bill raises his glass: "To us all and the North – where we do what we want!"'

In consequence of the strategy of the cabal, which includes Molloy's influence over chief officers, control of the WYMP's CID, and a self-interested commitment to protecting the WYMP's reputation, they are never detected. Only three people come close: Dunford in 1974, Whitehead in 1977, and Hunter in 1980. Dunford and Hunter are killed before they can make their suspicions public – Dunford likely by Rudkin and Hunter by Murphy and Alderman – and Whitehead has a mental health crisis from which he never recovers, courtesy of the influence of Laws. The cabal's first setback is the murder of Clare Kemplay in Wakefield in December 1974, which convinces Jobson that his initial suspicions about Marsh, Dawson, and Foster were right and motivates him to involve Dunford for the purpose of preventing the murder being pinned on the local travelling community. Marsh is indeed the murderer, part of a paedophile ring that includes Dawson and Laws. Jobson has the cabal's photo studio in Castleford burned down because it is connected to the paedophiles and Molloy succeeds in protecting the cabal by stage managing the Strafford Arms shooting. Foster is murdered by one of his OCG associates, Dawson commits suicide in order to avoid exposure as a paedophile, and The Swan Centre is never built. The identification of the Yorkshire Ripper brings unwanted media attention to the West Yorkshire sex trade in May 1977 and Eric Hall's relationship with Ryan brings unwanted anti-corruption attention to the WYMP the following month. At the same time, Molloy dies of cancer and Rudkin is forced to resign, emigrating to Australia. While Laws removes Whitehead as a threat, the Ripper inquiry continues to cause problems for the cabal, which is at its most vulnerable when Hunter and his team arrive in Leeds in December 1980. The combination of Hunter's perseverance and the Ripper's arrest prompts Craven to commit suicide so as to escape charges of murder and corruption, which provides the cabal with both a scapegoat and the opportunity to kill Hunter.

Hunter's intervention brings controlled vice to an end, but Foster's widow, Patricia, puts the cabal back on its feet by building The Ridings Centre, the first shopping centre with a food court in the

UK, in Wakefield in 1983 (Murphy 2013). Six months before the centre is due to open, the disappearance of Hazel Atkins brings unwanted media attention to the murder of Clare Kemplay, for which Michael Myshkin, a mentally and physically disabled man from Fitzwilliam (a mining village south-east of Wakefield), was convicted in 1975. Jobson killed Marsh, left his body in an abandoned mine, and then framed Myshkin to protect the cabal. When Hazel disappears, Jobson has doubts about whether Marsh was responsible. Angus once again prioritises reputation risk management, deciding that the cost of a wrongful conviction outweighs the benefits of publicly correcting institutional errors, and tries to dissuade Jobson from connecting Hazel with Clare. Jobson exploits Angus' unwillingness to reopen the case, protecting the cabal by framing an associate of Myshkin's for Hazel's murder and then arranging his death in custody. Hazel's murderer, Leonard Marsh (who was abused by his father, George), is detected by John Piggott, a solicitor who kills him in self-defence and in ignorance of the cabal's existence. The only remaining threat to the cabal is Barry James Anderson, who has returned to Fitzwilliam to take revenge on Laws, who has been abusing him for the last 16 years, since he was eight. Anderson takes his own mother hostage, kills Laws, and then commits 'suicide by police' when he turns his shotgun on Jobson. With Anderson dead, Jobson, Prentice, Alderman, and Murphy are free to retire on their superintendents' salaries and reap the rewards of their investment in The Ridings Centre.

6.3.2 Systemic Context

The covert inquiry Hunter is recruited to lead on Thursday 11 December appears both clearly defined and well-founded. Evans sets out Hunter's mandate as follows (Peace 2001: 15): 'Your brief is to review the case in its entirety, to highlight areas of concern, should any arise, to determine strategies, to pursue all avenues.' The rationale for the covert inquiry is that the institutions responsible for the governance of the WYMP have lost confidence in the constabulary's ability to detect the Ripper. This loss of confidence is in consequence of the combination of four circumstances. First, the increased public pressure to solve the case following the Ripper's perceived turn to 'respectable' women rather than sex workers since his murder of Thornton in May 1979. Second, since Thornton's murder the Home Secretary has authorised covert surveillance and the release of Department of Health and Social Security data that led to 200,000 interviews at a cost of £4 million without tangible results. Third, Oldman's inappropriate comments to the *Yorkshire Post*. Finally, the murder of Bell, who is not only the Ripper's 13th victim but the third 'respectable' woman in succession. Hunter is recruited by Evans, the Regional Inspector of Constabulary for Yorkshire and the North East; Reed, the Chief Inspector of Constabulary; and Warren, a civil servant employed by the Home Office.

The Home Office (Home Department) is the ministerial department responsible for citizen safety and national security in the UK. The Home Office is led by the Home Secretary (Secretary of State for the Home Department), who is currently supported by six Ministers of State, including the Minister of State for Crime, Policing and Fire. The Home Office is supported by the Ministry of Justice, which is responsible for the courts and prison and probation services (GOV. UK 2024). When the Metropolitan Police Force (now Metropolitan Police Service, MPS) was established in 1829, it was overseen by and accountable to the Home Secretary, who became the constabulary's police authority. The Home Secretary continued in this role until 2000, when the Metropolitan Police Authority was established – to be replaced by the Mayor of London in 2012 (Bowling, Reiner & Sheptycki 2019). When borough and county police forces were established in the 1830s, their police authorities were borough Watch Committees, which were replaced by Police Authorities in 1964 and Police and Crime Commissioners (PCCs, a category that includes Police, Fire and Crime Commissioners in some counties and the mayors of London, Manchester, and West Yorkshire) in 2012.[5] The Police Act 1964 was intended to establish a tripartite management system that would balance national and local priorities by sharing power among CCs, Police Authorities, and the Home Secretary, but the Home Secretary's control of operational policing increased substantially from 1994 to 2002 (Oliver 1997; Loader & Mulcahy 2003).[6] The Home Office Inspectorate of Constabulary (HMIC) was established in 1856 for the purpose of providing constabularies with a degree of central supervision. The role of His Majesty's Inspectorate of Constabulary and Fire & Rescue Services (HMICFRS 2024) has remained largely unchanged since: to represent the interests of the public by providing an independent assessment of the effectiveness and efficiency of constabularies (and, since 2017, fire and rescue services). The inspectorate is not part of the Home Office, but is one of the public bodies and agencies that supports the Home Office.

Evans leads Hunter's briefing and the presence of the head of HMIC and a single civil servant from the Home Office whose position is not disclosed suggests that the covert inquiry is being run by HMIC with the support of the Home Office. This is confirmed when Hunter is ordered to report directly and exclusively to Evans and the implication is that Evans will brief both his chief (Reed) and the Home Office (Warren) as the inquiry progresses. Warren briefs Hunter about the Super Squad and appears to be well-acquainted with the WYMP's chief officers, including Angus, Oldman, and Noble. He is also familiar with Hunter's career and with the details of his various investigations, including the planned investigation of Bradford Vice in 1977. In less than 36 hours, however, Evans' orders are countermanded and HMIC's covert inquiry undermined. Shortly after Hunter's arrival in Leeds on 12 December, Angus hands him a memorandum addressed to him, Evans, and Reed (Peace 2001: 42):

> The memorandum that in two sentences states that I have been invited by the West Yorkshire Metropolitan Police to review inquiries made into the murders and attacks attributed to the so-called Yorkshire Ripper; that I am to recommend any necessary changes to operational procedures, and that I am to make those recommendations directly to Chief Constable Angus. During the course of my review, should any evidence arise to suggest that any persons involved in the Ripper inquiry are themselves guilty or suspected to be guilty of any offences or negligence, then that evidence is to be immediately forwarded to the Chief Constable and no further or independent action is to be taken on the part of the review.

When Hunter phones Evans for clarification the next morning, Evans is noncommittal. Hunter presses him for an unequivocal response without success (Peace 2001: 51):

'So I should just ignore the letter?'
'Don't worry about it, I'll sort everything out.'
'I'm a bit concerned that…'
'Don't be. Leave the politics to me and just concentrate on the investigation. Any hint of obstruction on Yorkshire's part, pick up the phone and I'll put a stop to it.'
'Thank you.'
'Keep in touch, Pete.'

Someone has evidently informed Angus of the real purpose of the Super Squad and recommended that he take action to manage the risk to the WYMP's reputation. The likelihood is Warren, which suggests that the Home Office is concerned about protecting its own reputation as the ministerial department responsible for policing. Like the WYMP at the institutional level, the Home Office has weighed the benefit of correcting errors and eradicating corruption against the cost to its reputation and decided to prioritise the latter over the former. Angus' lack of cooperation at the institutional level is matched by his antagonism at the systemic level, at which he exploits the difference in priorities of HMIC and the Home Office to cast doubt on Hunter's authority and neutralise his efficacy. On Saturday 20 December Hunter is informed that Evans won't be available until after Christmas, which leaves him entirely on his own as Reed is on holiday in the Caribbean. Two days later, Angus tells Hunter that he spoke to Evans on Sunday and communicates what he represents as Evans' wishes. On Friday 26 December, Hunter is informed that allegations indicative of a disciplinary offence have been made against him and that these will be investigated by Angus. Angus tells him that his removal from the inquiry and replacement by Murphy have both been authorised by HMIC. In taking advantage of his relationship with Warren to exact revenge on Hunter, Angus plays into the hands of the cabal by appointing both Murphy and Jobson to key positions: Murphy will lead the inquiry whose actual aim is the detection of the cabal and Jobson will assist Angus in his investigation of Hunter. Angus' actions thus unite the WYMP, the Home Office, and the cabal in the common cause of maintaining the organised corruption in the WYMP.

The context within which the case is embedded includes 25 transcripts from *The John Shark Show*, a phone-in programme broadcast by BBC Radio Leeds, dated 29 May 1977 to 18 June 1977. The excerpts provide a sketch of the social, economic, and political circumstances of the period during which the two sets of crimes occur and a gauge of public opinion that reveals a nation divided by postcolonial melancholia, casual misogyny, and class antagonism (Smith 1989; Gilroy 2004; Beckett 2009). They also provide a commentary on the suitability of the criminal justice system for what most people take to be its primary purpose, the prevention, reduction, or control of crime. This commentary begins with the criminological concept of the dark figure of crime, which is discussed explicitly in two conversations, the first dated 31 May (Peace 2000: 50, emphasis in original):

CALLER: *During the past two or three decades criminologists in the US have been making systematic attempts to measure and analyse the dark figures of crime...*

JOHN SHARK: *The dark figures of crime?*

CALLER: *Yeah, the dark figures of crime, the proportions of people who have locked away their past offences quite unknown to the authorities or, if known, passed over. In a systematic study of sexual offences, Dr Raazinowicz doubted whether more than 5 in 100 ever came to light.*

JOHN SHARK: *That's outrageous.*

CALLER: *In 1964, he suggested that crimes fully brought into the open and punished represented no more than fifteen per cent of the great mass actually committed.*

JOHN SHARK: *Fifteen per cent!*

CALLER: *And that was in 1964.*

The dark figure of crime is a metaphor for crimes that remain unknown to the criminal justice system and the problem of measuring crime accurately became a core concern for criminology in the 1960s (Oba 1908; Radzinowicz 1964; Castelbajac 2014). Crimes that are neither reported by the public nor detected by the agencies responsible for law enforcement are necessarily unrecorded and, in consequence, necessarily unmeasured. The criminal justice system can only respond to the crimes it can measure and if unmeasured crime is a significant proportion of total crime, then regardless of how efficiently the system deals with measured crime, its effectiveness is severely limited. The criminal justice system and its constitutive institutions (including the police) are unlikely to be successful in controlling, reducing, or preventing crime if a significant proportion of it remains unknown to them.

The second conversation, dated 2 June, follows directly from the first (Peace 2000: 88, emphasis in original):

CALLER: *I'd like to ask Dr Rabonwick...*
JOHN SHARK: *Raazinowicz.*
CALLER: *Yeah, right, I'd like to ask him like, he's saying that all these crimes have been committed and no-one knows about them...*
DR RAAZINOWICZ: *Over eighty-five per cent, yes.*
CALLER: *Right. So my point is then, where are all the victims?*
DR RAAZINOWICZ: *The victims? The victims are everywhere.*

The caller is sceptical of the concept of the dark figure of crime and misunderstands its importance. The point is precisely that the number of victims of actual crimes greatly exceeds the number of victims of measured crimes and the creation of the National Crime Victimization Survey in the US in 1973 and the British Crime Survey (now the Crime Survey for England and Wales) in the UK in 1982 were attempts to measure crime beyond the scope of the criminal justice system (Bureau of Justice Statistics 2024; Office of National Statistics 2024). The criminological focus on victimisation furthermore suggests that the crucial issue may not in fact be crime but harm. In the first half of the 20th century, criminologists such as Willem Bonger (1905, 1938), Thorsten Sellin (1938a, 1938b), and Georg Rusche and Otto Kirchheimer (1939) established what would later be called the critical tradition of criminology, which is primarily concerned with legal harms, many of which are perpetrated by the state, business enterprises, and multinational corporations. As critical criminology expanded and diversified, zemiology (the study of harm) developed as a minor but nonetheless foundational field within the discipline (Schwendinger & Schwendinger 1970; Hillyard et al. 2004; Pemberton 2015). The criminal justice system and its constitutive institutions (including the police) can only respond to harms that are also crimes and to crimes that are reported or detected. Taken together, these limitations suggest that the criminal justice system in isolation is ineffective in the control, reduction, or prevention of harm.

The mechanism by which the criminal justice system controls, reduces, or prevents harm combines deterrence with incapacitation, i.e. dissuading people from offending or reoffending and restricting opportunities to offend or reoffend (Fassin 2018). Deterrence controls, reduces, or prevents harm by means of the public threat of punishment and the rehabilitation of individual offenders, but the former is notoriously difficult to measure and the latter has been regarded with increasing scepticism since the 1990s (Garland 2001; Farabee 2005; Tonry 2020; Brooks 2021). Incapacitation controls, reduces, or prevents harm by either removing offenders from society (prison) or limiting offenders' social interaction (probation), but mass incarceration is undesirable on both moral and economic grounds (Wacquant 2004; Alexander 2010; Wang 2018; Folan 2023). The effectiveness of both deterrence and incapacitation are thus limited. When one juxtaposes these limits with the limits on the scope of the criminal justice system established by crime that is unmeasured and harm that is not criminal, the full extent of its lack of fitness for the control, reduction, or prevention of harm is exposed. This, in turn, suggests that the effectiveness of the institutions of the criminal justice system in deterring harm is at least partly – and perhaps predominantly – determined by their reputations. These reputations are influenced by mass and social media, which shapes public perception of criminal justice effectiveness and the risk of victimisation. *The John Shark Show* transcript dated 6 June explores the relationship among public perception, the media, and the criminal justice system (Peace 2000: 163, emphasis in original):

JOHN SHARK: *Well, Sir Robert Mark said and I quote [reads]: The cancer of corruption which existed in the Obscene Publications Squad has been exposed and exorcised.*
CALLER: *Bollocks, John, that's what it is.*
JOHN SHARK: *You're not impressed?*
CALLER: *Course I'm not. He also said that none of it would have come to light if it hadn't been for the bleeding press. Not very bloody reassuring, that, is it? Relying on your lot.*
JOHN SHARK: *I believe Sir Robert said the whole country owes us a debt.*
CALLER: *Not from me you don't. Not from me.* [7]

The caller is equally sceptical of the police and the press, the former for being ineffective in controlling, reducing, or preventing harm and the latter for constructing, distorting, and amplifying the reality of that harm (Jewkes 2015; Ferrell, Hayward & Young 2015; Greer & McLaughlin 2023). The systemic context of conflicting and mediated public perceptions of police efficiency is not restricted to the juridical context, but includes the political context within which justice is administered. The transcript dated 17 June foregrounds the importance of the latter (Peace 2000: 372, emphasis in original):

CALLER: *You look through the paper and what do you see?*
JOHN SHARK: *I don't know, Bob, you tell me.*
CALLER: *[reads]: Baby battering claims six lives a week, injures thousands. Next page, every child in North waves at Queen. Then, seventy-four coppers quit every month and unemployment's up one hundred thousand. Rapes, murders, Ripper…*
JOHN SHARK: *What's your point, Bob?*
CALLER: *Callaghan bloody said it himself, didn't he? Govern or go.* [8]

As an institution situated in a systemic context, policing is limited by the effectiveness of both the criminal justice system and the incumbent government. Of equal – or, perhaps, greater – significance is the fact that the reputation of the institution of policing is partly determined by the reputation of the criminal justice system and the incumbent government. The institution of policing exerts no control over these reputations, in consequence of which its own reputation is extremely fragile, susceptible to public perceptions that it has no way of influencing. The investigations of the murders of the 13 women and six girls thus draw attention to the different ways in which the prioritisation of reputation risk management by the institution of policing, the vulnerability of the institution of policing to organised corruption, the impact of competition between government institutions, and the extent to which the criminal justice system is unfit for purpose detract from public protection.

Notes

1 GMP was formed by amalgamating Manchester and Salford Police with parts of Lancashire Constabulary, Chesire Constabulary, and West Yorkshire Constabulary (now West Yorkshire Police), becoming the second-largest constabulary in the UK. It is now the third-largest, behind the Metropolitan Police Service and Police Scotland.
2 I set out the differences among interpersonal, institutional, and systemic sexism and racism and between sexism and misogyny in Chapter 8.
3 George Marsh tortures and murders four girls from 1969 to 1974: Jeanette Garland (aged eight) in July 1969, Susan Ridyard (aged ten) in March 1972, Clare Kemplay (aged ten) in December 1974, and probably Christine Markham (aged nine) in May 1973. His son, Leonard Marsh, tortures and murders two girls: his first victim is unknown and his second is Hazel Atkins (aged ten) in May 1983.
4 The WYMP was formed in 1974, by amalgamating Leeds City Police and Bradford City Police with parts of West Yorkshire Constabulary. The constabulary's name was changed to West Yorkshire Police in 1986.
5 At the time of writing, all English and Welsh territorial constabularies are governed by a PCC with the exception of the City of London Police, which is governed by the Court of Common Council (Rogers 2017; City of London Police 2024).
6 I discussed these changes as part of my explanation of the politicisation of the UK police since the mid-1980s in Chapter 1.
7 Robert Mark founded A10, the UK police's first anti-corruption unit, in 1971 and was MPS Commissioner from 1972 to 1977.
8 James Callaghan is the incumbent Prime Minister, in office from 1976 to 1979. The reference to the Queen is to Elizabeth II's Silver Jubilee celebrations, which took place throughout 1977.

References

Alexander, M. (2010). *The New Jim Crow: Mass Incarceration in the Age of Colorblindness*. Revised ed. New York: The New Press.

Beckett, A. (2009). *When the Lights Went Out: Britain in the Seventies.* London: Faber & Faber.
Bonger, W.A. (1905/1916). *Criminality and Economic Conditions.* Trans. H. P. Horton. Boston, MA: Little, Brown Book Group.
Bonger, W.A. (1938/1943). *Race and Crime.* Trans. M.M. Hordyk. New York: Columbia University Press.
Bowling, B., Reiner, R., Sheptycki, J. (2019). *The Politics of the Police.* 5th ed. Oxford: Oxford University Press.
Brooks, T. (2021). *Punishment: A Critical Introduction.* 2nd ed. London: Routledge.
Bureau of Justice Statistics (BJS). (2024). National Crime Victimization Survey. Available at: https://bjs.ojp.gov/data-collection/ncvs#publications-0.
Castelbajac, M. de (2014). Brooding Over the Dark Figure of Crime: The Home Office and the Cambridge Institute of Criminology in the Run-up to the British Crime Survey. *The British Journal of Criminology: An International Review of Crime and Society,* 54 (5), 928–945.
City of London Police (2024). Police governance. Available at: www.cityoflondon.police.uk/police-forces/city-of-london-police/areas/city-of-london/about-us/about-us/police-governance.
Farabee, D. (2005). *Rethinking Rehabilitation: Why Can't We Reform Our Criminals?* Washington DC: The AEI Press.
Fassin, D. (2018). *The Will to Punish.* New York: Oxford University Press.
Ferrell, J., Hayward, K. & Young, J. (2015). *Cultural Criminology: An Invitation.* 2nd ed. London: Sage Publications.
Folan, E. (2023). The UK Has Its Own Mass Incarceration Crisis: It isn't just America. 2 January. *Novara Media.* Available at: https://novaramedia.com/2023/01/02/the-uk-has-its-own-mass-incarceration-crisis.
Garland, D. (2001). *The Culture of Control: Crime and Social Order in Contemporary Society.* Oxford: Oxford University Press.
Gilroy, P. (2004). *Postcolonial Nostalgia.* New York: Columbia University Press.
GOV.UK (2024). Home Office. Available at: www.gov.uk/government/organisations/home-office.
Greater Manchester Police (GMP) Museum & Archives (2024). History of Women in Policing. Available at: https://gmpmuseum.co.uk/collection-item/history-of-women-in-policing.
Greer, C. & McLaughlin, E. (2023). News power, crime and media justice. In: Liebling, A., Maruna, S. & McAra, L. (eds), *The Oxford Handbook of Criminology.* 6th ed. Oxford: Oxford University Press, 260–283.
Hillyard, P., Pantazis, C., Tombs, S. & Gordon, D. (eds) (2004). *Beyond Criminology: Taking Harm Seriously.* London: Pluto Press.

His Majesty's Inspectorate of Constabulary and Fire & Rescue Services (HMICFRS) (2024). About Us. Available at: www.justiceinspectorates.gov.uk/hmicfrs/about-us/what-we-do.

Jewkes, Y. (2015). *Media and Crime*. 3rd ed. London: Sage Publications.

Jones, S. (1986). *Policewomen and Equality: Formal Policy v Informal Practice?* Basingstoke: Macmillan Publishers.

Loader, I. & Mulcahy, A. (2003). *Policing and the Condition of England: Memory, Politics, and Culture*. Oxford: Oxford University Press.

Murphy, L. (2013). Landmark shopping centre celebrates 30 years. *Yorkshire Post*. 17 October. Available at: www.yorkshirepost.co.uk/business/landmark-shopping-centre-celebrates-30-years-1854701.

Oba, S. (1908). *Unverbesserliche Verbrecher und ihre Behandlung*. Berlin: Hermann Bahr.

Office of National Statistics (ONS). (2024). Crime Survey for England & Wales. Available at: www.crimesurvey.co.uk/en/index.html.

Oliver, I. (1997). *Police, Government and Accountability*. 2nd ed. Basingstoke: Macmillan Press Ltd.

Peace, D. (2000/2009). *Nineteen Seventy-Seven*. London: Quercus Books.

Peace, D. (2001/2009). *Nineteen Eighty*. London: Quercus Books.

Peace, D. (2002/2009). *Nineteen Eighty-Three*. London: Quercus Books.

Pemberton, S.A. (2015). *Harmful Societies: Understanding Social Harm*. Bristol: Policy Press.

Radzinowicz, L. (1964). The Criminal in Society. *Journal of the Royal Society of Arts*, 112 (5100), 916–929.

Richards, W.J. (1975). Greater Manchester Police Chief Constable's Report 1974 (1st April-31st December). Available at: www.ojp.gov/pdffiles1/Digitization/18856NCJRS.pdf.

Rogers, C. (2017). *Plural Policing: Theory and Practice*. Bristol: Policy Press.

Root, N. (2019). *Crossing the Line of Duty: How Corruption, Greed and Sleaze Brought Down the Flying Squad*. Stroud: The History Press.

Rusche, G. & Kirchheimer, O. (1939). *Punishment and Social Structure*. New York: Columbia University Press.

Ryan, W. (1971). *Blaming the Victim*. New York: Pantheon Books.

Schwendinger, H. & Schwendinger, J. (1970). Defenders of Order or Guardians of Human Rights? *Issues in Criminology*, 5 (2), 123–157.

Sellin, T. (1938a). Conflict and Crime. *American Journal of Sociology*, 44 (1), 97–103.

Sellin, T. (1938b). *Culture Conflict and Crime*. New York: The Social Science Research Council (Bulletin 41).

Smith, J. (1989/2013). *Misogynies*. London: The Westbourne Press.

Sugden, P. (1994). *The Complete History of Jack the Ripper*. London: Constable.

Tangney, J. P. & Dearing, R. L. (2002). *Shame and Guilt*. New York: Guilford Press.

Tonry, M. (2020). *Doing Justice, Preventing Crime*. New York: Oxford University Press.

Wacquant, L. (2004/2009). *Punishing the Poor: The Neoliberal Government of Social Insecurity*. Trans. anonymous. Durham, NC: Duke University Press.

Wang, J. (2018). *Carceral Capitalism*. South Pasadena, CA: Semiotext(e).

7
LOS ANGELES, 1947–1958

This chapter presents the third critical case study of the characteristics of policing as a practice and of policing as a situated practice. The case takes place in Los Angeles and is about the City of Los Angeles Police Department (LAPD) and County of Los Angeles Sheriff's Department's (LASD) investigations of a single, linked series, and multiple murder from January 1947 to May 1958. The context of the case is a history of police and political corruption that begins the day before the attack on Pearl Harbor in 1941, extends from Los Angeles to the rest of the US, Cuba, and South Vietnam, and ends in 1972, a little over a week after the death of J. Edgar Hoover. The critical case study is concerned with the involvement of three police officers in the three inquiries: LAPD Officer Dwight Bleichert's investigation of the Black Dahlia murder (1947), LASD Detective Deputy Sheriff Daniel Upshaw's investigation of the Wolverine Prowler murders (1949–1950), and LAPD Detective Wendell White's investigation of the Nite Owl massacre (1953). While all three of the cases are solved, none is solved quickly enough to prevent further murders, none of the perpetrators of the initial murders are prosecuted, and the unsatisfactory resolutions are only achieved at great personal cost to each of the officers. The focus on Bleichert,

DOI: 10.4324/9781003425922-10

Upshaw, and White demonstrates the significance of heroic struggle, edgework, absolute sacrifice, and worldmaking to police practice and provides insight into the different ways in which each can both contribute to and detract from public protection. An exploration of the tensions from which the four characteristics of policing as a practice are emergent in the case and its context provides insight into the ways in which the institution of policing and the systemic context of policing can detract from public protection. The 31-year-long history draws attention to the differential treatment of victims and the prioritisation of reputation risk management by the institution of policing and to the systemic racism and classism endemic to liberal democracy.

7.1 Case Summary

7.1.1 Black Dahlia Murder

On 15 January 1947, the mutilated corpse of 22-year-old Elizabeth Short is found in a vacant lot in Leimert Part, a neighbourhood in South Los Angeles. Her torso has been severed at the waist, with the intestines removed, and there is evidence of extensive torture. LAPD Chief Clemence Horrall details a squad of 100 detectives and plainclothes police officers to investigate. The squad is led by Detective Captain Jack Tierney (of Central Detectives), assisted by Detective Lieutenant Russell Millard and Detective Sergeant Harold Sears (both from Homicide), and includes the Central Division Warrants team, Sergeant Leland Blanchard and Bleichert. Short arrived in California from Boston in 1943 and spent the last four years making unsuccessful attempts to pursue a career in film, leading an itinerant life and surviving on charity from roommates and occasional sex work. She was a compulsive liar who exploited her associates ruthlessly and had dozens – possibly hundreds – of lovers, creating a large pool of suspects. Three days in, Bleichert interviews one of these lovers, Madeleine Cathcart Sprague, the daughter of Emmett Sprague, a Los Angeles property tycoon. Convinced that she has no connection to the murder, he accepts her offer to go out with him in return for omitting her name from the case files. They begin an initially brief relationship that fuels Bleichert's growing obsession with Short, which seems to be shared by Madeleine. Several of Short's other lovers are interviewed, but all active leads are exhausted by 5 February and the investigation is scaled back. Two days later, Bleichert exposes Detective Sergeant Fritz Vogel's brutal attempt to extract confessions from mentally ill suspects and is transferred back to uniform foot patrol for his disloyalty. Impressed by both Bleichert's integrity and intelligence, Millard keeps him on the case in an unofficial capacity.

The squad is dissolved on 15 March, with Millard and Sears continuing the investigation on overtime. In April, Bleichert goes to Mexico to look for Blanchard, who has been AWOL for two months, and finds his corpse, apparently the victim of his association with either corrupt police officers or an organised crime group (OCG). Bleichert marries and distances himself from the Short investigation for the sake of his mental health and his wife's wellbeing. He is unable to let the case go, however, and resumes his affair with Madeleine and his work with Millard in June 1949. On 29 June, the crime scene is discovered by a demolition crew working in the Hollywood Hills and Bleichert recovers the fingerprints of George Tilden, a former friend of Sprague's who is Madeleine's biological father. He withholds the information from Millard because he does not want to reveal his suppression of Madeleine's involvement in the case and confronts Tilden on his own. After killing Tilden in self-defence, Bleichert confides in Millard, who conceals Tilden's death to protect Bleichert's career. A week later, Bleichert realises that Short was killed by both Tilden and Ramona Cathcart Sprague, Madeleine's mother. Facing the same dilemma as before, he confronts her on his own and hears her confession. While deciding what action to take, he learns that Blanchard solved the case in 1947, blackmailed Sprague, and was murdered by Madeleine when he became too greedy. Bleichert arrests Madeleine and she confesses to Blanchard's murder, claiming to have been involved in a love triangle with him and Bleichert in order to protect her family from being connected to Short's murder. Bleichert corroborates her evidence, is dismissed from the LAPD on moral grounds, and the Black Dahlia case remains officially unsolved.

7.1.2 Wolverine Prowler Murders

On New Year's Eve 1950, the mutilated corpse of Martin Goines, a 33-year-old jazz musician, is found in a vacant lot in Allegro Street, West Hollywood, displayed to resemble the Black Dahlia. Upshaw is the LASD detective on call and identifies a suspect within the first 24 hours of the investigation. He asks his captain for assistance, but is told that he will only receive it if the victim is worthy of the resources, which seems increasingly unlikely as Goines appears to be a homosexual killed by one of his lovers.[1] Upshaw locates Goines' most recent address, which is in LAPD jurisdiction in North Tamarind, on 5 January. He breaks into the property, discovers that Goines was killed there, and finds evidence of a second and third murder the previous night. In consequence of the intensification of LAPD-LASD rivalry by a corruption scandal, Upshaw has been ordered to treat the LAPD with courtesy and decides against reporting the crime scene. The mutilated corpses of George Wiltsie and Duane Lindenaur are found in Griffith Park the next morning and LAPD Detective Sergeant Gene Niles is suspicious of the speed of Upshaw's response time. Goines' landlady alerts Niles to the crime scene the next day, but he is not interested in the case because both Wiltsie and Lindenaur are homosexuals with criminal records. Upshaw is given five more days to solve the Goines murder and pursues two leads on the mutilations, which were made with dentures constructed from wolverine teeth and a zoot stick, a weapon used by the LAPD during the Zoot Suit Riots of 1943.

On 8 January, Upshaw is recruited by Deputy District Attorney (DA) Ellis Loew, Lieutenant Malcolm Considine of the DA's Criminal Investigation Bureau, and Detective Lieutenant Dudley Smith of the LAPD Homicide Division for a grand jury investigation of communist influence in Hollywood. Upshaw agrees to infiltrate the 'brain trust' of the United Alliance of Extras and Stagehands (UAES) union as an undercover officer in return for leadership of an LASD-LAPD task force to investigate the Wolverine Prowler (Ellroy 1988: 15). He has, however, already visited Sunset Gower Studios to interview witnesses and is recognised as a police officer by UAES picketers. Upshaw is introduced to Claire De Haven, the linchpin of the brain trust, and her fiancé, Reynolds Loftis, on 13 January. That night, the Prowler murders a fourth man, Augie Duarte, leaving his corpse on the bank of the Los Angeles River. Duarte is associated with the brain trust and the Sleepy Lagoon Defense Committee, who were responsible for overturning the convictions of 17 Hispanic men for the murder of José Díaz in 1942. The following night, Claire exposes both Upshaw's cover and his repressed androphilia. Focusing on the Wolverine Prowler, he identifies Loftis' son, Coleman Masskie, as the murderer on 15 January. Masskie witnessed Smith commit the Sleepy Lagoon murder, had plastic surgery to conceal his identity, and has been trying to frame his father, with whom he had an incestuous relationship as an adult. When Niles' involvement in corruption results in his death, Smith encourages Deputy Chief Thaddeus Green, Chief of Detectives, to order Upshaw to take a lie detector test. Afraid of revealing his androphilia under the influence of sodium thiopental, Upshaw commits suicide. Considine and DA Special Investigator Turner Meeks complete Upshaw's investigation two weeks later. Masskie, Loftis, and Considine are killed in a botched arrest and Meeks flees Los Angeles after falling foul of his OCG associates, leaving the case officially unsolved.

7.1.3 Nite Owl Massacre

In the early hours of 14 April 1953, Delbert Cathcart, a sex offender and procurer with links to OCGs; Malcolm Lunceford, an ex-LAPD officer; and four other people are murdered in the Nite Owl Coffee Shop. The first detective on scene is Detective Sergeant Edmund Exley (of Hollywood Detectives) and LAPD Chief William Parker assigns the case to Deputy Chief Green, with Detective Lieutenant Smith (of Homicide) as his executive officer. Within a few hours, the sighting of a purple Mercury coupe in the vicinity is connected to earlier reports of young Black men discharging shotguns. A few hours later, Detective Sergeant John Vincennes (of Administrative Vice) and his partner arrest Raymond Coates, Leroy Fontaine, and Tyrone Jones. The suspects confess to kidnapping a woman at gunpoint and raping her multiple times before revealing her current whereabouts. White, a Homicide detective, rescues her and kills her abductor extrajudicially at Smith's bidding. The victim is unwilling or unable to specify the location of Coates, Fontaine, and Jones at the time of the murders and the investigation, which is taken over by Smith, focuses on finding the weapons used. While inquiring into Cathcart and Lunceford, White interviews Cathcart's girlfriend, Kathy Janeway, and establishes a link between the Nite Owl and a pornography case being investigated by Vincennes. Janeway is murdered on 20 April and White begins a long-term and unofficial investigation into the murders of seven sex workers from 1951 to 1958. On 25 April, LAPD officers find Coates' car and three shotguns, but the suspects escape from jail that night. The next day, Exley locates Coates, Fontaine, Jones, and an accomplice and kills all four of them, his excessive use of force motivated by fear. He is decorated for bravery and the case is closed.

In January 1958, Exley learns that the suspects did not commit the Nite Owl murders, but takes no action despite being head of Internal Affairs (IA). White discovers that the victim identified as Cathcart was an impersonator and leaks information to the media in February to embarrass Exley, whom he despises. A witness comes forward to exonerate the suspects and Parker reopens the case on 21 March. Smith is placed in command with Exley conducting an independent IA investigation using Vincennes and White. Vincennes determines that the impersonator was Dean Van Gelder, who had links to OCGs, and Exley connects the Nite Owl to Vincennes' pornography case and to control of the heroin trade in Los Angeles. White is only interested in the sex worker murders, suspects a musician named Spade Cooley, and confirms that the murderer is Arthur Perkins, one of his band members. Perkins was the driver for the Nite Owl, which was committed by John Stompanato, Lee Vachss, and Abraham Teitlebaum under the orders of Smith, who began a takeover of organised crime in Los Angeles when Mickey Cohen was imprisoned in 1951. On the morning of 29 March, Exley, White, and Vincennes bungle the arrest of Vachss and Teitlebaum, killing them in a shootout. Stompanato is in Mexico (and will shortly be killed by his girlfriend's daughter) so the only men who can testify against Smith are three convicts who were hired to kill Cohen in prison. Smith has arranged their escape from a prison train later that day and Exley's attempt to thwart it results in the Blue Denim Massacre, in which 28 prisoners (including the three witnesses), eight law enforcement staff (including Vincennes), and Perkins are killed. The case is closed for the second time and the murders attributed to an attempt by Perkins, Vachss, and Teitlebaum to expand their own OCG.

7.1.4 Bleichert, Upshaw, and White

The critical case study focuses on the practices of the three police officers who make the most significant contributions to the solutions of the Black Dahlia murder, Wolverine Prowler murders, and Nite Owl massacre respectively: Bleichert, Upshaw, and White. Bleichert is 29 years old and known as 'Bucky' because of his prominent front teeth. His father had a stroke in 1941, ten years after his mother's suicide, and he joined the LAPD to support him. In consequence of his father's German-American Bund membership, Bleichert was investigated by the Federal Bureau of Investigation (FBI) during his recruitment and succumbed to pressure to identify three of his Japanese American friends as subversives. They were all interned during the war and he has never forgiven himself. Bleichert was posted to foot patrol in Central Division after graduating from the LAPD Academy in July 1942 and met Blanchard a year later, during the Zoot Suit Riots. Bleichert and Blanchard are both former professional boxers and while Bleichert was working on radio car patrol in 1946, he was asked to fight Blanchard in a publicity stunt intended to encourage public support for a proposition to increase the LAPD's funding. He agreed, the proposition was passed, and he was rewarded with a transfer to Central Division Warrants, a plainclothes unit, in November. Bleichert is single and has a small social circle centred around Blanchard and Blanchard's girlfriend, Kay Lake. He is unaware of Blanchard's corruption and marries Lake in May 1947, shortly after Blanchard's murder. Bleichert is physically imposing – a lean and muscular six foot, three inches – and retains much of the strength, speed, and endurance he enjoyed as a professional athlete. His skill set includes competence with his baton and revolver and he very rarely resorts to excessive force in the performance of his duties. Bleichert's boxing career was hampered by his aversion to being hurt and he still feels fear during confrontations despite being physically courageous. He does not smoke and drinks alcohol in moderation.

Upshaw is 27 years old, single, and leads a solitary life. He is from San Bernadino and although he was brought up by his mother on her own, they are not close. Upshaw was a thrill-seeking car thief in high school and at San Bernardino Junior College, where he studied biology. His attempt to enlist when war was declared failed because of a punctured ear drum. He is a loner, but is not antisocial and was motivated to join the LASD in 1944 after witnessing the murder of a woman by two men. Upshaw's career progress has been rapid, from jail duty to uniformed patrol to detective in four and a half years, making him the youngest detective in the West Hollywood Substation by a decade. He has no personal life and is entirely focused on his police practice, to which he is dedicated to the point of devotion. He is highly-strung, restlessly energetic, and driven by a single-minded desire to protect the public. Upshaw hones his police practice both informally and formally, studying the work of contemporary criminologists and taking a forensic pathology course at the University of Southern California (USC). He is sexually naïve and voluntarily celibate. Expressions of sexuality by others make him uncomfortable, which appears prudish but is a component of the repression of his own sexuality for the purpose of avoiding his androphilia. Upshaw has a platonic relationship with Karen Hiltscher, the LASD dispatcher at West Hollywood, and occasionally takes advantage of her romantic interest in him. He is of medium height and build, physically fit, resilient, and robust. Upshaw does not smoke, is addicted to alcohol, and controls that addiction by restricting himself to four shots of bourbon a day.

White, who uses 'Bud' as his given name, is 34 years old and single with no family. His father was a violent alcoholic and his mother the victim of intimate partner violence. When White was 16, his father handcuffed him to his bed, beat his mother to death with a tyre iron, and fled. White was in the room with his mother's decomposing corpse and without water or food for a week until a truant officer found him. His father was arrested, convicted of manslaughter, and served 12 years in prison. White had a brief career as a professional football player that was cut short by injury before joining the LAPD. He has never recovered from the trauma of his childhood and decided to kill his father when he was released on parole, but was unable to locate him before he absconded and disappeared. Notwithstanding his awareness of his intellectual limitations, White's career goal was to become a detective. He joined Central Division Detectives before being transferred to the Homicide Adjunct Surveillance Detail (HASD, later known as the Mobster Squad) in 1952 and Homicide itself the following year. He is assigned to the Nite Owl case for the duration of the initial investigation. White is promoted to detective sergeant in 1958, detailed to Hollywood Division Detectives, and then seconded to IA when the Nite Owl is reopened. He is popular with women and begins a long-term but intermittent relationship with Lynn Bracken, a former sex worker, in 1954. White is over six foot tall, heavily built, and extremely strong. In spite of a permanent limp, he is highly proficient in physical confrontations, whether unarmed or armed, and has a well-deserved reputation as the toughest police officer in the LAPD. He smokes cigarettes and drinks alcohol, both in moderation. The police practice of White, Upshaw, and Bleichert provides insight into the different ways in which heroic struggle, edgework, absolute sacrifice, and worldmaking contribute to and detract from public protection.

7.2 Characteristics of the Practice

7.2.1 Heroic Struggle

The practice of policing is a heroic struggle because its purpose, public protection, can never be achieved in full. This limitation is underpinned by the unpredictability of the consequences of proactive policing and the inability of reactive policing to reduce anything more than the consequences of harm that has already been inflicted. Upshaw's police practice epitomises heroic struggle: the struggle was his motivation to join the police, is a characteristic of which he is continuously aware, and is a characteristic whose difficulty only makes him more determined to protect the public to the greatest extent possible. While his revelling in the difficulty of the struggle is not criminogenic, it is part of his repression of his sexuality and the combination of that repression with his determination increases his opportunities for career success. Ironically, the incident that caused Upshaw to join the LASD was his split-second witnessing of a woman being hacked to death with an axe while he was fleeing from the police in a stolen car in 1941. The image of the victim screaming as her arm was severed and his failure to do anything about it haunted him. Upshaw investigated the incident in an amateur capacity, identifying the woman as Kathy Hudgens, a missing person, and the murderers as Marty Sidwell, her lover, and Harland Jastrow, his friend. Sidwell died during the war, Jastrow disappeared, and Upshaw joined the LASD to 'to know WHY' people perpetrate acts of extreme violence (Ellroy 1988: 34, emphasis in original). He has searched for Jastrow unsuccessfully ever since and keeps a photograph of him as a reminder of both the difficulty and the value of the struggle to protect the public (Ellroy 1988: 74):

> A mug blowup of Harlan 'Buddy' Jastrow, Kern County axe murderer and the jolt that made him a cop, glared from the wall above his desk; some deputy who'd heard about his all-point want on the man had drawn a Hitler mustache on him, a speech balloon extending from his mouth: 'Hi! I'm Deputy Upshaw's nemesis! He wants to fry my ass, but he won't tell anybody why! Watch out for Upshaw! He's a college boy prima donna and he thinks his shit don't stink!'

The Wolverine Prowler case is a greater heroic struggle than the murder of Hudgens for several reasons. First, there is a more significant threat to the public. Upshaw begins his investigation after Masskie's first murder and Masskie kills three more victims before he is identified as the murderer. Second, the case is more complex, originating in a series of events that began several years before, confounded by Masskie's attempt to frame Loftis, and complicated by its connection to the UAES brain trust. Finally, Upshaw is faced with several institutional impediments – the perceived lack of quality of the first victim, the homosexuality of the second and third victims, and the hostility between the LASD and LAPD – that challenge and limit the investigation. In consequence, the Wolverine Prowler case supplants the Hudgens' murder as Upshaw's rationale for his police practice (Ellroy 1988: 194, emphasis in original):

> Danny paused, drank and sighted in on the mugboard around Jastrow's neck: Kern County Jail, 3/4/38. 'Sometimes I think that if I know who this guy [the Wolverine Prowler] is and why he does it, then I'll know something so big that I'll be able to figure out all the everyday stuff like cake. I can get on with making rank and handling meat and potatoes stuff because everything I ever sensed about what people are capable of came together on one job, and I nailed *why*. *Why*. Fucking *why*.'

The institutional impediments drive Upshaw to participate in the grand jury investigation, which brings him into the orbit of Smith, which leads to his death. As such, the Wolverine Prowler case is a classic heroic struggle, a fatal investigation that has to be picked up by someone else (Meeks), who also fails to achieve an official resolution.

White's childhood provided a first-hand example of the extent to which the criminal justice system fails to protect victims of violence against women and girls (VAWG) and his own victimhood has shaped a desire for retribution rather than justice. When he joins the Detective Bureau his partner and mentor, Detective Sergeant Richard Stensland, helps White to control his disposition for vengefulness so that it is enacted in acceptable (if not entirely legal) ways. White's particular set of skills and disposition are not only encouraged but exploited by his senior officers, including Chief Parker. In January 1952, Parker details him to crowd control at a film location because he 'wanted a muscle guy there to shoo away autograph hounds' (Ellroy 1990: 43). More ominously, Smith recruits him to the HASD three months later, introducing the unit as follows (Ellroy 1990: 342): 'Now, my job is to deter and contain organized crime in Los Angeles, and I have found that physical force often serves as the most persuasive corrective measure.' The HASD is a proactive policing tactic approved by Parker that involves threatening, intimidating, and if necessary assaulting any OCG affiliates suspected of attempting to fill the vacuum created by Cohen's imprisonment. Smith continues, calling it 'a duty that few men are fit for, but you were born for' (Ellroy 1990: 71). Unbeknownst to Parker and White, Smith is maintaining the vacuum in order to fill it with his own OCG, using heroin he stole from Cohen in 1950. White is not particularly enthusiastic about the HASD, but accepts the role because he is facing departmental and possibly legal action for excessive force and because he sees it as a means to the end of becoming a Homicide detective, which it is.

White's psychological struggle, which is inextricable from the heroic struggle of his police practice, is that he wants to be 'a real detective', a police officer who protects the public by negotiating the criminal justice system rather than by enacting personal vengeance (Ellroy 1990: 291). The combination of his lack of intellectual aptitude and the institutional exploitation of his skills and disposition thwarts this goal. When White meets Bracken in 1953, he opens up to her (Ellroy 1990: 238):

> Bud rambled on the Nite Owl, his strongarm job in the morning – sitting-duck stuff he couldn't take much more of. [...] He knew she knew the gist: he was frustrated because he wasn't that smart, he wasn't really a Homicide detective – he was the guy they brought in to scare the other guys shitless.

White is not only aware of his limitations, but tries to overcome them, attending criminology and forensic science classes at USC and the FBI's Criminal Investigation Procedures seminar, all at this own expense. The following year, he takes the sergeant's examination for the third time and achieves a score of 89%. At the same time, White exerts greater self-control over his desire for retribution, ceases his intimidation of the perpetrators of VAWG, and avoids any further excessive force accusations. Although he never loses his propensity for violence, he solves both the sex worker murders and the Nite Owl massacre (Ellroy 1990: 477):

> He [Exley] found detailed notes on White's prostitute-killing investigation. The notes were a limited man reaching for the stars, pulling most of them down. Limits exceeded through a brilliantly persistent rage. Absolute justice – anonymous, no rank and glory. [...] Room 11 at the Victory Motel – Wendell 'Bud' White seen for the first time.

In spite of this psychological victory, White's heroic struggle ultimately ends in failure as he is retired on medical grounds and unable to realise his potential as a real detective.

7.2.2 Edgework

The practice of policing is edgework because it involves a high risk of injury, which can be reduced by competence in a specific skill set and is accompanied by a specific sensation and set of emotions. These emotions can become addictive, especially when the work is demanding in terms of time, commitment, and lifestyle. The initial Nite Owl investigation does little to heighten the risk of injury to the police officers involved. The entire Detective Bureau is detailed to find three armed men who are rapists rather than murderers and have no intention of resisting arrest (although the detectives do not know this). White kills Sylvester Fitch, who is keeping Inez Soto captive as a sex slave, extrajudicially. After Coates, Fontaine, and Jones escape, Exley, who is on his own, finds them with their associate, Roland Navarette. Exley is afraid of physical confrontations and intimidated by the four men, even though they are unarmed and he is pointing a shotgun at them. When Coates taunts him for his cowardice, Exley is unable to control himself and shoots them all dead. As the five men killed by police in the course of the investigation are all Black, poor, and either ex-offenders or associates of ex-offenders, no departmental or legal action is taken against White or Exley. Exley is, in fact, awarded the LAPD's Medal of Valor and promoted two ranks, to detective captain, in order to protect the LAPD's reputation by creating a hero that the media can lionise. The second Nite Owl investigation is much more dangerous as it occasions direct conflict with the OCG established by Smith.

On 27 March 1958, Vincennes is shot five times by Pierce Patchett, Smith's partner in the drug and pornography trade, but saved by his ballistic vest. Patchett is killed by Stompanato, Vachss, and Teitlebaum before he can administer the *coup de grace* to Vincennes. Early on the morning of 29 March, Exley learns that the three witnesses to Smith's corruption are being transferred to San Quentin State Prison and that Vachss and Teitlebaum are meeting at Teitlebaum's deli. White suggests they arrest the two suspects on the premises. Exley weighs the risk of arresting two armed murderers in a public place against the speed with which Smith is covering up his connection to the Nite Owl and decides on immediate action.

As the detectives arrive at the deli, Exley realises he has forgotten his service revolver, further escalating the risk to them and to the public. He follows Vincennes and White inside (Ellroy 1990: 465–466):

> Chimes. Kikey [Teitlebaum] glanced over, reached under the register. Ed [Exley] saw Vachss make heat, make like he was smoothing his trousers. Metal flashing waist-high.
>
> People ate, talked. Waitresses circulated. Trash [Vincennes] walked toward the register; White eyeballed Vachss. Metal flashed: under the table coming up.
>
> Ed pulled White to the floor.
>
> Kikey and Vincennes drew down.
>
> Crossfire – six shots – the window went out, Kikey hit a stack of canned goods. Screams, panic runs, blind shots – Vachss firing wild toward the door. An old man went down coughing blood; White stood up shooting, a moving target – Vachss weaving back toward the kitchen. A spare on White's waistband – Ed stumbled up, grabbed it.
>
> Two triggers on Vachss. Ed fired – Vachss spun around grabbing his shoulder. White fired wide; Vachss tripped, crawled, stood up – his gun to a waitress' head.
>
> White walked toward him. Vincennes circled left; Ed circled right. Vachss blew the woman's brains out point-blank.
>
> White fired. Vincennes fired. Ed fired. No hits – the woman's body took their shots. Vachss inched backward. White ran up; Vachss wiped brains off his face. White emptied his gun – all head shots.

Teitlebaum has sustained a fatal chest wound and Exley and Vincennes question him while he is dying. White, whose attempts to control his desire for retribution have been only partially successful, kills him after his confession (Ellroy 1990: 467): 'White walked over, winked at Ed. "Thanks for the push," stepped on Kikey T.'s face until he quit breathing.' Like the decisions many police officers have to make, Exley's decision to effect the arrests at the deli has to be taken very quickly in spite of its serious consequences. Three bystanders are killed in the shootout and their relatives subsequently sue the LAPD for reckless endangerment. The arrest ultimately provides the information Exley seeks, which allows him to attempt to foil the prison escape Smith has orchestrated. Exley is, however, too late and the witnesses are killed in the Blue Denim Massacre, eliminating the final opportunity to connect Smith to the Nite Owl. Vincennes is also killed in the Blue Denim Massacre and White wounded so badly that he is retired on medical grounds. In retrospect, Exley's decision to arrest Vachss and Teitlebaum was wrong, although it was justified at the time it was taken.

While the LAPD discourages plainclothes police officers working alone from arresting suspects, LASD detectives are required to work on their own and expected to make arrests if necessary. Working alone either raises a police officer's risk of injury or limits the action she can take, or both. Upshaw's only means of communicating with the West Hollywood Substation is by telephone, which escalates the risk by delaying the speed with which he can request and receive assistance. As one might expect, Upshaw refuses to allow working on his own to limit his investigation, in consequence of which his risk of injury is raised and his competence in risk reduction tested. He begins by questioning nightclub staff in the 'Negro slums' of South Los Angeles (Ellroy 1988: 39). In Club Zombie, he actually interviews Masskie, who takes the opportunity to mislead him in to believing that Goines was homosexual. At Tommy Tucker's Playroom, Upshaw detains a man smoking cannabis in his car, learns the name of a local heroin dealer, and goes to his apartment, where he is threatened with a switchblade. Four nights later, Upshaw discovers the crime scene and decides to wait, on his own, in case the suspect returns to it. When Goines' burglary accomplice, Leo Bordoni, breaks into the apartment, Upshaw detains him without resorting to excessive force and continues his vigil after letting him leave.

Ironically, Upshaw is exposed to the greatest risk of injury when he is given assistance in the form of an LASD-LAPD task force on the tenth day of the Wolverine Prowler case. The cost of this command is the undercover operation for the Deputy DA, which is not particularly dangerous itself, but puts him under Smith's command. When Upshaw makes the connection among the Wolverine Prowler murders, UAES brain trust, and Sleepy Lagoon murder through Loftis, Smith is one step ahead of him. Smith has detected Upshaw's androphilia and has him questioned as a suspect in Niles' murder. Smith convinces Green that Upshaw is guilty and manipulates him in to allowing Upshaw to return home with his service pistol knowing that he has to face a polygraph test the following day. When Upshaw is released, Smith meets him outside City Hall (Ellroy 1988: 314–315):

> 'You're finished.'
> 'No, lad. You are. I've been talking to my old friend Felix Gordean, and he painted me a vivid picture of your emergence. Lad, next to myself Felix has the finest eye for weakness I've ever encountered. He knows, and when you take that lie detector test tomorrow, the whole world will know.'
> Danny said, 'No.'
> Dudley Smith said, 'Yes,' kissed him full on the lips and walked away whistling a love song.[2]

Upshaw discovers that his private case files have been stolen, realises that he will not be able to bring Smith to justice, and decides to commit suicide to avoid the destruction of his reputation.

7.2.3 Absolute Sacrifice

The practice of policing is an absolute sacrifice because public protection requires continuous self-sacrifice and the sacrifice of the interests of some others to other others, both of which are accompanied by an accumulated weight of responsibility. By the time

Short's corpse is discovered, Bleichert has been in Central Warrants for two months and on the trail of Raymond Nash for five days. Nash is a prolific and persistent violent and sexual offender with a criminal record of over two decades. Since his last prison sentence, he is suspected of committing a dozen armed robberies in San Francisco and has recently committed two in Leimert Park, the most recent of which resulted in the death of an elderly woman. Bleichert and Blanchard are looking for Nash in Leimert Park early on the morning of 15 January when they see three police cars parked half a block away and find Millard and Sears at the Short crime scene. Bleichert is immediately sceptical about the amount of resources dedicated to the case, but very quickly becomes obsessed with Short. He reveals his scepticism in a conversation with Blanchard later that day (Ellroy 1987: 72–73):

> Lee shook his head. 'Partner, this is *big*. Horrall and Thad Green were down here a couple of hours ago. Jack Tierney's been detached to Homicide to run the investigation, with Russ Millard backstopping. You want my opinion?'
> 'Shoot.'
> 'It's a showcase. A nice white girl gets snuffed, the Department goes all out to get the killer to show the voters that passing the bond issue will get them a bulldog police force.'
> 'Maybe she wasn't such a nice girl. Maybe that old lady that Nash killed was somebody's loving granny. Maybe you're taking this thing too personal, and maybe we let the Bureau handle it and get back to our job before Junior [Nash] kills somebody else.'

Bleichert is concerned about sacrificing Nash's recent and future victims – as well as the victims of the cases that the dozens of detectives will not be investigating – to Short.

Two days later, he asks Millard if he thinks Short's life is worth the resources being deployed and requests a return to Warrants. Millard refuses and asks him for his opinion, to which he replies (Ellroy 1987: 94):

'She said yes or no to the wrong guy, at the wrong time, at the wrong place. And since she's had more rubber burned on her than the San Berdoo Highway, and doesn't known how to tell the truth, I'd say that finding that wrong guy is going to be a hell of a job.'

Unlike many others and in spite of the language he uses, Bleichert neither judges Short's character nor holds her responsible for her own murder. His concern is that the case is unlikely to be solved despite the resources dedicated to it. Notwithstanding Millard's refusal to detach him, Bleichert spends five hours searching for Nash on Crenshaw Boulevard and South Western Avenue only to be asked by interviewees why he isn't searching for the Black Dahlia's murderer. Bleichert's obsession with Short begins with Madeleine, whom he sees for the first time that night. The following day he asks Millard to return to Warrants again, with the same result, and then interviews Madeleine, who is intentionally exaggerating her natural resemblance to Short. To Bleichert's dismay, further officers are detailed the day after, bringing the squad to its peak strength of 190 detectives and police officers on 19 January, which is when his relationship with Madeleine begins. Two days later, Nash robs a Japanese greengrocer, murdering the proprietor and his 14-year-old son, and is shot dead by an off-duty LASD detective. By the end of the month, Bleichert is fantasising that Madeleine is Short when they have sex, with her encouragement. His mental health deteriorates over the next two and a half years and he is unable to effect a recovery until the case is solved.

By 1958, the Nite Owl case is a 'dense series of criminal conspiracies at least five years old resulting in no fewer than four and perhaps as many as a dozen major crimes' (Ellroy 1990: 348). It is only solved because White decides to sacrifice his time and money to both improve his police practice and investigate the sex worker murders. Although this is an authentic sacrifice on his part, his motivation combines selfless and selfish reasons. White holds Exley responsible for Stensland's dismissal from the LAPD, his conviction for two murders committed during an armed robbery, and his execution in November 1954. While White has a genuine desire to improve his police practice, he takes an extended leave of absence in order to avoid working under Exley's supervision and pays for his studies during this time using stolen money left to him by Stensland. His authentic sacrifice becomes absolute sacrifice when he begins his own investigation into the Nite Owl, sacrificing the victims of the sex worker murders to the victims of the Nite Owl massacre. White's motivation is, once again, complex, a desire to embarrass Exley, but also a desire to protect the public by solving the case and become a real detective in the process. He was never convinced that Coates, Fontaine, and Jones were the Nite Owl murderers and always believed that the case was far more complex than Exley realised, starting with the connection to the pornography.

White makes significant progress on the Nite Owl in January 1958, when he finds Cathcart's corpse and confirms his suspicion that the victim at the Nite Owl (Van Gelder) was an impersonator. Although he does not yet know who was responsible, he realises that the murder is connected to organised crime in Los Angeles and begins leaking information to the press. In the middle of March, Lynette Kendrick is murdered. White suspects she is the seventh victim in the linked series and switches his extracurricular attention back to that case. Exley has been preparing for the reopening of the Nite Owl, recruits Vincennes as an ally, and coerces White to join them. A few hours after the investigation begins on 22 March, however, White leaves for San Francisco to investigate the murder of Chrissie Renfro (the fifth victim) in July 1956. In San Francisco, White makes the connection to Cooley and enlists the help of DA Loew. Loew tells him to stop his investigation and let a team from the DA's Bureau take over, but White doesn't trust him and spends the next six days hunting for Cooley in Los Angeles. White finds Cooley in an opium den on 28 March, defends himself against three assailants, and is intent on killing Cooley extrajudicially when he reveals that Perkins is the murderer. While questioning Stompanato on Perkins' whereabouts, White realises that he, Vachss, and Teitlebaum committed the Nite Owl massacre on Smith's orders (Ellroy 1990: 434):

> Bud whooped, punched the air, kicked boxes. Two cases made in one day – if anyone believed him. All dressed up and no one

to kill. Circumstantial Dudley evidence – no hard proof. Dudley too well placed to fall, nobody who cared like he did.
Except Exley.

White is overjoyed because Perkins is involved in both cases, meaning that he no longer has to sacrifice the victims of the one case to the victims of the other. He sets aside his hatred of Exley and makes a full disclosure of his discoveries. By the early hours of the next morning Exley has solved all but one of the major crimes peripheral to the Nite Owl and makes the decision to arrest Vachss and Teitlebaum.

7.2.4 Worldmaking

The practice of policing is worldmaking because its goal, public protection, requires the re-creation of social reality. This re-creation is achieved by negotiating the relationship between power and powerlessness by means of the exercise of authority and the employment of discretion. The Black Dahlia investigation can be divided into two discrete phases, although they are linked by the continuous investigation undertaken by Millard and Sears. The first lasts two months, from the discovery of Short's corpse on 15 January 1947 to the reassignment of all the detectives on 15 March. Bleichert's opportunities to re-create social reality during this period are limited and the most significant is his unofficial investigation of the Vogels' connection to Short. Detective Sergeant Fritz Vogel is seconded to the Black Dahlia investigation from Central Detectives and his son, Officer John Vogel, from foot patrol at Central Station. With the consent of Loew, Fritz Vogel takes four mentally ill suspects to a meat factory on the evening of 7 February. Seeking a confession, he seriously assaults them and is coercing them into mutilating the bisected corpse of a young woman when Bleichert activates the building's fire alarm. He succeeds in stopping Vogel, but the LAPD cover up the misconduct and Bleichert is taken off the case, dismissed from Central Warrants, and returned to foot patrol. Suspecting that there was more to the incident than Loew's desire for a confession, Bleichert breaks into the houses of father and son, discovering that Fritz arrested Short in June 1946 and that John may also have known her.

With Millard's help, he detains John, injects him with sodium thiopental, and questions him on 10 April. John admits that he had sex with Short three days before she was murdered. Bleichert arrests him on four charges, including obstruction of justice, and threatens to expose his father's corruption. Fritz commits suicide, John is dismissed from the LAPD for corruption, and Bleichert transferred to the Scientific Investigation Detail as an evidence technician, on the assumption that no police officer will work with him.

The second phase of the Black Dahlia investigation lasts 11 days, beginning on 26 June 1949, when Bleichert decides to stop trying to fight his obsession with Short and flies to Boston, and ending on 6 July, when he arrests Madeleine. Bleichert returns from Boston with a lead and acquires another when he threatens Turner Meeks with a pistol on 28 June, but their net result is the reconstruction of Short's final movements rather than the identification of a suspect in her murder. With Bleichert's costly and dangerous exercise of authority he does not possess exhausted, the crime scene is discovered the following day. He immediately suspects Tilden, albeit without a convincing reason. He retrieves fingerprints from the premises, bribes a janitor to let him into the Immigration and Naturalization Service's records after hours, and confirms that they are Tilden's. Bleichert realises he has no way of making the arrest without revealing that he withheld evidence on Madeleine in 1947 and decides he has only two options available, either let Millard and Sears make the arrest or administer justice extrajudicially himself. He confronts Emmett and Madeleine with the evidence against Tilden, Madeleine admits to procuring Short for Tilden (claiming that she thought he only wanted to have sex with her), and Emmett provides Bleichert with a list of his likely whereabouts. En route to the final address, Bleichert considers killing Tilden and wonders whether he will be able to live with himself if he does. The decision is taken out of his hands when Tilden attacks him with a pair of scalpels and he kills him in self-defence. Bleichert confesses his full involvement with Tilden and the Spragues to Millard, who decides to help him, burning Tilden's house down with his corpse inside. His worldmaking successful, Bleichert becomes suspicious of Emmett and Madeleine a week later and renews his investigation. He finds evidence that places Ramona at the scene of the crime, confronts her at home, and disarms her when she tries to shoot him. She confesses to murdering Short, with Tilden as her accomplice, and Bleichert once again considers his options. Arresting Ramona will reverse the re-creation of social reality he achieved with the help of Millard and he places Madeleine under surveillance while he makes his decision. When he overhears her telling a lover that she killed Blanchard, he arrests her. Madeleine confesses, but creates a narrative in which her, Blanchard, and Bleichert were in a love triangle in order to distance her family from the Black Dahlia case. Bleichert's final act of worldmaking is to corroborate Madeleine's testimony in order to protect Blanchard's posthumous reputation: he had in fact solved the Black Dahlia murder and was blackmailing Emmett. Bleichert is dismissed from the LAPD on moral grounds and Madeleine is convicted of Manslaughter Three.

Upshaw re-creates social reality in contravention of criminal justice procedure right at the very beginning of the Wolverine Prowler case. When he arrives at the Los Angeles County morgue, he finds Dr Katz, the Medical Examiner, drunk and bribes his assistant, who allows him to perform the preautopsy preparation of Goines' corpse in exchange for $25. Upshaw has the requisite knowledge and experience for the preparation, is convinced that the mutilation of the corpse will provide multiple clues to the identity of the murderer, and wants to make an immediate start on the investigation (even though he has not yet been assigned to it). Upshaw's second breach of criminal justice procedure, whose legality is questionable and which could well constitute an obstruction of justice, occurs on the fifth day of the investigation, when he discovers the crime scene. By this time Goines has been identified and Upshaw is notified of his most recent address, an apartment above a garage at 2307 North Tamarind. The residence is in LAPD territory and Dietrich has warned Upshaw to treat his city counterparts with courtesy in order to ease the counterproductive antagonism between the two law enforcement agencies. Following a hostile encounter with LAPD detectives on the first night of his investigation, however, he decides not to inform them. When the homeowner isn't in, Upshaw picks Goines' lock and enters his apartment. He immediately recognises that he has discovered the place where Goines was killed and that there is too much blood for a single corpse. He weighs the consequences of reporting his discovery against the chance of detecting and arresting the murderer and opts for the latter (Ellroy 1988: 115–116):

> Danny felt his stomach settle and his pulse take over, jolts like wires frazzling. Two other stiffs dumped someplace; a B&E on LAPD turf – Hollywood Division, where the Brenda Allen mess was the worst, where they hated the Sheriff's Department the most. His violation of Captain Dietrich's direct order: no strongarm, no prima donna in the City. No way to report what he found. An outside chance of the killer bringing number four here.[3]

Upshaw gathers as much evidence as he can from the crime scene while he is waiting and has the opportunity to interview Bordoni, Goines' friend, when he arrives. Upshaw is still in the apartment when Hiltscher informs him that the second and third corpses have been found in Griffith Park, which is also LAPD territory. His prompt arrival is met with rancour from Niles, who begins to suspect Upshaw is withholding information. Upshaw is lucky in that the crime scene is reported by Goines' landlady later that day, but the conflict with Niles hampers the effectiveness of the task force he is given to command and provides Smith with the opportunity to implicate him when Niles is murdered.

7.3 Situated Practice

7.3.1 Institution

Heroic struggle, edgework, absolute sacrifice, and worldmaking are characteristics of the practice of policing, the purpose of which is public protection. That practice is a situated practice, situated in both an institution and a systemic context. As the characteristics are emergent from the tensions among practice, institution, and systemic context, the Black Dahlia, Wolverine Prowler, and Nite Owl cases provide insight into the complexity of the relations among the characteristics of the practice of policing, policing as a situated practice, and public protection. An exploration of the tensions in the three cases and the 31-year-long history of police and political corruption provides insight into the ways in which the institution of policing and the systemic context of policing can detract from public protection. The heterogenous public is rarely protected uniformly and the most glaring example of the differential treatment of victims by the institutions of policing in the case study is the contrast between the respective police responses to the discovery of the corpses of Short and Goines. The murders themselves are very similar. To begin with, the corpses are separated in time and space by a little under three years and a little over seven miles. They have both been badly mutilated and Masskie imitated Tilden by leaving Goines' corpse naked in a vacant lot, hoping that the display would recall the earlier murder and make his murder more newsworthy (Ellroy 1988: 395): 'If he was lucky, victim number one would get just as much ink.' Short and Goines are both White, both casual workers in the entertainment industry, and both have criminal records for minor offences. Both murders also appear to be discrete crimes rather than part of a linked series as Goines is Masskie's first victim. Both cases also remain officially unsolved at their conclusion. The variation between Short and Goines is obvious, but does not appear nearly as significant as the similarities: gender (a woman and a man), age (Goines is 11 years Short's senior), and apparent sexuality (Goines and Short are believed to be homosexual and heterosexual respectively, although Goines is actually heterosexual and Short bisexual). The difference between the institutional responses could not be more extreme. While the LAPD forms a squad of 100 detectives and plainclothes police officers led by a detective captain to investigate Short's murder, the LASD assigns Goines' murder to a single, inexperienced detective deputy. The differential treatment of Short and Goines seems to be the result of their apparent sexuality and the influence of the media.

By the time Short's corpse has been removed from the place where it was discovered, the site has been visited by several reporters and Millard and Sears provide them with a handout that describes some of the details in order to enlist the press's assistance in the search for witnesses. Blanchard cynically but shrewdly predicts that the LAPD will exploit the initial media attention for the purpose of improving its reputation (Ellroy 1987: 72): 'It's a showcase. A nice white girl gets snuffed, the Department goes all out to get the killer to show the voters that passing the bond issue will get them a bulldog police force.'[4] He refers to Short's gender ('girl'), ethnicity ('white'), and class ('nice', meaning respectable and thus either belonging or aspiring to what can be called 'middle class', broadly construed). The implication is that the brutal murder of a person with these features is rich with news values and likely to be considered newsworthy by the media (Chibnall 1977; Fuller 1996; Bednarek & Caple 2017; Jewkes & Linnemann 2018). Blanchard is correct and the *Los Angeles Herald* morning headline is 'Hunt Werewolf's Den in Torture Slaying!' (Ellroy 1987: 75). Loew concurs with the LAPD's approach and regards the murder as a way of advancing his own reputation and political ambition. He not only refers to the killer as a werewolf, but summarises the murder as: 'Vivisection of a lovely young woman' (Ellroy 1987: 82). Short's promiscuity and lack of respectability are soon exposed, making her a less than ideal victim, so the media maintains interest by switching from 'Werewolf Murder' to 'The Black Dahlia', recalling *The Blue Dahlia*, a popular film noir with Alan Ladd and Veronica Lake which was released in April 1946 (Ellroy 1987: 89). The tactic is successful and the 'Black Dahlia' generates even more attention, including large numbers of confessions from mentally ill people. When the detectives learn that Short acted in a pornographic film, Loew wants to withhold the information from the press and makes several subsequent attempts to keep the less savoury aspects of Short's character and life private in order to preserve the newsworthiness of the murder in his own interest. The LAPD's commitment to the case reaches 190 police officers by the fifth day, 19 January. The pornographic film is discovered on 20 January, after which no further resources are committed. The detective squad is not, however, downsized for another two weeks and then only after all existing leads have been exhausted.

Masskie's plan to frame Loftis involves exploiting the newsworthiness of the Black Dahlia case by leaving Goines' naked, mutilated corpse in a place associated with homosexual liaisons

(Ellroy 1988: 395): 'He deposited Marty nude in a vacant lot on Allegro, prime fruit territory, a corpse on display like the Black Dahlia.' Masskie fails to realise that the link he establishes with homosexuality is much more consequential than the link he establishes with the Black Dahlia, in spite of the police immediately recognising both. Upshaw's first conversation with Dietrich after finding the corpse is illuminating (Ellroy 1988: 36):

> 'Shit. Captain, I want this one.'
> 'You can have it. No publicity, though. I don't want another Black Dahlia mess.'
> 'What about another man to work with me?'
> Dietrich sighed – long and slow. 'If the victim warrants it. For now, it's just you. We've only got four detectives, Danny. If this John Doe was trash, I don't want to waste another man.'
> Danny said, 'A homicide is a homicide, sir.'
> Dietrich said, 'You're smarter than that, Deputy.'
> Danny said, 'Yes, sir,' hung up, and rolled.

Goines has not yet been identified so the only indication that he might have been 'trash' is the location where his naked corpse was found, i.e. his presumed homosexuality. Almost all of the police officers involved in the case directly and indirectly are explicitly homophobic, use derogatory language to describe homosexuals, and regard homosexuals as being less than human and thus undeserving of police resources in the event they are victims of crime. Dietrich is no more homophobic than any of the other police officers and his attitude reflects institutional homophobia. This homophobia is not confined to the institution of policing or to the institutions of the criminal justice system, but is systemic, as reflected in state and federal law: sodomy was only decriminalised in the US in 2003 (Eskridge 2008).[5] The absence of reporters at the Allegro Street location and the LASD's decision to avoid recruiting the efforts of the media in solving the case are responsible for keeping it out of the headlines. In consequence of systemic homophobia, the discovery of the second and third victims' corpses does not increase the story's newsworthiness. Dr Norton Layman, the Assistant Chief Medical

Examiner for the City of Los Angeles, offers an insightful explanation (Ellroy 1988: 132–133):

> The Doc was convinced that a 'Reverse Black Dahlia Syndrome' was in effect – the three stiffs found so far had received a total of four inner section newspaper columns, city editors shying away because Marty Goines was trash and the whole thing was queer shit that you couldn't print without the Legion for Decency and Concerned Catholic Mothers on your ass.

The full extent of both institutional and systemic homophobia is most clearly and tragically revealed by Upshaw's decision to commit suicide when threatened with exposure by Smith.

On 1 January 1958 Inez Soto tells Exley that Coates, Fontaine, and Jones could not have committed the Nite Owl murders because they spent the entire night sexually abusing her. Exley, who is about to assume command of IA, is horrified but takes no action. The three suspects and their associate were all unarmed when he shot them dead so a reopening of the case could lead to criminal charges against him in addition to guaranteed public humiliation. His motive is to protect both his own reputation and that of the LAPD, as he reveals in his inaugural briefing to IA three days later (Ellroy 1990: 301):

> 'And, finally, we are the protectors of the public image of the Los Angeles Police Department. Know that when you read interdepartmental complaints filed against your brother officers and feel the urge to be forgiving. Know that when I assign you to investigate a man you once worked with and liked. Know that our business is stern, absolute justice, whatever the price.'

The price of absolute justice does not include the sacrifice of the LAPD's reputation, a sentiment with which Chief Parker agrees entirely.[6] A day later, White discovers Cathcart's corpse, realises that his scepticism about the solution to the Nite Owl case was correct, and contacts the press anonymously (in order to avenge Stensland's execution). *Whisper*, a New York magazine with a small circulation, publishes an article with the title '**WRONG MAN**

KILLED IN NITE OWL SLAUGHTER? WEB OF MYSTERY SPREADS...' in its February issue (Ellroy 1990: 319, emphasis in original). White's disclosure causes the murder of Peter and Bert Englekling, two witnesses in the Nite Owl case, in Gaitsville on 25 February. An article on the double murder is read by Otis Shortell, a prisoner at San Quentin, who reveals that he was one of the men who raped Soto and that all three of the suspects were with him and Soto at the time of the Nite Owl murders. The L.A. Daily News runs a story on the developments that closes with a challenge to the LAPD to reopen the case on 6 March.

Five days later, Parker tells the L.A. Times that he has no intention of reopening the case. On 16 March, Shortell's lawyer petitions the Attorney General (AG) of California to reopen the case and Parker reiterates that it has already been solved to his satisfaction. Three days later, public activism begins with people picketing the LAPD and flooding its phone lines with complaints. Parker remains unmoved and phones Exley to confirm his support. Exley takes the opportunity to tell him that he has doubts about the guilt of Coates, Fontaine, and Jones, but Parker is adamant (Ellroy 1990: 333–334): 'Don't interrupt me and don't tell me you're so suicidally naive as to think reopening the case will do a whit of good.' Parker's confidence in the AG's support is misplaced and when the AG orders a state investigation into the case, Parker has Loew file an injunction, which gives the LAPD two weeks from 21 March to reach a resolution themselves. Although Parker has social connections to Exley and recognises his brilliance as a detective, his multiple attempts to protect him are motivated by his dual desire to protect the reputation of the LAPD at all costs and to protect his own reputation for honouring Exley so soon after his killing of the three suspects (which was, in turn, a means of reputation risk management). Parker's protection of the LAPD is a career-spanning commitment: in January 1942 he failed to arrest ex-LAPD Chief James Davis for the murder of a Japanese American family on the basis of Davis' association with the department.

Although Exley solves the Nite Owl and all its peripheral cases, he does not acquire sufficient evidence to take action against Smith. Similarly, while Smith has successfully covered his tracks, his plans have suffered a major setback with the death of several key associates, most notably Patchett. As such, there is something of a stalemate between Smith and Exley in the summer of 1958, during which both men are promoted (Smith to detective captain and Exley to deputy chief) and both men set plans in motion (Smith to continue his corruption and Exley to thwart it). Smith's Mobster Squad remains a crucial component of his OCG and he recruits a new member, an amateur boxing champion named John Duhamel, straight out of the LAPD Academy to replace White. Smith does not know that Duhamel has been planted by Exley and is working as an undercover officer for IA. On the evening of 30 October 1958 there is a burglary in Mid-Wilshire, at the home of J.C. Kafesjian, a drug dealer who is an LAPD informant. Detective Captain Daniel Wilhite, commander of the Narcotics Division, asks Detective Lieutenant David Klein, commander of the Administrative Vice Division, to attend in order to prevent the local detectives from inquiring too deeply into Kafesjian's affairs. Narcotics is notoriously corrupt and Wilhite has contacted Klein because Klein has been affiliated with OCGs for at least half of his two decades in the LAPD. Klein complies, but the following day Exley details him and one of his detective sergeants to investigate the burglary regardless of Wilhite or Kafesjian's wishes.

Exley is interested in Kafesjian because he was initially recruited as an informant by Smith in 1937 on the understanding that he would be allowed to sell drugs as long as he restricted his sales to South Los Angeles (i.e. to a primarily Black clientele) and limited the violence employed. Exley hopes that Klein's investigation will threaten Smith and predicts that Smith will attempt to strike a deal with Klein in consequence of his reputation for corruption. On 18 November, however, Smith abducts Klein, drugs him, coerces him to kill Duhamel, and films the murder – neutralising both of Exley's agents. Early the next morning, Klein is detained by Special Agent Willis Shipstad of the FBI, who is investigating LAPD corruption in South Los Angeles. Klein becomes the central figure in the tripartite struggle among Exley (who wants to bring Smith to justice), Smith (who wants to outmanoeuvre Exley), and Shipstad (who wants evidence of LAPD corruption). Klein agrees to cooperate with all three and detains the burglar, a mentally ill ex-offender named Wylie Bullock. He uses Bullock to negotiate with Exley and Smith and he and Smith are both intending to kill one another when they meet on 28 November. Klein is saved by Bullock, who attacks Smith with a meat cleaver, leaving him brain damaged, paralysed, partially blinded, and in need of constant care. Klein takes refuge with his OCG associates, has plastic surgery, and flees to Brazil. Taking advantage of Smith's disability and Wilhite's suicide, Exley holds a press conference on 8 December in which he represents the Narcotics Division as an isolated instance of corruption in the LAPD and announces that he will personally be providing evidence against them to a grand jury. It is an act of reputation risk management that allows the LAPD to retain some credibility, as an institution prepared to take action against its own police officers when required. In spite of his hatred of Smith, Exley represents him as a hero wounded in the line of duty and awards him a special pension to cover the cost of care for the rest of his life on 3 January 1959. Like Parker's, Exley's protection of the LAPD's reputation is a career-long commitment.

7.3.2 Systemic Context

All of the police officers in the case study are White supremacists in the sense of believing that 'race' is a biological and moral category, that there is a natural hierarchy of races, and that the White race is at the apex of this hierarchy (Sussman 2014; Saini 2019; Andrews 2021). All of the police officers, including Bleichert, Upshaw, and White, make frequent use of racial slurs and derogatory language to express this superiority, including: 'boogie', 'coon', 'jig', 'jigaboo', 'nigger', 'shine', and 'spook' (to refer to Black people); 'Mex', 'spic', and 'wetback' (to refer to Hispanic people); 'Chink' and 'Jap' (to refer to East Asian people); and 'breed', 'halfbreed', and 'mulatto' (to refer to people of mixed race). Neither the offensive language nor the attitudes that underpin it are challenged in either the LAPD or LASD and both law enforcement agencies are institutionally racist. The most striking example of institutional racism is the investigation of the Nite Owl massacre. The second Exley sees the shotgun shells at the crime scene, he recalls recent reports that 'a carload of Negro youths were seen discharging shotguns into the air in the Griffith Park hills' (Ellroy 1990: 99). Within a few hours, the entire Detective

Bureau is on the trail of Fontaine, Coates, and Jones, dispatched by the chief in person. It is only through Vincennes' restraint that the three suspects are not killed extrajudicially, but Exley's lack of restraint reverses the situation, bringing about the resolution Parker (and of course Smith) wanted. There can be no doubt that the suspects would have been treated differently if they were White, notwithstanding the repugnance of the crimes they did commit. Institutional racism is insufficient to explain these circumstances, which are the consequence of a more ubiquitous and persistent racism, referred to as both 'structural' and 'systemic'. As structural racism is also used as a synonym for institutional racism, I shall use systemic racism and distinguish between the two levels as follows: (1) institutional bias and prejudice is the perpetuation and aggravation of disadvantage by means of complex, coherent, and cooperative human activities (practices) sustained by structures of power and status (institutions); and (2) systemic bias and prejudice is the perpetuation and aggravation of disadvantage by means of the material, administrative, ideological, and cultural environment (context) within which structures of power and status (institutions) are situated (Ture & Hamilton 1967; MacIntyre 2007; Bates 2014; Lingayah 2021). The extent and impact of systemic racism is scrutinised in the part of the history of police and political corruption that begins at the end of 1958 and ends in the middle of 1972.

This history explores the complexity of the connections among several domestic and international events: the Bay of Pigs Invasion (April 1961), Operation Mongoose (from November 1961, aimed at removing the communists from power in Cuba), the assassination of John Fitzgerald Kennedy (JFK, November 1963), the escalation of America's involvement in Vietnam (March 1965), the assassination of Martin Luther King Jr (April 1968), the assassination of Robert Francis Kennedy (June 1968), the exposure of the FBI's Counter Intelligence Program (COINTELPRO, March 1971, the surveillance and harassment of civil rights and other groups since August 1956), and the death of J. Edgar Hoover (May 1972). All three federal governments and the nexuses of power within which they are embedded are revealed as promoting White supremacism and anti-unionism domestically and prioritising American exceptionalism and anti-communism internationally. The myth of the 'Camelot' of JFK's administration is debunked by Peter Bondurant, Ward Littell, and Kemper Boyd, the ruthless and resourceful agents of Hoover, Howard Hughes, James Hoffa, Sam Giancana, Carlos Marcello, and Santo Trafficante Jr (Hersh 1997: 190).[7] The myth of counterculture, progress, and liberation under Lyndon B. Johnson and Richard Nixon is replaced with the reality of unaccountability, cruelty, and oppression as Wayne Tedrow Jr, Donald Crutchfield, Dwight Holly, and Robert Bennett pick up where their predecessors left off, carving out the will of the powerful men they serve. While Hoover's death is not as dramatic as the Kennedy or King assassinations, it is nonetheless momentous given that he was a White supremacist and head of the FBI (and its predecessor, the Bureau of Investigation) for an incredible 48 years, serving eight presidents (McKnight 1998; Weiner 2012). The exposure of COINTELPRO is largely the work of Joan Klein, a Jewish communist revolutionary who spends most of her life fighting fascism in its multiple guises both within and without America.[8] As a woman whose selflessness, integrity, and humanity are beyond question, the '*Red Goddess Joan*' stands in stark contrast to Bondurant, Littell, Boyd, Tedrow, Crutchfield, Holly, and Bennett (Ellroy 2009: 640, emphasis in original). The history concludes with the revelation that it has been authored by Crutchfield and dedicated to Klein, who is 83 years old in 2009.

Crutchfield is a young private investigator from Los Angeles who works for Operation Mongoose, the Mafia, and the FBI before falling in love with Klein, joining her crusade against Hoover, and fathering her child. The narrative of 1958 to 1972 is thus literally his story – *history* – meticulously and scrupulously compiled over a period of 37 years (Ellroy 2009: 639, emphasis in original): '*Forty thousand new file pages buttress my recall. I burned all of my original paper. I built paper all over again, so I might tell you this story.*' *This story* is not simply history or even alternative history, but a disclosure of the origin and causes of mass harms perpetrated or facilitated by individuals and agencies of the federal government, with a particular emphasis on racism. As such, Crutchfield's narrative (1958–1972) and the overarching narrative that it concludes (1941–1972) constitute a critical criminology (McGregor 2021). The critical tradition of criminology began with the critique of Cesare Lombroso's prototypical positivist criminology by his contemporaries in the 19th century and developed critiques of capitalist economics and biological determinism in the early 20th century (Swaaningen 1999).[9] Howard Becker (1963) criticised unproblematised conceptions of crime with his sociology of deviance in the 1960s, which led to the tradition's emphasis on harms (whether criminalised or not) rather than crime the following decade. In the 21st century, critical criminology is contrasted with 'conventional' or 'mainstream' criminology and delineated by Walter DeKeseredy (2022: 12) as 'a perspective that views the major sources of crime and social control as the unequal class, race/ethnic, and gender relations that control our society'. Criminology is thus the study of harm rather than crime and classism, racism, and sexism are mass harms. Crutchfield's critical criminology explores all three, with a focus on the causes and consequences of racism at the individual, institutional, and systemic levels. Liberal democracy and free market capitalism are represented as complicit in systemic racism in virtue of the precedence they accord individual freedom over collective responsibility and their facilitation of the accumulation of vast amounts of wealth by egotistic and enterprising individuals. American society from 1941 to 1972 is not shaped by its citizens or even by the elected representatives of those citizens, but by those who wield power in virtue of their money, mercilessness, or both, i.e. men like Hoover, Hughes, Hoffa, Giancana, Marcello, and Trafficante. There is one man in particular who exemplifies the era with which Crutchfield is concerned, Dudley Liam Smith.

The three investigations that constitute the critical case study are linked by Smith: he is Short's biological father, the Sleepy Lagoon murderer, and gave the orders for the Nite Owl massacre. He also links the case studies to the history of police and political corruption, recruiting Bennett to the LAPD in 1941 and becoming Joan Klein's guardian for two months in 1942. Smith is most accurately described as a sociopath, completely lacking in empathy but able to control his antisocial impulses, sustain long-term relationships, and prosper socially and economically. He was born in Dublin in 1905, to a Catholic family with strong nationalist sympathies. When his father was killed by the British Army, Smith's mother turned to alcohol and physically abused him. His older brother, James, suffered the same fate as his father in 1919 and Smith killed his first man, the soldier who shot James, at the age of 14. Smith saw action in 1921 in the Anglo-Irish War and in 1922 in the Irish Civil War. He was recruited as a bootlegger by Joseph Kennedy, moved to Boston, and joined the LAPD in 1928 after killing one of Kennedy's enemies by accident. During the Second World War, Smith served as a major in first the US Army's Military Intelligence Division (in Mexico) and then the Office of Strategic Services (in Paraguay). He was promoted to detective lieutenant on his return to the LAPD and worked in Homicide until his promotion to detective captain in 1958. Smith was medically retired from the LAPD in 1959, at the age of 53, and spent the rest of his long life in a care home.

The first mention of Smith is in Kay Lake's diary, on 6 December 1941, as 'a suavely brutal cop named Dudley Smith' who is a detective sergeant in Homicide (Ellroy 2014: 29). That afternoon, Smith and Detective Sergeants Michael Breuning and Richard Carlisle perpetrate the extrajudicial killing of a suspected serial rapist using sawn-off shotguns (Ellroy 2014: 43):

> Jerome Joseph Pavik stepped from his car and eyed the world, shit-faced. He gawked a vacant lot, catty-corner. It was full of palm trees and high grass.
> He staggered into the lot. He walked up to a palm tree and pulled out his dick. He launched a world's record piss.
> Dudley said, 'Now, lads.'
> The street was no-one-out quiet. They beelined to the lot. Soft dirt covered their footsteps. The rape-o swayed and sprayed grass.
> They came up behind him. He didn't hear shit.
> Dudley said, 'Those grand girls won't be the same now. This prevents recurring grief.'
> He started to turn around. He started to say 'Say what?'
> Six triggers snapped. The rape-o blew up. Bone shards took down palm fronds. Carlisle's glasses got residual-spritzed.
> Big booms overlapped. Note those buckshot-on-wood echoes. 3:30 church bells pealed through all of it.

The last mention of Smith is by David Klein, when he decides to return to the US in 1992 (Ellroy 1992: 349, emphasis in original): *'I'm going to kill Carlisle, and make Dudley fill in every moment of his life – to eclipse my guilt with the sheer weight of his evil.'* The last time Klein saw Smith was on 28 November 1958, when Smith was attacked by Klein's prisoner (Ellroy 1992: 321–322, emphases in original):

> Bullock went at him cleaver-first.
> Wild swings – the handcuffs fucked his grip up – the blade ripped Dudley's mouth ear to ear. Roundhouse coup de grace – the cleaver hit asphalt.
> 'EYEBALL MAN!' – Bullock on Dudley.
> Biting.
> Clawing.
> Ripping at his eyes.
> Look:
> One gushing red socket.
> 'NO!' – *my* scream/my gun out/aiming at them tangled up together.
> I fired twice – two misses – ricochets off the pavement.
> Two more shots braced against the hood – Bullock's face exploded.
> Bone sprayed in my eyes.
> Firing blind – ricochet zings, a jammed slide.
> Dudley on Bullock – prying at his hands.
> Dudley weaving, screaming exultant – his eye cupped back to his face.
> I grabbed the money and ran. Echoes boomed behind me: 'EYEBALL MAN! EYEBALL MAN!'

The extraordinary violence of both the extrajudicial killing and the foiled ambush are typical of Smith, who regards excessive force as an essential component of his practice of policing and his practice of policing as nothing more than a means to the end of acquiring wealth, status, and power. His abuse of his authority is carefully calculated and completely remorseless, stated calmly and concisely as (Ellroy 2014: 236): 'I am in no way constrained by the law.'

Smith is able to flourish in America because he is perceptive enough to realise that its liberal democracy is underpinned by a political economy which is complicit in systemic classism and racism (as well as sexism). He arrives in the US in the employment of the socioeconomic elite, ingratiates himself with the Kennedys, and remains under their protective wing during his careers in the police and military. Smith is not merely a White supremacist, but a private National Socialist with a horror of miscegenation who kills six Black looters in February 1942 and José Díaz at the Sleepy Lagoon six months later. He is nonetheless able to maintain professional and even personal relationships with individuals he considers biologically and morally inferior if those relationships are in his interests. Smith is an entrepreneur *par excellence*, exploiting his official status in the LAPD, systemic racism in the US, wartime geopolitics, and his official status in the US Armed Forces for personal gain. His most ambitious plan is to expand his organised corruption within the LAPD to establish an OCG of his own that will maximise profit by selling heroin to Los Angeles' Black population and exotic pornography to its White population (Ellroy 1990). The plan will minimise risk by capitalising on Smith's position in the LAPD, Chief Parker's desire to rid Los Angeles of OCGs, antiblack racism that ignores addiction in Black neighbourhoods, and the vices of the financially solvent. The scheme is only foiled by White's dogged persistence with the Nite Owl investigation and the sale of heroin in Black neighbourhoods is subsequently used by the Central Intelligence Agency to fund Operation Mongoose. Smith takes advantage of the precedence accorded to individual freedom over collective responsibility by liberal democracy to use all legal and illegal means to advance his wealth, status, and power. By the time he is medically retired, he has achieved a position somewhere in between the power elite of Hoover, Hughes, Hoffa, Giancana, Marcello, and Trafficante and the men who do their bidding, like Bondurant, Littell, Boyd, Tedrow, Crutchfield, and Holly. Smith's final years, over three decades in a care home, seem to be his just deserts, but he retires with his reputation intact thanks to Exley. He is more than the thread that links the three cases to one another and to the overarching narrative; he is a product and an exemplar of liberal democratic America from 1941 to 1972. There is consequently a sense in which Smith's malpractice of policing – or, more accurately, his failure to practice policing – is more illuminating than the practices of Bleichert, Upshaw, and White, at least with respect to the systemic context within which the institution and practice of policing are situated. The history of police and political corruption thus draws attention to the differential treatment of victims and the prioritisation of reputation risk management by the institution of policing and to the relationship between liberal democracy and systemic racism and classism.

Notes

1 All anal and oral sex was illegal in California at the time and sexual offenders classified as morally or sexually perverted were liable to be sterilised (Eskridge 2008).
2 Gordean is a heterosexual procurer of homosexual male sex workers for 'the Hollywood elite and old money LA' (Ellroy 1988: 143).
3 The cause of the antagonism between the LASD and the LAPD is a corruption scandal involving Hollywood procurer Brenda Allen and the LAPD's Administrative Vice Division. The scandal began with the arrest of Allen in 1948 and resulted in the resignation of LAPD Chief Clemence Horrall in 1949 (Buntin 2009).
4 This quote is part of a longer quotation I cited in my discussion of absolute sacrifice in the previous section.
5 Homosexual acts were decriminalised in the UK in 1967 (Joyce 2022). I define both institutional and systemic prejudice and bias in my discussion of systemic context below.
6 The concept of absolute justice is central to Exley's police practice and revised over the course of his career, most notably after he gains insight into White's police practice, as revealed in a reflection I quoted in my discussion of heroic struggle in the previous section.
7 Giancana, Marcello, and Trafficante held leadership positions in the Mafia.
8 Joan Klein is not related to David Klein.
9 I introduced the critical tradition of criminology in the second critical case study (Chapter 6).

References

Andrews, K. (2021). *The New Age of Empire: How Racism and Colonialism Still Rule the World*. London: Allen Lane.

Bates, L. (2014). *Everyday Sexism*. London: Simon & Schuster.

Becker, H. (1963). *Outsiders: Studies in the Sociology of Deviance*. New York: Free Press.

Bednarek, M. & Caple, H. (2017) *The Discourse of News Values: How News Organizations Create Newsworthiness*. New York: Oxford University Press.

Buntin, J. (2009). *LA. Noir: The Struggle for the Soul of America's Most Seductive City*. New York: Crown Publishing Group.

Chibnall, S. (1977). *Law and Order News: Crime Reporting in the British Press*. London: Tavistock Publications.

DeKeseredy, W.S. (2022). *Contemporary Critical Criminology*. Abingdon: Routledge.

Ellroy, J. (1987/1988). *The Black Dahlia*. London: Mysterious Press.

Ellroy, J. (1988). *The Big Nowhere*. New York: The Mysterious Press.

Ellroy, J. (1990). *L.A. Confidential*. New York: The Mysterious Press.

Ellroy, J. (1992). *White Jazz*. New York: Alfred A. Knopf.

Ellroy, J. (2009/2010). *Blood's a Rover*. London: Windmill Books.

Ellroy, J. (2014). *Perfidia*. London: William Heinemann Ltd.

Eskridge, W.N. (2008). *Dishonorable Passions: Sodomy Laws in America 1861–2003*. New York: Viking Press.

Fuller, J. (1996). *News Values: Ideas for an Information Age*. Chicago: University of Chicago Press.

Hersh, S. (1997). *The Dark Side of Camelot*. London: HarperCollins Publishers.

Jewkes, Y. & Linnemann, T. (2018). *Media and Crime in the U.S*. Thousand Oaks, CA: Sage Publications.

Joyce, J.P. (2022). *Odd Men Out: Male Homosexuality in Britain from Wolfenden to Gay Liberation*. 2nd ed. Manchester: Manchester University Press.

Lingayah, S. (2021). It takes a system: The systemic nature of racism and pathways to systems change. London: Beyond Race/Race on the Agenda. Available at: www.rota.org.uk/publications/systemsreport2021.

McGregor, R. (2021). James Ellroy's Critical Criminology: Crimes of the Powerful in the Underworld USA Trilogy. *Critical Criminology: An International Journal*, 29 (2), 349–365.

MacIntyre, A. (2007). *After Virtue: A Study in Moral Theory*. 3rd ed. London: Duckworth Books.

McKnight, G. (1998). *The Last Crusade: Martin Luther King, Jr., the FBI, and the Poor People's Campaign*. New York: Basic Books.

Saini, A. (2019). *Superior: The Return of Race Science*. London: 4th Estate.

Sussman, R.W. (2014). *The Myth of Race: The Troubling Persistence of an Unscientific Idea*. Cambridge, MA: Harvard University Press.

Swaaningen, R. van (1999). Reclaiming Critical Criminology: Social Justice and the European Tradition. *Theoretical Criminology*, 3 (1), 5–28.

Ture, K. & Hamilton, C.V. (1967/1992). *Black Power: The Politics of Liberation*. New York: Vintage Books.

Weiner, T. (2012). *Enemies: A History of the FBI*. London: Penguin Books.

PART 4
The Solution

8
PUBLIC PROTECTION AND POLICE LEGITIMACY

The purpose of this chapter is to present the findings from the case studies, identifying the different ways in which the practice of policing, the institution of policing, and the systemic context of policing undermine police legitimacy. Police legitimacy is undermined in two distinct ways, by the use of coercion rather than consent to protect the public and by failure to protect the public. The case studies demonstrate the circumstances in which heroic struggle, edgework, absolute sacrifice, and worldmaking undermine police legitimacy in both of these ways. Coercive tactics include the use of excessive force to detain suspects, the use of torture to interrogate suspects, and the use of undercover policing to secure evidence for prosecution. While undercover policing need not be coercive, it undermines public trust, on which police legitimacy is supervenient. The practice of policing can fail to protect the public in consequence of the interaction among the four characteristics, police procedure, and political policies. The practical challenges to police legitimacy and public protection are summarised as: inappropriate tactics and procedural limitations. As the characteristics of the practice of policing are emergent from the tensions among the practice, the institution, and the systemic context, the case studies also demonstrate the ways in which policing as a situated practice undermines police legitimacy. They identify four ways in which the institution of policing undermines police legitimacy by failing to protect the public: competition for resources among law enforcement agencies and constabularies; the safeguarding of law enforcement agency and constabulary reputations; corruption within law enforcement agencies and constabularies; and the reinforcing of racism, sexism, and homophobia. Similarly, the case studies identify four ways in which the systemic context of policing undermines police legitimacy by failing to protect the public: competition for resources among different institutions of the criminal justice system; the reinforcing of racism, sexism, and homophobia; public perception of the criminal justice system; and a political context in which social inequality is prevalent. The institutional and systemic challenges to public protection and police legitimacy are summarised as: competition, reputation safeguarding, corruption, public perception, and social inequality. These findings provide the foundation for the radical framework for recovering police legitimacy that is set out in Chapter 10.

8.1 Policing as a Practice

Recall from Chapter 4 that the three case studies were selected for their strategic significance in exploring both the four characteristics of the practice of policing and policing as a situated practice. The four characteristics – heroic struggle, edgework, absolute sacrifice, and worldmaking – were delineated in Chapter 3 and are the results of my (McGregor 2021) autoethnographic study. The analytic autoethnography was based on my service as a police officer in the Durban City Police (DCP) in South Africa from 1992 to 1998. The exploration of the four characteristics was consequently limited to my own experiences, which were first representative of those of my colleagues, constituting the sample of the study, and then representative of police officers in the US (in virtue of the legal and social similarities between the US and South Africa) and the UK (in virtue of the DCP being modelled on the Metropolitan Police Service [MPS], unique to South Africa at the time), constituting the population of the study.[1] My intention was that the case studies would explore all four of the characteristics of policing in significantly more detail than I had been able to do in my autoethnography and would explore the relation among the characteristics, their situation, and public protection. In Chapter 1, I defined police legitimacy as *public recognition of the right of the institution of policing to exercise its legal powers* and noted that recognition was likely to be revoked if the institution of policing was either perceived as relying on coercion (rather than consent) to protect the public or perceived as failing to protect the public (regardless of whether policing is consensual or coercive). My summary of the evidence from the case studies deals with each of the four characteristics of the practice of policing individually, but it is worth bearing in mind that they interlock to characterise the practice in its entirety such that the relevant relations are among the full set of characteristics, public protection, and police legitimacy.

8.1.1 Heroic Struggle

The practice of policing is a heroic struggle because its purpose, public protection, can never be achieved in full. This limitation is underpinned by the unpredictability of the consequences of proactive policing and the inability of reactive policing to reduce anything more than the consequences of harm that has already been inflicted. The characteristic is derived from the work of Lois Presser (2008), who identifies a relation between heroic struggle and toxic masculinity and argues that heroism is criminogenic when the difficulty of the struggle is inadvertently or deliberately conflated with the morality of the struggle. Considered as a characteristic of the practice of policing, the implication is that heroic struggle can, when it becomes criminogenic, undermine both public protection and police legitimacy. Detective Sergeant Wendell White exhibits a great deal of toxic masculinity, which is why Detective Lieutenant Dudley Smith recruits him to the Homicide Adjunct Surveillance Detail (HASD). The HASD is a proactive policing unit that deploys extrajudicial means to reduce the impact of organised crime groups (OCGs) in Los Angeles and is interesting for two reasons. First, if Smith was not using it to establish his own OCG it may well have simultaneously contributed to public protection (reducing particular types of crime) while threatening police legitimacy (by relying on coercion). The relationship between public protection and police legitimacy is thus, as one might expect given the complexity of policing as a situated practice, not entirely straightforward. Second, the HASD is reminiscent of the tactics associated with colonial policing rather than Anglo-American Democratic Policing (AADP) and anticipates concerns about the militarisation of policing that would emerge four decades later.

In contrast to White, Detective Deputy Sheriff Daniel Upshaw's approach to heroic struggle is to keep its difficulty at the forefront of his mind (as evinced by his photograph of Jastrow) and to use that difficulty as motivation to succeed as fully as possible without using extrajudicial means. This might seem to be a counter-example to Presser's claims about conflation, but it is not. What is important about Upshaw's attitude to heroic struggle is that he recognises both the difficulty and the morality, in consequence of which his self-awareness of the characteristic contributes to both public protection and police legitimacy in his investigation of the Wolverine Prowler murders. The exchanges between Detective Sergeant Antigone Bezzerides and Vera Machiado suggest a once again complex relation among the four characteristics, public protection, and police legitimacy, drawing attention to Peter Manning's (2010) difference principle, which I cited in Chapter 1 as: *given the current range of inequalities in education, opportunity, income, and skills, any police practice, especially that driven and shaped by policy, should not further increase extant inequalities.* In spite of good police work and good intentions, Bezzerides leaves everyone involved worse off than before her intervention, which could well detract from police legitimacy by the perception of Machiado and her sister that the police has failed to protect them. While the example is less dramatic than the others in the case studies, it also cuts to the very core of heroic struggle: that good police work, motivated by good intentions, can increase extent inequalities and contribute to a loss of legitimacy in cases where the increase of inequalities is perceived as a failure of public protection.

8.1.2 Edgework

The practice of policing is edgework because it involves a high risk of injury, which can be reduced by competence in a specific skill set and is accompanied by a specific sensation and set of emotions. These emotions can become addictive, especially when the work is demanding in terms of time, commitment, and lifestyle. The risk of injury is dependent on numerous variables, including the duty to which a particular police officer is assigned and the location and timing of that duty, but is nonetheless omnipresent and is omnipresent regardless of the extent to which that police officer has or has not mastered the sets of excellences and skills required to protect the public. All police officers should be competent in the specific skill set of dealing with physical confrontations because competence both reduces their own risk of injury and facilitates their ability to protect others from injury by other others. One of the reasons for the revocation of police legitimacy is failure to protect the public and a police service full of officers who are physically incapable of protecting the public is a police service that is likely to be perceived as ineffective. All eight of the officers in the three case studies are competent in dealing with physical confrontations, from the obvious examples of White and Officer Paul Woodrugh to the less obvious, such as Detective Sergeant Helen Marshall, whose edgework during her two investigations is restricted to dealing with a death threat. Bezzerides reflects on the additional challenge edgework poses to women police officers in virtue of the combination of toxic masculinity, gender stereotypes, and sex differences.

Edgework as a risk of injury is not just a feature of the reactive paradigm or of the targeting of police officers, but of the proactive paradigm and planned police operations. In planned operations, the specific skill set must include the reduction of the risk of injury to the police officers involved and any members of the public likely to be in the vicinity as well as – ideally – to the suspects themselves. Such situations combine edgework with the excellence of the practice of policing I referred to as judgement in Chapter 3. The three most striking examples in the case studies are the arrest of Lee Vachss and Abraham Teitlebaum, the Blue Denim Massacre, and the Vinci Massacre. Detective Captain Edmund Exley (in 1958) and Bezzerides (in 2013) are able to justify their respective decisions, but all three operations fail to produce the desired result at the cost of unnecessary loss of life and there is a negative impact on police legitimacy in at least the first, where the City of Los Angeles Police Department (LAPD) is sued for reckless endangerment. While the addictive quality of edgework is only explicit in the examples of Woodrugh (who misses the exhilaration of combat he experienced in the military) and White (whose use of excessive force is motivated by both retribution and exhilaration), it is present in all eight of the police officers. Addiction to edgework is both strong and subtle for Assistant Chief Constable Peter Hunter and Marshall who, in spite of being mature, calm, and responsible officers, take risks over and above those demanded by public protection. Addiction extends beyond edgework to substances (alcohol and drugs) and high-risk activities (gambling) for three of the other four officers.

8.1.3 Absolute Sacrifice

The practice of policing is an absolute sacrifice because public protection requires continuous self-sacrifice and the sacrifice of the interests of some others to other others, both of which are accompanied by an accumulated weight of responsibility. In his treatise on the dysfunctionality of the US criminal justice system, Michael Huemer (2021) argues that government employees are disproportionately likely to enjoy exerting power. This seems to require empirical substantiation, but Huemer's logic is impeccable: exerting power is the core function of government so people who do not enjoy or object to the exertion of power are less likely to apply for positions in government. Not all government employees will enjoy exerting power, but the proportion of those who do will be above average when measured against the population as a whole. The exertion of power – especially direct, physical power – is a core component of public protection, in consequence of which the institution of policing attracts a disproportionate number of recruits who are likely to abuse their power and endanger the legitimacy of that institution by an over-reliance on coercion. The exploration of absolute sacrifice in all three of the case studies suggests that the institution of policing also attracts a disproportionate number of recruits who are likely to take responsibility for the life chances of others. The claim follows from Huemer's logic: absolute sacrifice is a core component of the practice of policing (and probably other practices within public service), in consequence of which people who do not enjoy taking responsibility for others are less likely to apply for positions in the police. All eight of the police officers take responsibility for others over and above the requirements of public protection and the weight of this responsibility is particularly evident in Hunter, Bezzerides, and White. Taking too much responsibility can detract from public protection, police legitimacy, or both when it motivates extrajudicial action or has a negative impact on a police officer's mental health.

Like edgework, absolute sacrifice is a feature of planned police operations. With respect to absolute sacrifice, planned operations include uniformed patrols, plainclothes investigations, and in fact all allocations of police resources: increasing a police presence in one location usually means decreasing it in another location, but always means not increasing it in that other location. Absolute sacrifice is thus to at least some extent exacerbated for police supervisors and police chiefs, who are responsible for the allocation of resources in both the proactive and reactive paradigms of policing. Although he is not a supervisor, Officer Dwight Bleichert is acutely aware of the LAPD's sacrifice of the interests of the recent and future victims of other crimes to the interests of Elizabeth Short as soon as he realises the extent of the response to the discovery of her corpse. While Bleichert's specific concern is the interruption of Central Warrants' search for Raymond Nash, a serial rapist who makes his living from armed robbery and is expected to either rape or kill again in the near future, he is aware of the broader sacrifice LAPD Chief Clemence Horrall is making in detailing 100 detectives and plainclothes police officers to investigate Short's murder. Nash murders two people six days after the investigation begins and the implication is that these deaths could have been avoided had Horrall not seconded Central Warrants to the Short investigation. The situation is reversed in the Wolverine Prowler investigation, where the County of Los Angeles Sheriff's Department (LASD) sacrifices the interests of Martin Goines and the murderer's next three victims to the interests of the victims of the crimes Upshaw's colleagues are investigating.

8.1.4 Worldmaking

The practice of policing is worldmaking because its goal, public protection, requires the re-creation of social reality. This re-creation is achieved by negotiating the relationship between power and powerlessness by means of the exercise of authority and the employment of discretion. Worldmaking usually threatens police legitimacy when police officers exercise an authority they do not possess or use extrajudicial means to re-create social reality, such as Detective Raymond Velcoro's interrogation of Irving Pitlor (although, like the HASD, his actions could simultaneously be contributing to public protection). All three of the case studies feature a tactic from the proactive paradigm of policing that can result in a revocation of police legitimacy in spite of being both authorised and legal: undercover operations. Bezzerides and Upshaw take part in undercover operations in order to re-create social reality, Bezzerides because there is no other way to pursue the lead acquired by Velcoro and Upshaw because there is no other way to establish a task force for the Wolverine Prowler investigation. Upshaw is not particularly invested in the operation, which is low risk (as he is not infiltrating a criminal organisation) and has no chance of success in consequence of him being identified as a police officer and physically incapable of seducing Claire de Haven (or any other woman). Bezzerides is completely invested in her operation, which is very high risk, and although it is an extreme example it reveals crucial rather than contingent problems with undercover policing as a tactic. First, there is the high risk of injury to the police officers working undercover. The heightened risk itself is unlikely to impact on police legitimacy, but it increases the risk that the officers will have to use force to defend themselves and if that force results in injury or death, then that injury or death has been precipitated by the police rather than the suspects (even if the suspects attack an undercover officer).

Second, and more importantly, there is an even higher risk that undercover police officers will have to participate in illegal activity themselves to maintain their cover. If this illegal activity involves the consumption of illegal substances, then this may reduce the extent to which the undercover officer is a reliable witness, which may defeat the whole purpose of an undercover operation. Marshall appears to have emerged from her high-risk undercover operation for Manchester and Salford Police's Vice Squad relatively unscathed, but she was nonetheless required to actually work as a pornographic model, which the cabal of corrupt police officers attempts to use against her. Finally, as police legitimacy is supervenient on public trust in the police, the deceptive character of the tactic may damage the reputation of the institution of policing. When undercover policing involves the exploitation of vulnerable people it undermines legitimacy directly by using coercion to protect the public. Amia Srinivasan (2019) advocates collective feminine worldmaking over individualistic masculine worldmaking and Marshall's worldmaking is a rare example of the former in the practice of policing, the forfeiture of one's own re-creation of reality for a co-created representational order. Given Srinivasan's justification for her advocacy, it seems that individualistic worldmaking is more likely to be a threat to police legitimacy than collective worldmaking, but Bezzerides' undercover operation complicates any straightforward relation because it is a collective re-creation of social reality by her, Woodrugh, and Velcoro.

8.2 Policing as an Institution

8.2.1 Counterproductive Competition

The institution of policing has a clearly defined relationship with both public protection and police legitimacy. Recall from Chapter 2 that the purpose of the institution of policing is not public protection but self-sustenance: the institution sustains itself and, in so doing, sustains the practice of policing, whose purpose is, in turn, public protection (MacIntyre 2007). Police legitimacy is, however, defined in terms of the institution of policing (rather than the practice of policing) as it is recognition of the right of the institution (rather than the rights of individual police officers) to exercise its legal powers. Institutions distribute money, power, and status and compete for money, power, and status. With respect to the institution of policing, competition is with other institutions – either other police services or other institutions within the criminal justice system – and usually aimed at securing funding or resources from one or more levels of government for the purpose of self-sustenance. This is the sense in which *the ideals and creativity of the practice are always vulnerable to the acquisitiveness of the institution, in which the cooperative care for common goods of the practice is always vulnerable to the competitiveness of the institution.* The most striking example of competition among different institutions of policing in the case studies is the formation of the special detail to investigate Caspere's murder in 2013. Each of the three law enforcement agencies involved has a different goal: the Ventura County Sheriff's Office (VCSO) to solve the murder; the Vinci Police Department (VPD) to protect both its own reputation and that of the mayor's office; and the California Highway Patrol (CHP), which is working for the Attorney General (AG), to gather intelligence on VPD corruption for a grand jury. In a further series of complications, Deputy AG Katherine Davis instructs Bezzerides to recruit Velcoro as a witness against the VPD and Detective Teague Dixon has the same instructions as Velcoro, meaning that none of the four detectives in the special detail are supposed to prioritise solving the murder. It is only because Bezzerides, Velcoro, and Woodrugh ignore their orders that progress in the investigation is made, although this is undermined by Dixon, who has also ignored his orders and is seeking evidence he can use to blackmail his former accomplices.

Like the confidential special investigation's undercover operation, this is an extreme example, which is similarly useful in drawing attention to two crucial rather than contingent aspects of institutional competition. The first is obvious, but important: the more individual institutions of policing there are, the more likely there is to be competition among them. The discovery of Caspere's corpse potentially involves three law enforcement agencies and three more are implicated in the broader investigation (the LAPD, the City of Ventura Police Department, and the LASD). Competition for money, power, and status is much more likely to detract from public protection than contribute to it. When competition among different institutions of policing does detract from public protection, it places the legitimacy of the institution as a whole at risk on the basis of ineffectiveness. The second aspect is that while an excess of police services encourages counterproductive competition, the existence of police services at different levels – local, regional, and national – has value in both deterring and detecting corruption. The CHP is a regional law enforcement agency and the VPD a local one; the VCSO could be considered either, but given the large number of small Sheriffs' Offices noted in Chapter 2 is more accurately described as regional in the taxonomy I have used. When Bezzerides realises that the corruption extends from the local to the regional, she plans to take the case to the national level (the Federal Bureau of Investigation [FBI]), but is unable to do so.

8.2.2 Reputation Management

An institution's *reputation* is the set of stakeholder perceptions of and beliefs about that institution. Stakeholder confidence is a condition of institutional success and sustainability and stakeholders are confident in an institution when it is perceived to be meeting or exceeding their expectations. A *risk* to the reputation of an institution is a risk to stakeholder confidence, which is a risk to the institution's capacity to sustain itself (Fombrun 1996; Rayner 2003; Power 2007). *Reputation risk management* is the anticipation and acknowledgement of changing stakeholder perceptions of and beliefs about the institution in order to prevent or minimise the loss of stakeholder confidence (Larkin 2003; Szwajca 2018). In the institution of policing, stakeholders include both the public for whose protection the institution is responsible and the government institution or institutions that provide funding and resources for the institution. The link between the public as stakeholders and police legitimacy is clear: the public expects the institution of policing to provide protection by consensual means and when the institution is perceived or believed to be either ineffective or relying on coercion, there is a loss of confidence and a revocation of legitimacy, i.e. the public no longer recognises the right of the institution to exercise its legal powers because it is no longer meeting their expectations. As stakeholders, government institutions expect the institution of policing to be effective (in public protection) and efficient (in its use of financial and other resources). In consequence of the direct relation between the confidence of the public as stakeholders and police legitimacy, police chiefs often prioritise reputation risk management over both transparency and public protection (Mawby 2002; Colbran 2022; Harper 2022). Two things are important to note here. First, that as the head of an institution of policing, a police chief is justified in attempting to minimise reputational damage as long as the practice the institution supports is still protecting the public. Second, following from the first, police chiefs may have public-spirited rather than selfish reasons for prioritising reputation risk management.

The reputation of an individual institution of policing is fragile for a variety of reasons, which include its construction, distortion, and amplification by the media and its relationship with the reputations of the criminal justice system and incumbent government that constitute the systemic context within which the institution is situated. This fragility is best illustrated by the circumstances of the West Yorkshire Metropolitan Police (WYMP) at the end of 1980. The institution has been under intense stakeholder pressure to solve the Ripper inquiry since 1977, when the murders were identified as a linked series and the murderer achieved national notoriety as the Yorkshire Ripper. Since the murders of Rachel Johnson and Janice Ryan in June 1977 the WYMP's reputation has suffered on the basis of public perception that it has been ineffective in detecting the Ripper and, in consequence, protecting the public. By the time the Super Squad and covert inquiry are established in December 1980, the Ripper has murdered seven more women, which has lowered the constabulary's reputation even further. The very formation of the Super Squad reduces the reputation of the WYMP still further: an acknowledgement by the Home Office as a stakeholder that the institution is ineffective, which will contribute to a similar perception by the public as stakeholders, which will in turn contribute to a revocation of legitimacy. Similarly, the formation of the covert inquiry reduces the reputation of the WYMP for those who are aware of the inquiry's existence and has the potential to reduce the reputation (and, in consequence, legitimacy) of the service if either inefficiency or corruption are uncovered and made public. Chief Constable Ronald Angus' attempts to manage and outmanoeuvre

Hunter are thus entirely rational (if not justified), on the basis that one of his priorities is sustaining the WYMP as an institution.

8.2.3 *Organised Corruption*

All three case studies also demonstrate the vulnerability of the institution of policing to corruption when that corruption is organised rather than isolated, collective rather than individual. By 1980 the WYMP is host to a cabal of four corrupt police officers, who are either detective superintendents or detective chief superintendents and conspiring with a detective chief superintendent in Greater Manchester Police (GMP). The cabal is able to manipulate the chief constables of both constabularies and is particularly adept at exploiting those chiefs' concerns about risks to the reputations of their respective institutions. The combination of this unwitting support from chief constables and other chief officers with the cabal's relationship with OCGs and contacts in the building industry enables them to neutralise the threats posed by Hunter and two investigative journalists and retire in prosperity once The Ridings Centre opens in October 1983. The corruption in the VPD has a different organisational structure and is more reliant on the corrupt police officers' relationships with corrupt municipal officials. The corruption began in the LAPD, with William Holloway, Kevin Burris, Dixon, and Benjamin Caspere, and migrated to Vinci, where the inclusion of Austin Chessani provides Holloway with a level of protection the WYMP cabal does not enjoy. Chessani is the police authority for the VPD, the individual whose role is to ensure that the law enforcement agency is protecting the public and to whom allegations of corruption are likely to be reported, which decreases the likelihood of detection. Smith's corruption in the LAPD differs in structure from both the VPD and the WYMP, involving fewer police officers and more OCG members. Although it is impossible to be certain it seems that the only two police officers who are knowingly complicit in Smith's attempt to establish his own OCG in Los Angeles are Detective Sergeants Michael Breuning and Richard Carlisle, who have worked closely with him for over a decade. Like the WYMP cabal, Smith is very good at manipulating other police officers into playing either a supporting or active role on his OCG's behalf without realising what they are doing. For example, LAPD Chief William Parker authorises Smith's HASD in order to prevent a war between OCGs seeking to fill the vacuum created by Mickey Cohen's incarceration in 1951 and White joins the HASD as a means to end of achieving his goal of becoming a Homicide detective.

Traditionally, police corruption was treated like any other breach of discipline, with the investigation, trial, and sentencing being conducted by an officer of appropriately senior rank. In 1971, MPS Deputy Commissioner Robert Mark established the UK's first anti-corruption unit, A10, in response to endemic corruption in the constabulary's criminal investigation department (Root 2019). These units spread to other police services and are now usually known as professional standards departments. The Police Complaints Board, an independent non-departmental public body that oversees the police complaints system in England and Wales, was established in 1977 (Maguire & Corbett 1991). Since 2018, it has been known as the Independent Office for Police Conduct (IOPC). Most accusations of misconduct are still investigated by constabularies' own professional standards departments, with serious cases referred to the IOPC (IOPC 2024). The decentralised structure of the institution of policing in the US makes it difficult to trace corresponding developments, but the first dedicated internal affairs division of a law enforcement agency was probably the City of New York Police Department's (NYPD) Confidential Squad, which was established in 1914 (Lardner & Repetto 2000). Rachel Moran (2016) notes both that most complaints about police conduct in the US are handled by internal affairs units and that there are no national standards for these units. She (Moran 2016: 844) refers to the system as 'frankly, farcical' and speculates that it is designed for reputation risk management rather than public accountability. In serious cases of corruption, police authorities have established *ad hoc* commissions to investigate, such as the LAPD's Christopher Commission in 1991 and the NYPD's Mollen Commission in 1992 (Domanick 2015; Albrecht 2017). The Violent Crime Control and Law Enforcement Act of 1994 authorises the US Department of Justice to intervene if a law enforcement agency is accused of violating people's federal rights.

8.2.4 Differential Treatment of Victims

The case studies reveal the impact of both the differential treatment of victims and the differential treatment of suspects on public protection. I focused on the former at the level of policing as an institution and on the latter at the level of the systemic context of policing, but both types of differential treatment occur at both levels. The differential treatment of victims and suspects is a function of a variety of prejudices, most obviously: racism, sexism, homophobia, and classism. In spite of these prejudices sharing an identical structure, they are not typically approached in a uniform way in either the US or UK. For example, unlike the 'isms', prejudice against homosexual people is labelled a phobia, i.e. an irrational fear. As noted in Chapter 7, prejudices like these are often divided into two or more categories: individual or interpersonal and one or more of institutional, systemic, or structural. Interpersonal prejudice is the prejudice of an individual against a particular group. Institutional, systemic, and structural prejudice is more complex. I shall define interpersonal and institutional racism, sexism, and homophobia in this section and discuss systemic racism, sexism, and homophobia in the next, along with classism, which I explore as part of the broader problem of inequality.

(1) *Racism* is a belief in the inferiority of people of other races, people with different phenotypic traits, or people of other ethnicities that manifests in the deployment of racial stereotypes and prejudicial discrimination
(Fanon 1952; Davis 1989; Haney-López 1994; Sussman 2014)[2]

(2) *Sexism* is a belief in the inferiority of women or females that manifests in the deployment of gender stereotypes and prejudicial discrimination
(Beauvoir 1949; Lerner 1986; Connell 1987; Alcoff 2006)[3]

(3) *Homophobia* is a belief in the inferiority of non-heterosexual or non-cisgender people that manifests in the deployment of LGBTQ+ stereotypes and prejudicial discrimination
(Foucault 1984; Butler 1999; Califia 1997; Ásta 2018)[4]

In keeping with the lack of consistency in defining and describing these terms, 'misogyny' is often distinguished from sexism as follows:

(4) *Misogyny* is the distrust, dislike, or hatred of women or females that manifests as hostility or violence towards women and girls
(Smith 1989; Anderson 2015; Cameron 2023)

There appears to be no direct equivalent for racism and homophobia and racist and homophobic violence would be referred to as bias crimes in the US and hate crimes in the UK. As violence against women and girls is not considered either a bias or hate crime, the term is a useful description of a particular type of violence, but less useful as a description of hostility, which is a component of all three of the prejudices defined above.

In Chapter 7, I distinguished institutional prejudice from both interpersonal and systemic prejudice and the definition I employed can be applied to racism, sexism, and homophobia as follows:

(1*) *Institutional racism* is the perpetuation and aggravation of disadvantage on the basis of race, phenotypic traits, or ethnicity by means of complex, coherent, and cooperative human activities sustained by structures of power and status.

(2*) *Institutional sexism* is the perpetuation and aggravation of disadvantage on the basis of gender or sex by means of complex, coherent, and cooperative human activities sustained by structures of power and status.

(3*) *Institutional homophobia* is the perpetuation and aggravation of disadvantage on the basis of sexual orientation or gender identification by means of complex, coherent, and cooperative human activities sustained by structures of power and status.

The case studies reveal the LAPD and LASD as institutionally racist and institutionally homophobic and the LAPD, LASD, WYMP, and GMP as institutionally sexist. When institutional racism, sexism, or homophobia is the cause of the differential treatment of victims, both public protection and police legitimacy are undermined.

8.3 Systemic Context of Policing

8.3.1 Counterproductive Competition

The practice of policing is a situated practice, situated within an institution and a systemic context. The practice and the institution are situated in a context that includes both the criminal justice and political systems. The institution of policing is one of the three constitutive institutions of the criminal justice system in the US and the UK, but its relation to the political system differs in the two countries – and, indeed, within the US – in consequence of some US police chiefs being elected by the public and thus part of the political system. In the UK, police chiefs are career civil servants and not directly involved in politics. The purpose of the criminal justice system is, as set out in Chapter 2, to resolve conflict by identifying those who are deserving of punishment and each of the policing, judicial, and penal institutions makes a specific contribution towards this goal. In the previous section, I claimed that the most striking example of competition among different institutions of policing in the case studies is the formation of the special detail to investigate Caspere's murder because each of the three law enforcement agencies involved has a distinct goal, only one of which involves solving the case. While this is true, it is also an oversimplification because the CHP is only involved as a proxy for the California Department of Justice (CA DOJ), which wants to use the investigation of Caspere's murder as a means to the end of investigating Vinci corruption. The goals of the CA DOJ may not undermine public protection – because the detection of corruption may well be more important to public protection than the detection of Caspere's murderer – but it is nonetheless likely to undermine police legitimacy because of the public's perception of the core responsibilities of the police, one of which is investigating murder.

The covert inquiry in West Yorkshire provides an example of counterproductive competition between the institution of policing and institutions within the political system. The inquiry is initiated by both the Home Office and Her Majesty's Inspectorate of Constabulary (HMIC, now His Majesty's Inspectorate of Constabulary and Fire & Rescue Services), an independent body whose role is to support the Home Office. Hunter is briefed by representatives from both government bodies and it is not clear who is in charge, although the presence of the Chief Inspector of Constabulary suggests HMIC. Notwithstanding Hunter's brief to *review the case in its entirety, highlight areas of concern, determine strategies, and pursue all avenues*, someone does not want him to succeed.

The likelihood is Michael Warren, from the Home Office, and the likely reason reputation risk management, i.e. the Home Office does not want incompetence or corruption exposed in the WYMP because it will reflect poorly on the Home Office's own reputation. If so, then the counterproductive competition is between two institutions in the political system, but it has a direct impact on the institution of policing, undermining public protection by hindering both of Hunter's investigations. The impact of this competition on police legitimacy is less clear. The significance of public perception and the police's reputation to legitimacy suggests that the Home Office's action may actually be maintaining police legitimacy while sacrificing public protection. The problem with this kind of reputation risk management is that should it be exposed to the public, the reputations and legitimacy of both the Home Office and the WYMP would suffer. The potential for competition between political institutions and the institution of policing or among institutions within the political system provides an extra layer of complexity to the systemic context of policing. Where there is a more direct relation between the political system and the institution of policing, such as in the US, the potential for counterproductive competition increases in consequence of there being individual as well as institutional competition. The more competing interests there are, the greater the likelihood of interpersonal or institutional conflict.

8.3.2 Differential Treatment of Suspects

In Chapter 7 I argued for the need to distinguish institutional racism from a more ubiquitous and persistent type of racism on the basis that institutional racism alone provided an insufficient explanation of the LAPD's handling of the Nite Owl massacre investigation and suggested 'systemic racism' as the most appropriate term. Systemic prejudice can be applied to the taxonomy of prejudice I established in the previous section of this chapter as follows:

(1**) *Systemic racism* is the perpetuation and aggravation of disadvantage on the basis of race, phenotypic traits, or ethnicity by means of the material, administrative, ideological, and cultural environment within which structures of power and status are situated.

(2**) *Systemic sexism* is the perpetuation and aggravation of disadvantage on the basis of gender or sex by means of the material, administrative, ideological, and cultural environment within which structures of power and status are situated.

(3**) *Systemic homophobia* is the perpetuation and aggravation of disadvantage on the basis of sexual orientation or gender identification by means of the material, administrative, ideological, and cultural environment within which structures of power and status are situated.

Mirroring the institutional level, I do not think that there is any point in distinguishing systemic sexism from systemic misogyny unless one is referring to acts of violence, in which case the latter term is more appropriate. The relationship between systemic prejudice and both public protection and legitimacy seems straightforward: a criminal justice system that resolves conflict by identifying only some of the people who are deserving of punishment is protecting some of the public at the expense of others and does not, in consequence, have the right to exert its legal powers.

If one considers the contexts as well as the cases, the studies clearly reveal the differential treatment of suspects, from the twice-sanctioned execution of Raymond Coates, Leroy Fontaine, and Tyrone Jones in the Nite Owl massacre investigation to the WYMP's torture of some but not all suspects in the investigations of both sets of crimes against women and girls from 1969 to 1983, to the various attempts by the VPD, Arkansas State Police (ASP), and FBI to charge people from ethnic minorities or of low socioeconomic status (or both) for the various murders and abductions that took place from 1980 to 2012. This can be contrasted with the relative immunity of the wealthy and powerful from arrest, prosecution, and conviction, and the ease with which they are, when arrested, able to negotiate, exploit, and manipulate the criminal justice system to their advantage.[5] The extension of this differential treatment from the police to other institutions within the justice system suggests a more ubiquitous prejudice, but this could perhaps be accounted for by stretching the definition of institutional prejudice to include the criminal justice system as an institution rather than a system. The best example of the need for a distinct third tier of prejudice is the Wolverine Prowler murders investigation. The main difference between the response of the LASD to Goines' murder and the response of the LAPD to Short's murder is the presumed homosexuality of Goines. The interpersonal homophobia of the majority of police officers directly or indirectly involved in the investigation of what quickly becomes a linked series has a reciprocal relation with both institutional homophobia and the wider material, administrative, ideological, and cultural environment that includes, for example, the law. The political system and the public it is intended to serve are homophobic, regarding homosexuality as psychologically harmful and immoral. Restricting this ubiquitous and pervasive prejudice to one or more institutions both minimises and misrepresents the problem. Returning to my discussion of systemic racism, it is worth noting that all three of the Black Dahlia, Wolverine Prowler, and Nite Owl cases take place before the Civil Rights Era, in consequence of which it is hardly surprising that the LASD and LAPD are also institutionally racist.

8.3.3 Lack of Fitness for Purpose

In Chapter 6 I explored the ineffectiveness of the criminal justice system in terms of a mismatch between its perceived purpose and pragmatic limitations. Public perception of the criminal justice system, which is shaped by the mass media and by politicians, is that its primary purpose is the prevention, reduction, or control of crime. The system's capacity to perform this function is, however, severely limited by at least two constraints. First, it can only respond to reported or detected crime, which excludes the majority of crimes committed. Second, it can only respond to *crime*, i.e. criminalised acts, which excludes the majority of harm caused by the state, businesses enterprises, and multinational corporations. In Chapter 2 I described the purpose of the criminal justice system as *conflict resolution by the identification of those who are deserving of punishment* and while the successful resolution of conflict is likely to contribute to the prevention, reduction, and control of crime, it is quite obviously not going to prevent, reduce, or control crime in isolation. David Rose (1996) and William Stuntz (2011) make more sophisticated and more robust arguments for the criminal justice system's lack of fitness for conflict resolution, referring to a 'collapse' characterised by the combination of ineffectiveness and unfairness in both Britain and America. The context of their studies is the Transatlantic shift from a culture of welfarism to a culture of control in the early 1990s, which David Garland (2001) diagnoses as the result of the mass media's reporting on three decades of rising crime. For Rose (1996: 309), a 'state which sends innocent people to goal for life but cannot reliably bring offenders to justice fails to protect its citizens from itself and from themselves'. The primary cause of collapse in Britain is growing inequality. For Stuntz (2011: 2), the criminal justice system is unsuccessful in 'keeping crime in check while maintaining reasonable limits on criminal punishment'. The primary cause of collapse in America is the replacement of the rule of law with official discretion.

Rose (1996: 9) acknowledges the significance of public perception of and public confidence in the criminal justice system and notes that 'as time went on, public blame for the crisis focused more and more on the police'. As the public face of the criminal justice system – or, at the very least, the part of the criminal justice system that the public are most likely to see on a day-to-day basis – the institution of policing is more susceptible to criticism and censure than the judicial and penal institutions. This confirms another claim I made in Chapter 6, that the reputation of the institution of policing is partly determined by the reputations of the criminal justice system and the incumbent government. In other words, when the criminal justice system or the incumbent government are perceived as failing to protect the public, police legitimacy can be revoked in consequence of the institution of policing being part of the criminal justice system and in service to the incumbent government. When one considers the impact of the mass media on the reputations of and public confidence in the government, the criminal justice system, and the institution of policing, the complexity of the situation and fragility of police legitimacy increase dramatically. When one considers the impact of social media over and above the impact of the mass media, the complexity and fragility increase exponentially. There are no conclusive studies on the combined impact of social and mass media on police legitimacy (social media platforms and channels change so quickly that it may not be possible to reach a conclusion that will not immediately be out of date), but the evidence of the impact of the mass media on the acquittal of the four LAPD officers accused of assault in April 1992 and the impact of social and mass media on the killing of George Floyd in May 2020 are sufficient indication of its power. In the third decade of the 21st century, the police take responsibility for the failures of the criminal justice system and the incumbent government while under unprecedented surveillance and scrutiny, with almost every person in every public place carrying an audio-visual recorder.

8.3.4 Politico-Economic Inequality

I have already noted the significance of race and class in the prejudicial treatment of suspects by the LAPD, WYPD, VPD, ASP, and FBI. In Chapter 2, I cited Richard Wilkinson and Kate Pickett (2009, 2018) on inequality: of the world's 50 richest nations, the US and UK had the second and fourth biggest gaps between rich and poor respectively and the first and third worst health and social problems respectively. These inequalities were exacerbated by the impact of the COVID-19 pandemic in both countries from January 2020 to May 2023. As opposed to social democracy, liberal democracy is a deeply unequal political system and the neoliberal hegemony established in the 1990s remains unchallenged (Garland 2001; Wacquant 2004; Reiner 2021). Although liberal democracy is committed to the protection of the rights of the individual, its integration with the neoliberal emphasis on the value of competition in all spheres of life has created a compatibility with systemic racism (and perhaps systemic sexism). Classism and racism work together to widen the gap between rich and poor, maximising the profits of the former by decreasing the salaries and increasing the precarity of the latter (Robinson 1983; Harvey 2005; Hall 2011). My main example of the combination of inequality, classism, and racism in the case studies was Smith – or, more specifically, his success as *a product and an exemplar of liberal democratic America from 1941 to 1972*. His exemplary status is more rather than less relevant in 21st century neoliberal democratic America and Britain.

Inequality has an impact on both public protection and police legitimacy and I briefly discussed the causal relation between inequality and health and social problems in Chapter 2. If the criminal justice system is believed to be either sustaining or exacerbating existing inequality, then it is likely to be perceived as not only ineffective in preventing, reducing, or controlling crime, but actively harmful to those most in need of its protection. An obvious way in which the criminal justice system maintains (or perhaps exacerbates) inequality is the extent to which wealth protects one from becoming embroiled within that system. Manning (2010) alludes to this injustice when he recommends his difference principle for police practice. Being wealthy provides one with more privacy, not only private spaces in which to consume illegal substances and abuse those who live with us, but private spaces that keep us away from those with whom we are likely to come into conflict and away from the prying eyes of the police and the public who might call them for service. Once one is embroiled within that system, wealth matters even more, as Huemer (2021: 98) points out in his discussion of the exorbitant prices of legal services'. Being wealthy provides one with a better quality and quantity of legal expertise and the ubiquity of plea bargaining means that those who cannot afford to pay for their own criminal defence are subjected to systemic injustice. This is true of the US and the UK (see: Rose 1996; Smith & Cape 2017; Nobles & Schiff 2020). As noted above, the situation of the institution of policing within the criminal justice system is such that when the system is perceived to be failing to protect the public, protecting only some of the public, or actively harming some of the public, police legitimacy can be revoked regardless of perceptions of the police. Jake Monaghan (2023: 27) makes a pithy observation that extends beyond the failures of the criminal justice system to the political system: 'The pathologies of policing therefore depend on pathologies in other parts of society.' Having identified the different ways in which the practice of policing, the institution of policing, and the systemic context of policing can all undermine police legitimacy, I address three sets of objections to my findings in the next chapter.

Notes

1 The population of the autoethnography has the potential to include police officers in Canada, Australia, and New Zealand given the extension of Peter Manning's (2010) concept of Anglo-American Democratic Policing, but policing in these countries is beyond the scope of my inquiry in this book.
2 One can believe in the inferiority of one's own race or ethnicity, but this is not the way the prejudice usually manifests.
3 Sexism could also be a belief in the inferiority of men or males, but this is not the way the prejudice usually manifests.
4 My definition of homophobia is more inclusive than usual, including prejudices against all LGBTQ+ people on the basis of their close relation and frequent concurrence. LGBTQ+ is the 'acronym for lesbian, gay, bi, trans, queer, questioning and ace' people (Stonewall 2024). *Queer* denotes the rejection of specific labels, *questioning* the exploration of different labels, and *ace* a general lack of sexual attraction to others.
5 I return to and expand on this point at the end of this chapter.

References

Albrecht, J.F. (2017). *Police Brutality, Misconduct, and Corruption: Criminological Explanations and Policy Implications*. Cham, Switzerland: Springer Nature.

Alcoff, L.M. (2006). *Visible Identities: Race, Gender, and the Self*. New York: Oxford University Press.

Anderson, K.J. (2015). *Modern Misogyny: Anti-Feminism in a Post-Feminist Era*. Oxford: Oxford University Press.

Andrews, K. (2018). *Back to Black: Retelling Black Radicalism for the 21st Century*. London: Zed Books.

Ásta (2018). *Categories We Live By: The Construction of Sex, Gender, Race, and Other Social Categories.* New York: Oxford University Press.
Bates, L. (2014). *Everyday Sexism.* London: Simon & Schuster.
Beauvoir, S. de (1949/2010). *The Second Sex.* Trans. C. Borde & S. Malovany-Chevallier. New York: Vintage Books.
Butler, J. (1999). *Gender Trouble: Feminism and the Subversion of Identity.* 2nd ed. New York: Routledge.
Califia, P. (1997/2001). *Sex Changes: The Politics of Transgenderism.* Jersey City, NJ: Cleis Press.
Cameron, D. (2023). *Language, Sexism and Misogyny.* Abingdon: Routledge.
Colbran, M. (2022). *Crime and Investigative Reporting in the UK.* Bristol: Policy Press.
Connell, R.W. (1989/1998). *Gender and Power: Society, the Person and Sexual Politics.* Cambridge: Polity Press.
Davis, A.Y. (1989/1990). *Women, Culture, and Politics.* New York: Vintage Books.
Domanick, J. (2015). *Blue: The LAPD and the Battle to Redeem American Policing.* New York: Simon & Schuster, Inc.
Fanon, F. (1952/2008). *Black Skin, White Masks.* Trans. R. Philcox. New York: Grove Press.
Fombrun, C.J. (1996). *Reputation: Realizing Value from the Corporate Image.* Boston, MA: Harvard Business School Press.
Foucault, M. (1984/1992). *The Use of Pleasure: The History of Sexuality Volume 2.* Trans. R. Hurley. London: Penguin Books.
Garland, D. (2001). *The Culture of Control: Crime and Social Order in Contemporary Society.* Oxford: Oxford University Press.
Hall, S. (2011). The Neo-Liberal Revolution. *Cultural Studies*, 25 (6), 705–728.
Haney-López, I. (1994). The Social Construction of Race: Some Observations on Illusion, Fabrication, and Choice. *Harvard Civil Rights-Civil Liberties Law Review*, 29 (1), 1–62.
Harper, T. (2022). *Broken Yard: The Fall of the Metropolitan Police.* London: Biteback Publishing.
Harvey, D. (2005). *A Brief History of Neoliberalism.* Oxford: Oxford University Press.
Huemer, M. (2021). *Justice Before the Law.* London: Palgrave Macmillan.
Independent Office for Police Conduct (IOPC) (2024). A guide to the complaints process. Available at: www.policeconduct.gov.uk/complaints/guide-to-complaints-process. Accessed 3 March 2024.
Lardner, J., & Repetto, T. (2000). *NYPD: A City and Its Police.* New York: Henry Holt and Company.
Larkin, J. (2003). *Strategic Reputation Risk Management.* Basingstoke: Palgrave Macmillan.

Lerner, P. (1986). *The Creation of Patriarchy*. New York: Oxford University Press.

Lingayah, S. (2021). It takes a system: The systemic nature of racism and pathways to systems change. London: Beyond Race/Race on the Agenda. Available at: www.rota.org.uk/publications/systemsreport2021.

MacIntyre, A. (2007). *After Virtue: A Study in Moral Theory*. 3rd ed. London: Duckworth Books.

MacKinnon, C.A. (1989). *Towards a Feminist Theory of the State*. Cambridge, MA: Harvard University Press.

Macpherson, W., Cook, T., Sentamu, J. & Stone, R. (1999). The Stephen Lawrence Inquiry. February. London: GOV.UK. Available at: https://assets.publishing.service.gov.uk/government/uploads/system/uploads/attachment_data/file/277111/4262.pdf.

Maguire, M. & Corbett, C. (1991). *A Study of the Police Complaints System*. London: Her Majesty's Stationery Office.

Manning, P.K. (2010/2016). *Democratic Policing in a Changing World*. Abingdon: Routledge.

Mawby, R.C. (2002). *Policing Images: Policing, Communication and Legitimacy*. Cullompton: Willan Publishing.

McGregor, R. (2021). Four Characteristics of Policing as a Practice. *Policing: A Journal of Policy and Practice*, 15 (3), 1842–1853.

Monaghan, J. (2023). *Just Policing*. New York: Oxford University Press.

Moran, R. (2016). Ending the Internal Affairs Farce. *Buffalo Law Review*, 64 (4), 837–905.

Nobles, R. & Schiff, D. (2020). The Supervision of Guilty Pleas by the Court of Appeal of England and Wales – Workable Relationships and Tragic Choices. *Criminal Law Forum*, 31 (4), 512–552.

Perez, C.C. (2019). *Invisible Women: Exposing Data Bias in a World Designed for Men*. London: Penguin.

Power, M. (2007). *Organized Uncertainty: Designing a World of Risk Management*. Oxford: Oxford University Press.

Presser, L. (2008). *Been a Heavy Life: Stories of Violent Men*. Champaign, IL: University of Illinois Press.

Rayner, J. (2003). *Managing Reputational Risk: Curbing Threats, Leveraging Opportunities*. Chichester: John Wiley & Sons Ltd.

Reiner, R. (2021). *Social Democratic Criminology*. Abingdon: Routledge.

Robinson, C. (1983/2000). *Black Marxism: The Making of the Black Radical Tradition*. Chapel Hill, NC: University of North Carolina Press.

Root, N. (2019). *Crossing the Line of Duty: How Corruption, Greed and Sleaze Brought Down the Flying Squad*. Stroud: The History Press.

Rose, D. (1996). *In the Name of the Law: The Collapse of Criminal Justice*. London: Jonathan Cape Ltd.

Smith, J. (1989/2013). *Misogynies*. London: The Westbourne Press.

Smith, T. & Cape, E. (2017). The Rise and Decline of Criminal Legal Aid in England and Wales. In: Flynn, A. & Hodgson, J. (eds), *Access to Justice and Legal Aid: Comparative Perspectives on Unmet Legal Need*. London: Hart Publishing, 63–86.

Stonewall (2024). List of LGBTQ+ terms. Available at: www.stonewall.org.uk/list-lgbtq-terms. Accessed 3 March 2024.

Stuntz, W.J. (2011). *The Collapse of American Criminal Justice*. Cambridge, MA: The Belknap Press.

Sussman, R.W. (2014). *The Myth of Race: The Troubling Persistence of an Unscientific Idea*. Cambridge, MA: Harvard University Press.

Szwajca, D. (2018). Dilemmas of Reputation Risk Management: Theoretical Study. *Corporate Reputation Review*, 21 (4), 165–178.

Ture, K. & Hamilton, C.V. (1967/1992). *Black Power: The Politics of Liberation*. New York: Vintage Books.

Wacquant, L. (2004/2009). *Punishing the Poor: The Neoliberal Government of Social Insecurity*. Trans. anonymous. Durham, NC: Duke University Press.

Wilkinson, R. & Pickett, K. (2009). *The Spirit Level: Why Greater Equality Makes Societies Stronger*. New York: Bloomsbury Press.

Wilkinson, R. & Pickett, K. (2018). *The Inner Level: How More Equal Societies Reduce Stress, Restore Sanity and Improve Everyone's Wellbeing*. London: Allen Lane.

9
REVIEWING THE EVIDENCE

This chapter reviews the evidence from the case studies by addressing potential objections to the findings summarised in Chapter 8 preparatory to setting out the framework for recovering police legitimacy in Chapter 10. In keeping with the approach developed throughout this book, the objections are addressed in the order of policing as a practice, policing as an institution, and the systemic context of policing. There are two objections to my presentation of policing as a practice. First, that there is a methodological mismatch with an autoethnography based on uniformed patrol and case studies based on plainclothes detection. Second, that the characteristics of the practice of policing duplicate the extensive body of existing research on police occupational culture, more commonly referred to as 'cop culture'. My response is that the apparent mismatch yields further insight into policing as a practice and that the overlap with cop culture is both minimal and illuminating. Most reform initiatives have targeted policing as an institution and the objection to my presentation is that it is redundant because all that is required to recover police legitimacy is the implementation of already-existing proposals. I examine the recommendations that followed the murders of George Floyd and Sarah Everard – from the *Investigation of the City of Minneapolis and the Minneapolis Police Department* (DOJ & USAO 2023) and *Baroness Casey Review: Final Report* (Casey et al. 2023) – and contend that while they are indeed likely to improve police legitimacy, they are also insufficient to effect its recovery. There are two objections to my presentation of the systemic context of policing. First, that my approach fails to account for the racist origins of policing in both the UK and the US. Second, that by according the systemic context the same or more significance than the institution and the practice, I have inadvertently or deliberately absolved police officers and police chiefs from responsibility for the crisis of legitimacy. My response is that the argument for racist origins is most usefully applied to revisit the distinction between the high and low functions of policing and that recognition of the impact of the systemic context of policing provides a more fine-grained account of what the public should expect from police officers and police chiefs.

9.1 Policing as a Practice

9.1.1 Methodological Mismatch?

My methodology consists of two parts, an autoethnography (summarised in Chapter 3) and three case studies (introduced in Chapter 4). The purpose of the former is to set out the four characteristics of policing as a practice and the purpose of the latter to explore the four characteristics and policing as a situated practice. The methodological objection is that there is a mismatch between the autoethnography, which is based on my for the most part uniformed service in the Durban City Police (DCP), and the case studies, all three of which involve multiple murders investigated by police detectives. If the DCP had a criminal investigation department (CID) or if one of the case studies involved patrol duties the dichotomy would not be so obvious, but there appear to be two discrete types of police work that are too distinct to be linked by the four characteristics of policing as a practice. In Chapter 2, I explained Anglo-American Democratic Policing (AADP) in terms of three features, one of which is its basic assumptions or paradigm, consisting of two parts: proactive policing (*focused on deterrence and prevention*) and reactive policing (*reactive and responsive to public concerns*). The former originated with uniformed night patrol and the latter with plainclothes daytime detection and each paradigm may involve a distinct practice.

I discussed my critical case study selection process in Chapter 4, setting out the shortlist of nine from which the three were chosen. The second of my three criteria for this shortlist was *a critical case study of the four characteristics of the practice of policing and policing as a situated practice* without reference to whether that practice was uniformed patrol or plainclothes detection. It did not occur to me to seek out one or the other or a mix of the two (as I did with the third criterion, which requires at least one from the US and one from the UK). Of the nine complex narrative fictions selected, two were concerned with uniformed patrol (ABC's *High Incident* and BBC One's *Happy Valley*) and a third with both uniformed patrol and plainclothes detection (Joseph Wambaugh's five police procedurals). The relevant point is not the difference between interrupting a violent assault while on patrol and investigating a murder, but the extent to which both types of police work are characterised by heroic struggle, edgework, absolute sacrifice, and worldmaking. My initial autoethnography and subsequent exploration of the four characteristics in the case studies clearly show that they are. There is *one* practice of AADP, which includes two paradigms and multiple roles in which the individual characteristics may be more or less prominent. I am tempted to say that a detective has more opportunity for worldmaking than I did on foot patrol, but I probably had more opportunity to exercise discretion on each shift than my detective counterparts in the South African Police Service (SAPS).[1] I could also say that edgework was more pertinent to my specialisation as a dog handler than that of a typical detective, but my colleague and role model Carl Devlin was a detective inspector in the SAPS when he was killed in an ambush after several years of distinguished service as a dog handler. Subdividing the practice of policing seems both inaccurate and unnecessary. I am, in consequence, confident that the objection can be dismissed, although it is useful in prompting further reflection on the characteristics of the practice of policing as ubiquitous across a wide variety of roles (which includes different duties or details and specialisations as well as different ranks within the institution of policing).

9.1.2 Cop Culture?

A more compelling objection is that the four characteristics of policing as a practice either duplicate the extensive body of existing research on police occupational culture or, at best, make a minimal contribution to that research. Before reviewing this objection, it is necessary to identify the specific subject of the existent literature, which has accumulated a bewildering terminology over the last five decades. The most common contemporary term is probably 'cop culture' (Reiner 1982: 166), but the following terms have also been used to describe an identical or similar phenomenon: 'working personality' (Skolnick 1966: 57), 'organizational codes' (Wilson 1968: 83), 'socialization' (Cain 1973: 198), 'occupational subculture' (Goldsmith 1974: 1), 'occupational culture' (Manning 1997: 9; Holdaway 1983: 2), 'street cop culture' (Reuss-Ianni 1983: 1), 'police culture' (Smith & Gray 1985: 337), 'canteen culture' (Fielding 1994: 51), and 'force culture' (Rowe 2023: 4).[2] The first distinction to make is between the organisation and the occupation. To deploy the approach I have developed from Alasdair MacIntyre (2007), organisational culture is a feature of the institution of policing and occupational culture a feature of the practice of policing. Organisational codes and force culture are thus distinct from the rest of the terms. Ben Bowling, Robert Reiner, and James Sheptycki (2019) note the significance of distinguishing canteen culture from cop culture, on the basis that the latter refers to the values and beliefs demonstrated while on duty and the former to the values and beliefs expressed while off duty. As such, I shall employ 'cop culture' as inclusive of working personality, socialisation, occupational sub/culture, street cop culture, and police culture.

The concept originated in a series of empirical studies of the sociology of policing conducted in the 1960s and 1970s, most notably Michael Banton's (1964) *The Policeman in the Community*, Jerome Skolnick's (1966) *Justice Without Trial: Law Enforcement in Democratic Society*,

William Westley's (1970) *Violence and the Police: A Sociological Study of Law, Custom and Morality*, and Maureen Cain's (1973) *Society and the Policeman's Role* (Charman 2017; Bowling, Reiner & Sheptycki 2019). These studies were significant in revealing the error of the widely held view that police practice was primarily determined in a top-down direction, by the law, government policy, and organisational procedures, in imitation of the functioning of the military. The idea that police practice might also be determined in a bottom-up direction, by informal or implicit occupational norms or rules, was popularised in the 1980s, at the same time as the concept of organisational culture emerged in the discipline of organisational studies (Reiner 1982; Rowe 2023). The sophistication – or lack thereof – of these early studies is disputed on at least two points. First, conflict over whether cop culture is homogenous across roles, ranks, institutions, and nations or whether the concept has always been heterogenous, admitting of variations along several axes. Second, conflict over the explanatory power of the concept, which ranges from being the primary determinant of police practice to obscuring the actual determinants of police practice. A third feature of both early and subsequent studies, the characterisation of cop culture as racist, sexist, and classist, is widely accepted, but has nonetheless been challenged by a handful of compelling studies (Waddington 1999; Sklansky 2007; Charman 2017). The contemporary and continuing relevance of the concept is that it has the potential to explain the reservation with police reform I expressed in Chapter 1, which is that several decades of it have neither averted nor ameliorated the Transatlantic crisis of police legitimacy. If a recalcitrant set of informal occupational norms partly or mostly determines the practice of AADP, then it is not surprising that neither institutional reforms nor changes in police demographics have improved police legitimacy (Sklansky 2006; Loftus 2009; Paoline & Terrill 2014; Bacon 2016).

Cop culture can be defined as a patterned set of understandings that shapes beliefs, attitudes, and behaviours that are either emergent, enduring, or extinguished over time and in to which successive generations of police officers are socialised (Holdaway 1983; Charman 2017; Bowling, Reiner & Sheptycki 2019). Cop culture is related to police legitimacy to the extent that it determines everyday encounters between police officers and members of the public and its widespread (but not universal) condemnation is in virtue of its negative impact on police legitimacy. The initial conception of cop culture, Skolnick's (1966) working personality, described that personality as: suspicious, loyal, isolated, and conservative.[3] Bowling, Reiner, and Sheptycki (2019) expanded this early model to seven core characteristics: a sense of mission, suspicion, isolation/solidarity (includes both loyalty and isolation), conservatism, machismo, racial prejudice, and pragmatism. Sarah Charman (2017) is sceptical about both the pervasiveness and maliciousness of cop culture, identifying its emerging and enduring characteristics as: cynicism, communication (reliance on interpersonal skills), comradeship, a code of self-protection, categorisation (a mapping of social reality that includes police and public), and compassion. In consequence of the extent to which cop culture is held to undermine police legitimacy and resist top-down reform, it is important to identify its causes. This inquiry is classic criminology in the sense of identifying a phenomenon or behaviour that is harmful, investigating the causes of that phenomenon or behaviour, and proposing a theory-led, evidence-based solution that controls, reduces, or prevents the harm by reducing or removing its cause.

The most popular understanding of cop culture is that it is caused by the mandates, pressures, strains, and stresses of the practice of policing, particularly but not exclusively the mandates, pressures, strains, and stresses of policing in a democracy. Skolnick (1966) initially attributed cop culture to the combined pressure of the authority exerted and danger faced by police officers and more recent studies have drawn attention to systemic pressures, with Bowling, Reiner, and Sheptycki (2019) focusing on the exacerbation of inequality and Bethan Loftus (2009) on the exacerbation of social divisions. Charman (2017) is concerned less with the causes of cop culture than its function and argues that it is a tool for coping with stress, for legal vacuum-packing (exercising discretion), for reinforcing a sense of mission, and for learning (for recruits). If cop culture is also harmful, then it seems to be as complex a problem as the crisis of legitimacy itself with no obvious or easy solution. The most popular position on the explanatory power of cop culture is that it is one of several determinants of police practice rather than the primary determinant (Paoline & Terrill 2014; Charman 2017; Bowling, Reiner & Sheptycki 2019; Caveney et al. 2020). In contrast, Mike Rowe (2023) is not only sceptical of the existence of cop culture, but regards the concept as obscuring the actual determinants of police practice. His argument is a development of his work with Geoff Pearson (Pearson & Rowe 2020: 194), in which they conclude that cop culture provides neither a determinant nor an explanation of police practice. Rowe (2023) refers to their analysis of police officer decisions to stop and search and arrest suspects, which found that training, procedures, supervision, and time provided a comprehensive set of causal factors. Their ethnography, which involved work with 78 police officers based at 38 police stations in three different constabularies over six years, did not find evidence of any shared culture. His (Rowe 2023: 13) aim in writing *Disassembling Police Culture* is thus 'to clear the idea of culture out of the way so that we can see more clearly the webs and associations and to open up the black box'.

There does indeed appear to be an overlap between the various characteristics of cop culture and the four characteristics of policing as a practice established in my (McGregor 2021) autoethnography. Bowling, Reiner, and Sheptycki's (2019: 172) sense of mission, policing as 'a way of life with a worthwhile purpose' is very similar to heroic struggle. The sense of mission includes adrenaline addiction and 'the thrills of the chase, the fight, the capture' (Bowling, Reiner & Sheptycki 2019: 172), which – along with Skolnick's (1966: 40) 'danger' as one of the two principal variables of the police officer's role – is similar to, if not identical with, edgework. Charman's (2017: 336) 'compassion' shares features with absolute sacrifice and with worldmaking. So it seems as if I may have done little more than reshuffle existing taxonomies of cop culture and extracted the set of characteristics that most closely matched my own experience. Recall from Chapters 2 and 3, however, that my approach begins with policing as a practice in MacIntyre's (2007) conception of practices, which are constituted by a set of excellences and require mastery of those excellences and a specific set of skills in order to achieve the purpose of the practice. Public protection requires both the skills and the excellences of the practice and the former are acquired by formal training and the latter by informal norms. The characteristics of the practice of policing are distinct from the skills and the excellences, a product of the tensions between the practice and its situation. Are the informal norms into which police officers are socialised – courage, self-restraint, integrity, and judgement – cop culture? I defined cop culture as *a patterned set of understandings that shapes beliefs, attitudes, and behaviours that are either emergent, enduring, or extinguished over time*, which is – again – similar to but not identical with the mastery of the excellences of the practice of policing. As such, I am open to dialogue about the relationship between cop culture and the excellences of the practice. Ultimately, however, like Pearson and Rowe (2020), I maintain that the combination of the excellences, skills, and characteristics provides a comprehensive account of the practice of policing in the absence of cop culture. More importantly for my purpose in this book, the characteristics of the practice have the greatest explanatory power with respect to the loss and recovery of police legitimacy.

9.2 Policing as an Institution

9.2.1 DOJ & USAO Investigation

In reflecting on their own study of US police reform following the Ferguson unrest of 2014 to 2015, Ross Deuchar, Vaughn Crichlow, and Seth Fallik (2021) rightly warn against reinventing the wheel when approaching any substantial changes to policing. In Chapter 1, I mentioned the Christopher Commission on the City of Los Angeles Police Department (LAPD) in 1991 and the Macpherson report on the Metropolitan Police Service (MPS) in 1999. Their recommendations for reform are as – if not more – relevant today than they were in the 1990s so perhaps the solutions to the Transatlantic crisis of police legitimacy are already well known and what I should be researching is the reasons for the failure to implement them.[4] One can extend this admonition against reinventing the wheel beyond police reform to policing more generally. The idea of 'depolicing', for example, is not new at all and is discussed by Donald Black (1980: 196) in *The Manners and Customs of the Police*, one of the early monographs on cop culture (as noted in Chapter 1). My description of the crisis of police legitimacy in Chapter 1 focused on two murders by police officers as exemplifying the loss of public trust: the murder of George Floyd by Officer Derek Chauvin in 2020 and the murder of Sarah Everard by Constable Wayne Couzens in 2021. The murders precipitated investigations of the Minneapolis Police Department (MPD) and MPS, by the US Department of Justice Civil Rights Division (DOJ) and US Attorney's Office District of Minnesota Civil Division (USAO) and Louise Casey respectively, both of whom published their reviews in 2023.[5]

Minneapolis is the largest city in Minnesota, with a population of approximately 425,000 people, and the MPD is the largest law enforcement agency in the state, with an establishment of 731 police officers. The *Investigation of the City of Minneapolis and the Minneapolis Police Department* (DOJ & USAO 2023) begins with four findings and concludes with 28 recommendations. The findings identify the MPD's failures as: excessive use of force; discrimination against Black, Native American, and disabled people; and violations of the right to free speech. The recommendations for reform are divided into the following areas: use of force (5); identification and reduction of racial disparities (3); protection of First Amendment rights (2); response to people with behavioural health issues (3); accountability (7); transparency (1); supervision (3); training (3); and wellness (1). These reforms are focused on the use of force and departmental discipline. The DOJ and USAO found that the MPD repeatedly and even routinely uses force when it is not justified and excessive force when it is necessary to use force. In July 2017, for example, Officer Mohamed Noor shot Justine Diamond, an unarmed White woman who had called the MPD to report a possible rape-in-progress, dead because she ran up to his police car and startled him. The DOJ and USAO (2023: 67) note that some MPD officers appear to be unconcerned about either departmental or legal accountability and describe the disciplinary system as 'fundamentally flawed'. Complaints against MPD officers are investigated by the department's Internal Affairs unit, the city's Office of Police Conduct

Review (OPCR), or the two together. Of the complaints investigated by the OCR only half were resolved within 12 months and a quarter remained open after 24 months. Of those complaints resolved by referring officers for 'coaching', less than a quarter of the officers referred actually received coaching (DOJ & USAO 2023: 73). As an example, Officer Ty Raymond Jindra was disciplined for abusing his authority to conduct unconstitutional searches for the purpose of seizing narcotics for personal use in November 2017, but was not suspended until the MPD received nine further complaints.

Clearly, the DOJ and USAO's recommendations regarding use of force and departmental discipline would make a significant contribution to the MPD's recovery of legitimacy by controlling, reducing, or preventing its use of coercion to protect the public of Minneapolis. There are nonetheless at least two senses in which the review falls short, both of which involve failing to set out the implications of and limitations imposed by the systemic context within which the institution is situated. The very title of the review recognises that public protection (including crime control, reduction, and prevention) is not performed by the police in isolation. This understanding of policing as a situated practice is commendable, but only two of the 28 recommendations involve the city rather than the MPD. The significance of the political context of policing in the city is reinforced by the first sentence of the first section of the review after the executive summary, which reads (DOJ & USAO 2023: 3): 'Minneapolis is a diverse, prosperous city marked by stark racial inequality.' The next two pages set out precisely how stark this inequality is, with the close alignment of the division of rich and poor with that of White and Black. Policing of the poor is overdetermined for a wide variety of well-known reasons and if the poor of Minneapolis are disproportionately Black, then Black residents are much more likely to have encounters with the police before one even considers whether the MPD employs racist officers or is institutionally racist. If the institution of policing responsible for a city in which there is a large gap between the richest and poorest residents is to avoid being perceived as punishing rather than protecting the poor, then its deployment must be changed at the strategic level.

The DOJ and USAO review has a similar approach to the impact of militarisation on the MPD, to which it both draws attention and fails to set in its systemic context. The first thing that struck me about the descriptions of the misuse of force is the extent to which it is paramilitary rather than civilian. I am not suggesting that the MPD or any US law enforcement agency should be unarmed – in a country with so much legal and illegal gun ownership and so little effective gun control this would be immoral rather than just irresponsible. Notwithstanding, in addition to their firearms, MPD officers appear to be routinely equipped with tasers, chemical irritants, baton rounds, and blast balls, all of which are regularly used unnecessarily or in excess of what is necessary. The paramilitary practices of the MPD extend from equipment to tactics: hog-tying suspects was only prohibited in 2015 and neck restraints in 2020 (after Floyd's murder). Both of these are potentially deadly and almost always unnecessary uses of force. The practice of restraining a suspect by kneeling on either their neck, back, or both for long periods – also potentially deadly – was standard in the MPD. Chauvin, for example, knocked a handcuffed woman to the ground and knelt on her neck and back in June 2017 and knelt on the neck and back of a 14-year-old Black suspect for over 15 minutes in September 2017. What is perhaps even more damning is the review's revelation that MPD officers have to be trained to exercise their legal duty to intervene if they witness a colleague using excessive force against a suspect and that there were 'numerous' failures to intervene witnessed by the DOJ and USAO (2023: 26) *during their investigation*. The review also reveals the prevalence of the military practice to which I drew attention in Chapter 1, the failure of police officers to render first aid to suspects that have been injured, including those who have been shot.

9.2.2 Casey Review

London is the largest city in the UK, with a population of approximately 9 million people, and the MPS is the largest constabulary in the UK, with an establishment of 34,372 police officers.[6] The Casey review (Casey et al. 2023) begins with eight conclusions and 16 recommendations.[7] The conclusions identify the MPS' failures as: inadequate organisational management; failure to manage integrity; an organisational culture that is resistant to reform; the collapse of neighbourhood policing; inadequate protection of women and children; a lack of accountability and transparency; toleration of discrimination; and the loss of legitimacy. The recommendations call for significant reform along a comparable scale to that of the Patten report (Patten et al. 1999) on the Royal Ulster Constabulary (RUC) and are divided into the following areas: radical reform of the MPS' disciplinary and vetting processes (5); radical reform of the protection of women and children (2); rebuilding trust (3); rebuilding neighbourhood policing (2); new leadership and management (1); new oversight and accountability (1); and independent progress reviews of the proposed reforms (2). These reforms are focused on ineffective public protection and ineffective service discipline. The MPS' failure to protect the public is a consequence of its response to the various Conservative governments' austerity measures, which involved: reorganisation from 32 Borough Operational Command Units (BOCU) to 12 Basic Command Units (BCU); the prioritisation of response and specialist policing over neighbourhood policing; and the despecialisation of detectives dealing with crimes against women and children (Public Protection Teams). To take just one of these issues as an example, the shift from BOCUs to BCUs was problematic because where the 32 BOCUs corresponded with the 32 boroughs of the Greater London Authority, each BCU is now responsible for policing two to four boroughs. The problem is exacerbated by the limited autonomy of the BCUs and the limited authority of the chief superintendents who lead them (Casey et al. 2023: 97): 'BCUs are treated like satellites of New Scotland Yard, rather than being able to set their own direction.' Ineffective service discipline is a consequence of the MPS' fundamentally flawed structure, poor line management, misconduct and vetting systems that are not fit for purpose, and formal and informal resistance to change. The MPS' misconduct system is even less efficient than the MPD's, with the average time required to finalise a case being 400 days. As an example, Constable David Carrick was allowed to join the MPS in 2001, to join the Parliamentary and Diplomatic Protection unit in

2009, and to escape suspension from duty subsequently despite a history of misogynist violence that resulted in his conviction for 24 rapes and 25 other offences against women in February 2023.

Clearly, Casey's recommendations regarding ineffective public protection and ineffective service discipline would make a significant contribution to the MPS' recovery of legitimacy by improving its ability to protect the public of London. Like the DOJ and USAO review, there are nonetheless at least two senses in which Casey fails to set out the implications of and limitations imposed by the systemic context within which the institution is situated. She commendably goes to great lengths to explain the impact of austerity on the MPS, but seems to base her recommendations on the idea that the police uplift programme of 2019 to 2023 will provide sufficient resources (Grierson, O'Carroll, Osborne & Partington 2019; HM Treasury 2019; NPCC 2024). A detailed explanation of austerity is necessary because it has to at least some extent been hidden. From 2010 to 2022, the 'real terms impact' of austerity was an 18% cut in funding (Casey et al. 2023: 61). The MPS responded to this systemic change by prioritising warranted police officers, with numbers falling from just under 32,000 in 2012 to a low of just under 30,000 in 2018 before reaching 34,372 at the end of 2022. Maintenance of police officer levels was, however, at the expense of support staff, which included the reduction of Police Community Support Officers (full-time, unsworn) by 58%, the reduction of civilian staff (including analysts) by 24%, and the reduction of special constables (part-time, fully sworn) by 66%. During this period, the resignation rate doubled, creating a situation where over 30% of response officers and over 40% of CID detectives were still in probation by 2022 (Casey et al. 2023). The broader impact of austerity is less well documented. Austerity had – and continues to have – an impact across all public services and the London Boroughs reduced their spending on community safety by 42% from 2010 to 2016, with a slow return to 2015 levels by 2021. Perhaps more importantly, austerity has shrunk the social safety net and caused an increase in non-crime demand on the police, as discussed in Chapter 1. Casey cites a 2018 Her Majesty's Inspectorate of Constabulary and Fire & Rescue Services report on policing and mental health, but does not consider its consequences in detail (cited in Casey et al. 2023: 46): 'Too many aspects of the broader mental health system are broken; the police are left to pick up the pieces.' Austerity has caused an increase in unmet demand and a decrease in arrests, undermining police legitimacy by eroding the MPS' capacity for public protection.

Casey's second failure to identify the limitations of the MPS' systemic context is in her conclusions about the constabulary's toleration of discrimination. 'Systemic' is used 16 times in the Casey review (one of which is a direct quote) and 'systematically' once. In each case it is used as a synonym for 'institutional'. Casey (Casey et al. 2023: 257, 285 & 329) states that the MPS is 'institutionally homophobic' and 'institutionally sexist and misogynistic' and that she 'found institutional racism in the Metropolitan Police'. The evidence for these four – or perhaps three, because it is unclear whether 'sexist' and 'misogynist' are also being used as synonyms – varies in strength and is most convincing with respect to racism, where Casey (Casey et al. 2023: 289, emphasis in original) distinguishes between the '*internal culture*' and '*external face*' of the MPS and explores the relationship between them. Combining the definitions I used in Chapters 7 and 8, the three levels of racism, sexism, and homophobia can be defined as follows:

(1) *Interpersonal bias and prejudice*: the perpetuation and aggravation of disadvantage by means of individual beliefs, values, and behaviour.
(2) *Institutional bias and prejudice*: the perpetuation and aggravation of disadvantage by means of complex, coherent, and cooperative human activities sustained by structures of power and status.
(3) *Systemic bias and prejudice*: the perpetuation and aggravation of disadvantage by means of the material, administrative, ideological, and cultural environment within which structures of power and status are situated.

Casey's review focuses on the relationship between (1) and (2), but ignores (3). In the same way that I described institutional racism as an insufficient account of the LAPD's handling of the Nite Owl massacre investigation in Chapter 7, interpersonal and institutional racism, sexism, and homophobia are an insufficient account of Casey's findings. I return to the relationships among (1), (2), and (3) in the next section.

9.3 Systemic Context of Policing

9.3.1 Radical Approach?

If the framework for the recovery of police legitimacy I set out in Chapter 10 is radical, then it is radical in virtue of two features. First, the framework has been developed by cutting directly to the root causes of the Transatlantic crisis of police legitimacy, focusing on policing as a practice and working from the bottom up (Davis 1989). Second, the framework occupies common ground between the conventional and critical traditions of criminology, seeking the solution to a conventional problem through a critical lens (Lea 2016). Fundamental to both of these features is the distinction between the institutional and systemic levels of policing and the recognition that the latter is at least as important as the former. A potential objection to my approach is that it does not cut directly to the root causes of the crisis with which I am concerned because it ignores the racist origins of policing. As noted in Chapter 1, much abolitionist research argues that AADP began with colonial policing, which was initially performed by the military and included militias and slave patrols. Colonial policing was both militarised and politicised, using paramilitary equipment and tactics for the social control of a racialised population (Schrader 2019; Maher 2021; Day & McBean 2022; Go 2023). Micol Siegel (2018) identifies the beginning of this tradition of radical scholarship as *Policing the Crisis: Mugging, the State, and Law and Order*, in which Stuart Hall and colleagues (1978: 379, emphasis in original) contended that inner cities in the UK had become '*internal colonies*' in the postcolonial era. Alex Vitale (2021) regards the maintenance of social inequality as a crucial rather than contingent function of the police, describing the Peel model as an adaptation of colonial policing from the periphery of the British empire to its core for the purpose of controlling the emerging urban working class.

The objection can be divided into two related questions: are the abolitionist arguments for the origins of AADP correct and, if so, are the colonial origins of AADP relevant to its contemporary practice? While there is strong evidence for the former, particularly in the US, my view is that AADP originates with the Peel model and that the Peel model was a departure from rather than development of colonial policing. My rationale is based on, *inter alia*, the widespread lack of militarisation across AADP practice. Again, the US might be produced as a counter-example, but the very fact that militarisation has been highlighted as a relatively recent and highly problematic trend suggests that it is not – or should not be – part of AADP. The second question is more important because even if the abolitionists are right, the burden of proof rests on them to demonstrate the contemporary relevance of the colonial origins of policing. I give two personal examples by way of response, beginning with an analogy. The origin of the institution of education in the UK is, indisputably, the Christian Church (Simon 1966; Lawson & Silver 1973; Vernon 2004). I am not only an atheist, but believe that the Big Five world religions (Hinduism, Buddhism, Judaism, Christianity, and Islam) are all 'harmgenic' in virtue of their contributions to the mass harms of ecocide, racism, and sexism (Presser 2018: 2; see: McGregor 2023, Chapter 4). My views on religion do not, however, commit me to the abolition of education in the UK (or to the abolition of the UK institution of education). The pertinent question is whether the institution of education remains sufficiently Christian for me to judge that it is more detrimental than beneficial, which is clearly not the case. In Chapter 3, I summarised the history of policing in South Africa, tracing the colonial origins of the SAPS to first the South African Police (SAP) and then the SAP and South African Mounted Riflemen, which was a paramilitary and regular military pairing before the former absorbed the latter. The SAP was the main instrument of apartheid from 1948 to 1994, was responsible for crimes against humanity in the Sharpeville massacre (1960) and Soweto uprising (1976), and maintained its own death squad for counter terrorism operations (1981 to 1993) (Pauw 1991; Davenport

& Saunders 2000; Jansen 2015). I contrasted the SAP with the DCP, which was modelled on the MPS and deployed for political purposes on only a single occasion (in 1985). The dismantling of apartheid began in 1989 and while my SAPS colleagues may well have found it more difficult to adapt than my DCP colleagues, the transformation of the SAP to the SAPS in 1995 was precisely for the purpose of undoing this legacy, a parallel to the transformation of the RUC to the Police Service of Northern Ireland (PSNI) in 2001. As such, the colonial origins of the SAP and RUC provide insufficient evidence for the abolition of the SAPS and PSNI.

The contention that AADP originated in colonial policing does, however, raise an interesting point given the militarisation and politicisation associated with the latter. In Chapter 1, I discussed the militarisation of the US police from the late 1980s and the politicisation of the UK police from the mid-1980s as processes that have contributed to and exacerbated the Translatlantic crisis of police legitimacy. Although I did not use the term, both of these processes are systemic, militarisation beginning with the War on Drugs and politicisation with the Miners' Strike. These systemic problems have been institutionalised over the last three decades and have a great deal of explanatory power with respect to the problems highlighted by the DOJ and USAO and Casey reviews. One of the two key areas for reform of the MPD was its inappropriate – and often illegal – use of force and I commented on its deployment of paramilitary equipment and tactics in the previous section. One of the two key areas for reform of the MPS was its failure to protect the public, one of the causes of which is its core-periphery model of management, in which individual BCUs are expected to implement policing strategies from New Scotland Yard regardless of whether they are suited to the local community to whom that BCU is responsible. As discussed in Chapter 6, the MPS has always maintained a closer relationship with the Home Office than the UK's other territorial constabularies and the authoritarian management of the police initiated by the Home Office in the 1990s has been internalised and implemented by the MPS in the 2010s. Both militarisation and politicisation are more closely associated with the high function of policing than the low function of policing.

In Chapter 2 I delineated high policing as the set of national security functions and low policing as the set of routine domestic functions. Both sets of functions are performed by police services at the national, regional, and local levels, which are all involved in an almost unlimited range of duties that includes emergency response, crime reduction, border control, and counter terrorism. Several police services at the national level, such as the United States Border Patrol, US Immigration and Customs Enforcement, Border Force, and Immigration Enforcement, are nonetheless dedicated to high policing exclusively while others, such as the Federal Bureau of Investigation, United States Secret Service, and Ministry of Defence Police, are dedicated to both high and low policing functions. National security functions necessarily require more militarisation and more politicisation than routine domestic functions. Counter terror policing, for example, originates in military counterinsurgency and requires paramilitary equipment and tactics as well as access to intelligence acquired from espionage in order to control, reduce, or prevent heavily armed and well-planned attacks on the public and on the national infrastructure.[8] In consequence of the significant threat to life, counter terror strategy can be characterised as pre-crime rather than post-crime, i.e. prioritising prevention over prosecution, and thus in tension with the principles and ideals of the criminal justice system (Zedner 2007; McCulloch & Wilson 2016; Mythen & Walklate 2016). The impact of high policing on police legitimacy should be considered carefully, particularly where – as Casey (Casey et al. 2023) suggests with respect to the MPS – low policing functions are sacrificed to high policing functions when funding is not available for both. I return to this issue in Chapter 10.

9.3.2 Absolving Responsibility?

The inclusion of the systemic context of policing involves study of the political economy of AADP, a subject that has received attention from only a handful of researchers in the sociology of policing, most notably Reiner (1978, 1984, 2011, 2021), Peter Manning (1997; 2010), Tim Newburn (Lewis et al. 2011; Newburn 2022; Newburn & Jones 2022), and Daanika Gordon (2022).[9] Like the relation between policing and empire, the relation between policing and political economy has been more widely researched by abolitionists, with Mark Neocleous (2021) and Vitale (2021) making particularly powerful contributions. The objection to my findings is that by according the systemic context of policing at least as much significance as the institution of policing, I have inadvertently – or perhaps, given my former career, deliberately – absolved police officers and the law enforcement agencies and constabularies that employ them from responsibility for the Transatlantic crisis of police legitimacy. Recall, for example, the controversy in March 2023 when MPS Commissioner Mark Rowley refused to accept that the MPS was institutionally racist, misogynist, or homophobic. Rowley's reason was that the term is ambiguous and although his own meaning was opaque, I criticised the Casey review for failing to distinguish between the institutional and systemic levels of bias and prejudice in the previous section (Dodd & Grierson 2023; McHardy 2023; BBC 2023). Extending the objection beyond a particular police service to the institutions of policing in the UK and US, one might regard the systemic context of policing as providing the following alibi: the police are part of the criminal justice system and the liberal democratic state and will inevitably reflect various juridical and political inequalities, prejudices, and biases over which they have little or no control.

My response begins with an article called 'Abolishing Institutional Racism', in which Adam Elliott-Cooper (2023) proposes the discontinuation of the use of the term as a description of a particular type of racism.[10] His conceptual analysis is a critique of both the Macpherson (Macpherson et al. 1999) and Commission on Race and Ethnic Disparities (Sewell et al. 2021) reports and a debunking of the latter's conclusion that the institutions of the Conservative government could no longer be regarded as racist according to the definition of the former. Elliott-Cooper argues that the racialised order of the British Empire has been reproduced by the contemporary state and makes three criticisms of the Macpherson report, that it: dehistoricises racism, ignores capitalism, and fails to engage with the relationship between politics and power. The absence of a historical context is problematic because it disconnects contemporary racism from the racial hierarchy that was used to justify White supremacism and from the role of the police in maintaining that hierarchy. Once the racism of an institution such as the MPS is isolated from 'a historically constituted system of exploitation, violence and control' it is reduced to either intentional or unintentional interpersonal prejudice, which is framed as a psychological or moral deficiency (Elliott-Cooper 2023: 106). In 21st-century Britain, the racial hierarchy of the Empire is realised in and by capitalist political economy, which exploits workers on the basis of their racial identity. Finally, the Macpherson report denies that the law and the policies it underpins are racist, restricting racism to their practical application. Elliott-Cooper does not use the term 'systemic racism' (or 'structural racism'), but refers to historically constituted systems and norms that require dismantling before interpersonal racism can be controlled, reduced, or prevented. His (Elliott-Cooper 2023: 113) conclusion includes a concise and pithy statement of the impact of the systemic context of policing on the reputation of the institution of policing sketched in Chapter 8: 'Policing is generally more visceral and visible than the slower violence experienced through unemployment and exploitation at work, poor housing and education, or unequal access to healthcare and other vital services.'

Elliott-Cooper recalls Bowling, Reiner, and Sheptycki (2019: 183) on the relationship between cop culture and political economy, specifically 'the embeddedness of police culture in the deep structure of policing an unequal society, with policy reforms producing at best cosmetic alterations'. Similarly, Gordon (2022: 8) refers to 'the central role that policing plays in the urban growth politics of post-industrial cities and the spatial and racial inequalities that result'. Policing is a situated practice, which means that it is sustained by an institution and that both the practice and the institution exist in a systemic context that includes the juridical and political systems of a nation state.[11] The practice and institution of policing will thus reflect the various prejudices and inequalities of the systemic context, over which police chiefs and police officers have no control. What police chiefs and officers can both do, however, is prioritise Manning's (2010) difference principle: *given the current range of inequalities in education, opportunity, income, and skills, any police practice, especially that driven and shaped by policy, should not further increase extent inequalities*. Even here, however, the practice of police officers will be limited by police procedures and the institutional policies of police chiefs by the juridical and political contexts in which the institution is situated. In his critique of cop culture, Rowe (2023: 15) makes a related point about racial disproportionality in the patterns of police choices:

> officers are policing as intended. Officers are directed to police particular neighbourhoods in ways that will produce, and reproduce, a disproportionate attention on young men in those places [...]. That is what they are tasked to do. And that can be changed.

Rowe's observation matches the Casey's (Casey et al. 2023: 317) commentary on racial disproportionality in the MPS' use of stop and search:

> Indeed, the Met accepts that it is used disproportionately. They have said publicly that this happens because they target areas of high crime which tend to be poorer areas where Black communities are more likely to live. It has also said that the Met is saving young Black lives by using stop and search in the way they do, as young Black boys and men are not only more likely carry a knife, but also more likely to suffer from someone else using that knife.[12]

The relevance of the difference between the institutional and systemic levels of policing is that systemic causes will bring the police into contact with a disproportionate number of people from ethnic minorities, low socioeconomic status, or both. The institutional response to these contacts can be changed, but it remains limited by systemic factors. Rowe (2023) recognises this when he suggests a refocusing of policing on the vulnerability of the individuals involved in drug and violent crime, which would require a fundamental change to the purposes for which the police are used that is beyond the reach of the institution. Without this systemic change diversifying recruitment and providing implicit bias training will not succeed in recovering the legitimacy that is lost by the public's perception of police racism.[13] Gordon (2022) regards the purposes for which the police are used in River City as primarily determined by urban austerity rather than public safety and is sceptical of the capacity of the police to reduce either racial or socioeconomic inequality without an expansion of the welfare state. In the absence of such an expansion, policing and segregation are likely to remain in a mutually reinforcing vicious circle. The identification of the systemic context of policing and its significance does not preclude criticism of or excuse discriminatory policing. Policing as a practice and an institution should follow Manning's difference principle and when it is not followed either police officers or police chiefs are responsible for this failure. What the systemic context does is show that policing is limited by the justice, equality, and fairness of the juridical and political systems within which it is situated. I elaborate on these limitations in Chapter 10, which sets out my radical framework for recovering police legitimacy.

Notes

1 This is one of the reasons I described uniformed patrol as the apotheosis of the contrast between power and powerlessness in my introduction to worldmaking in Chapter 3.
2 In consequence of the already broad scope of my study, I have restricted my discussion of cop culture to research undertaken in either the US or the UK, which excludes several valuable contributions to the subject; for example, two monographs by Janet Chan (1997; Chan, Devery & Doran 2003).
3 I introduced Skolnick's working personality in Chapter 3, as part of my delineation of edgework.
4 The subject is unquestionably worthy of further research, although it is beyond the scope of both this book and my expertise.
5 Casey's official title is The Baroness Casey of Blackstock DBE CB, but I can neither condone nor be complicit in an honours system that is both derived from and actively promotes the British Empire (c.1583–1997).
6 The MPS is the third-largest police service in the UK and the US, behind US Customs and Border Protection, with 47,000 law enforcement agents, and the City of New York Police Department, with 36,000 police officers (Brooks 2022; NYPD 2024).
7 For a related investigation that remains in progress at the time of writing, see: Angiolini (2024).

8 I use 'terrorism' for convenience only. My preference is for 'insurgency' to describe all organised, ideologically motivated violence regardless of its scale as it lacks the pejorative connotations of 'terrorism'. One of the reasons that national security is a necessarily political function is because decisions about which groups are insurgent organisations and which people are permitted to cross the border are themselves ideological.
9 There is a related field in political philosophy, which focuses on the relationship between policing minorities and liberal democracy. See: Kleinig (1996, 2019); Del Pozo (2022); Monaghan (2023); and Heath (2023).
10 I introduced Elliott-Cooper in Chapter 1, in my discussion of defunding (depolicing).
11 In describing the systemic context of policing in this way I do not mean to suggest that this is the only – or even the best – characterisation of this context or that Elliott-Cooper's prioritisation of the historical context of policing is flawed. I have selected the juridical and political contexts of policing because they appear to be the most relevant to my concern with police legitimacy.
12 Casey is critical of this rationale, maintaining that the stated intention does not match the reality of the use of the tactic, which is that there are fewer arrests for weapons than both drugs and theft. See also: Head (2023). For a contrasting view, based on research conducted in Chicago, see: Skogan (2023).
13 This is in fact Rowe's (2023: 149) main objection to the concept of cop culture, that it obscures and hinders the identification of the real cause of 'aberrant behaviours', which is the role of policing within the criminal justice system and the nation state.

References

Angiolini, E. (2024). The Angiolini Inquiry: Part 1 Report. 29 February. GOV.UK. Available at: https://assets.publishing.service.gov.uk/media/65e06493b8da630f42c862e5/_HC_530__-_The_Angiolini_Inquiry_Part_1_Report.pdf.

Bacon, M. (2016). *Taking Care of Business: Police Detectives, Drug Law Enforcement and Proactive Investigation*. Oxford: Oxford University Press.

Banton, M. (1964). *The Policeman in the Community*. London: Tavistock Publications.

BBC (2023). Baroness Casey urges Met Police chief to accept problems are institutional. 29 March. *BBC News*. Available at: www.bbc.co.uk/news/uk-65110300.

Black, D. (1980). *The Manners and Customs of the Police*. New York: Academic Press.

Bowling, B., Reiner, R., Sheptycki, J. (2019). *The Politics of the Police*. 5th ed. Oxford: Oxford University Press.

Brooks, C. (2022). *Federal Law Enforcement Officers, 2020 – Statistical Tables*. September. US Department of Justice. Available at: https://bjs.ojp.gov/sites/g/files/xyckuh236/files/media/document/fleo20st.pdf.

Cain, M. (1973). *Society and the Policeman's Role*. London: Routledge & Kegan Paul Ltd.

Casey, L., Caddie, D., Callan, S., Fisher, I., Gilbert, C., Hilton, L., Kincaid, S., Lumley, J., Mohan, N., O'Connor, N., Rahman, N. & Williams, S. (2023). Baroness Casey Review: Final Report: An independent review into the standards of behaviour and internal culture of the Metropolitan Police Service. March. Metropolitan Police. Available at: www.met.police.uk/SysSiteAssets/media/downloads/met/about-us/baroness-casey-review/update-march-2023/baroness-casey-review-march-2023a.pdf.

Caveney, N., Scott, P., Williams, S. & Howe-Walsh, L. (2020). Police reform, austerity and 'cop culture': time to change the record? *Policing and Society: An International Journal of Research and Policy*, 30 (10), 1210–1225.

Chan, J.B.L. (1997). *Changing Police Culture: Policing in a Multicultural Society*. Cambridge: Cambridge University Press.

Chan, J.B.L., Devery, C. & Doran, S. (2003). *Learning the Art of Policing*. Toronto: University of Toronto Press.

Charman, S. (2017). *Police Socialisation, Identity and Culture: Becoming Blue*. Cham, Switzerland: Palgrave Macmillan.

Davenport, T.R.H. & Saunders, C. (2000). *South Africa: A Modern History*. 5th ed. Basingstoke: Macmillan Press Ltd.

Davis, A.Y. (1989/1990). *Women, Culture, and Politics*. New York: Vintage Books.

Day, A.S. & McBean, S.O. (2022). *Abolition Revolution*. London: Pluto Press.

Del Pozo, B. (2022). *The Police and the State: Security, Social Cooperation, and the Public Good*. Cambridge: Cambridge University Press.

Dodd, V. & Grierson, J. (2023). Khan criticises Rowley's refusal to describe Met as institutionally biased. 21 March. *The Guardian*. Available at: www.theguardian.com/uk-news/2023/mar/21/khan-criticises-rowley-refusal-describe-met-police-institutionally-misogynistic-racist-homophobic.

Elliott-Cooper, A. (2023). Abolishing institutional racism. *Race & Class*, 65 (1), 100–118.

Fielding, N. (1994). Cop canteen culture. In: Newburn, T. & Stanko, E. (eds), *Just Boys Doing Business? Men, Masculinities and Crime*. New York: Routledge, 46–63.

Go, J. (2023). *Policing Empires: Militarization, Race, and the Imperial Boomerang in Britain and the US*. Oxford: Oxford University Press.

Goldsmith, J. (1974). Introduction. In: Goldsmith, J. & Goldsmith, S. (eds), *The Police Community: Dimensions of an Occupational Subculture*. Pacific Palisades, CA: Palisades Publishers, 1–14.

Gordon, D. (2022). *Policing the Racial Divide: Urban Growth Politics and the Remaking of Segregation*. New York: New York University Press.

Grierson, J., O'Carroll, L., Osborne, H. & Partington, P. (2019). Will there really be 20,000 new police officers? 11 November. *The Guardian*. Available at: www.theguardian.com/politics/2019/nov/11/election-fact-check-will-there-really-be-20000-new-police-officers.

Hall, S., Critcher, C., Jefferson, T., Clarke, J. & Roberts, B. (1978/2013). *Policing the Crisis: Mugging, the State, and Law and Order*. Basingstoke: Palgrave Macmillan.

Head, T. (2023). Against Serious Violence Reduction Orders: Discriminatory, Harmful and Counterproductive. November. Runnymede Trust. Available at: https://assets-global.website-files.com/61488f992b58e687f1108c7c/654e3ee9fc29a51c7a3a4dc6_Runnymede%20SVRO%20Report%20v6%20(1).pdf.

Heath, J. (2023). The challenge of policing minorities in a liberal society. *Journal of Political Philosophy*. Available at doi:10.1111/jopp.12313.

HM Treasury (2019). Spending Round 2019. London: Her Majesty's Stationery Office. Available at: https://assets.publishing.service.gov.uk/government/uploads/system/uploads/attachment_data/file/829177/Spending_Round_2019_web.pdf.

Holdaway, S. (1983). *Inside the British Police: A Force at Work*. Oxford: Basil Blackwell.

Jansen, A. (2015). *Eugene De Kock: Assassin for the State*. Cape Town: Tafelberg.

Kleinig, J. (1996). *The Ethics of Policing*. Cambridge: Cambridge University Press.

Kleinig, J. (2019). *Ends and Means in Policing*. New York: Routledge.

Lawson, J. & Silver, H. (1973). *A Social History of Education in England*. Abingdon: Routledge.

Lea, J. (2016). Left Realism: A Radical Criminology for the Current Crisis. *International Journal for Crime, Justice and Social Democracy*, 5 (3), 53–65.

Lewis, P., Newburn, T., Taylor, M., McGillivray, C., Greenhill, A., Frayman, H. & Proctor, R. (2011). *Reading the Riots: Investigating England's summer of disorder*. London: The London School of Economics and Political Science and *The Guardian*. Available at: https://eprints.lse.ac.uk/46297/1/Reading%20the%20riots(published).pdf.

Loftus, B. (2009). *Police Culture in a Changing World*. Oxford: Oxford University Press.

McCulloch, J. & Wilson, D. (2016/2017). *Pre-crime: Pre-emption, Precaution and the Future*. Abingdon: Routledge.

McGregor, R. (2021). Four Characteristics of Policing as a Practice. *Policing: A Journal of Policy and Practice*, 15 (3), 1842–1853.

McGregor, R. (2023). *Literary Theory and Criminology*. Abingdon: Routledge.

McHardy, M. (2023). Met Police commissioner privately admits force is institutionally racist despite public denials, Labour claims. 24 March. *The Independent*. Available at: www.independent.co.uk/news/uk/crime/met-police-mark-rowley-instutional-racism-b2307426.html.

MacIntyre, A. (2007). *After Virtue: A Study in Moral Theory*. 3rd ed. London: Duckworth Books.

Macpherson, W., Cook, T., Sentamu, J. & Stone, R. (1999). The Stephen Lawrence Inquiry. February. London: GOV.UK. Available at: https://assets.publishing.service.gov.uk/government/uploads/system/uploads/attachment_data/file/277111/4262.pdf.

Maher, G. (2021). *A World Without Police: How Strong Communities Make Cops Obsolete*. London: Verso Books.

Manning, P.K. (1997). *Police Work: The Social Organization of Policing*. 2nd ed. Prospect Heights, IL: Waveland Press, Inc.

Manning, P.K. (2010/2016). *Democratic Policing in a Changing World*. Abingdon: Routledge.

Monaghan, J. (2023). *Just Policing*. New York: Oxford University Press.

Mythen, G. & Walklate, S. (2016). Counterterrorism and the Reconstruction of (In)Security: Divisions, Dualisms, Duplicities. *The British Journal of Criminology: An International Review of Crime and Society*, 56 (6), 1107–1124.

National Police Chiefs' Council (NPCC) (2024). Police Uplift Programme. Available at: www.npcc.police.uk/our-work/police-uplift-programme.

Neocleous, M. (2021). *A Critical Theory of Police Power: The Fabrication of Social Order*. 2nd ed. London: Verso Books.

Newburn, T. (2022). The inevitable fallibility of policing. *Policing and Society: An International Journal of Research and Policy*, 32 (3), 434–450.

Newburn, T. & Jones, T. (2022). Policing, punishment and comparative penalty. *The British Journal of Criminology: An International Review of Crime and Society*, 62 (5), 1196–1212.

NYPD (2024). About NYPD. Available at: www.nyc.gov/site/nypd/about/about-nypd/about-nypd-landing.page.

Paoline, E.A. & Terrill, W. (2014). *Police Culture: Adapting to the Strains of the Job*. Durham, NC: Carolina Academic Press.

Patten, C., Hayes, M., Lynch, G., O'Toole, K., Shearing, C., Smith, J., Smith, P. & Woods, L. (1999). *A New Beginning: Policing in Northern Ireland: The Report of the Independent Commission on Policing for*

Northern Ireland. September. CAIN Archive. Available at: https://cain.ulster.ac.uk/issues/police/patten/patten99.pdf.
Pauw, J. (1991). *In the Heart of the Whore: The Story of Apartheid's Death Squads*. Midrand: Southern Book Publishers.
Pearson, G. & Rowe, M. (2020/2022). *Police Street Powers and Criminal Justice: Regulation and Discretion in a Time of Change*. Oxford: Hart Publishing.
Presser, L. (2018). *Inside Story: How Narratives Drive Mass Harm*. Oakland, CA: University of California Press.
Reiner, R. (1978). *The Blue-Coated Worker: A Sociological Study of Police Unionism*. Cambridge: Cambridge University Press.
Reiner, R. (1982). Who Are the Police? *The Political Quarterly*, 53 (2), 165–180.
Reiner, R. (1984). *The Politics of the Police*. Brighton: Wheatsheaf Books.
Reiner, R. (2011). *Policing, Popular Culture and Political Economy: Towards a Social Democratic Criminology*. Aldershot: Ashgate Publishing.
Reiner, R. (2021). *Social Democratic Criminology*. Abingdon: Routledge.
Reuss-Ianni, E. (1983/2017). *Two Cultures of Policing: Street Cops and Management Cops*. Abingdon: Routledge.
Rowe, M. (2023). *Disassembling Police Culture*. Abingdon: Routledge.
Schrader, S. (2019). *Badges Without Borders: How Global Counterinsurgency Transformed American Policing*. Oakland, CA: University of California Press.
Sewell, T., Aderin-Pocock, M., Chughtai, A., Fraser, K., Khalid, N., Moyo, D., Muroki, M., Oliver, M., Shah, S., Olulode, K. & Cluff, B. (2021). *Commission on Race and Ethnic Disparities: The Report*. 31 March. GOV.UK. Available at: https://assets.publishing.service.gov.uk/media/6062ddb1d3bf7f5ce1060aa4/20210331_-_CRED_Report_-_FINAL_-_Web_Accessible.pdf.
Siegel, M. (2018). *Violence Work: State Power and the Limits of Police*. Durham, NC: Duke University Press.
Simon, J. (1966/1979). *Education and Society in Tudor England*. Cambridge: Cambridge University Press.
Sklansky, D. (2006). Not Your Father's Police Department: Making Sense of the New Demographics of Law Enforcement. *The Journal of Criminal Law and Criminology*, 96 (3), 1209–1243.
Sklansky, D. (2007). Seeing Blue: Police Reform, Occupational Culture, and Cognitive Burn-In. In: O'Neill, M., Marks, M. & Singh, A. (eds), *Police Occupational Culture: New Debates and Directions*. Oxford: JAI Press, 19–46.
Skogan, W.G. (2023). *Stop & Frisk and the Politics of Crime in Chicago*. New York: Oxford University Press.

Skolnick, J.H. (1966). *Justice Without Trial: Law Enforcement in Democratic Society*. New York: Wiley.
Smith, D.J. & Gray, J. (1985). *Police and People in London: The PSI Report*. Aldershot: Gower Publishing Ltd.
US Department of Justice Civil Rights Division & US Attorney's Office District of Minnesota Civil Division (DOJ & USAO) (2023). Investigation of the City of Minneapolis and the Minneapolis Police Department. 16 June.US Department of Justice. Available at: www.justice.gov/d9/2023-06/minneapolis_findings_report.pdf.
Vernon, K. (2004/2014). *Universities and the State in England, 1850–1939*. Abingdon: Routledge.
Vitale, A. (2021). *The End of Policing*. 2nd ed. London: Verso Books.
Waddington, P.A.J. (1999). Police (canteen) sub-culture. An appreciation. *The British Journal of Criminology: An International Review of Crime and Society*, 39 (2), 287–309.
Westley, W. (1970). *Violence and the Police: A Sociological Study of Law, Custom and Morality*. Cambridge, MA: MIT Press.
Wilson, J.Q. (1968/1978). *Varieties of Police Behavior: The Management of Law and Order in Eight Communities*. Cambridge, MA: Harvard University Press.
Zedner, L. (2007). Pre-crime and post-criminology? *Theoretical Criminology*, 11 (2), 261–281.

10

THE RADICAL FRAMEWORK

This chapter concludes my study by presenting a radical framework for recovering police legitimacy. A comprehensive framework must integrate measures at all three of the levels at which legitimacy is undermined: the practice of policing, the institution of policing, and the systemic context of policing. My framework consists of ten recommendations across these three levels and across the spectrum of short, medium, and long term. There are three changes to the practice of policing, the first of which is directed at tactics and equipment that should be restricted so as to minimise coercive public protection and maximise public trust: no-knock warrants, police paramilitary units, police animals, and undercover policing. The second change is to recruitment, selection, and initial training, which should reflect the heroic struggle, edgework, absolute sacrifice, and worldmaking that characterise the practice of policing. The third change, which is related to the second, is that initial and in-service training should emphasise the significance of edgework to public protection. There are three reorganisations to the institution of policing. First, a complete overhaul of the structure of the institution of policing in the US and the absorption of all tiny US law enforcement agencies and local constabularies in the UK into larger police services. Second, no local or regional police agency should retain primary responsibility for high policing functions. Third, the reduction of institutional racism by all available means short of positive discrimination. There are four transformations of the systemic context of policing, two aimed at its juridical context and two at its political context. First, public discourse about the purpose of the police and the criminal justice system should acknowledge the complex reality of crime causation and crime control. Second, governments at all levels should invest in the criminal justice system for the purpose of facilitating reform. Third, the influence of the political context of the practice of policing on that practice should be decreased by changing the appointment of criminal justice officials in the US and replacing police and crime commissioners (PCCs) in the UK. Finally, inequality should be reversed by an evolution from liberal democracy to social democracy. Systemic transformation and perhaps even institutional reorganisation are unlikely to be implemented. Even if they are, the most expedient will require several years before their effects are felt. In consequence, I close with a description of how police chiefs can initiate a short-term recovery of legitimacy within the constraints imposed by the systemic context of policing.

10.1 Practical Change

In Chapter 9, I described my framework for the recovery of police legitimacy as radical in virtue of working from the bottom up and occupying common ground between the conventional and the critical traditions of criminology. The situation of the practice of policing in both an institution and a systemic context is crucial to my approach, which is why a comprehensive framework must include measures aimed at all three levels. In Chapter 1, I defined police legitimacy as *public recognition of the right of the institution of policing to exercise its legal powers* and noted that recognition was likely to be revoked if the institution of policing was perceived as either relying on coercion to protect the public or as failing to protect the public. In Chapter 8, I summarised the findings of the case studies as providing evidence of the use of coercion and failure to protect the public in the practice of policing and failure to protect the public in the institution and systemic context of policing. The measures targeting each of these levels loosely align the practice, institution, and systemic context of policing with the short, medium, and long terms respectively. Weighing the scope of the required changes against the timescales of historical and contemporary reviews, I define short term as within two years, medium term as two to ten years, and long term as more than ten years (Patten et al. 1999; The White House 2022; Casey et al. 2023).

10.1.1 Police Tactics and Equipment

I summarised the practical challenges to police legitimacy as inappropriate tactics and procedural limitations. Inappropriate tactics undermine police legitimacy by the use of coercion and deception to protect the public and procedural limitations undermine police legitimacy by failure to protect the public. Although inappropriate tactics and procedural limitations undermine police legitimacy in distinct ways, they are both closely related to the characteristics of the practice of policing introduced in Chapter 3 and explored in the case studies: inappropriate tactics are a response to policing as edgework and procedural limitations and the four characteristics collectively are all emergent from the tensions among the practice, institution, and systemic context of policing. In Chapter 9, I discussed the contention that the practice of Anglo-American Democratic Policing (AADP) originated in the practice of colonial policing, which was militarised and politicised, using paramilitary tactics and equipment for the social control of a racialised population. I rejected the abolitionist argument for this position while noting that the contemporary trends of militarisation and politicisation are inconsistent with AADP and a threat to police legitimacy. Militarisation in the US began with the War on Drugs in the late 1980s and threatens legitimacy by using coercion to protect the public. Politicisation in the UK began with the deployment of the police in the Miners' Strike of 1984 to 1985 and threatens legitimacy by failing to protect (all of) the public.

In consequence of these threats to police legitimacy, my first recommendation is:

(1) *Tactics and equipment associated with militarisation and politicisation should be restricted so as to minimise coercion and deception.* These include:

   a   *No-knock warrants*: there is ample evidence that failure to knock and announce is an unnecessarily coercive tactic which often raises risk for police and public alike. The killing of Breonna Taylor in Louisville in March 2020 is a particularly compelling example (DOJ & USAO 2023; see also: Balko 2021).

   b   *Paramilitary police units*: should be used only for the purpose they were intended (very-high-risk incidents that require specialist training and equipment for safe resolution) and use only the equipment necessary.[1] No other police units should use paramilitary or military equipment, which would prevent scenes such as those in Ferguson in August 2014, where (mostly) White police officers – in battle dress uniforms, with equipment indistinguishable from the military and armoured fighting vehicles – confronted Black protesters (see: Swaine & Holpuch 2014).

   c   *Police animals*: my (McGregor 2021) experience as a dog handler leaves me in no doubt that the police dehumanise the public when they deploy dogs to hunt, threaten, or attack them. Horses may seem innocuous, but consider the images of 42 mounted police officers charging unarmed protesters at Orgreave coking plant in June 1984 and of (White) US Customs and Border Protection agents corralling (Black) Haitian migrants in Texas in September 2021 (see: Conn 2017; Sullivan & Kanno-Youngs 2021). In addition to coercion, there are concerns about the welfare of the dogs and horses being used as paramilitary police equipment. The police use of animals should be restricted to detection dogs.[2]

   d   *Undercover policing*: the use of police officers to infiltrate criminal and political organisations is always deceptive, often coercive, and sometimes politically motivated. The tactic undermines public trust, on which police legitimacy is supervenient (see: Hadjimatheou 2017; Schlembach 2024). In addition, there are the practical problems with undercover policing revealed by the case studies.[3]

All four parts of the recommendations apply to the US and the UK. The restriction of no-knock warrants could be implemented immediately. The restriction of paramilitary police units and police animals and the cessation of undercover policing could be achieved in the short term. While there would be arguments that public protection was being reduced, there would be savings in terms of both finances and resources that could be used elsewhere. I also take the position that any paramilitary police officer, dog handler, mounted police officer, or undercover police officer that would rather resign than return to uniform patrol or plainclothes detection is no great loss to a police service.

10.1.2 Police Fitness

My approach in this book began with policing as a practice in Alasdair MacIntyre's (2007) conception of practices. A practice is a *coherent and complex form of socially established cooperative human activity* and the aim of the practice of policing is public protection. The practice of policing is constituted by a set of excellences (courage, self-restraint, integrity, and judgement) and achieved by a set of skills (effective communication, physical prowess, technical proficiency, and first aid). The practice also has a distinct set of characteristics that are emergent from the tension between its aim and its situation in an institution and a systemic context: heroic struggle, edgework, absolute sacrifice, and worldmaking. The characteristics can either help or hinder police officers in achieving their aim and are thus of particular significance with respect to police legitimacy. A police officer who is fit for duty is a police officer who has mastered all three of the sets of excellences, skills, and characteristics of the practice. By mastery of the characteristics I mean a police officer who is able to deploy them in the service of public protection or, at the very least, is able to cope with them to the extent that they do not detract from public protection. Developing my delineation in Chapter 3, a 'good cop' is a cop who has mastered the excellences, skills, and characteristics of the practice. I am tempted to say that one can be a good cop without mastering all of the skills. In the UK, for example, technical proficiency in response driving and with firearms are neither part of initial training nor mandatory in-servic training. It is nonetheless desirable that all police officers in the UK are competent to respond to crimes-in-progress at high speed and effective communication, physical prowess, and first aid are similarly (if not more) significant to public protection so I see no reason to distinguish the skills from the excellences and the characteristics.

Broadly speaking, current police officer training in the US and UK focuses on the acquisition of the skills and the furnishing of a foundation for the acquisition of the excellences at the expense of coping with the characteristics. The characteristics of the practice of policing have become more rather than less important in the 21st century, an era in which almost every person in every public place carries an audio-visual recorder and the police are subjected to unprecedented surveillance and scrutiny. In a time of crisis, members of the public are more likely to use their smartphones to record an officer struggling with a suspect than to call for assistance. One of several consequences of the ubiquity of the smartphone is the exacerbation of policing as a heroic struggle: not only can good police work, motivated by good intentions, increase extent inequalities and contribute to a loss of legitimacy, but a good police officer, who has mastered all of the excellences, skills, and characteristics and is motivated by good intentions, can find herself going viral on social media and be subject to the humiliation and abuse that entails. The relationship between the characteristics of the practice and police legitimacy and between the characteristics and good policing is sufficient reason to recommend:

(2) *The characteristics of the practice of policing should be reflected in recruitment, selection, and training*: the pitfalls associated with each should be acknowledged from the very beginning of the process and addressed as fully as possible in police training.[4]

One of the benefits of implementing this recommendation would very likely be an increase in police officer retention. The Transatlantic crisis of legitimacy has caused recruitment problems in both the US and the UK (BBC 2022; Brown, Jennings & Brown-Clark 2022; Leonard & Blankstein 2023; Westneat 2023). In England and Wales, the problem has to some extent been addressed by the uplift programme of 2019 to 2023, but this has created problems of its own, including an acceleration of voluntary resignations (Clinton 2022; Tyson & Charman 2022). Sarah Charman (Charman & Bennett 2022; Charman & Tyson 2023) has, once again, provided exemplary research on this phenomenon and her criminological inquiry into its causes suggests that greater awareness of and an ability to master or cope with the characteristics would reduce resignations.

Policing is distinguished from most other practices by the legitimate use of force and the use of force has a direct impact on police legitimacy: if excessive, the police are perceived as relying on coercion rather than consent; if inadequate, the police are perceived as failing to protect the public. Uses of force are more likely to be recorded by the public and more likely to go viral than other interactions between police and public. Every public police use of force now has the potential to be seen by millions of people and use of force is, by its very nature, unpredictable, messy, and unpleasant to watch – even when it is legal, reasonable, and competent. To take just one example, a CBC News (2016) video clip on YouTube shows Metropolitan Police Service (MPS) officers confronting a mentally ill man walking along a residential street with a machete. When the incident starts, there are nine police officers, most of whom have their batons drawn. When the incident ends, there are approximately 25 police officers at the scene, several with shields in addition to batons. The detention is an exemplary use of force with a serious threat to the public being neutralised without any serious injuries to either the suspect or the officers, but it does not *look* professional. Many recorded incidents often exclude the precursor to the police use of force and watching a few seconds of violence without any context increases the likelihood of a prejudicial judgement against the officers involved. In such circumstances, one may well wonder if it is even possible to retain, let alone recover, police legitimacy, a point to which I return at the end of this chapter. In Chapter 8, I noted that a police service full of officers who are physically incapable of protecting the public is a police service that is likely to be perceived as ineffective. Policing is edgework and there is a close relationship among all three of edgework, use of force, and police legitimacy such that:

(3) The significance of edgework should be emphasised in initial and in-service police training.

In Chapter 8, I mentioned the additional challenge to women police officers in virtue of the combination of toxic masculinity, gender stereotypes, and sex differences, which was explored in the Southern California, 2013–2014 case study. I revisit this point here because both the Casey review (Casey et al. 2023) and the Police Foundation's Strategic Review of Policing in England and Wales (Muir et al. 2022) assume that gender parity is desirable, with Casey noting that the MPS has only 29% women police officers in contrast to 52% of London's population.[5] My concern is that their shared position fails to recognise policing as a fundamentally physical job. It has always seemed strange to me that firefighting is uncontroversially regarded as a practice requiring considerable physical prowess whereas policing is not. At present, only 8% of firefighters in England and Wales are women, as opposed to 51% of the population. The equivalent in policing is 32% (GOV.UK 2021, 2023c). The apparent consensus that 8% is acceptable and 32% problematic fails to recognise the similarity of the physical demands of the two practices. I am not suggesting that recruitment should not target more women or that the institution of policing is not sexist, but that gender parity should be considered in the context of the characteristics of the practice of policing.

10.2 Institutional Reorganisation

10.2.1 Structure and Size

I summarised the institutional challenges to police legitimacy as: competition for resources among law enforcement agencies and constabularies; the safeguarding of law enforcement agency and constabulary reputations; corruption within law enforcement agencies and constabularies; and the reinforcing of racism, sexism, and homophobia. Each of these challenges undermines police legitimacy by failing to protect the public or, more specifically, by subverting the practice it sustains, whose purpose is public protection. Competition between law enforcement agencies and constabularies is a function of the number of law enforcement agencies and constabularies with overlapping jurisdictions or responsibilities. The safeguarding of reputations, corruption, and institutional prejudice can all be reduced by more robust governance and more robust service discipline, which require, in turn, effective leadership and efficient organisation. I shall, in consequence, address all four of these challenges by examining the structure and the size of the institutions of policing in the US and the UK. There was only one sentence in the Casey review (Casey et al. 2023: 86) that genuinely shocked me: 'For example, the Met could not tell us how many trained drivers they needed across the force, or how many detectives they needed.' How can a constabulary not know how many drivers or detectives it needs or has? Driving has become the core component of uniformed patrol with the sacrifice of neighbourhood policing to response policing and detectives are the core component of criminal investigation. In addition, this observation was made at a time when the MPS claimed to be prioritising both response policing and Public Protection Teams. If there might not be a driver to respond to an emergency call or a detective to investigate a reported crime, then the beliefs, attitudes, and behaviours of the drivers and detectives hardly matter. The practice of policing will only be effective in an institution that is at least minimally efficient, which requires a little more than knowing how many drivers and detectives one has.

How much worse, then, is a nation that does not know how many law enforcement agencies it has? In my discussion of the institution of policing in the US in Chapter 2, I stated that there are *approximately 18,000* law enforcement agencies. I am not even sure this figure is accurate (if the precise number is, for example, closer to 17,000) in spite of research based on US Department of Justice (DOJ) reports published from 2016 to 2022 and corroborated with a variety of academic sources. In their DOJ report, Duren Banks and colleagues (2019: 1) note that the 'decentralized, fragmented, and local nature of law enforcement in the United States makes it challenging to accurately count the number of agencies and officers'. One might respond by claiming that as the US is a federal republic, the pertinent question is the number of law enforcement agencies in each state. I am not convinced that this question would be any easier to answer, but even if it was, the existence of 83 federal law enforcement agencies demonstrates the need for some degree of coherence among the national, regional, and local levels (Brooks 2022). Stephen Rushin (2017: 17) draws attention to one of the problems with the fragmented character of the institution: 'Several inherent characteristics of American policing – local political accountability, decentralization, significant frontline discretion, and the general lack of federal oversight – allow a handful of police departments to violate individual rights with virtual impunity.' Decentralisation hinders reform and Jamiles Lartey (2023) cites James Comey, Director of the Federal Bureau of Investigation (FBI) from 2013 to 2017, on his chagrin at having less data on lethal uses of force than both *The Guardian* and *The Washington Post* newspapers in 2015. Lartey goes on to criticise the FBI's efforts to remedy this situation, which involved establishing a programme that only began in 2019, is voluntary, and is supported by only two thirds of US law enforcement agencies. He is similarly critical of President Joe Biden's Executive Order 14074 of May 2022, which had failed to meet its initial deadlines by February 2023 (The White House 2022). Simply put, the fragmented structure of the institution of policing in the US precludes consistency in professional standards crucial to sustaining the practice of policing, such as leadership, discipline, equipment, training, and recruitment.[6]

Recall my claim from Chapter 2 that if the US institution of policing was structured along UK lines there would be 290 law enforcement agencies rather than 18,000 (and that if the UK institution of policing was structured along US lines there would be 4,286 constabularies rather than 69). I also distinguished the two institutions by the different levels at which the majority of police officers are employed: 63% of law enforcement agents in the US are employed at the local level (in contrast with 0.2% in the UK) and 8% of police officers in the UK are employed at the regional level in contrast with 20% in the US). I noted that neither of these sets of statistics reveal the most significant difference between the two institutions of policing, which is that 30% of law enforcement agencies in the US employ less than ten agents. Banks and colleagues

(2016: 1) describe the situation as: 'The most common type of agency is the small town police department that employs 10 or fewer officers.' The problem of consistency in professional standards is exacerbated in these tiny law enforcement agencies. At the other end of the scale, the City of New York Police Department (NYPD) is the second-largest police service in the US and UK, with approximately 36,000 police officers (behind US Customs and Border Protection, which has 47,000 agents) (Brooks 2022; NYPD 2024). The MPS is the largest police service in the UK and the third-largest in the US and UK, with an establishment of 34,372 police officers (Casey et al. 2023). Both the NYPD and the MPS are considerably larger than the next-largest police service in each country.

The Casey review (Casey et al. 2023: 25, emphasis in original) implies that the MPS is too big to function efficiently and the last sentence of her recommendations suggests '**dividing up the Met into national, specialist and London responsibilities**' if its public protection does not improve in the next two to five years. Plans to reduce England and Wales' 43 constabularies to 13 'superforces' in 2006 were rejected and the Casey review appears to provide evidence in support of this decision (Loveday 2006: 25). In contrast, while the NYPD has been the subject of several scandals since the publication of the Mollen Commission report (Mollen et al. 1994) – including the killing of Amadou Diallo in 1999, the discriminatory surveillance of Muslim communities from 2002 to 2014, and the killing of Eric Garner in 2014 – its legitimacy has been called into question because of its use of coercion, not failure to protect the public. Indeed, the New York City Council Resolution on Police Reform of March 2021 (NYC 2021) addresses classism, racism, and accountability rather than effectiveness or efficiency.[7] As such, the problem with the MPS does not seem to be that it is too big, but that it is poorly led and poorly organised. The structural reorganisation of policing should thus be focused on the smaller law enforcement agencies. As this reorganisation is complex, I divide my recommendation into two parts:

(4) *The institution of policing should be restructured:*

    a   *Long-term goals (US)*: the employment of the majority of law enforcement agents at the regional level, a substantial

reduction of the number of law enforcement agencies, and meaningful oversight by the DOJ.
b *Short-term goals (US and UK)*: US law enforcement agencies with ten or fewer agents and all local UK constabularies should be absorbed by appropriate police services.

The existence of local constabularies in the UK is not particularly problematic because of the insubstantial proportion of constables they employ – even though three of the 17 have more than 50 police officers, which makes them large by US standards – but they raise the same concerns about professionalism as the tiny US law enforcement agencies. Local constabularies could either be absorbed into the territorial constabularies or have their police officers replaced with security guards. My inclination is to raise the minimum number of law enforcement agents to significantly more than 11 for the retention of a US law enforcement agency, but keeping the number at 11 would enable institutional change that is both substantial and swift. There are two further points worth mentioning with regard to this structural reorganisation. First, as noted in Chapter 2, the number of law enforcement agencies with fewer than ten agents decreased by 1.3% from 2013 to 2020 (Reaves 2015; Goodison 2022). This may appear to be a negligible figure, but 1.3% of 18,000 means the loss of 234 law enforcement agencies in seven years. Second, following the Police Act 1964, the number of constabularies in England and Wales was reduced from 117 to 43 from 1966 to 1974, remodelling UK policing as a regional rather than local institution in eight years (Loader & Mulcahy 2003). A comparative remodelling of the US institution of policing is therefore an achievable long-term goal. As in the previous section, I take the position that any police officer who would rather resign than work for a larger police service is no great loss to the institution of policing.

10.2.2 Decolonising Policing

I use 'decolonising' here as an abbreviation for maintaining the distance between AADP and colonial policing in the face of militarisation and politicisation. In Chapter 9, I discussed the relationship between colonial policing and high policing, arguing that the set of national security functions necessarily requires more militarisation and politicisation than the set of routine domestic functions. Maintaining as much distance as possible between high and low policing would contribute to the maintenance of the distance between AADP and colonial policing – which would be an indirect, or perhaps in some cases direct, corrective to institutional racism. I make this claim because border control has historically focused on people of colour, on people from the Americas south of the border in the US and on people from the periphery of the former empire in the UK (Tyler 2010; DOJ 2011; Yeng 2014). Since 2001, counter terrorism has focused on Islamist groups, which has created conflict between the police and Muslim communities in the US and the UK (McCulloch & Wilson 2016; Elshimi 2017; Nguyen 2019). An initial attempt to maintain the distance between high and low policing is:

(5) *No local or regional police service should have primary responsibility for high policing functions.*

National police services should be responsible for those functions.

In Chapter 9, I also stated that the Casey review makes the strongest case for institutional racism (as opposed to sexism and homophobia), which begins with a statistical analysis. London's population of 9 million people (swelled by large numbers of visitors throughout the year) is the most ethnically diverse in the UK, with only 54% of Londoners identifying as White (as opposed to 74% in England and Wales). In contrast, 84% of MPS officers identify as White (as opposed to 92% in England and Wales) (Casey et al. 2023; GOV.UK 2023a, 2023b).[8] While the MPS is thus more ethnically diverse than the institution of English and Welsh policing (and UK policing), it does not reflect the diversity of the public it is sworn to protect. This dichotomy between police and public is exacerbated by the fact that the majority of MPS officers do not live in London.[9] As with gender, Casey seems to take it for granted that precise proportionality is desirable, noting that ethnic parity could only be achieved in a decade if the MPS increased its Black, Asian, and minority ethnic recruitment to a minimum of 50% immediately. Given the explicit parallel with the Patten report, I wondered if she was going to include this recommendation in her proposed reforms. The Patten report introduced a 50% quota of Police Service of Northern Ireland (PSNI) recruitment from Northern Ireland's Catholic minority in order to diversify the overwhelmingly Protestant composition of the former Royal Ulster Constabulary (RUC). The measure was discontinued in 2011, once the Catholic proportion of the constabulary had reached 30% (Patten et al. 1999; Muir et al. 2022).

Casey (Casey et al. 2023: 24) does not recommend a similar measure for the MPS, drawing back to: 'A narrowing in the gap between the diversity of the Met's workforce, including its officers and senior officers, and the make-up of the city it polices.' The Police Foundation (Muir et al. 2022: 100) is more convinced, however, contending that positive discrimination in recruitment was crucial to the 'refounding' of the RUC as the PSNI in 2001. In consequence, their (Muir et al. 2022: 100) 20th recommendation (of 56) is:

> The government should develop a plan to improve workforce diversity, setting targets for female and ethnic minority recruitment for each police force. In order to facilitate this the government should legislate to allow police forces to introduce time limited positive discrimination policies until such time as these targets are achieved.

The parallel with Northern Ireland is an oversimplification. Northern Ireland was – and to some extent remains – a country deeply divided into two groups distinguished by religious affiliation. In contrast, the statistics I cited from Casey represent only a single aspect of London's incredibly diverse population (I have not, for example, included nationality or religion). In addition, while a likeness between a police service and the public it protects is obviously desirable, it is a guarantee of neither public protection nor police legitimacy.

The Baltimore City Police Department (BPD) achieved notoriety in 2015 following the death in custody of Freddie Gray and again in 2017 with the indictment of its Gun Trace Task Force for racketeering (DOJ 2016; Fenton 2021). Baltimore's population at the time was 621,000, 63% of whom were African American. The BPD had an establishment of 2,600 police officers, 42% of whom were African American, i.e. roughly equal numbers of Black and White officers.[10] Notwithstanding, the DOJ's (2016) *Investigation of the Baltimore City Police Department* found that the law enforcement agency demonstrated patterns of discrimination against African Americans, excessive uses of force, and unconstitutional exercises of power. The ratio between African American police officers and public is similar in the Chicago Police Department (CPD), which is the sixth-largest law enforcement agency in the US and was subject to an equally scathing investigation by the US Department of Justice Civil Rights Division and US Attorney's Office Northern District of Illinois in 2017 (DOJ & USAO 2017; Holliday & Backlund 2015).[11] The DOJ report on the BPD noted that 75% of officers live outside of the city they police, mirroring concerns in both the MPS and NYPD. The CPD, however, requires all of its officers to live within the city and this policy has not improved public protection any more than the law enforcement agency's relatively high level of ethnic diversity. In summary, there is at present insufficient evidence to recommend temporary positive discrimination measures in recruitment:[12]

(6) *Institutional racism should be reduced by all available means short of positive discrimination.*

10.3 Systemic Transformation

10.3.1 Juridical Investment

I summarised the systemic challenges to police legitimacy as: competition for resources among different institutions of the criminal justice system; the reinforcing of racism, sexism, and homophobia; public perception of the criminal justice system; and a political context in which social inequality is prevalent. Each of these challenges undermines police legitimacy by failing to protect the public or, more specifically, by providing a context in which the aim of the situated practice of policing, public protection, is subverted. The four challenges can be addressed by two measures that are as obvious as they are unlikely to be implemented: a well-resourced, publicly funded criminal justice system and social democratic governance. The first measure is aimed at the juridical context of the practice of policing and the second at its political context. There is a second measure targeting the juridical context that may not be as important as resourcing and funding, but precedes questions of criminal justice system efficiency. In Chapter 8, I stated that public perception of the primary purpose of the criminal justice system is the prevention, reduction, or control of crime. This misconception is exploited by politicians seeking popular support and President Barack Obama's administration is the only government in the US and UK not to have represented itself as 'tough on crime' (or words to that effect) in (at least) the last three decades. As the public face of the criminal justice system, the reputation of the institution of policing is particularly vulnerable to the fallacy that the system is primarily an instrument of – and the primary instrument of – crime prevention, reduction, or control. Crime is a complex phenomenon with economic, social, psychological, and political causes and neither the institution of policing nor the criminal justice system are likely to control, let alone reduce or prevent, it in isolation. The purpose of the criminal justice system is conflict resolution and the purpose of the situated practice of policing public protection.

Police chiefs, justice officials, and politicians should be honest about what the system and its constituting institutions are intended and able to achieve. This may seem redundant, but a sample of four regional police service crime plans and strategies from similarly-sized services in the US and UK suggests otherwise.[13] The title of Lancashire Constabulary's police and crime plan is *Leading the Fight Against Crime* (Snowden 2021) and the first part (of two) of the first pillar (of three) of Merseyside Police's police and crime plan is 'Fighting Crime' (Spurrell 2021: 13). Police chiefs and the government officials to whom they are responsible all know that 'crime fighting' is both a misnomer and a relatively small part of the practice of policing. The Phoenix Police Department changed from a strategic plan in 2021 to a *Crime Reduction Plan* in 2023 and the latter is exclusively focused on 'the prevention and control of criminal activity in the City of Phoenix' (Sullivan 2023: 4). The Las Vegas Metropolitan Police Department's strategic plan is considerably better, with a vision to 'be the safest community in America' and a mission to provide 'exceptional police services in partnership with the community' (Lombardo 2020: 8). Public safety is the criterion against which the institutions sustaining the practice of policing should be judged, not crime reduction. When the public expects the police to reduce crime there is a greater chance of legitimacy being revoked on the basis of ineffectiveness. My recommendation is thus that:

(7) *Police chiefs and justice and government officials should acknowledge the complexity of the causes of crime and the limited capacity of the criminal justice system to abate those causes.*

After my discussion of public misconception in Chapter 8, I moved on to David Rose (1996) and William Stuntz's (2011) studies of the criminal justice systems in the UK and the US, both of which were concerned with what they respectively refer to as 'collapses'. Two more recent studies suggest that the situation has not improved in either the UK in the last 28 years or the US in the last 13. Jon Robins and Daniel Newman (2021: 176) argue that the social inequality on which Rose focused has transformed the criminal justice system: 'We have a two-tier legal system: open to those who can afford it; but increasingly closed to the poor and the vulnerable and the not-so-poor.'[14] The primary cause of this juridical inequality is the various Conservative governments' reduction of legal aid as part of austerity. Michael Huemer (2021) expands Stuntz's exploration of injustice to include: over criminalisation, lack of access to justice, the replacement of jury trial with plea bargaining, over-incarceration, and the lack of accountability of criminal justice officials. The primary cause of this injustice is the development of a philosophy of law that prioritises respect for authority over the demands of justice for the individual, which has been embraced across the political spectrum. At the time of writing, the criminal justice system in England and Wales is widely considered to be in a state of accelerated collapse, with every institution affected: the police are experiencing a crisis of legitimacy; the backlog of Crown Court cases is in the dozens of thousands (Topping 2023); and the prison system is so full that cell space rather than public safety is determining sentencing (Siddique & Dodd 2023). If the system is t have any hope of resolving conflict effectively and efficiently, the judicial and penal institutions are going to require a commitment to public sector investment along similar lines to the recent police uplift programme. If plea bargaining, which is a feature of both the US and UK systems but regarded as particularly problematic in the former, is reduced, then there will be significantly more pressure on the system. In consequence, my recommendation is:

(8) *Governments at all levels should invest in those criminal justice systems that are insufficiently resourced so as to facilitate reform.*

Resourcing and funding should be used to ensure efficient justice rather than to expand an unjust system.[15]

10.3.2 Political Evolution

In Chapter 8, I explained the difference between liberal and social democracy, describing the former as a deeply unequal political system that is responsible for increasing inequality and decreasing social mobility. I stated that liberal democracy was compatible with systemic racism (and possibly systemic sexism) in spite of its commitment to the protection of the rights of the individual and that classism and racism work together to widen the gap between rich and poor at both local and global levels. I referred to my discussion of the various harms of inequality, many of which have a direct impact on the practice of policing, in Chapter 2. The College of Policing's (2020: 16) prediction of trends in the next two decades begins with rising 'inequality and social fragmentation'. The implications for policing are summarised as: increasing violence, increasing drug abuse and mental illness, and decreasing public trust. I am not suggesting that deprivation or relative deprivation is the primary cause of crime or harm, but both causes clearly make significant contributions to both effects. A political system that exacerbates inequality is harmgenic. In Chapter 9, I mentioned that only a handful of researchers have attended to the political economy of AADP, the first and most prolific of whom is Robert Reiner. In his latest monograph, he (Reiner 2021) argues for a social democratic criminology based on the following principles: (i) deprioritisation of the problem of crime; (ii) the political and moral economy of capitalism as the root cause of harm; (iii) justification of penal interventions by harm reduction alone; (iv) ineffectiveness of the criminal justice system in crime reduction; and (v) social democratic governance. Reiner's position on the root cause of harm is supported by zemiologists such as Steve Hall (2012) and Simon Pemberton (2015), but even if capitalism is only one of several primary causes of harm, there are significant criminological gains to be made in operationalising his final principle:

(9) *Rising social inequality should be reduced by means of a peaceful political evolution from liberal democracy to social democracy.*

A social democracy would also reduce competition for resources among different institutions of the criminal justice system by increasing public funding and reduce racism, sexism, homophobia, and classism by prioritising collective responsibility over individual freedom.

At present, a social democratic evolution seems unlikely in the UK and almost impossible in the US. The Conservative Party has been in power in the UK since 2010 and become increasingly right wing (and corrupt) since at least the Brexit referendum of 2016. Obama's presidency was followed by Donald Trump, an openly racist, sexist, and homophobic billionaire in 2017. It seems much more likely that inequality will rise in both countries to the extent where social democracy is only achievable by means of a violent revolution, which would itself cause mass harm. A more modest transformation that would nonetheless contribute to the recovery of police legitimacy would be the de-politicisation of the practice of policing at the level of its political context. As noted in Chapter 1, some police chiefs and many criminal justice officials in the US are elected. In the UK, the introduction of elected PCCs in 2012 was an attempt to reverse the trend of centralisation, but has re-politicised the police in virtue of an overwhelming Conservative majority. My final recommendation is:

(10) *Increase the distance between policing and politics.*

    a   *Long term (US)*: replace elected police chiefs and criminal justice officials with career civil servants.

b *Medium term (UK)*: replace PCCs with sufficiently empowered police authorities.

In the US, the measure would have the additional benefit of reducing competition for resources among different institutions of the criminal justice system by restricting that competition to institutions rather than both institutions and individuals.

10.3.3 Policing Now?

At the beginning of this section, I claimed that the two most important systemic transformations – financial investment in the criminal justice system (8) and the evolution from liberal democracy to social democracy (9) – are as unlikely as they are obvious. At the beginning of this chapter, I claimed that systemic transformation was loosely aligned with the long term, which is certainly the case for (9). Like (8), public discourse about the purpose of the criminal justice system (7) and the removal of PCCs in the UK (10b) could be achieved in the medium term. The de-politicisation of the police in the US (10a) is much more complex and would extend to the long term. Of the institutional reorganisations, the distancing of regional and local police services from the high function of policing (5) is a medium-term objective and the reduction in the number of law enforcement agencies in the US (4a) a long-term objective, although the process would be set in motion by the absorption of 30% of the country's law enforcement agencies by larger agencies in the short term. The longer a transformation or reorganisation takes, the lower the chance of its implementation because extension across one or more election terms requires continuous commitment by succeeding governments and when those governments are from different political parties, they are less likely to honour the promises of their predecessors. This is both the strength and the weakness of democracy: it allows an ignorant bigot like Trump to become President, removes him from office in four years, indicts him on federal and state charges in six, and could see him either back in the White House or in prison in eight. In my discussion of Adam Elliott-Cooper (2023), Mike Rowe (2023), and Daanika Gordon's (2022) studies in Chapter 9, I argued that the systemic context of policing places significant – severe, even – restrictions on both institutional reorganisation and practical change. John Van Maanen (1973: 416) made the same point more concisely and more eloquently half a century ago: 'To change the police without changing the police role in society is as futile as the labors of Sisyphus.' Even if I am being overly pessimistic about the likelihood of the transformations and reorganisations, however, none of them are going to alleviate the crisis immediately or recover police legitimacy in the short term. Legitimacy is nonetheless a property of the institution of policing, which makes it primarily the responsibility of police chiefs, so the question I shall close with is what police chiefs can do about the crisis *now*.

First, police chiefs can push on with the practical changes. The deployment of no-knock warrants (1a) and police paramilitary units (1b) for the purposes they are intended could be implemented immediately – police chiefs do not have to wait for legal reforms, such as 'Breonna's Law' in Louisville (Shepherd 2020). The safe restriction of police animals (1c) and withdrawal of undercover police officers (1d) would take longer, but are achievable in the short term. Changes to recruitment, selection, and training to reflect the four characteristics of the practice of policing (2) and to training to emphasise edgework (3) are also achievable in the short term, though it would take longer for their full benefits to be realised. A commitment to these measures would show that police chiefs were taking public opinion seriously and taking steps to improve public protection.

Second, police chiefs can implement zero tolerance policies on interpersonal and institutional racism immediately (6). The chiefs of tiny law enforcement agencies in the US and local constabularies in the UK can also initiate dialogue about their absorption by larger police services immediately (4b). In discussing police use of force in the era of the smartphone, Danny Shaw (2023) argues that police chiefs should prioritise transparency over reputation risk management: 'Phone footage and social media have exposed police practices and behaviour that have been largely hidden from view. Some of it we are questioning; some of it we don't understand; some of it we really don't approve of.' While I agree with Peter Manning (2010) that the transparency of the institution of policing will always be limited, it is no longer the sequestered world it was for most of the 20th century. I would thus extend Shaw's claim about the counterproductiveness of reputation risk management to all reputational threats: the real risk to reputations in the 21st century is covering up ineffectiveness or misconduct that is almost certain to be revealed at a later date.

Third, police chiefs can initiate change in the discourse about the purposes of policing and the criminal justice system in the short term, although I suspect it would take considerably longer for justice officials and politicians to follow suit, which is why I designated (7) a medium-term measure. For all the criticism he has received, MPS Commissioner Mark Rowley has been exemplary in this regard, drawing attention to the strain calls for mental health service place on response policing and the strain hyperbolic increases in criminal justice bureaucracy place on detectives (Dodd 2023; Fouzder 2023). To take one of many examples from the US, Fresno Police Department Chief of Police Paco Balderrama has drawn attention to the ways in which well-intended criminal justice reforms undermine public protection and defended alternative approaches to public order policing (Ray 2022). Even in the UK, where police chiefs are career civil servants rather than directly elected officials, they usually only say what needs to be said in interviews given after their resignation, which is too late.

What this book has demonstrated is that the Transatlantic crisis of police legitimacy is not the responsibility of police officers and police chiefs alone because its causes include institutional and systemic problems that are beyond their control. The consequence is that the recovery of police legitimacy to the extent where most of the public supports the police most of the time is unlikely (albeit not impossible). Recognition of these limits does not absolve police officers and police chiefs from responsibility for the crisis, but sets realistic and achievable goals and expectations. The goal is that police officers and police chiefs recover public support incrementally and protect the public in its entirety, regardless of its level of support. To this end, police officers should be held accountable for their pursuit of excellence in the practice of policing. Police chiefs should be held accountable for maintaining discipline and increasing effectiveness internally and for changing the existing discourse and shaping public expectations externally. Speaking up about the limitations the situation of the practice of policing places on public protection will be met with criticism from all directions, including from within the institution of policing. This should come as no surprise because policing is no less a heroic struggle for police chiefs than it is for police officers. I am reminded of a considerate note I once received from a detective I never met: 'No one can expect you to do any more than your best.'[16] Any police officer or police chief who is not prepared to be judged against that standard is no great loss to the institution of policing.

Notes

1. If this were the case in the US, the number of these units would be reduced dramatically.
2. At the time of writing, the College of Policing (2023a, 2023b) has launched a public consultation as part of its revision of authorised professional practice for the use of police dogs and horses in England and Wales.
3. While the use of confidential informants by law enforcement agencies and constabularies is problematic in several ways, it does not pose the same threat to police legitimacy as undercover policing (see: Murji 1998; Kamali 2017).
4. The implementation of this recommendation to recruitment, selection and training in the US and UK (and of the third recommendation below to initial and in-service training) are beyond the scope of this study, but would use my exploration of the four characteristics of the practice of policing as its foundation. I applied for funding to sketch such an implementation in England and Wales while writing this book.
5. The New York City Council's (NYC 2021) Resolution on Police Reform of March 2021 also prioritises the recruitment of women police officers.
6. For a brief but enlightening discussion of the relationship among recruitment, training, and legitimacy in US policing, see: McArdle 2023; Lehman 2023.
7. For an exploration of the NYPD's resistance to reform, see: Cheng (2024).
8. There is inconsistency in the exact percentages of White MPS officers reported by Casey, who mentions 82% (Casey et al. 2023: 9) and 84% (Casey et al. 2023: 64) once each. I have used the latter as it appears on page that presents multiple sets of statistics, suggesting corroboration.
9. The NYC's Resolution on Police Reform has a similar concern about NYPD police officer residency (NYC 2021).
10. These statistics are from the DOJ (2016) report, which does not provide the percentage of White police officers in the BPD. A later report in *The*

Washington Post (Wood 2019) confirmed the 63% African American population and recorded 40% of BPD officers as African American and 45% as White.
11 Chicago has a population of 2.7 million, 33% of whom are African American. The CPD has an establishment of 12,000 police officers, 23% of whom are African American.
12 For a contrasting view, see: Quinlan (2024).
13 This was very much a convenience sample as the two English constabularies are those local to my work and home respectively. I matched them with similar-sized regional law enforcement agencies in the US, also selected by convenience (the ease with which I was able to access them online).
14 Huemer (2021) makes a similar critique of the US criminal justice system, as noted both here and in Chapter 8.
15 For examples of resourcing and funding aimed at efficient rather than expanded public protection, see: Braga and Cook (2023); Pughsley (2023).
16 The missive was from Bill Ingram, a detective warrant officer in the Commercial Branch of the South African Police CID.

References

Balko, R. (2021). *Rise of the Warrior Cop: The Militarization of America's Police Forces*. 2nd ed. New York: Public Affairs.
BBC (2022). Police Scotland applicants fall 50% in one year. 5 July. *BBC News*. Available at: www.bbc.co.uk/news/uk-scotland-62040344.
Braga, A.A. & Cook, P.J. (2023). *Policing Gun Violence: Strategic Reforms for Controlling Our Most Pressing Crime Problem*. New York: Oxford University Press.
Brooks, C. (2022). Federal Law Enforcement Officers, 2020 – Statistical Tables. September. US Department of Justice. Available at: https://bjs.ojp.gov/sites/g/files/xyckuh236/files/media/document/fleo20st.pdf.
Brown, J.D., Jennings, O. & Brown-Clark, L. (2022). 'It's changing': As police officers quit the profession in droves, an opportunity for change emerges. 7 October. *News21*. Available at: https://inpursuit.news21.com/stories/its-changing-as-police-officers-quit-the-profession-in-droves-an-opportunity-for-change-emerges.
Casey, L., Caddie, D., Callan, S., Fisher, I., Gilbert, C., Hilton, L., Kincaid, S., Lumley, J., Mohan, N., O'Connor, N., Rahman, N. & Williams, S. (2023). Baroness Casey Review: Final Report: An independent review into the standards of behaviour and internal culture of the Metropolitan Police Service. March. Metropolitan Police. Available at: www.met.police.uk/SysSiteAssets/media/downloads/met/about-us/baroness-casey-review/update-march-2023/baroness-casey-review-march-2023a.pdf.

CBC News (2016). UK Cops Disarm Man Wielding a Machete. 2 August. YouTube. Available at: www.youtube.com/watch?v=9mzPj_IaMzY. Accessed 3 March 2024.

Charman, S. & Bennett, S. (2022). Voluntary resignations from the police service: the impact of organisational and occupational stressors on organisational commitment. *Policing and Society: An International Journal of Research and Policy*, 32 (2), 159–178.

Charman, S. & Tyson, J. (2023). Over and out: the damaged and conflicting identities of officers voluntarily resigning from the police service. *Policing and Society: An International Journal of Research and Policy*, 33 (7), 767–783.

Cheng, T. (2024). *The Policing Machine: Enforcement, Endorsements, and the Illusion of Public Input*. Chicago: The University of Chicago Press.

Clinton, J. (2022). Police: 1,800 officers recruited under Boris Johnson scheme 'have resigned'. 30 December. *The Guardian*. Available at: www.theguardian.com/uk-news/2022/dec/30/police-1800-officers-recruited-under-boris-johnson-scheme-have-resigned.

College of Policing (2020). Policing in England and Wales: Future Operating Environment 2040. 11 August. Available at: https://assets.college.police.uk/s3fs-public/2020-08/future-operating-environment-2040.pdf.

College of Policing (2023a). Police dogs authorised professional practice – Consultation. November. Available at: https://assets.college.police.uk/s3fs-public/2023-11/Police-dogs-APP-consultation.pdf.

College of Policing (2023b). Mounted police authorised professional practice – Consultation. November. Available at: https://assets.college.police.uk/s3fs-public/2023-11/Mounted-police-APP-consultation.pdf.

Conn, D. (2017). The scandal of Orgreave. 18 May. *The Guardian*. Available at: www.theguardian.com/politics/2017/may/18/scandal-of-orgreave-miners-strike-hillsborough-theresa-may.

Dodd, V. (2023). Met wins battle with NHS over not attending mental health calls. 17 August. *The Guardian*. Available at: www.theguardian.com/uk-news/2023/aug/17/met-police-mental-health-calls-nhs-mark-rowley.

Elliott-Cooper, A. (2023). Abolishing institutional racism. *Race & Class*, 65 (1), 100–118.

Elmsley, C. (1983). *Policing and its Context 1750–1870*. London: The Macmillan Press Ltd.

Elshimi, M.S. (2017). *De-radicalisation in the UK Prevent Strategy: Security, Identity, and Religion*. Abingdon: Routledge.

Fenton. J. (2021). *We Own This City: A True Story of Crime, Cops and Corruption in an American City*. London: Faber & Faber Limited.

Fouzder, M. (2023). 'Costly and bureaucratic': Met Police chief calls for criminal justice reform. 12 September. *The Law Society Gazette*.

Available at: www.lawgazette.co.uk/news/costly-and-bureaucratic-met-police-chief-calls-for-criminal-justice-reform/5117202.article.

Goodison, S.E. (2022). Local Police Departments Personnel, 2020. November. US Department of Justice. Available at: https://bjs.ojp.gov/sites/g/files/xyckuh236/files/media/document/lpdp20.pdf.

Gordon, D. (2022). *Policing the Racial Divide: Urban Growth Politics and the Remaking of Segregation.* New York: New York University Press.

GOV.UK (2021). Fire and rescue workforce and pensions statistics: England, April 2020 to March 2021. 5 November. Official Statistics. Available at: www.gov.uk/government/statistics/fire-and-rescue-workforce-and-pensions-statistics-england-april-2020-to-march-2021.

GOV.UK (2023a). Population of England and Wales. 4 April. *Ethnicity facts and figures.* Available at: www.ethnicity-facts-figures.service.gov.uk/uk-population-by-ethnicity/national-and-regional-populations/population-of-england-and-wales/latest.

GOV.UK (2023b). Police workforce. 26 May. *Ethnicity facts and figures.* Available at: www.ethnicity-facts-figures.service.gov.uk/workforce-and-business/workforce-diversity/police-workforce/latest.

GOV.UK (2023c). Male and female populations. 2 August. *Ethnicity facts and figures.* Available at: www.ethnicity-facts-figures.service.gov.uk/uk-population-by-ethnicity/demographics/male-and-female-populations/latest.

Hadjimatheou, K. (2017). Neither Confirm nor Deny: Secrecy and Disclosure in Undercover Policing. *Criminal Justice Ethics*, 36 (3), 279–296.

Hall, S. (2012). *Theorizing Crime and Deviance: A New Perspective.* London: Sage Publications Ltd.

Holliday, D. & Backlund, H. (2015). For Black Officers in Chicago, City's Police Crisis Calls for Action. 7 December. *City Bureau.* Available at: www.citybureau.org/stories/2016/7/31/for-black-officers-in-chicago-citys-police-crisis-calls-for-action.

Huemer, M. (2021). *Justice before the Law.* London: Palgrave Macmillan.

Kamali, S. (2017). Informants, Provocateurs, and Entrapment: Examining the Histories of the FBI's PATCON and the NYPD's Muslim Surveillance Program. *Surveillance & Society*, 15 (1), 68–78.

Lartey, J. (2023). Biden Promised a Police Misconduct Database. He's Yet to Deliver. 4 February. *The Marshall Project.* Available at: www.themarshallproject.org/2023/02/04/biden-promised-a-police-misconduct-database-hes-yet-to-deliver.

Lehman, C.F. (2023). How to Build a National Police Academy: And why we should. 15 June. *City Journal.* Available at: www.city-journal.org/article/how-to-build-a-national-police-academy.

Leonard, A. & Blankstein, E. (2023). LAPD shrinks below 9,000 officers, the fewest cops in a generation. 7 August. *NBC News.* Available at: www.

msn.com/en-us/news/us/lapd-shrinks-below-9000-officers-the-fewest-cops-in-a-generation/ar-AA1eVELx.

Loader, I. & Mulcahy, A. (2003). *Policing and the Condition of England: Memory, Politics, and Culture*. Oxford: Oxford University Press.

Lombardo, J. (2020). Las Vegas Metropolitan Department Strategic Plan 2020–2024. 13 November.Latin Chamber of Commerce Las Vegas. Available at: https://fliphtml5.com/krha/vqff/basic.

Loveday, B. (2006). Size Isn't Everything: Restructuring Policing in England and Wales. March. Policy Exchange. Available at: https://policyexchange.org.uk/wp-content/uploads/2006/03/size-isnt-everything-mar-06-2.pdf.

MacIntyre, A. (2007). *After Virtue: A Study in Moral Theory*. 3rd ed. London: Duckworth Books.

McArdle, M. (2023). America Needs a West Point for Police Officers. 5 June. *The Washington Post*. Available at: www.washingtonpost.com/opinions/2023/06/05/police-criminal-justice-west-point.

McCulloch, J. & Wilson, D. (2016). *Pre-crime: Pre-emption, precaution and the future*. Abingdon: Routledge.

McGregor, R. (2021). Four Characteristics of Policing as a Practice. *Policing: A Journal of Policy and Practice*, 15 (3), 1842–1853.

Manning, P.K. (2010/2016). *Democratic Policing in a Changing World*. New York: Routledge.

Mollen, M., Baer, H., Evans, H. & Tyler, H.R. (1994). The City of New York Commission to Investigate Allegations of Police Corruption and the Anti-Corruption Procedures of the Police Department: Commission Report. 7 July.The City of New York. Available at: www.nyc.gov/assets/doi/images/content/timeline/MollenCommissionNYPD.pdf.

Muir, R., Higgins, A., Halkon, R. & Walcott, S. (2022). The Final Report of the Strategic Review of Policing in England and Wales: A New Mode of Protection: Redesigning policing and public safety for the 21st century. March. Police Foundation. Available at: www.policingreview.org.uk/wp-content/uploads/srpew_final_report.pdf.

Murji, K. (1998/2019). *Policing Drugs*. Abingdon: Routledge.

Nguyen, N. (2019). *Suspect Communities: Anti-Muslim Racism and the Domestic War on Terror*. Minneapolis, MN: University of Minnesota Press.

NYC (2021). City Council Passes Comprehensive Police Reform Resolution to Confront Legacy of Racialized Policing and Deepen Accountability, Trust between Police and Communities. 25 March. Office of the Mayor. Available at: www.nyc.gov/office-of-the-mayor/news/222-21/city-council-passes-comprehensive-police-reform-resolution-confront-legacy-racialized.

NYPD (2024). About NYPD. Available at: www.nyc.gov/site/nypd/about/about-nypd/about-nypd-landing.page.

Patten, C., Hayes, M., Lynch, G., O'Toole, K., Shearing, C., Smith, J., Smith, P. & Woods, L. (1999). A New Beginning: Policing in Northern Ireland: The Report of the Independent Commission on Policing for Northern Ireland. September. CAIN Archive. Available at: https://cain.ulster.ac.uk/issues/police/patten/patten99.pdf.

Pemberton, S. (2015). *Harmful Societies: Understanding Social Harm*. Bristol: Policy Press.

Pughsley, A. (2023). The Policing Productivity Review: Improving outcomes for the public. October. National Police Chiefs' Council. Available at: https://assets.publishing.service.gov.uk/media/655784fa544aea000dfb2f9a/Policing_Productivity_Review.pdf.

Quinlin, T.L. (2024). *Police Diversity: Beyond the Blue*. Bristol: Policy Press.

Ray, J. (2022). Fresno Police Chief Paco Balderrama on misconceptions about cops, criticism over anti-mask protester. 23 February. *Los Angeles Times*. Available at: www.latimes.com/california/story/2022-02-23/fresno-police-chief-paco-balderrama-la-times-q-and-a.

Reaves, B.A. (2015). Local Police Departments, 2013: Personnel, Policies, and Practices. May. US Department of Justice. Available at: https://bjs.ojp.gov/content/pub/pdf/lpd13ppp.pdf.

Reiner, R. (2021). *Social Democratic Criminology*. Abingdon: Routledge.

Robins, J. & Newman, D. (2021). *Justice in a Time of Austerity: Stories From a System in Crisis*. Bristol: Bristol University Press.

Rose, D. (1996). *In the Name of the Law: The Collapse of Criminal Justice*. London: Jonathan Cape Ltd.

Rowe, M. (2023). *Disassembling Police Culture*. Abingdon: Routledge.

Rushin, S. (2017). *Federal Intervention in American Police Departments*. Cambridge: Cambridge University Press.

Schlembach, R. (2024). *Spycops: Secrets and Disclosure in the Undercover Policing Inquiry*. Bristol: Policy Press.

Shaw, D. (2023). The police are struggling to operate in a smartphone world. 28 July. *The Spectator*. Available at: www.spectator.co.uk/article/the-police-are-struggling-to-operate-in-a-smartphone-world.

Shepherd, K. (2020). Louisville bans 'no-knock' warrants after police killing of Breonna Taylor inside her home. 12 June. *The Washington Post*. Available at: www.washingtonpost.com/nation/2020/06/12/louisville-breonna-taylor-law.

Siddique, H. & Dodd, V. (2023). England and Wales judges told not to jail criminals as prisons full – report. 12 October. *The Guardian*. Available at: www.theguardian.com/law/2023/oct/12/england-and-wales-judges-told-not-to-jail-criminals-because-prisons-full-report.

Snowden, A. (2021). Leading the Fight Against Crime: The Police and Crime Plan for Lancashire 2021–2025. December. Lancashire Police Crime

Commissioner. Available at: www.lancashire-pcc.gov.uk/wp-content/uploads/2021/12/Police-Crime-Plan-Full-document-PDF-Copy.pdf.

Spurrell, E. (2021). Merseyside Police and Crime Plan 2021–2025. October. Merseyside Police and Crime Commissioner. Available at: www.merseysidepcc.info/media/esgbbj0b/final-police-and-crime-plan-2021-25.pdf.

Stuntz, W.J. (2011). *The Collapse of American Criminal Justice*. Cambridge, MA: The Belknap Press.

Sullivan, E. & Kanno-Youngs, Z. (2021). Images of Border Patrol's Treatment of Haitian Migrants Prompt Outrage. 21 September. *The New York Times*. Available at: www.nytimes.com/2021/09/21/us/politics/haitians-border-patrol-photos.html.

Sullivan, M.G. (2023). Crime Reduction Plan. 5 June. Phoenix Police Department. Available at: www.phoenix.gov/policesite/Documents/Crime_Reduction_Plan.pdf.

Swaine, J. & Holpuch, A. (2014). Ferguson police: a stark illustration of newly militarised US law enforcement. 14 August. *The Guardian*. Available at www.theguardian.com/world/2014/aug/14/ferguson-police-military-restraints-violence-weaponry-missouri.

The White House (2022). Executive Order 14074 of May 25, 2022: Advancing Effective, Accountable Policing and Criminal Justice Practices To Enhance Public Trust and Public Safety. *Federal Register*, 87 (104) 32945–32963.

Topping, A. (2023). Delays to rape trials in England and Wales 'devastating' for victims. 27 March. *The Guardian*. Available at: www.theguardian.com/society/2023/mar/27/delays-to-trials-in-england-and-wales-devastating-for-victims.

Tyler, I. (2010). Designed to fail: A biopolitics of British citizenship. *Citizenship Studies*, 14 (1), 61–74.

Tyson, J. & Charman, S. (2022). Police officer resignations have risen by 72% in the last year – we asked former officers why. 1 November. *The Conversation*. Available at: https://theconversation.com/police-officer-resignations-have-isen-by-72-in-the-last-year-we-asked-former-officers-why-188616.

US Department of Justice Civil Rights Division (DOJ) (2011). United States Investigation of the Maricopa County Sheriff's Office. 15 December. *The New York Times*. Available at: www.documentcloud.org/documents/274910-justice-department-findings-in-its-investigation.

US Department of Justice Civil Rights Division (DOJ) (2016). Investigation of the Baltimore City Police Department. 10 August. US Department of Justice. Available at: www.justice.gov/d9/bpd_findings_8-10-16.pdf.

US Department of Justice Civil Rights Division & United States Attorney' Office Northern District of Illinois (DOJ & USAO) (2017). Investigation o the Chicago Police Department. 13 January. US Department of Justice. Available at: www.justice.gov/d9/chicago_police_department_findings.pdf.

US Department of Justice Civil Rights Division & United States Attorney's Office Western District of Kentucky Civil Division (DOJ & USAO) (2023). Investigation of the Louisville Metro Police Department and Louisville Metro Government. 8 March. US Department of Justice. Available at: www.documentcloud.org/documents/23698446-doj-report-on-louisville-pd.

Van Maanen, J. (1973). Observations on the Making of Policemen. *Human Organization*, 32 (4), 407–418.

Westneat, D. (2023). In Seattle, the cops keep leaving, while the backup never comes. 15 February. *The Seattle Times*. Available at: www.seattletimes.com/seattle-news/in-seattle-the-cops-keep-leaving-while-the-backup-never-comes.

Wood, P. (2019). Baltimore-area police departments are much whiter than the people they serve. 23 September. *The Washington Post*. Available at: www.washingtonpost.com/local/public-safety/baltimore-area-police-departments-are-much-whiter-than-the-people-they-serve/2019/09/23/855f4d98-d4ed-11e9-9343-40db57cf6abd_story.html.

Yeng, S. (2014). *The Biopolitics of Race: State Racism and U.S. Immigration*. Lanham, MD: Lexington Books.

INDEX

abolition 17, 22–24, 272–274
absolute sacrifice 74–75, 78–79, 128–132, 166–169, 206–210, 236–237, 290–291
Abt, T. 7–8, 22
Anglo-American Democratic Policing (AADP) 4–5, 41–44, 74–75, 259–261, 273, 288–290, 297–298
Arkansas State Police (ASP) 138–140, 147–148, 249–250
authentic sacrifice 78, 130, 208–209
autoethnography: analytic 62–68, 74–75, 102–103, 232, 259–260; evocative 62–65
auto-ethnography *see* autoethnography: analytic

Baltimore Police Department (BPD) 65–66, 299–300
Bezzerides, Detective Sergeant A. 119–120, 122–130, 132–134, 136–137, 234, 235, 238, 239, 241
Black Dahlia murder 107, 192–193

Bleichert, Officer D. 197–198, 206–208, 210–212, 220, 237

Cain, M. 261–262
California Highway Patrol (CHP) 116–117, 240
case selection *see* fieldwork model of research
case study 89–92, 100–107
Caspere murder investigation 116–119
characteristics: absolute sacrifice *see* absolute sacrifice; edgework *see* edgework; heroic struggle *see* heroic struggle; of policing as a practice *see* policing: practice of; worldmaking *see* worldmaking
Charman, S. 261–264, 291–292
Chauvin, Officer D. 15–16, 266, 268
Chicago Police Department 300
City of Los Angeles Police Department (LAPD) 10, 116, 130–132, 192–197, 213–221, 235–237, 243–244, 246, 250,

252, 291; Christopher Commission 18–19, 244, 265
City of New York Police Department (NYPD) 11, 244, 296, 300
classism 9, 75, 183, 215, 223, 226, 253, 262, 296, 303–304; *see also* inequality
coercion 7–8, 9–12, 233–234, 236, 239, 241, 267, 287–290, 292, 296
Cohle, Detective R. 140–142, 145–147
consent 5–6
cop culture *see* informal occupational norms
counterproductive competition: institutional 135–138, 239–241, 293–294; systemic 142–145, 179–183, 247–248
counter terrorism *see* policing: high
County of Los Angeles Sheriff's Department (LASD) 194–195, 214–217, 220, 237, 240, 246, 250
Couzens, Constable W. 16, 23
COVID-19 *see* pandemic
Craven, Detective Superintendent R. 152–157, 165–167, 176–178
Cray, Senior Constable (later Sergeant) C. 67–68, 73–74, 76
criminal justice system 4–7, 24, 48–50, 142–146, 183–187, 247, 249–254, 275, 300–305
criminology 93–94, 102, 107, 183–185, 222–223, 263, 272, 303–304
critical case study *see* case study

data sampling *see* fieldwork model of research
Defunding *See* Depolicing
democracy 4–9, 12–14, 41, 142–143, 263, 305; liberal 36, 40, 48, 50–52, 148, 223–227, 252–254, 276; social 18, 50–52, 252, 303–304
depolicing 17, 20–22, 265–266
Derrida, J. 50, 78–79, 87,
Devlin, Detective Inspector C. 260
difference principle 9, 22, 52, 234, 253, 277–279

differential treatment: of suspects 8–9, 15, 50, 148, 248–250; of victims 50, 214–217, 245–246
Dora Lange murder 140–142, 145–147
Durban City Police (DCP) 67–74, 76–80, 259–260
Durban Metropolitan Police Service *see* Durban City Police

edgework 74–78, 125–128, 161–166, 203–206, 234–236, 288–293
Elliott-Cooper, A. 20, 276–277, 305–306
Ellroy, J.: 102; hendecad 103–106; *L. A. Quartet* (novel series) 105–107
ethnography 62
Everard, S. 16, 266
excellences: definition 36–38; of policing *see* policing: practice of
Exley, Detective Sergeant (later Chief) E. 195–197, 203–205, 217–221, 235–236

Federal Bureau of Investigation (FBI) 138, 145–146, 197, 202, 219, 221–222, 241, 249, 275, 295
fieldwork model of research 89–90, 93, 100–105
Fleetwood, J. 20–21, 94
Floyd, G. 15–16, 19, 23–24, 252, 266, 268
Flyvbjerg, B. 87–89, 91–93, 100, 105
Fresno Police Department 307

Gordon, D. 275–277, 279, 305–306
Greater Manchester Police 157, 159–160, 243, 246

Hart, Detective M. 140–142, 145–147
Hays, Detective W. 138–140, 147–148
Her Majesty's Inspectorate of Constabulary *see* Her/His Majesty's Inspectorate of Constabulary and Fire & Rescue Services

Her/His Majesty's Inspectorate of Constabulary and Fire & Rescue Services (HMICFRS) 7, 16–17, 152, 154, 180–183, 247–248, 270–271
heroic struggle 74–76, 122–125, 158–161, 199–203, 233–234, 291–292, 308
Home Office 7, 152, 154, 180–183, 242, 247–248, 274
Home Secretary 13–14, 180–181
homophobia: institutional 214–217, 246, 250; interpersonal 216, 245, 250; systemic 216–217, 250
Hoover, J.E. 103, 221–223, 226
Huemer, M. 18, 49, 139, 142, 236–237, 253, 302
Hunter, Assistant Chief Constable P. 156–164, 168–172, 236–237

inappropriate tactics 288–290
Independent Office for Police Conduct (IOPC) 244
induction (logic) 64, 66
inequality 8–9, 50–52, 147–148, 245, 251–254, 263, 267, 272–273, 279, 300–304; *see also* classism
informal occupational norms 73, 261–265
Ingram, Detective Warrant Officer W. 308
institution: definition 37–38; of policing *see* policing: institution of
institutional reorganisation 293–300

Jobson, Detective Chief Superintendent M. 174, 176–179, 182–183

Lancashire Constabulary 301
Las Vegas Metropolitan Police Department 301–302
Lea, J. 20–21, 272
legitimacy 4–8, 44–45; definition 7; Transatlantic crisis 8–17, 52–53, 305–308

Los Angeles Police Department *see* City of Los Angeles Police Department
Los Angeles Sheriff's Department *see* County of Los Angeles Sheriff's Department
Louisiana State Police (LSP) 140–142, 145–147
Lyng, S. 76–77

MacIntyre, A. 35–42, 44, 47, 53, 62, 72, 75, 87, 89, 221, 261, 264–265, 290
Manning, P. 4–7, 9, 12, 22, 41–45, 47–48, 52, 75, 80, 234, 253, 261, 275–279, 307
Marshall, Detective Sergeant H. 157–158, 160–161, 164–168, 172–173, 235–236, 239
media 8–9, 15–17, 23, 43–44, 50, 72, 96, 129, 140–141, 146, 175–176, 178–179, 183–187, 196, 203, 214–217, 242, 250–252, 291, 306–307
Menye, Police Constable S. 67
Merseyside Police 301
Metropolitan Police Service (MPS) 5, 13, 16–17, 69, 180, 232, 244, 274–278, 292–294, 296, 300, 307; Macpherson report 18–19, 265, 276–277; Casey review 266, 268–272, 274, 293, 296, 298–299
Metropolitan Police *see* Metropolitan Police Service
militarisation 9–12, 268, 273–275, 288–290, 297–298
Minneapolis Police Department (MPD) 11–12, 15–16; US Department of Justice and Attorney's Office investigation 266–268, 274
misogyny 128, 165–167, 183, 246, 249, 269–271, 276; *see also* sexism
Mitchell, Police Constable (later Inspector) C. 68
Muir, W.K. 42–43, 76–79

narrative: criminology 93–94; definition 96; epistemology 89, 97–100, 105; fiction 94–96, 99–103; thickness 93, 95–101, 105
New York Police Department *see* City of New York Police Department
Newburn, T. 19–20, 52–53, 275–276
Nite Owl massacre 197–199

organised corruption 243–244

pandemic 14–17, 24, 51, 252
Peace, D. 68, 107; *Nineteen Eighty* (novel) 106–107; *Red Riding Quartet* (novel series) 104–106
Peel, R. 4–6, 41–42, 272–273
phenomenological knowledge 97–100
Phoenix Police Department 301
phronetic social science 87–92
Pizzolatto, N. 107; *True Detective* (television series) 104–106; *True Detective 2* (television season) 106–107
Police and Crime Commissioners (PCCs) 14, 180, 304–305
police fitness 290–293
police paramilitary units (PPU) 9–10, 288–290
Police Service of Northern Ireland (PSNI) 274; Patten report 269, 298–299
policing: colonial 22, 69, 234, 272–274, 288, 297–298; decolonising 297–300; evidence-based (EBP) 18; high 12, 42, 273–275, 297–298, 305; institution of 4, 7, 44–47, 239–246, 293–300; juridical context of 47–50, 300–303; low 12, 42, 274–275, 287–298; political context of 47, 50–53, 303–305; practice of 41–44, 232–239, 287–293; situated practice of 44, 135–148, 173–187, 213–227, 267, 277; systemic context of 44, 47–53, 247–254, 300–305; undercover 13–14, 16–17, 132–134, 136–137, 164–166, 194–195, 219, 238–239, 288–290
politicisation 12–14, 274–275, 288–290, 297–298, 304–305
positive discrimination 299–300
positivism 64, 223
practical changes 287–293
practice: definition 37–38; of policing *see* policing: practice of
Presser, L. 75–76, 94, 96, 234, 273
procedural justice theory 5–7, 19–20
procedural limitations 233–239, 277–278, 288
public perception 24, 185–187, 233–235, 241–243, 247–248, 250–254, 267, 278–279, 287, 292, 300–301
public protection 6–9, 12, 24, 43–44, 72–75, 81, 232–233, 239–240, 247, 305–308
public safety *see* public protection

racism: institutional 10, 18–19, 220–222, 246, 262, 271–272, 276–277, 297–300; interpersonal 220, 222, 245; systemic 221, 223, 249–250, 252–253, 276–277, 303–304
Radebe, Police Constable T. 79
radical framework 287–305
Reagan, R. 8
realism 64, 94
recommendations *see* radical framework
reform 17–20, 262–263, 265, 277, 295
Reiner, R. 4, 6, 9, 12–13, 18, 42–43, 48, 50–51, 148, 180, 252, 261–264, 275–277, 303–304
reputation management 241–243
reputation risk management *see* reputation management
Ripper inquiry 152–156
Rose, D. 251–253, 302
Rowe, M. 42–43, 261–262, 264–265, 278–279, 305–306
Royal Ulster Constabulary *see* Police Service of Northern Ireland

Rubin, A. 89–90, 92–93, 101, 104

Seattle Police Department 23–24
self-ethnography *see* autoethnography: evocative
sexism: institutional 157–158, 160–161, 246, 262, 271, 293; interpersonal 160–161, 245; systemic 249; *see also* misogyny
skills: set of *see* policing: practice of
Smith, Detective Lieutenant (later Detective Captain) D.L. 194–197, 218–220, 223–227
social inequality *see* inequality
South African Police *see* South African Police Service
South African Police Service (SAPS) 69, 71–72, 80, 260, 273–274
Special Constabulary 66, 270
Special Weapons and Tactics *see* police paramilitary units
Srinivasan, A. 79–80, 239
Stuntz, W. 48–49, 142–143, 251, 302
systemic transformation 300–308

Taylor, B. 289, 306
Thatcher, M. 8, 13
trust 6–8, 48, 51–52, 239, 266, 269, 289, 303

Upshaw, Detective Deputy Sheriff D. 198–201, 205–206, 208–210, 212–213, 234, 238

Velcoro, Detective R. 120–123, 125–130, 134–135, 238–239
Ventura County Sheriff's Office (VCSO) 136–137, 240–241
Vinci Police Department (VPD) 135–138, 240, 243, 249–250
Vitale, A. 21–23, 272–273, 276

West, Detective (later Detective Lieutenant) R. 138–140, 147–148
West Finger missing persons 138–140, 147–148
West Yorkshire Metropolitan Police (WYMP) 173–183, 242–243, 246, 248–250
White, Detective (later Detective Sergeant) W. 198–199, 201–205, 233, 235–237, 244
Wolverine Prowler murders 194–195
Woodrugh, Officer P. 121–123, 125–127, 130–132, 236–236, 239
worldmaking 74–75, 79–80, 132–135, 169–173, 210–213, 238–239, 291–292